Puppet Master Complete

Puppet Master Complete
A Franchise History

NAT BREHMER

McFarland & Company, Inc., Publishers
Jefferson, North Carolina

ISBN (print) 978-1-4766-7630-2
ISBN (ebook) 978-1-4766-4519-3

Library of Congress and British Library
cataloguing data are available

Library of Congress Control Number 2021039179

© 2021 Nat Brehmer. All rights reserved

No part of this book may be reproduced or transmitted in any form or by any means, electronic or mechanical, including photocopying or recording, or by any information storage and retrieval system, without permission in writing from the publisher.

Front cover: Poster art featuring the characters Blade, Pinhead and Torch from the 1990 film *Puppet Master II* (author collection)

Printed in the United States of America

*McFarland & Company, Inc., Publishers
Box 611, Jefferson, North Carolina 28640
www.mcfarlandpub.com*

For my father, Donald Brehmer.

Acknowledgments

This book could not have been made without the help and guidance of so many people. But I wouldn't be doing this without Chris Ward, who got me into it, and my dad—as much as he'd hate to hear it—for letting me rent *Puppet Master* in the first place. The biggest thanks to Kieran Fisher and James McCormick, who I told to talk me out of writing a *Puppet Master* book and said the opposite. Thanks to Kat Ellinger and Lee Gambin for their guidance on crafting a book of this type. A huge thank you to the following contributors, without whom this book would not exist: Kenneth J. Hall, Lee MacLeod, Richard Band, Glenn Lumsden, Chris Endicott, C. Courtney Joyner, Jeff Burr, Jay Woelfel, Dave Parker, Rick Phares, Jeff Farley, Shane Bitterling, Tom Devlin and Shawn Gabborin. Thanks to Charles Band and David Schmoeller for kickstarting this whole thing and all the cast and crew that followed for carrying the torch over the years. Thanks to the support of my family and my wife, Shelley. To everyone I left out, thank you, too. And a forever thank you to David Allen, for being the wonderful wizard he was.

Table of Contents

Acknowledgments — vi
Preface — 1
Introduction — 3

CHAPTER ONE. Fall of an Empire and a Full Moon Rising — 7
CHAPTER TWO. *Puppet Master* — 13
CHAPTER THREE. The Eternity Comics — 31
CHAPTER FOUR. *Puppet Master II* — 37
CHAPTER FIVE. *Puppet Master III: Toulon's Revenge* — 54
CHAPTER SIX. *Puppet Master 4* and *5* — 72
CHAPTER SEVEN. *Puppet Wars*: The Unmade Trilogy — 88
CHAPTER EIGHT. *Puppet Master: The Action Figure Series* — 99
CHAPTER NINE. *Curse of the Puppet Master* — 114
CHAPTER TEN. *Retro Puppet Master* — 126
CHAPTER ELEVEN. *Puppet Master: The Legacy* — 140
CHAPTER TWELVE. *Puppet Master vs. Demonic Toys* — 152
CHAPTER THIRTEEN. *Puppet Master: Axis of Evil* — 168
CHAPTER FOURTEEN. *Puppet Master: Axis Rising* — 175
CHAPTER FIFTEEN. The Action Lab Comics — 185
CHAPTER SIXTEEN. *Puppet Master: Axis Termination* — 195
CHAPTER SEVENTEEN. *Puppet Master: The Littlest Reich* — 204
CHAPTER EIGHTEEN. *Blade: The Iron Cross* — 214
CHAPTER NINETEEN. The Fans — 223
CHAPTER TWENTY. The Future — 228

Chapter Notes — 235
Bibliography — 239
Index — 241

Preface

In the annals of movie history, there are very few franchises that are truly, entirely unique to themselves, but the *Puppet Master* series is certainly one of them. It came from humble beginnings. Following on the heels of a failed independent horror and sci-fi production company, it was the debut film for an even *smaller* company. It was a straight-to-video horror flick about a troupe of terrifying toys, only a year after the blockbuster success of *Child's Play*. It, in short, should not have worked. But it did. Not only that, it succeeded no doubt beyond the company's wildest dreams and even beyond any reasonable expectations that could have been perceived at the time. This little killer puppet movie became a huge video hit. Then it naturally spawned a sequel, and another, and another, not by any means an unheard-of trend for horror. But as of 2021, it has spawned 14 films in total to date. That includes all eleven entries in the "official" franchise, a crossover battle royale for the Sci-Fi (now SyFy) channel, a 2017 theatrical reboot, and a spinoff movie for the series' most iconic puppet, Blade. It is incredible that a little low-budget horror effort like *Puppet Master* launched one of the longest-running horror franchises of all time, as well as launching Full Moon as a studio that has gone on to make hundreds of other quirky, weird and wild movies since.

But in many ways, it's stuff outside of the movies that truly makes *Puppet Master* such an unbelievable phenomenon. While they may not have even have the number of sequels, there are plenty of straight-to-video horror franchises. *Puppet Master*, however, is so much more than that. It has spawned two comic book series, not to mention appearances by the puppets in the Full Moon comic crossover *Dollman Kills the Full Moon Universe* and a prequel tie-in comic to the *Blade* movie. There have been countless models and replicas over the years. Even Halloween costumes. Most astonishingly, this straight-to-video horror franchise spawned an action figure series that started out being sold in comic shops and, as its success ballooned, wound up in stores ranging from Spencer's to Toys "R" Us.

This book is meant to examine *all* of these things, because they are all a part of *Puppet Master* history. It is as much all of these other things as it is a series of films, and it always has been. It's a symbiotic relationship. The movies spawn the toys, which generate the interest to spawn more movies, and so on, and so forth. At the same time, it's incredible that something that started so small could see its characters become so iconic, that the look of these characters would stand out enough to grab the interest of kids and adults who had never seen nor heard of the films the characters came from. That's a testament not only to Charlie Band for seizing each of these opportunities from the very beginning, but especially to David Allen and his entire puppet crew for creating and animating these inanimate props and—essentially—instilling them with life to the point that they feel like genuine characters. Without the dynamic designs of the puppets themselves, there's no doubt in probably anyone's mind that none of this would have ever happened.

The story of *Puppet Master* is essentially the story of a franchise that refuses to die, hopefully in the best way possible. It's engaging, I'd like to think, whether you've seen the movies or not. This is the story of a single feature designed to cater to the video rental market that then launched a series that has outlasted video stores themselves. At the same time, there have been obvious struggles. Yes, the movies are still being made, but without the video market, the budgets are almost impossibly small. The resilience of the series is now cemented in the resilience it takes to make a single new entry, for barely a fraction of the cost of the early movies, on schedules of often less than a week. Many fans note the diminishing returns, the loss of budget and in some cases a largely perceived decline in quality. There's no doubt an objective truth to that. But at the same time, it's amazing to even see a movie come together at all under those conditions and look even half as good as it does.

It's easy to dismiss *Puppet Master* as a series that refuses to die. That is, however, an incredible thing. It *refuses* to die. It has had to adapt to everything from the loss of video stores to the rise of streaming. It's a franchise that has often run out of money, but never really run out of steam. As the recent comics can attest, there are countless great stories to be told even thirty-plus years later, and the mythology can still be expanded in any number of ways.

In this book, we're going to cover all of these hurdles, the challenges that have forced the franchise to adapt to new financial realities, new release models, and an ever-changing industry in general. We're looking at every single film, as well as the comics, the toys, and everything that has been done to keep the *Puppet Master* brand alive over time. So please join me on this weird and wonderful journey, one about movies and comics and toys and surviving the independent marketplace. Of course, it's also about puppets. Puppets who, despite all odds, display individual quirks and personalities despite never uttering a single line. Puppets who are sometimes villains, sometimes heroes, who sometimes vomit leeches and sometimes play laser tag, and in doing so, are puppets who never do exactly what they're expected to do. And it is, ultimately, about how a franchise that refuses to die can sometimes be a miraculous feat in and of itself.

Introduction

"Why Puppet Master?"

That is probably the question I've been asked most in my life. "How do you pronounce that last name?" "Where are you from?" "Why *Puppet Master*?" And the truth is, it's a complicated thing to answer. It might, in fact, take an entire book to truly explain it. Like many horror fans, I got hooked on the genre at a young age. The '90s were full of horror-adjacent family fare that made for excellent, if small, first steps into the darkness. Things like *Nightmare Before Christmas*, *Casper*, *The Addams Family*—not to mention shows like *Goosebumps* and *Are You Afraid of the Dark?*—all did their part in building an interest, but I wanted more. By the time I was in first grade, my friends had already introduced me to the concepts of Freddy and Jason and I would endlessly browse the horror aisle at the local video store, imagining what each movie could possibly be about. That's where I must have seen Full Moon's output for the first time, but to my surprise to this day, I found *Puppet Master* under genuinely child-friendly circumstances.

On a whim, while browsing a bookstore with my dad, I picked up a toy magazine because it had my favorite *X-Men* villain on the cover. I took the magazine home, had a friend come over. We flipped through it and marveled at the cool, unique toys we were never going to buy, as we always did. And then I flipped to a two-page spread in the middle of the magazine and my eyes bulged out of my head. These toys were completely different than anything else contained within those pages. Scary, yet accessible. Immediately endearing.

It was a spread detailing Full Moon Toys' lineup of *Puppet Master* figures for the upcoming year. I was genuinely, completely hooked the moment I saw them. It's amazing, in retrospect, because some of them were in the background and barely visible. I forced my best friend, the one who'd gotten me into horror in the first place, to draw more detailed pictures of the ones I couldn't quite see, particularly Blade and Six-Shooter. I tacked those police sketches on my wall, as I would also wind up doing with the magazine itself. Within no time, I sought out and rented the original film.

From that point on it was a full-blown obsession. I'd rent *Puppet Master* almost every weekend, only really alternating with *II* and *III*, which were also available at the local video store. I would draw the characters endlessly, look for the movies anywhere I went on the off chance that they would be there. That was when my parents first started asking the question. "Why *Puppet Master*?"

In the late '90s, the franchise was virtually inaccessible. The toys weren't sold anywhere near me, a couple of the movies were available for rent, but all of them were out of print, so they couldn't be bought anywhere. That inaccessibility made it all the more endearing. Because I couldn't buy the toys, I'd stare at ads in magazines. When I did finally come across figures, they'd be obscure side characters like Mephisto and I'd still treat them like the Holy Grail. I'd scan through *TV Guide* like a hawk to see if any of the films would be scheduled to play on the Sci-Fi Channel.

A one-page ad for *Retro Puppet Master* felt like the announcement of *The Empire Strikes Back.* I would keep renting the movies, taping them from TV whenever I found them. Finally, one Christmas morning I would walk downstairs and open my presents to find the entire set of the action figure series. No doubt my parents would hope that finally having those toys would scratch the itch and I would finally be able to move on to more healthy obsessions. But instead, it only cemented a lifelong love of these characters and this series.

I would seek the first opportunity I could to try and get my friends into these movies. Having the toys to show them proved to be great for that. I became the *Puppet Master* Child Recruitment Service. But eventually they would grow out of the genre and especially out of the franchise, and I wouldn't. That was when my friends started to ask me, more and more, the question my parents had hounded me with for years. "Why *Puppet Master*?"

Even now, even among people who eat and breathe horror for a living, I'll get the same question. It's a beloved, successful franchise, but it's also a weird hill to die on. Much of my professional career has been devoted to providing thoughtful responses to things I didn't know how to respond to as a child. I love *Halloween* for its filmmaking, for its seasonal mystery and its rhythm. I love *Texas Chain Saw Massacre* for its rawness, for the fact that it is relentlessly bleak and treated as utterly realistic as possible, that it's both the death knell for Gothic horror as well as the perfect evolution of it.

Puppet Master has always been harder to explain.

If anything, I've thought so hard about it that I've come up with hundreds of different answers. The puppets themselves are iconic. They are the imagery that sells the franchise. Their designs are outwardly creepy, they wear their eccentricities on their sleeve—sometimes on their head, too. They're barely more than two feet tall, but capable of unleashing incredible amounts of damage.

But it also fascinates me that they're the good guys, even when they're not. The original film shows that with their puppet master, they are harmless. But if they fall into the wrong hands, they're capable of incredible chaos. That concept by itself makes for an incredibly diverse franchise, in which the central characters can be the villains and heroes in almost equal measure.

As a very quiet kid I also likely related to the fact that these puppets could not speak, but always got their point across, always remained perfectly in synch with one another. It could even be that I discovered the series around the same time that my parents informed me of their divorce and diving headfirst into these films and their world helped me to take my mind off it. It could be that I don't need to explain why, necessarily, because I'm far from the only one who loves *Puppet Master* as much as I

Introduction 5

do. Every fan has their own story of how they got into it, why they love it, and what it means to them.

Puppet Master became something of a phenomenon, and it is in many ways the most unlikely phenomenon in movie history. Almost every major decision made from its inception has been a gamble. Some of those gambles have paid off, some of them haven't, but despite incredibly high highs and devastatingly low lows, the series has kept on going. Created to cater to the video market, it survived the death of video stores. It survived several studio bankruptcies, increasingly low budgets, a deal with the Sci-Fi Channel and even now it is still surviving. In fact, with a new film having just been released, the recent comic series and the remake from Cinestate, it might even be *flourishing*.

Even at its most unsuccessful, this is ultimately a success story. A franchise that spawned fourteen films, models, action figures, statues, comic books and Halloween costumes without ever going to theaters once. It is the backbone of the Full Moon Empire, something fans continue to celebrate, and something people are constantly rediscovering—or even discovering for the first time. Fans continue to make their own versions of the puppets, their own fan films, art and even video games, all in tribute to the foundation Full Moon put in place almost thirty years ago.

Why *Puppet Master*?

You'll see.

CHAPTER ONE

Fall of an Empire and a Full Moon Rising

Throughout the 1980s, Empire Pictures consistently lived up to its name on video store shelves. Charles Band had created a company that offered incredibly different films than what people were used to seeing on the big screen, especially at the height of the slasher era. Featuring a range of different, bizarre creatures—at a wide range of sizes, no less—Empire's films proved to be impressively diverse, but always remained consistent within a singular style. Even in the most extremely different scenarios, the Empire brand always remained intact. But that's the nature of Charles Band as a producer and, by all accounts, it always has been. Judging by the hundreds of films to his credit as producer, he can and will make anything as long as it appeals to his sensibilities, which can be impressively expansive and jarringly specific all at the same time. Rubber monsters, women in peril, little people in starring roles—as long as a movie could include these elements, subject matter and genre rarely seemed to matter.

Raised in Italy, son of producer/director Albert Band, Charles Band not only grew up on low-budget movie sets but got to witness that country's horror renaissance of the '60s and '70s firsthand.[1] Long before creating his own studio with Empire, Band did one other crucial thing that proves incredibly important to the story of *Puppet Master*: he brought Italian horror to the states and began to build the foundations of horror video. Creating his own labels, Wizard Video and Media Home Entertainment, Band brought many of the biggest horror of the era with him overseas, introducing American viewers to the films of Lucio Fulci, particularly titles like *Zombie Flesh Eaters* and *The Beyond*. He would also distribute incredibly controversial features like Mier Zarchi's *I Spit on Your Grave*, creating the now iconic poster image, for which he cast a young Demi Moore—an actress he would go on to work with later on *Parasite*.[2]

Through Wizard, Band even found his way into the video game industry in its earliest days. After the success and notoriety of films like *The Texas Chain Saw Massacre* and *Halloween*, Band produced video game tie-ins for both for the then-new Atari system. The *Texas Chain Saw Massacre* game in particular caused incredible controversy from parents who were shocked to discover that their children could play as the chainsaw wielding maniac Leatherface, even though the graphics made it impossible to tell what was even happening in the game, let alone who was killing who. The important thing, though, was that even as a distributor, Band had begun to gain notoriety in the horror world.

Wizard Video became incredibly successful, presenting its films in recognizable "big box" packages. It was a design that allowed fans to always immediately know these movies when they saw them on the video store shelf. From the beginning, that was clearly an important thing for Band: to present a recognizable brand, something that would distinguish his features from everyone else's. On that level, it should have come as absolutely no surprise when he started making features of his own.

Formed in 1983, Empire International Pictures became a theatrical distribution company not all that different from Wizard Video, with one major exception: it would allow Band to conceive, produce and even direct his own movies, all overseen by himself. Band was not new to producing films by any stretch, but his previous years producing films like *Laserblast* and *Tourist Trap*, though they had seen success, had not allowed him the opportunity to build a brand. Empire would launch many careers, but there would never be any doubt of who exactly was running this ship. Band was in an interesting position, an auteur who always had a clear vision for how he wanted things to be, yet almost always let that vision be carried out by others. From the very beginning, his career was compared to the legendary success of B-Movie producer Roger Corman. Corman was still incredibly active in those days—and, as a matter of fact, has remained an active producer to this day—so the comparison started turning heads in the indie horror world almost immediately. An interview at the time even labeled Corman the "King of B-Movies," while Band could optimistically be referred to as the Prince.

The Empire name first appeared in trade ads in 1983, in the pages of Variety while Band sought funding for a sequel to his film *Parasite,* with the words "EMPIRE PICTURES presents *PARASITE II.*"[3] The Empire name almost overshadowed the title of the film, and that was likely the point. In fact, *Parasite II* did not even wind up happening at all. But it didn't matter; it was a means to an end to introduce Empire Pictures to the world. Empire's first release would actually turn out to be 1984's *The Dungeonmaster.*

An anthology consisting of several segments bridged by a single protagonist, *Dungeonmaster* could almost be seen as an announcement for the major players who would go on to define Empire throughout its success. Segment directors like David Allen, John Carl Buechler, Ted Nicolau and Peter Manoogian would all go on to direct multiple films for Empire and Full Moon. David Allen would become one of the most important people to ever work with Band, creating the dazzling stop-motion effects for many Empire features before creating the now-iconic designs for *Puppet Master.* Virtually anyone involved with the franchise would agree that if there was one person more integral to the success of the *Puppet Master* series than even Band himself, that person would be David Allen.

In general, it's fascinating that Empire's very first release would be perhaps the most crucial to this narrative, as without *Dungeonmaster* it is entirely possible that there would be no *Puppet Master* at all, at least not as we know it. The connection between the two titles is no coincidence, as Band liked the title of the former so much that he conceived the latter simply because he wanted another feature with the word "master" in it, according to his introduction to the *Puppet Master* Blu-ray.

While *Dungeonmaster* has gone on to become something of a cult classic—for example, the line "I reject your reality and substitute my own!" has been embraced by pop culture thanks to the show *Myth Busters*—the film was not by any means a breakout success. This was a low-budget distribution company in an era just before the boom of the video market. Before the Wild West of infinite streaming platforms, movies really had to battle it out for theatrical distribution and the lower tier, independent horror pictures almost never came out on top. Receiving a limited release, *Dungeonmaster* still earned enough for Empire to keep going, and so they did.

The film had, after all, showcased a style very different from everything else on the market, blending sci-fi, horror and fantasy all together in one uniquely weird offering. This would truly become the Empire model and Band had faith that it would find an audience that would not just respond to the company's strangeness, but truly embrace it.

To their shock, they found that lightning in a bottle it in their very next film. While *Dungeonmaster* carved out a niche, it still took its basic concepts from things that were popular at the time, namely Disney's *Tron* and the role-playing game *Dungeons and Dragons*. Even if the stylistic direction would be completely different, the initial influence was clear. Empire leaned even harder into this model with *Ghoulies*. Released in 1985, less than a year after the box-office phenomenon of *Gremlins*, *Ghoulies* isn't even a movie that sounds different from Joe Dante's blockbuster. The title is so similar that it screams of Asylum mockbusters like *Transmorphers* and *Atlantic Rim*. And yet in terms of plot and style, the two films share almost nothing in common. *Ghoulies,* like *Gremlins,* does feature a cast of slimy little monsters, but they're not even the stars. For the most part, it kind of forgets about them.

But even if *Ghoulies* was designed to simply ride the coattails of *Gremlins'* success, that would *not* be the thing that would skyrocket its popularity. That honor fell entirely to the marketing. When conceiving a feature, Band would tend to start in a very similar way to Corman: with only a title and a poster. In this instance, he had a clear vision for the art that would sell the feature. One of the Ghoulies is creeping up out of the toilet bowl underneath the sinister, coy tagline "They'll get you in the end." It's an image that people immediately responded to, so absurd that it made people feel like they needed to see it, likely against their better judgment. The image was both hilarious and haunting, selling a horror movie on toilet humor alone, yet offering the promise of doing for bathrooms what *Jaws* did for beaches.

The trouble, unfortunately, was that nothing on that poster was included in the film itself. As more theaters demanded the poster, Band surely realized that people would expect something at least similar to what they were promised in the film, so he quickly shot an insert of a Ghoulie's head popping out of the toilet bowl. This barely made up for what truly felt like an egregious mismarketing, but it evidently worked. Whether they were simply hooked on the poster art or enjoyed the weird mix of pint-sized creatures and Satanic Cults that the film had to offer, *Ghoulies* was Empire's first true box office hit.

Moving forward, the company finally had what it had lacked before: a reputation. People knew what they were getting into with Empire now after the success of *Ghoulies*. That same year, Band would come in at the end of production to help finance a little film from a first-time director, called *Re-Animator*. It would obviously go on to become one of the biggest cult classics of the 1980s, retaining a wide and loyal fan base to this day. Equally important, it would begin Band's long career of collaboration with director Stuart Gordon. Throughout his career, Gordon's work straddled the line between the B-List and the A-List. He would always work with small budgets, always make horror that—while it pushed the boundaries—at least offered a healthy sense of humor. Gordon would continue to collaborate with Band several times, well into the Full Moon era, and would become the most well-known of Empire's rotating list of directors, even going on to helm two episodes of the Showtime series *Masters of Horror*.

Band had very little to do with *Re-Animator*, striking a deal with producer Brian Yuzna to distribute the film theatrically while also offering post-production services. But it led to him immediately re-teaming with Gordon for two back-to-back Empire hits.[4]

Finished before *From Beyond*, though released after, *Dolls* is incredibly important to forming the wet clay of what would eventually become *Puppet Master*. During a storm, a group of strangers find themselves stranded at an old mansion well off the beaten path. The house is run by an eccentric elderly couple and is filled with dolls from top to bottom. Despite the fact that the movie features genuinely creepy old-school Victorian dolls doing increasingly macabre things—especially removing a woman's eyes to replace them with glass doll's eyes—there is a sense of wonder and fun throughout. It's meant to scare the audience in places, sure, but not to terrify and that's an important distinction. *Dolls* presents a story that is scary but fun, even feeling as though it invites kids along for the ride. The protagonist is a young girl and the film overall has a recurring theme of getting in touch with one's inner child. While the tone would largely be more serious, the *Puppet Master* series would adopt the same model of creating content that would straddle the line of what would generally be thought of as kids' horror and adult horror.

On paper, there are immediate and obvious similarities between a movie about killer dolls running around an empty house and a movie about killer puppets running around an empty hotel. But the truth is that aside from their obvious parallels, the two features are very different. *Dolls* has a sense of whimsy that the early *Puppet Master* entries would mostly lack. The biggest connection to be made, truthfully, is that the eccentric old doll maker is played by the late, great Guy Rolfe. With an impressive career as a character actor, spanning decades, Rolfe would go on to become the actor most identified with the *Puppet Master* franchise after taking the titular role of Andre Toulon in *Puppet Master III: Toulon's Revenge*. He would be the only actor to play Toulon more than once, as well, returning for three more sequels, making him somewhat equivalent to the Robert Englund or Doug Bradley of this franchise.

The origin of *Dolls* proved to be very different from *Re-Animator*. Whereas that movie had seen Gordon team with screenwriter Dennis Paoli to craft their Lovecraft adaptation from the ground up, after its success, Gordon was invited to look over any project Empire already had brewing, where he settled on the already-existing *Dolls* treatment by Ed Naha. According to Gordon in an interview with *Fangoria*, it was the fantasy, fairy tell element of *Dolls* that intrigued him the most, as well as the opportunity to make his sophomore feature—while still obviously a horror film—so different from his first.[5] After *Dolls,* Gordon would re-team with the bulk of the *Re-Animator* crew for another H.P. Lovecraft adaptation, *From Beyond.* Band would be much more involved this time, a producer from the beginning in a refreshingly different picture than *Re-Animator,* taking heavy cues from Carpenter and Cronenberg in the wake of *The Thing*'s revolutionary FX.

As Empire pushed into the second half of the decade, its output increased exponentially. Whereas they had released one or two films a year to start, they quickly found themselves releasing nine or ten, sometimes more. And while many of those features, such as *Troll* and *TerrorVision* clearly bore the Charles Band seal of approval, others such as *Rawhead Rex, Intruder* and *Prison* were simply pick-ups that weren't met with much of any involvement by Band at all. His role on them was simply as an executive. Band had founded Empire for one reason: to make his own movies his own way. But by the late '80s, that was proving to be harder and harder as Empire began distributing more and more films. Despite his role as a producer, Band had never shown an interest in simply slapping his name on someone else's movie as an executive. Always dreaming up new, bizarre ideas, he had longed for the hands-on approach. Not just distributing films but creating them all in-house.

In an interview with *Cult Films and the People Who Made Them,* Band said, "That started off as one thing and became another. The first few films were my films and the last year I think of the twelve films that were released only two were films I was directly involved in."[6]

At the same time, the Empire films never quite recaptured the box office success of *Ghoulies.* That's not to say that they were not successful, of course. They were made for very little money and always earned more than they cost to make. Less and less of that money was coming in from theaters, though. By this point in the late '80s, the video boom had begun in earnest. Band had already seen success in that area distributing the Wizard Video and Media Home Entertainment titles. This is not to mention that the films were becoming cheaper and cheaper, both in-house and in the independent pick-ups. TransWorld Entertainment, under the newly put together Epic Holdings, commenced a takeover to seize all assets of the dwindling studio.[7] Empire was folding and there was nothing Band could do to prevent it from happening, but there was never a question of whether or not he would continue to produce and distribute films, only a question of how exactly he would do it. As fantastic as the Empire model had been, it hadn't ultimately worked and it became clear that something new and different would need to take its place.

By the end of Empire Pictures' nearly ten-year run, it had become clear that the films were much more successful on video than they had been in their often-meager theatrical releases. In theaters, these features would come and go. But on video store shelves, it proved to be a completely different story. Older horror fans and young kids alike would be dazzled by the gripping artwork and the promise of weird and unusual creatures. The theatrical market was getting bigger and meaner, more competitive every day. But the video market was newer and, therefore, largely untested. The decision to create feature films exclusively for video retailers was an incredible gamble, but with Empire behind him, Band didn't really have anything to lose.

Paramount proved willing to provide the home video distribution for Band's new company, Full Moon Entertainment. All it would need to either prove its success or prove that this risky idea simply could not work was a single movie. Full Moon could not enter the video market without, well, a video to market. So Band sought out to produce a debut feature that would put his new company on the map. Something that would be done as a straight-to-video affair, but with all the passion and ambition of a theatrical release. Something that would prove that the Full Moon model could work.

He only needed to decide exactly what that would be.

But *Dungeonmaster* had been a pretty great title, hadn't it?

Chapter Two

Puppet Master

He had a title. Like Roger Corman before him, Band's films often began life with two things: a title and a piece of artwork, though it is unclear whether the original artwork or the original script came first, as they appear to have been made independently of one another. In the case of the original poster, the artwork featured a variety of very unrefined, almost unfinished looking puppets, sitting in an open-faced old trunk. The puppets depicted in the artwork came in all shapes and sizes. One had a drill on his head, another was a werewolf, another looked like a kind of lizard, while one had guns for hands, another one was a brute of a puppet with a small head on a burly body, while the last two had knives for hands and a skull-like face, respectively. At first glance, these puppets bore almost no resemblance to what people would eventually see in the finished movie. But those design elements are incredibly important. Even if they mixed and matched, every single puppet in that original piece of art would be referenced in the designs of puppets and creatures that would appear in the franchise eventually. The poster was designed by Lee MacLeod, who had worked with Band in the Empire days and would go on to become Full Moon's go-to artist throughout most of the '90s. He describes the process of creating the poster as follows: "For that one, I met with Charlie and he described what he wanted: the puppets in a trunk. If memory serves, he had the puppets already figured out and I basically designed them according to his description," MacLeod says. "The pre-production puppets I drew up were sort of cool, but in no way as great as what David Allen would produce."

With an idea, a basic visual concept and a title all ready to go, one more crucial, obvious thing was needed: a story. To write the script, he approached Kenneth J. Hall, who he had worked with as an FX artist dating all the way back to *Ghoulies*. A writer as well, Hall had first penned *The Tomb* for Fred Olen Ray, which saw an evil, immortal woman rise from the grave after her tomb had been desecrated. It starred Sybil Danning and John Carradine. After that, he had gone on to write *Evil Spawn* (which he also directed), *Terror Night* and *Nightmare Sisters*. But Hall's relationship working for Band dated back even before the creation of Empire Pictures. As he explains, "I worked on *Metalstorm*, which was before Empire. I foam-fabricated the body of the Energy Monster. When they started Empire, I did P.A. work on *Sword Kill*, which was eventually released as *Ghost Warrior*. That's when I got to know Charlie's wife, Debra Dion. She saw a photo of a werewolf I had created back in Florida and asked if I still had it. I did, so I wore it in a segment of *Dungeonmaster*. It was there I met John Carl Buechler.

"I went on to work at John's shop after helping out as an extra puppeteer on *Ghoulies*, later doing effects on a number of their shows. However, I wanted more to be a writer and, eventually, a director, so I kept trying to get Debra to read my scripts. I even gave her one that was an adaptation of a Lovecraft story prior to *Re-Animator*. She told us they didn't make horror films! I honestly believe she didn't like the genre even though that's what they were making.

"It wasn't until my friend David DeCoteau brought me in to write what became *Dr. Alien* that she took notice of me. I approached the project as a teen comedy with some sci-fi elements, which she really liked. After that, I formally met with Charlie for the first time and I was slated to write and direct a number of projects."

All things considered, getting the job writing *Puppet Master* proved relatively easy. As Hall explains: "It was about nine months after the overseas banks shut down Empire. Charlie had started Bandcompany and had an office on Sunset Boulevard. Debra called me in for a meeting and that's when it happened…. Charlie had a title and the list of puppets. He told me the killers in the story would be about fifteen inches tall. I replied, 'Like *Ghoulies*.' He said, 'No, these characters are carved out of wood.' I said, 'Oh, like *Dolls*.' He had no idea I was teasing him for going to the same well over and over again."

From the beginning, Hall's original script for *Puppet Master* proved to be very different from the film that people would wind up seeing. This story centered on a coven of New Age witches who wind up traveling to an abandoned hotel to get in touch with the renowned puppet master who had died there, only to inadvertently awaken his legion of terrifying, killer puppets. Tonally, it felt much more in line with the early Empire productions like *Ghoulies* and *Dolls*. This was something done with a much more bombastic, tongue-in-cheek style. At the same time, it was a much more effects-heavy script than the finished *Puppet Master* would prove to be. Hall's script featured numerous killer puppets, some of which were totally original creations, some of which were depicted on the artwork he was shown when Band commissioned him to write the script. "It centered around a group of contemporary witches, warlocks and other occult types who were looking for a missing member," explains Hall. "My original opening was akin to *The Big Chill*, where they learn he's dead through the psychic grapevine. This reference was lost on Charlie because he apparently only watches genre films. However, there was a similar sequence in the final film.

"The group of witches in my script were far more malevolent than the parapsychologists they were changed to. They hijack their lost friend's coffin at the gravesite and torment his girl in attempt to learn what he was up to all these years."

Ultimately, Hall's version proved a little too ambitious for the scope that Band was aiming to achieve. That script laid the foundations—a group of people making their way to an abandoned hotel to be picked off one by one by the master's puppets. While Band was apparently satisfied with the script, its director proved not to be.

David Schmoeller, who had worked with Band on multiple pictures beginning with *Tourist Trap*, was Band's first choice for director and agreed to do it on one condition: he be allowed to rewrite the script from top to bottom. In an interview with *Love It Loud*, Schmoeller explained how he came to direct *Puppet Master*, as well as

Chapter Two. Puppet Master

why he rewrote Hall's original script. "When Charlie made a deal with Paramount to release his Full Moon films, he hired me to direct the first film. He called me in, gave me a script he wanted me to direct called *Puppet Master*. The original idea was Charlie's and the draft I was given was written by Kenneth J. Hall. I think Charlie considered me a skilled director who was also very dependable—in terms of schedules and budgets....

"Charlie also knew that I had to write my own scripts in order to direct them. So, he knew he had to hire me to rewrite *Puppet Master*—so that I could direct it. The process of me rewriting Kenneth J. Hall is no reflection on his work (although I'm sure he was not happy—what writer would be?). It's just that I have to rework the story to make it my own—and put it into a cinematic form that I can direct."[1]

Trusting Schmoeller as both a director and an economically minded storyteller, Band agreed. According to the director, 90 percent of what is there in the finished film is his. He made most of the changes that resulted in the film that fans have now grown up on for thirty years. Instead of a coven of New Age witches, Schmoeller went for the scaled-back, somewhat classier notion of a group of paranormal psychologists ranging from University professors to carnival fortunetellers.

With less puppet carnage, the script instead focused on mystery. It is less centered on exactly what the puppets were doing as much as who is the one telling them to do it. There would still be plenty of horror and mayhem, particularly a cut sequence involving Pinhead pulling the fire alarm to alert all of the other puppets to someone attempting to leave the hotel, which would have been admittedly fascinating to see.

Given Schmoeller's involvement, *Puppet Master* bears many interesting similarities to the director's previous cult classic Charles Band collaboration, *Tourist Trap*. Both films are about people being terrified by doll-like inanimate figures—mannequins, in the case of *Tourist Trap*—and both are about those figures being controlled by a character not fully revealed until the end of the film. Like Richard Band's score for *Puppet Master,* the great Pino Donaggio's music for *Tourist Trap* conveys equal doses of whimsy and dread. If there is a major difference between the two, other than the stylistic differences as *Puppet Master* aims to be slightly more slick and refined than its predecessor, it's that in *Tourist Trap* the mannequins are not actually alive. They are controlled by another character, like the puppets, but they are controlled telekinetically. He consciously manipulates their every movement. The puppets, on the other hand, have their individual personalities. They will do what they are called upon to do, but there are character quirks that set them apart from the very first time the audience is introduced to them, and those moments in which the character of these wooden creations come through would ultimately prove to be the success of not just the movie, but also the very thing that would launch the *Puppet Master* brand.

Puppet Master was sold at the now-defunct MIFED film market in September of 1988.[2] Together, Band and Schmoeller began assembling a slew of familiar Empire faces behind the camera. Cinematographer Sergio Salvati had shot numerous Empire films such as *Cellar Dweller, Ghoulies II* and Schmoeller's own *Crawlspace*. He had also served as Lucio Fulci's director of photography on some of the director's best, including *City of the Living Dead* (aka *Gates of Hell*) and *The Beyond* and many, many

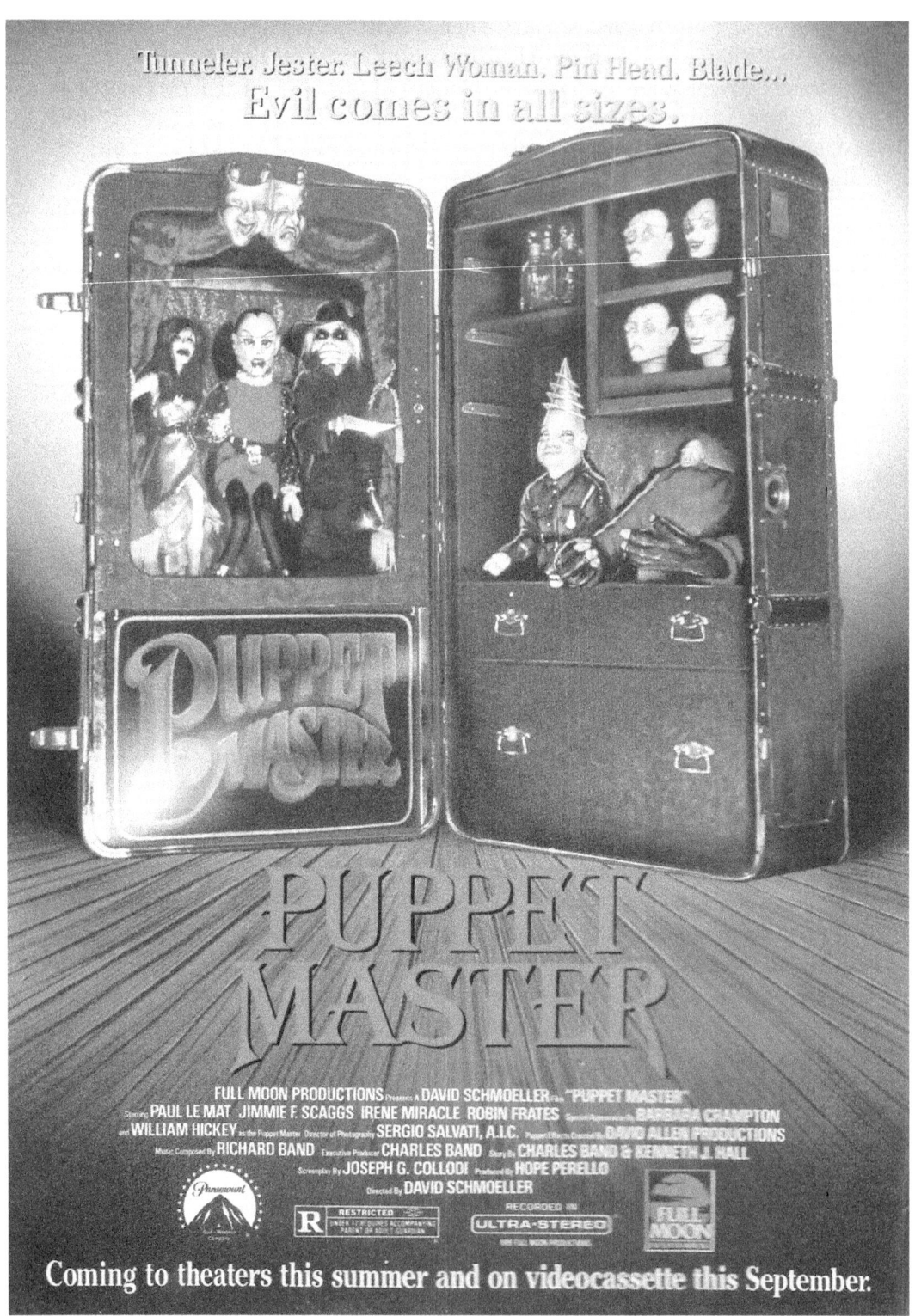

Puppet Master magazine ad (Author Scan).

more. He had even worked in the camera department on the cinematic classic *The Good, the Bad and the Ugly*. While Salvati was no doubt hired because of his previous work with Band and Schmoeller, he provided a distinctly Italian look that would not only call back to his films with Fulci, but—perhaps because of that connection—would also completely benefit the movie's occasionally dreamlike, surrealist nature.

John Myhre was also brought on board as production designer. Whereas Salvati was a seasoned vet of a cinematographer, Myhre was largely unproven in his field. *Puppet Master* was his first film as production designer after working as a prop master on *Night of the Comet* and *Creature*. Thankfully, he proved himself up to the task, providing the artistic, prestigious Old Hollywood look would be needed for the film's primary setting, the Bodega Bay Inn. *Puppet Master* turned out to be Myhre's big break. He went on to work as production designer on such huge films as *Memoirs of a Geisha, Chicago, Ali, X-Men, Dreamgirls* and *Pirates of the Caribbean: On Stranger Tides*. Myhre has now won two Oscars with a total of five nominations in the Set Decoration category. He has even worked on such huge Disney productions as *Mary Poppins Returns* and is set to provide production design for *The Little Mermaid*. And that road to monumental success began with *Puppet Master*.

Perhaps the most important team assembled behind the camera, however, was that of David Allen and his group of puppeteers. Allen had previously worked with Band on several features, providing stop-motion sequences for *Laserblast, Dolls, Ghoulies II* and many more beginning in the mid–1970s. On most of these films, the stop-motion work had been relatively small. After all, these were small productions that didn't necessarily have the time to devote to lengthy, Harryhausen-esque sequences. Still, Allen's few shots of Victorian dolls creeping around an old mansion in Stuart Gordon's *Dolls* had made an impact on audiences, brief as they were. With *Puppet Master*, there was an opportunity to go bigger, bolder and scarier when it came to the FX and practical creations. It was something that both Allen and his crew sought to achieve.

The team behind the creation of the puppets consisted of Allen, Dennis Gordon, Mark Rappaport, Cindy Sorensen, John Teska and Brett White. Each would have their own specific duties, but each of them also wore many different hats on the journey to bring this movie to life.

Going off of the accumulated puppet descriptions over the course of the script's evolution, Allen and his crew set to work designing the film's five diminutive stars. Schmoeller had dictated that the film's prologue featuring the death of the titular puppet master, Andre Toulon, be a period piece set during the late 1930s, which meant that the puppet designs would have to match their era. Jester, the film's evolution of *Dolls*' Mr. Punch, would serve as the comic relief, a relatively harmless and only vaguely sinister puppet, whose face would be split into three sections that could spin on their own in order to magically rearrange in order to form different expressions. While a puppet who served the basic function as Jester appeared in Hall's original script, the character was very different. According to Hall, "The spy puppet in my script was a character called Skull. He was replaced by Jester and his skeletal features were given to Blade."

Pinhead would be just as the name would make him sound: a burly, sweatered brute of a puppet with a very small head. Tunneler, another character that had existed from the very first artwork, changed almost entirely from the original design. Sticking to the period notions, Tunneler's visual cues stemmed from Italian fascist Benito Mussolini, and the only thing he still had in common with the concept art was the namesake drill atop his head. Blade (named Switchblade on set according to the *Fangoria* set report but was either a typo or changed sometime before release) was an amalgamation of several ideas over the course of previous drafts of the script and the initial concept artwork.

Both the original concept art and Kenneth J. Hall's original script displayed a character with a skull-like face and another with a knife for a hand, though they were two separate characters. Blade in the script proved to be very different from the finished film. As Hall notes, "Blade himself had multiple sword-wielding arms, similar to Kali from *The Golden Voyage of Sinbad*. We already had a puppet in the script, Six-Shooter, who had more than two arms, but Charlie liked the concept of Blade." When the roster of puppets lessened significantly, certain traits were combined. It would be director David Schmoeller himself who would provide the final inspiration for the puppet. At this point in time, Schmoeller had something of a rivalry with infamous German actor Klaus Kinski, calling him a nightmare to work with on the director's previous film, *Crawlspace*. Whether out of resentment or respect for Kinski's ability to instill fear, Schmoeller suggested that the actor's pallid face and long, wispy white hair be put to use in the puppet.[3] The end result of this hodgepodge of inspirations proved to be a dynamic image, a grinning, expressionistic, Neo Gothic puppet with a knife for one hand and a hook for another. While each puppet's design proved perfectly suited for the film, it's easy to see how Blade would take off to become the striking, sinister icon at the center of Full Moon Productions.

Blade appears in the hallway (courtesy Chris Endicott).

Amazingly, though—and much like Pinhead in *Hellraiser* before it—nobody seemed to predict this at the time. Blade was almost mentioned as an afterthought during the *Fangoria* set visit interview and was largely just thought of as another of the five puppets causing destruction and mayhem throughout the film. If anything, there seemed to be an indication that Pinhead, out of all the puppets, was expected to become the breakout star. But it would be Blade's pasty, goth-chic face on much of the marketing, and viewers were immediately intrigued by the puppet's design. Because of that, it continues to be his face on the marketing to this day. In fact, Blade's standout success was perhaps cemented with the announcement of his solo film, *Blade: The Iron Cross,* in 2019.

The last of the puppets in the film, though far from the least, would be the group's most distinctive member in many different ways. She is the only female puppet in the film, even including the dozens of puppets on the wall in Toulon's workshop displayed during the prologue. She would also be the only puppet who didn't wear her special ability as a physical trait. She's the only puppet for which it isn't obvious exactly how she is going to kill someone. Because of that, she is also both the most surprising and the most disgusting of the group. Her name, however, gives her abilities away: Leech Woman.

At first glance, Leech Woman is only vaguely creepy. Her long dark hair and dark eyes may be slightly unnerving, but hardly threatening when compared to her counterparts. She's meant to be pretty, to disarm the victim until she can get close enough to do what she is truly designed to do: vomit large, poisonous leeches all over her prey. Because of its impractical nature, her method of killing usually requires assistance from at least one of the other puppets or requires the victim to be otherwise restrained. With that in mind, her introduction and standout sequence in the film itself is all too perfect.

Hall, however, was much less of a fan, though he praised the other puppets. "My only real complaint was the Leech Woman," he says, "because I thought it was ridiculous that she spits leeches on people. That may be gross, but they are hardly deadly. My puppet had a body of clear glass with a metal forked tongue to drain people's blood. At one point, she is draining a victim who starts struggling with her and breaks her in half. He bleeds to death while her upper torso crawls out of the room, leaving a trail of blood behind."

David Allen based the designs of the puppets as a collective entity on the French Grand Guignol theater, which specialized in macabre horror shows depicting displays of violence and gore.[4] The full title *Le Theatre du Grand Guignol* in English directly translates to "Theatre of the Great Puppet." Guignol, specifically, was a famed French puppet that specialized in satirical political commentary in a very similar style to Punch and Judy. Grand Guignol theater was often reliant on special effects, stunning audiences not just with extreme imagery, but by leading them to wonder how exactly these grisly feats were being pulled off, like watching a magic show. In most Grand Guignol plays, the violence would be relatively sparse until culminating in an extremely gruesome climax, which is certainly the case in *Puppet Master,* making the film at least a modern-day descendant carrying on the classic Grand Guignol tradition.

Pinhead emerges from a coffin (courtesy Chris Endicott).

For Allen it seemed important that the puppets be at least somewhat disarming. While some have criticized *Puppet Master* for lightening its diminutive characters too much, rarely making them completely outwardly sinister, that was exactly what makes them so endearing in the original film and is likely a huge part of their ongoing success. He made it clear that these characters could be believably tamed, and that they were not necessarily eager to do terrible things but that they were *capable* of doing those terrible things, and that's where the fear—or at least the discomfort—was meant to stem from. These puppet characters were in their own way cute, and were meant to be at least somewhat, but they were *also* deadly. And that juxtaposition of those two concepts, which should be completely opposite, may be the very thing that has become the key to *Puppet Master*'s success, from the films to the merchandising and everything in between. These are characters that are meant to be enjoyed, dazzling even if they're unsettling, and there is an immediate attraction to bringing those concepts together.

In an interview with *Cinefantastique*, Allen explained his thoughts on the animation process. "I do not find it relaxing. It's a very intense experience…. There's a paranoia that hangs over the whole process which is based on the fact that it's a time-lapsed process. The only thing that is supposed to be disturbed over a period of hours or even days is the thing that you, yourself are consciously disturbing. Nothing else is even supposed to move. You're asking for a complete suspension of all the physical laws and properties that can befall something that's at rest. It may all go to smash because something fell over or a light blew out. And you don't know if it's worked until the next day. But the results *are* a lot of fun."[5]

Chapter Two. Puppet Master

With the design and creation of the film's tiny terrors underway, it was time to move onto casting the movie's human stars as well. What had begun as a group of New Age witches would now be a cast of psychics, coming to the Bodega Bay Inn after receiving a distress call from an estranged colleague, only to find to their shock that he has taken his own life. Leading this group of psychics is actor Paul Le Mat as Yale professor Alex Whittaker. Beginning his acting career with the TV movie *Firehouse*, Le Mat would find much larger success with his very next film, *American Graffiti*. The biggest film from George Lucas prior to *Star Wars*, *American Graffiti* continues to be celebrated as a coming-of-age classic. Le Mat co-starred alongside Richard Dreyfuss and Ron Howard, who would both go on to be huge industry talents. In 1979, Le Mat reprised his role as John Milner for *More American Graffiti* before starring in the acclaimed *Melvin and Howard* in 1980. Le Mat's Alex Whittaker is the most soft-spoken and certainly the least eccentric of the psychics making up the main cast of the film. Other than occasionally reminding both the other characters and the viewer that he dreams the future, Alex basically comes across as the average, stoic college professor.

Starring opposite Le Mat would be relative newcomer Robin Frates as Megan Gallagher, widow of the psychic's former colleague, Neil Gallagher. Frates had only accumulated few acting credits prior to her leading role in *Puppet Master*, consisting only of the film *Big Man on Campus* and an episode of the TV series *Anything but Love*. Frates' relative newness to the industry proved perfect for the character, as she naturally embodied the doe-eyed innocence and endless naiveté that Megan needed in order to work in the way she was intended.

Filling out the cast of psychics would be Irene Miracle as "The White Witch" Dana Hadley, as well as Matt Roe and Kathryn O'Reilly as Frank Forrester and Clarissa Stamford. Miracle continued to accentuate the film's Italian flavor, as she was already well known to horror fans at the time for her memorable appearance in Dario Argento's *Inferno*, the second of his "Three Mothers" trilogy beginning with *Suspiria*. In that film, Miracle has an extended, beautifully shot underwater sequence leading to her grisly death at the hands of the film's supernatural killer. In an interview with *House of Freudstein*, Miracle explained that it was the chance to work with the director that attracted her to *Puppet Master*. "He's a fine director who deserves to work with much more than he has. Ironically, he only made *Puppet Master* with the idea that it would be a sounding board to some of these other more sensitive and psychologically complex films that he had written."[6]

The late Matt Roe had made several TV appearances prior to *Puppet Master*, in shows ranging from *Murder, She Wrote* to *Werewolf, L.A. Law* and *Who's the Boss?* This would only be his second feature film appearance after *Double Revenge* and his first lead role. After *Puppet Master*, Roe would make several other appearances in movies like *Black Scorpion* and *Naked Gun 33⅓: The Final Insult*. Most intriguingly, he also put in a cameo in the *other* killer toy franchise, portraying a police officer in *Child's Play 2*. While each of the other psychics has some kind of specific gimmick, Roe's Frank Forrester appears to be a general by-the-numbers psychic, but often links his own gifts with the more riveting powers of his lover and colleague, Clarissa Stamford.

Portraying Clarissa, Kathryn O'Reilly was called upon to have a sexual reaction to just about any object she came into contact with throughout the film, as her character can read and feel the entire history of objects and places just by touching them. O'Reilly is an actress with only six credits to her name, but *Puppet Master* is proof that she could easily have had a career as a cult scream queen had she wanted one. Prior to this film, her only film appearances were as a sex worker in the previous year's *Jack's Back* and as a member of the Vampirettes in the spoofy sequel *Saturday the 14th Strikes Back*.

Although her character is as smart and professional as the others, O'Reilly doesn't have much to do as Clarissa unless the scene takes a sexual turn, allowing her to vividly describe the history of an elevator or bed. While this might not make the best use of her character, it allows for a very clear distinction between when Clarissa is using her psychic abilities and when she is not. Her typically stiff-upper-lip nature allows for an interesting contrast to her more unhinged, wildly sexual scenes.

If Clarissa's defining trait is her potential nymphomania, Frank's is his greed. Of the psychics, he was the closest to Neil, something that the movie only casually mentions but which becomes incredibly obvious once the bigger picture is revealed. He and Neil together were interested in the legends of Andre Toulon, the famous puppet master who shot himself in this hotel, particularly in the rumors that he had found some sort of key to immortality through a way to bring inanimate objects to life. When Frank so bluntly says that if he discovered Toulon's secrets he'd "rule the world," it's hard to tell if even he thinks he's joking or not. Once everything becomes clear in the third act, it's hard to wonder if the film might not have played out exactly the same had Frank gotten to Toulon's secret before Neil did.

Dana stands out against these other psychics, even though she is the most immediately antagonistic. A hard drinking woman who spends the bulk of the film talking to a dead dog, Dana is hardly approachable. She even comfortably, proudly refers to herself as a "nasty bitch." But even though she is easily the most confrontational of the psychics, she is the only one actively trying to protect everyone else in the hotel, even warning the maid Theresa not to go near the fireplace where she will meet her eventual end. This juxtaposition, along with the smirking style in which Miracle portrays the character, makes her the most vibrant and interesting person to watch in the whole movie.

The last of the psychics is the dearly departed Neil Gallagher, a man missed by his wife, but not so much by the people who truly knew him. Dana is quick to refer to Neil as a "despicable, greedy bastard" who screwed them over in his pursuits of Toulon's secret, which clearly led him to this hotel. By the end of the film, it's revealed that Neil Gallagher is actually alive and well. He did find Toulon's magic and used it on himself, bringing his colleagues to the hotel in order to murder them before they could pick up on the fact that he had survived his own death or that he had found the secret of life for himself. He also claims that he needs new bodies with which to experiment with the boundaries between life and death, noting that the first experiments consisted of the murder of his wife's parents.

Playing Neil Gallagher with sadistic glee is the late Jimmie F. Skaggs, who had appeared as a drug dealer in *Lethal Weapon* and a pagan in *Dragnet* alongside several other supporting roles and TV guest spots. He had portrayed a villain the year prior to *Puppet Master* in Empire Picture's *Ghost Town,* an undead revenge Western with terrific cover art. In that, he brought much of the same manic energy and sleaziness that make his role in *Puppet Master* work so well.

The film shot at the historic Castle Green Apartments in Los Angeles. The massive structure proved perfect for the Bodega Bay Inn, providing both the sense of isolation that the suspense in the script required, as well as a distinctive classic Hollywood feeling, allowing the film to more readily feel like a spiritual successor to the likes of shock-masters Alfred Hitchcock and William Castle, both of whom served as clear influences. The film opens with a literal bang, introducing audiences to a seemingly kind old puppet master by the name of Andre Toulon.

William Hickey as Toulon, with Jester (courtesy Chris Endicott).

Even though he is only in one scene, casting Toulon proved to be one of the most crucial aspects of the movie. William Hickey proved to be the right choice for the part. The late, great actor had a long career in Hollywood and saw numerous successes both before and after *Puppet Master.* This was only a few years after his Oscar-nominated turn in 1985's *Prizzi's Honor.* In 1993, he would appear on the other end of the stop-motion spectrum as the mad scientist Dr. Finklestein in Tim Burton and Henry Sellick's *The Nightmare Before Christmas.* Hickey would also make appearances throughout the '90s in films like *Major Payne* and *Mouse Hunt,* as well as an Arnold Schwarzenegger–directed episode of *Tales from the Crypt* before his death in 1999. Hickey's performance as the titular puppet master is even more impressive when taking into account the fact that it was entirely shot in all of six hours.

For the purposes of *Puppet Master,* Hickey proved to be perfect in his one scene role as Andre Toulon. An apparently kindly old man, there's something nonetheless eccentric about him that makes the viewer start to believe that he could have built these morbid, puppet creations, even if they appear to be relatively harmless. The prologue sequence does a great job not just of establishing the mystery, but in disarming the puppets as well.

Given that this was a straight-to-video production, people had already picked up the videocassette and seen the designs of the puppets before watching the film. They knew what to be scared of. But in the opening, the puppets are as domesticated as family pets, with Jester appearing warm and loving in the arms of his creator and Blade racing around the hotel in a nervous frenzy played much more for comic relief than scares. This opening allows the viewer to let their guard down when it comes to the puppets. Seeing that they are harmless in the arms of their creator, people were completely unprepared for the kind of carnage that the puppets would wind up wreaking later on.

Admittedly, it takes a long time for that carnage to begin in earnest, with most of the early portions of the film centering on establishing the characters and the mystery of both why Neil Gallagher shot himself and why none of the other psychics knew about it before they arrived. In addition to that, there are no shortage of dream sequences and surreal visions. Alex has a dream of Megan (who he has yet to meet) and Neil (who he has yet to learn is dead) dancing in the Inn's ballroom while Neil wears a faceless white mask, a dream that continues to reoccur until the third act. His dream ends in seeing himself covered in leeches, something that might confuse first time viewers and might be one of the strangest bits of foreshadowing in horror history, once Leech Woman in unveiled later on in the feature.

The first sign that even lets the viewer in on the fact that the puppets are still at large in the hotel is also possibly the most creepily effective shot of the entire film. A long, lingering dolly move toward the open casket housing Neil Gallagher's apparent corpse also sees the introduction of Pinhead as the puppet rises out of the coffin and leaps down to the floor. For such a quick moment, it is a complicated blend of stop-motion and puppetry that took two days to properly execute, shining a light on just how hard Allen and his crew worked on getting the effects just right, even on the limited timeframe of a small, independent horror film.[7]

The first major scare sequence of the movie also involves Pinhead, as the maid Theresa does exactly what she was warned not to do and goes to tend the fireplace by herself. In a scene with much better build up than payoff, Theresa hears someone playing the piano, but can't find any sign of anyone else in the room and returns to the fireplace just in time for Pinhead to whack her in the side of the head with the poker. Interestingly enough, this kill was apparently not originally meant to be Pinhead's. In an on-set interview with *Fangoria*, Schmoeller noted that Jester would be the one to kill the maid.[8] At some point in time, that detail was changed. It's easy to assume that may have been budgetary, as Theresa's death is far less complicated than any of the other kill sequences in the movie. There's simply a shot of Pinhead's hand picking up the poker and a cutaway to blood being splattered across the fireplace, so it's more than likely that this was retooled during the post-production FX shoot when time or budget would not allow the sequence to happen as originally planned.

It seems like a natural explanation as every aspect of that death scene is an insert shot. This is admittedly somewhat disappointing, though, as it would not only have been Jester's only kill in the film, but his only kill in the entire franchise as even after twelve movie appearances the puppet has yet to actually claim a victim.

After much more exposition following Theresa's death, the characters settle into their hotel rooms, providing a voyeuristic look into their private kinks—from Frank and Clarissa's bondage to Dana's ability to hold conversation with her stuffed dog, Leroy. These voyeuristic moments are not without intention, as it's not just the viewer spying on the characters once they settle into their separate rooms, but the puppet Blade. We follow him from room to room as he spies on each of the psychics, picking out potential victims. In these scenes, Blade is characterized similarly to the opening prologue, walking the thin line between being sinister and being comedic. The fact that this morbid looking puppet is spying on hotel guests without them even realizing it is certainly unsettling, but when Blade's eyes literally pop at the sight of Frank and Clarissa's kinky sex, it's absolutely played for comedic effect. Even though Schmoeller cited Jester as the film's comic relief, Blade plays that role in more than a few of the film's major sequences as well.

These scenes also show that Blade's scouting out his *own* victims in particular. After spying on Frank and Clarissa, he steps aside to let Tunneler have his moment in the spotlight. That puppet is revealed in a spectacular fashion as well, first seen through the keyhole, with a long shadowed silhouette turning to a full reveal as the door slowly creaks open. Seeing the door wide open, Clarissa worriedly tells Frank that she thinks someone has entered the room and that she can hear someone moving around even if she can't see them. Frank, blindfolded, is naturally worried and begs her to untie him, which she ignores. This scene originated in Hall's original script. "Humorously," he says, "Charlie insisted on keeping a bondage scene I had written, despite that it made far less sense that a pair of scientists would be engaging in this activity in the middle of an investigation."

As a movie about killer toys, this scene makes for one of the most iconic images and the most natural progression of the theme. Like a startled child, Clarissa bends down to check under the bed, at first seeing nothing and then discovering Tunneler, blinking at her curiously before he takes a running start into her mouth. The death is grisly, but we don't see any of it before it cuts away to a shot of Clarissa's bloody hand raising up to grab onto the bed. It is as squeamish as it is practical, smart on both the part of the puppet and—obviously—the script. With Frank on the bed, anything else would have caused a scream and alerted him or potentially anyone else in the hotel. Taking her mouth out of the equation makes a twisted kind of sense.

With Clarissa dead, Leech Woman makes her debut only seconds later, taking advantage of poor Frank while he lays helpless and restrained on the bed. At first, he somehow mistakes the puppet's small hands and mouth for Clarissa and continues to think this is Clarissa even after hearing her regurgitate a leech. It's only once the leech begins to make its painful presence known that Frank forces himself to look at what's actually happening. Much unlike Clarissa, he screams and screams in pain as he has the blood sucked out of him by poisonous, deadly leeches. Over time, fans have often

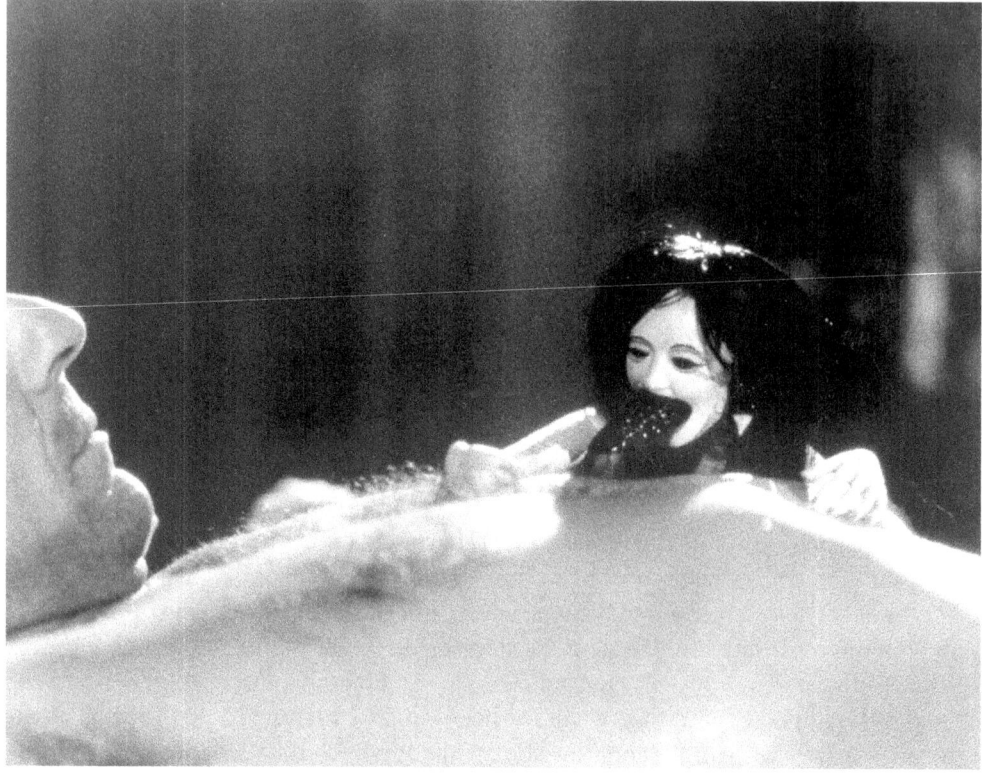

Leech Woman does her thing (courtesy Chris Endicott).

pointed out that leeches would not naturally be fatal—but then again, they're not naturally spat up by puppets either.

There is a sexual connotation to both of these deaths that is hard to ignore as they come right on the heels of Frank and Clarissa's bondage scene. Despite the practical reasons for it, one can't help but notice the implications of Tunneler drilling Clarissa through the mouth. Immediately following that, Frank somehow mistakes Leech Woman's touch for that of Clarissa, and despite the pain believes the first leech to be an "undisclosed sexual aid." Clarissa is bored by a phallic drill, while Frank is quite literally drained of fluids. These moments only exaggerate the bizarre eccentricity of this scene as a whole, especially for what is otherwise a largely sexless movie. These brief moments of fetish do occasionally continue to pop up throughout the franchise but are never made as prominent or obvious as they are here.

The action seems to quiet down as it transitions into Dana discovering Gallagher's body in her hotel room, making it clear that she knows more than she's letting on, even that she might have already realized that Neil himself is behind everything strange going on in the hotel. Within moments, this turns into the extended puppet chase leading up to Dana's death at the hands of both Pinhead and Blade. As exciting as both of these death scenes are—mostly being the highlight of the movie—they showcase the film's larger pacing issues. After an hour of next to no puppet scenes, the bulk of the deaths happen in rapid succession, one right after the other.

This is highlighted immediately after Dana's death, when Alex has a dream about a conversation with Megan that happens in the very next scene. It's a very awkward scene that plays almost like a built-in bathroom break moment. But it leads directly into the final revelation, in which Neil Gallagher both reveals he's alive and lays out his evil ambitions. This scene truly hammers home *Puppet Master*'s Agatha Christie inspirations. From the location to the atmosphere to many of the character interactions, *Puppet Master* almost plays like old-school murder mystery theater. The classic horror elements feel so much in-keeping with films like *House on Haunted Hill* and even Hitchcock's *Rope*, with the knowledge that someone is pulling the puppets' strings and attempting to figure out who may or may not be in on it—as both Frank and Dana acknowledge that they know more than they are letting on. Skaggs is embracing cheesy sleaziness as he explains all of the horrific things he's done both up to his suicide and after his return from death, but the scene takes a drastic change when he makes the mistake of announcing that he plans to toss the puppets by the wayside in favor of experimenting with reanimated humans instead.

They trap Neil in the elevator, saving the film's most grisly death scene for last, as all of the puppets—with the exception of Jester, who is a spectator throughout the entire film, never getting directly involved—gang up to take down this new puppet master at once. This scene was so grisly in concept that it needed to be altered in order for the film to receive an R rating.

During Neil's death, his blood is green, which viewers have noticed as being particularly jarring and unrealistic. The reason for this has been long rumored to be that the filmmakers knew that the color of the blood had to be changed. This honestly makes a great deal of sense. That same sequence with red blood would have proved to be too much and simply wouldn't fly by the MPAA but changing the color of the blood to green would mean that censorship would not be as large of a problem. As random a change as this might have been, Neil's green blood wound up contributing something crucial to the *Puppet Master* mythology that would become more and more important as the film series progressed: the green serum that gives the puppets life. In context with the sequel, which delves much further into the serum and its importance, the confusing emerald splatter of this death scene makes much more sense, as it effectively explains why Neil had green fluid running through his veins during the original film's climax.

Still, Neil's death is certainly effective. The puppets truly unleash their vicious potential as they unleash the "total destruction of this body" that Neil accidentally let slip would be the only way in which to kill him for a second time. With Blade removing his fingers and Tunneler taking out his leg in order to incapacitate him, Leech Woman returns for her second scene in the movie to deliver the killing blow, dropping a large leech down into Gallagher's mouth.

This is an interesting and uncommon turn of events for a horror film that makes *Puppet Master* all the more unique and intriguing. At the end, the monsters are not dispatched, but rather take matters into their own hands and strike out at the villain who has been manipulating them instead of setting their sights on the heroes of the piece. They may be the cause of most of the carnage unleashed throughout the running time, but they both begin and end the film as relatively benevolent forces.

Moments like these make the puppets' full-blown turn into antiheroes later on in the franchise much easier to digest.

Adding the final piece of the puzzle would be Charlie Band's brother, Richard, who composed the music for several Empire releases, including the cult classic *Re-Animator*. The score for *Puppet Master* would have slight echoes of Pino

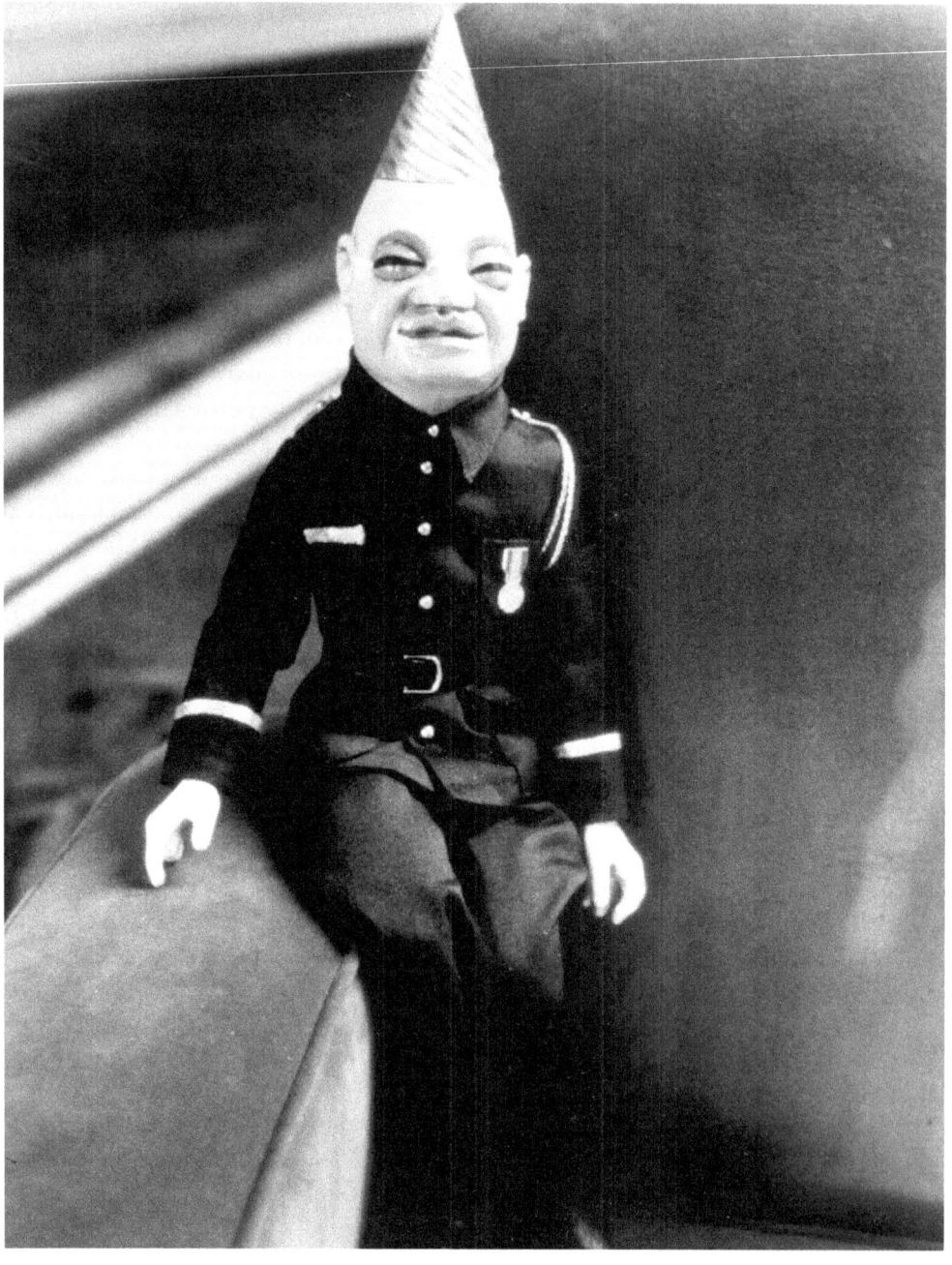

Tunneler appears (courtesy Chris Endicott).

Donaggio's themes for Schmoeller's own *Tourist Trap*, but certainly proved to be its own thing. The *Puppet Master* score is haunting, somewhat whimsical, evoking the necessary feelings of toys and childhood that has been twisted and contorted. Most importantly, the opening theme proved to be instantly recognizable, a must for any horror film that wanted to stand out and survive in the era of franchise icons like Michael Myers, Freddy Krueger and Jason Voorhees, each of whom carried a distinct sound with them in each of their appearances. "At that point, to the best of my recollection," says Richard Band, "Empire was kind of winding down. So things were going through a bit of a change. At that time in my career, I hadn't had a lot of experience just yet with electronics. I was formally trained, so most of my work was orchestrally based, as it has been through most of my career. At that point, my knowledge of it was very limited, as opposed to now, where I've been doing it for twenty, twenty-five years. But back then I had very little knowledge. And the reason I bring up Empire and the state of being at that time is because slowly the budgets for the movies had been diminishing significantly. And when *Puppet Master* came up, there was like no money for an orchestral score. And so it was kind of an interesting challenge, because I wanted to do the movie but wasn't sure exactly how to get it done. I heard certain things in my mind as to what I wanted it to sound like and again my inclination was more of an orchestral type of sound for it.

"I don't remember much input from either Charlie or David Schmoeller, to be honest. Obviously at that point they trusted me, since I had done a myriad of other films. So they knew that I would handle it right. So there wasn't a lot of input on anybody's part … we all knew where we wanted to go with it."

Puppet Master hit video on October 12, 1989. Lee MacLeod returned to design the now-iconic poster and video art, which was essentially a version of his original poster, only depicting the puppets as they actually appeared in the film. MacLeod explains the creation of the poster: "The final poster that I did was created once he [Allen] had created the puppets and the trunk. I, along with several other illustrators in L.A., were experimenting with illustrating over photography … sort of a poor man's Photo Shop, which did not yet exist. We would assemble all sorts of photos, color copies and art work on a board, photograph it, pull a print and go into it with air brush, prisma colors, brushed paint and anything else that would help. The idea was to come up with imagery that was very real and still transcended a photo. Without the actual puppets, this would not have worked."

As Full Moon's first release, it had everything riding on it. Any kind of success could only be good for anyone involved, but for Band it meant nothing more or less than the future of his brand-new production company. To everyone's surprise, *Puppet Master* exceeded any and all expectations. It sold out its first run almost immediately and gained the coveted title of a Platinum release, a distinction kept for videocassette releases which proved to be particularly profitable. *Fangoria* gave the movie mild praise, acknowledging the effects while noting that the movie wasn't all that scary.[9] B-Movie guru Joe Bob Briggs, on the other hand, loved it and in his review called it "one of the best of '89."[10] Viewers responded to the atmosphere, the clever kills and above all to the puppets themselves. Even though the film was a straight-to-video release, it was a definite hit, creating minor horror icons and launching Full Moon as an independent studio. From its success, Band was free to launch a slate of similarly themed films to cater to the cult and horror audience. While the future of Full Moon was unclear, though exciting, one thing became abundantly obvious: the success of *Puppet Master* was going to demand a sequel.

Chapter Three

The Eternity Comics

Development of *Puppet Master II* began almost immediately after the figures came back for *Puppet Master*'s rental success, but it was not the only development related to that title going on at the same time. Because of its proven success, Band sought out potential marketing ventures as quickly as he could, both in attempt to cement the Full Moon brand and in realizing that he had (whether intentionally or inadvertently) created genuine new horror icons in the form of the film's central puppets. While the sequel was still in production, Band teamed with a small comic press named Eternity, a division of Malibu, itself a division of Marvel, to produce an original *Puppet Master* comic book series.

Band himself had been a longtime comic book fan since the Marvel boom of the early '60s, admiring the art of Jack Kirby and the varied range of fascinating characters with roots in horror and science fiction, from Doctor Strange to the Fantastic Four. Band had also clearly responded to the interconnectivity of Marvel comics. They told their own stories, but they all existed in the same universe and that potential for crossover was something Band echoed in Full Moon from its earliest incarnation.[1] As the studio found its footing and established itself, characters would regularly go on to appear in each other's movies, with direct mashups and crossovers like *Dollman vs. Demonic Toys* being a part of everyday life in the Full Moon universe. With this in mind, it is only natural that Band would be excited to create characters and oversee stories that would lend themselves to the same kind of comic book storytelling that had inspired him.

The only problem with the notion of a *Puppet Master* comic book was the fact that the mythology had barely established itself yet. Yes, the movie had been successful and Full Moon was at work getting a sequel off the ground, but all that Eternity had to go off of was one film with several unanswered questions. Those questions, however, proved to be the jumping off point for a brand-new *Puppet Master* story.

Eternity hired the writer/artist team of David DeVries and Glenn Lumsden to create a four-part comic series that would address the film's biggest unanswered question: who was Andre Toulon and *why* did he bring his puppets to life? The opening prologue of *Puppet Master* is barely addressed throughout the rest of the film. Yes, the viewer is led to understand that Toulon was a kindly old toymaker who did not want his secrets to fall into the wrong hands, but how did he obtain those secrets and who's hands specifically did he not want them to fall into? Confirming that the German assassins in that opening sequence were Nazis, as most viewers suspected, DeVries set out to pen a story that would serve as both a prequel and sequel to the first film's opening sequence. As Lumsden recalls, "Our relationship with Malibu grew fairly quickly, starting with the repackaging of a lot of the stuff we had done in Australia, expanding into doing a bit of new stuff and doing some covers for their other books as well. When *Puppet Master* came along, they thought of asking Dave and me ... for which I am very grateful! The guys at Malibu were bloody fantastic to work with and for, and it is one of my happiest memories of my time doing comics in the States."

Not surprisingly, considering the fact that it had just come out, neither DeVries nor Lumsden had seen *Puppet Master* prior to getting the job on its comic book counterpart. As an artist meant to draw the likenesses of these characters, Lumsden was not given many references to base his artwork on. As he recalls, "From memory, all I had was the video of the first movie, which I watched on a friend's VHS player in his caravan (hah, I didn't own a video player at that stage!) I did sketches off the screen at first, then I got the idea to buy a tripod for my camera and I would freeze-frame the movie and take a picture. From this I was able to build up a photo library of characters, costumes, locations, etc."

Luckily, Lumsden admits to enjoying the film after seeing it. "I thought the movie was a better-than-average low budget flick, and I do love the concept of evil puppets scuttling around in the shadows causing bloody mayhem. My one bugbear has always been their tiny size! They're so small, you're forever having to invent ways the victim can trip over or get themselves stuck so the little monsters can do their stuff! I would have made them mid-thigh height if I'd been in charge!"

There had to have been a few specific notes from Full Moon on the sequel's direction—largely that the resurrected Toulon would still be seeking revenge for the death of his beloved wife, Elsa, and that the puppets would be brought to life by a serum that they appeared to be running out of. These elements (especially Elsa's name) were introduced in the sequel, so it's hard to think the comic could have been made with no knowledge of the next movie, but if there was knowledge it certainly wasn't much and the creative team was not "in the know" as to what exactly the sequel would hold. In fact, Lumsden even admits, "I can't recall knowing anything about the *Puppet Master II* plot at all." DeVries crafted an opening issue set in 1938, a year before the opening of the movie. It sees Andre Toulon living in Berlin as a successful puppeteer, catching the attention of the Reich for the political satire at the core of his shows. When the Nazis storm in to shut the place down, they wind up murdering Toulon's wife. Vengeful and heartbroken, Toulon uses the Egyptian secrets of life to instill Elsa's soul into the puppet Leech Woman. He then uses his puppets to strike out against the Nazis, bringing the full attention of the Reich down on himself after using his puppets to assassinate General Mueller.

If these details sound particularly familiar, they should, as every single one of them would wind up being present in the later sequel *Puppet Master III: Toulon's Revenge*. Because of this, the importance of the early comic book series cannot be understated. So much of the mythology that fans know and love stems from these early comics. Toulon's need to lash out at the Nazis over Elsa's murder, Elsa becoming Leech Woman and, much more than that, the notion that the puppets themselves are inhabited by human souls *all* come from these early comic books. Even if they had the original film to work with and a few specific details as to where the sequel was headed, DeVries and Lumsden laid much of the groundwork for the entire franchise within these pages.

"I haven't seen *Puppet Master III,* which probably sounds terrible from the POV of a *Puppet Master* fan," says Lumsden, "But after the books, we began to get offers from the larger companies, like Valiant, DC and Marvel, and the treadmill of producing monthly comics just took over my life completely! All I did for most of the '90s was draw and fall asleep. Usually with the help of too much booze. So my knowledge of '90s popular culture, etc. is a vacuum. Ironic really, when you consider that my job for that period was to produce stuff for the popular culture! I remember [DeVries] saying that he could see a lot of our *Puppet Master* comic in one of the films, and he was pleased as punch!"

The second, third and fourth issues of the miniseries picked up after Toulon's suicide, introducing many plot threads that would *not* wind up being used in the movies but which made for fun comic storytelling nonetheless. Issue two reveals that the Bodega Bay Inn is run by Toulon's much younger American cousin, Paul. The tragedy has attracted all kinds of unwanted attention, with two couples seeking to stay in that room in particular after the death. The first of them is a horror actor with a sexual fascination with the morbid, hoping to seduce a young starlet in the same room where the puppet master committed suicide. The second couple consists of one of the German spies and a female colleague as they continue their search for Toulon's secrets in the hotel. The puppets fend off the spies and use their serum to bring their recently deceased master back to life. Andre ropes a horrified Paul into his continuing attempts to keep his puppets and his secrets out of the Nazis' hands, leading to an exciting third issue that hops throughout Cairo before a finale finishing things off at the hotel.

Although the series is well plotted and full of interesting ideas, with that third issue in particular feeling like a Full Moon version of *Raiders of the Lost Ark,* the idea that the puppets attempted to bring Toulon back to life before the events of *Puppet Master II* almost lessens that film's plot, especially as—much like the sequel—it doesn't end well. It seems awkwardly set up to ease fans of the first film into the idea of Toulon returning from the grave, even showing him in a precursor to the bandaged appearance he would sport in the sequel. But again, the idea of Toulon's return from the grave should not be shocking considering that the plot of the original *Puppet Master* hinges on someone doing just that.

Eternity's *Puppet Master* was treated as a major event for the small, independent publisher. This turned out to be their first full-color title ever, something they kept up through each of their Full Moon titles that followed. For the introduction to the first issue, Eternity tapped none other than Full Moon and Empire director extraordinaire Stuart Gordon. As the director of Band's previous production, *Dolls,* Gordon had remained relatively quiet throughout the development of *Puppet Master.* For fans worried that the latter may have been a rip-off of the former, it was no doubt a relief to see that Gordon was good natured about the movie, understood the differences in the concept, and gave the budding *Puppet Master* franchise his full support.[2]

The *Puppet Master* comic book was so successful that Eternity green-lit a sequel

miniseries almost immediately. Titled *Puppet Master: Children of the Puppet Master,* this series ran a short and sweet two issues, half the length of the previous one. Lumsden explains how it came together: "The first series we did went well enough to warrant a sequel. From memory, there was interest from another country.... Italy, perhaps? They wanted a *Puppet Master* story they could run in installments, so Dave wrote *Children of the Puppet Master* so every six pages or whatever, it would be a kind of self-contained unit ... but it could still be read as a complete story. I remember thinking at the time, 'that's so clever!'" Reading back through the two-issue miniseries with this in mind, the structure Lumsden notes becomes incredibly clear. While the two issues do tell one story, there are breaks every few pages so that each individual scene almost feels like a self-contained chapter, which is one of a couple details that help *Children of the Puppet Master* to feel like a very different entity than the first series, even though it came from the same creative team.

Whereas the first series had been a prequel set long before the events of *Puppet Master,* this bookended nicely as a sequel set almost directly after the events of the film. The first issue, in fact, is mostly an adaptation of the movie, walking through the plot beat for beat in order to bring new readers up to speed before continuing on with those characters after their ordeal at the Bodega Bay Inn. While characters from the movie, like Alex Whittaker and Megan Gallagher, play a major role, they look nothing like their cinematic counterparts.

This version of Alex bears some similarities to a much younger Paul Le Mat, casting aside the lightened mullet for a look more similar to his *Melvin & Howard* days. Megan, meanwhile, is reimagined as a blond, and much more intriguingly, the comic reveals a bit more about her backstory and family history. With her malevolent husband now out of the picture, Megan reverts back to her maiden name: Toulon. It's a fun twist to reveal that Megan is descendant of the hotel owner Paul Toulon from the previous miniseries. While it doesn't gel with the film itself—given how often Toulon is talked about, it's definitely something she would have seen fit to mention— it blends in nicely with the comic's own sense of larger mythology and continuity.

The comic book also wonderfully provides an explanation for Leroy the dog's return to life at the end of the original movie, revealing that Megan transferred Neil's soul into the dog in order to punish him for his manipulation of her and for the murder of her parents. Leroy's second life (and Neil's third) is cut painfully short, though, when he meets his end at the hands of the puppets once again. This time, now that *Puppet Master II* promotion was in high gear, the puppets would be joined in the comic by their newest member, Torch. With the amount the first miniseries goes through to sell itself as a prequel to *Puppet Master II, Children of the Puppet Master* undercuts all of that by casually sliding in Torch as if he's been there the whole time, even including him in flashbacks, despite the fact that the puppet is shown being built in the sequel.

Once again, however, it works if the comics are taken as their own continuity. Torch is teased at the end of the first miniseries, when undead Toulon is seen carving the head of this new puppet, claiming that the last of the Nazi assassins coming to

Opposite: **Puppet Master #1 cover artwork.**

take his life would be a perfect life force to instill into his brand-new creation. Taking only the first movie into continuity—and even then reimagining it for their purposes—the Eternity comics are their own little side universe in which anything can be imagined, and also serve as both a darker, gorier and altogether more erotic universe than had ben depicted in the film itself.

While the sequel elements and larger shocks of the second issue of *Children of the Puppet Master* are interesting—particularly seeing the puppets in the snow and Alex Whittaker waking from one of his dreams only to have Blade slit his throat—they mostly play second fiddle to a burgeoning romantic subplot between Megan and Alex's sister. While clearly played as lacy erotica used to lure in young male readers that weren't already sold on the prospect of killer puppets, this plot can't help but serve as a clever commentary on the complete lack of either romantic or sexual tension between Megan and Alex in the first film.

Their romantic interlude is cut short when the puppets come for Megan after learning that she plans to abandon them and sell off the hotel. This leads to an exciting chase scene throughout the house, seeing Megan step up as a gun-toting, almost Ripley-esque heroine (albeit in her underwear) as she fends off the puppet siege. At the end, Megan escapes and leaves the puppets trapped inside as the house apparently burns down, sealing the fate of Toulon's puppets once and for all. Again, if these comics are to be taken as their own separate continuity, then the ending of *Children of the Puppet Master* provides a suitable finale for this corner of the mythology as a whole.

The *Puppet Master* comic books have become highly sought after by fans over the years, with many collectors cherishing them among the rarest pieces in their collections. They have never been reprinted, though they often pop up online at reasonable prices, totaling six individual issues as well as a trade paperback collecting both issues of *Children of the Puppet Master*. Even now, the Eternity comics remain an interesting enigma. They represent a unique standalone interlude in the development of the franchise, as they largely ignored continuity for their own purposes, and yet wound up giving the franchise some of its strongest elements, cornerstone pieces of the mythology that continue to be represented and prove their importance to this day.

Chapter Four

Puppet Master II

Before the comics had even been announced, development had already begun on *Puppet Master II*. Following the positive response of the first *Puppet Master*, Full Moon released its next two features—*Crash & Burn* and *Meridian*—to varying degrees of success. The former, starring Paul Ganus, Megan Ward and Bill Moseley, finds a crew picked off one by one as they struggle to maintain a TV station for the company Unicom, which has risen to become a singular global corporate entity. Very dry, but with a good turn by Moseley, it was released in most European markets as *Robot Jox 2*, a sequel to Stuart Gordon's giant robot feature for Empire. It was marketed as an extremely similar movie in general, with the trailer focusing heavily on the film's one and only scene featuring a massive robot, which came right at the very end. *Meridian*, meanwhile, starred *Twin Peaks*' Sherilynn Fenn as a young woman who finds love with a cursed man-beast after inheriting an Italian castle. This *Beauty and the Beast* riff would see Charlie Spradling as Fenn's best friend. Dominating every scene with her beauty, charm and wit, Spradling wound up making several Full Moon appearances to the point that she would actually briefly become the spokeswoman for the entire company.

While Full Moon continued to branch out with different types of films, from sci-fi to fantasy to borderline erotica, *Puppet Master II* remained a huge priority. Whereas the original saw several changes of hands between various incarnations of the script, Band hired David Pabian to write the sequel, which stuck very closely from the page to the screen. In this case, Pabian's own interests as a horror fan dictated the sequel's approach and tone. Gone were be the Italian and Hitchcockian influence of the first. Instead, *Puppet Master II* would take its inspirations from the classic Gothic Universal monster movies of the 1930s and '40s. The *Ten Little Indians* approach was axed in favor of a classic, old school haunted house movie. The numerous gothic influences are apparent right from the film's opening scene, showing the puppets digging up the grave of their beloved creator, Toulon. The corpse's hands rise from the dirt, outstretching as the movie segues into the opening titles, a shot that easily feels as though it could have been directly lifted out of a classic E.C. comic book.

The most obvious influences from the Universal heyday would be apparent in the new look for Andre Toulon himself. Covering his decaying form in bandages and a long coat, the undead Toulon is almost a spitting image for Claude Rains' Invisible Man. The character's arc for the sequel borrows much from the Universal movies as well. Taking a more central presence this time, Toulon proved to be mentally scarred from his time in the dirt, driven insane and mistaking the film's young lead for his reincarnated wife. This reincarnation plot is lifted directly from 1932's *The Mummy*, something that Pabian was very aware of as it was one of the writer's favorite horror movies. The fact that she *isn't* actually the reincarnation of Elsa only hammers home the movie's more energetic, inventive approach to the story and makes Toulon that much more sympathetic in his genuine rage and insanity.

Apart from the inclusion of Toulon as a major character, Pabian's script for *Puppet Master II* would prove very similar to the original, covering extremely similar ground. Like *Friday the 13th Part 2* before it, it's almost a cleaner, more refined version of the first. Instead of a group of psychics, the sequel focuses on a team of paranormal researchers. Intrigued by the ramblings of Alex Whittaker, who has now wound up in an asylum—which is interesting, as he seemed barely affected by anything that had happened when he left the hotel at the end of the original—they make their way to the hotel to see if there's any truth to Whittaker's ramblings of supernatural mayhem at the Bodega Bay Inn.

Much like the first, Band would continue to serve as executive producer. When *Puppet Master*'s producer Hope Perello went on to direct *Howling VI: The Freaks*, David DeCoteau came aboard to produce the sequel. Having previously directed *Dreamaniac* and *Creepozoids* for Empire, DeCoteau was no stranger to working with Band and would prove to be one of the most important figures to the *Puppet Master* franchise over time, eventually directing four of them in total.

Perhaps most excitingly for fans of the original and longtime Empire fans as well, *Puppet Master II* marked the directorial debut of David Allen. With most of the praise for *Puppet Master* focusing on the dazzling stop-motion effects and puppet sequences, there was no doubt on the studio's part that the sequel would need to be bigger, better and altogether more exciting when it came to animating its diminutive stars. With that in mind, there was no better person to take over as director for the second installment. While David Allen would never direct another film after *Puppet Master II*, the sequel showcases a clear talent and passion. Allen's direction is lean and stylistic, especially for the budget. With both his talent and interest in the field, it's a shame that it was not something he got the chance to do more of.

With Allen in the director's chair, and with the film having at least twice as many puppet sequences this time around, his crew of puppeteers certainly had their work cut out for them. Largely, they consisted of the same team from the first film. Mark Rappaport, John Teska and others were joined by new faces like Chris Endicott and Yancy Calzada. Chris Endicott explains how he came to work at David Allen Productions: "I had always been interested in stop-motion. I had done it since I was a kid, so of course he was one of my heroes. I came to L.A. David DeCoteau and I were high school friends. I had helped Dave DeCoteau on some of his earlier movies. When he started working with Charlie, I worked on those in various capacities. When it turned out that he was going to work on a film that David Allen was working on, he actually facilitated an introduction with me and David. I had never met David Allen before, but I had done work shooting inserts at David's studio for *Meridian* before he did *Crash & Burn*. Dave DeCoteau called me, I was doing stop-motion on a commercial downtown and said, 'Get over here. I'm at David Allen Productions right now

Chapter Four. Puppet Master II

Puppet Master II magazine ad.

and we're shooting inserts.' So I dropped everything and went over to David's studio in Burbank. Sherilynn Fenn was downstairs on a stage and they were shooting some kind of close ups of her for *Meridian*. I went upstairs to David's office and introduced myself and talked about his career, I told him I was interested in stop-motion and I was just getting into the business. I told him I was going to be doing sound work on *Crash & Burn*, because I'd been doing some boom operating on *Sorority Babes in the Slimeball Bowl-a-rama*, *Creepozoids* and things like that to pick up some extra money on the side. I said that I would be more than willing to help him on the puppet effects for *Crash & Burn*, so that's what happened. I made myself invaluable to him. I just worked my butt off to make myself somebody who was irreplaceable. So I started working with him ever since. For ten years, starting on that show, anything to make myself usable."

The puppets were just the same as fans of the first knew and recognized them. Leech Woman proved to be something of a problem, however. Band has claimed in interviews and on the *Puppet Master II* commentary that the higher ups at Paramount were impressed by the rental numbers for *Puppet Master* and had a meeting to discuss the potential sequel, explaining that they didn't care what Band did with it as long as it killed her off as they did *not* care for the Leech Woman character and simply considered her to be too gross.[1] She was a disgusting puppet and they wanted the sequel to get rid of her, so Band, according to this account, begrudgingly agreed. Screenwriter David Pabian notes that the direction to take Leech Woman out early on in the sequel came from Band himself.

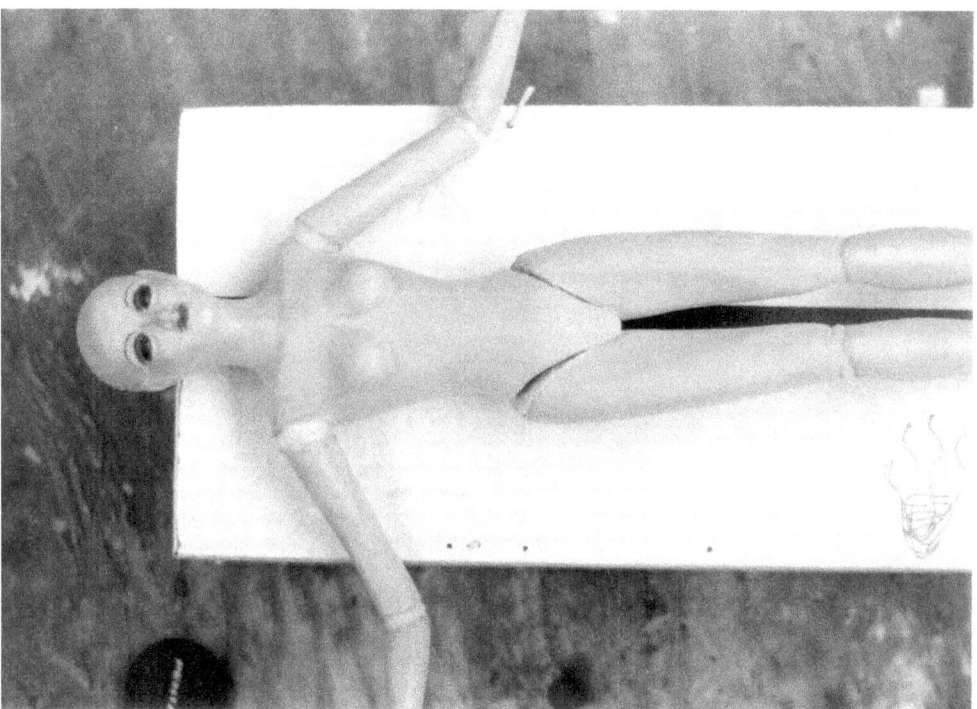

Painting a new Leech Woman rod puppet for *Puppet Master II* (courtesy Chris Endicott).

Chris Endicott recalls the decision to take Leech Woman out during the scripting stage: "I remember the discussion. I don't think I was there for it, but when David came and told us about the fact. David came away from the discussion, not when it was first revealed, because it wasn't something that happened on set, but David came to me and on the set for the barn, the scene where she gets killed, he gave us the impression that Charlie just found that kind of stuff distasteful and he just did not like the character. But I don't know if, in retrospect, if that was something that Paramount put into his head and he was just kind of regurgitating that point of view. For example, though, he hated *Re-Animator*. He didn't think it was a good idea to make that kind of movie that gross and he only kind of embraced it after it became so popular. I would probably hold to the idea that it just didn't appeal to him."

Whoever was responsible for the decision, the end result is the same. In only her second scene, when the puppets are sent to kill redneck couple Martha and her husband Mathew, Leech Woman is killed by Martha after cutting into the husband's brain. Martha engages in a bit of a chase around the small cabin, hunting the puppet with her shotgun in hand, eventually tossing Leech Woman into the furnace so that she—and the audience, thanks to the lingering camera—can sit and watch her burn. There's definitely no love lost for the little puppet in this mean-spirited sendoff.

Leech Woman's death is twofold, though. Not only does she die to appease the producer and/or studio, she immediately makes room for a new puppet. It became a tradition for *Puppet Master* sequels to each introduce at least one new puppet to the mythology as they went along. That tradition began right here in *Puppet Master II* with the introduction of Torch. Design-wise, Torch immediately fit the same '40s German aesthetic as the others, with the only difference being that he is welded out of metal instead of carved out of wood. With the loss of both Leech Woman and Tunneler (who was caught and dissected by the parapsychologists after killing one of them) and the appearance of Torch, *Puppet Master II* introduced viewers to the series' ever-changing puppet roster. To this day, the widely considered eight "main" puppets (Blade, Pinhead, Tunneler, Leech Woman, Jester, Six-Shooter, Torch, Decapitron) have never appeared all together as an ensemble in a single film.

The technical requirements to bring this new puppet to life dwarfed anything seen in the previous movie. This wasn't just a puppet that needed a blend of rod puppetry, animatronics and stop-motion animation to bring to life, as each of the others were—this was a puppet required to shoot a flame on a closed set. Having been shot in 1990, *Puppet Master II* hailed from a time long before CGI became everyday use in films. Torch lived up to his name, being a puppet with a flamethrower replacing his right hand—an aesthetic very similar to Blade—and when he shot a flame, it was an actual flame being shot across the set, with lengths reaching up to twenty feet. Creating this puppet required so much more precaution than *any* of the others. The effects crew needed to work out the mechanics of building a working flamethrower out of a two-foot puppet, but it also required safety and stunt regulations usually reserved for bigger fire stunts on much larger, blockbuster movies.

Endicott notes that, all things considered, the flamethrowing aspects of Torch were comparatively easy: "Honestly, when he was a flamethrower, he was a prop. He was a stiff, steel rod armature thing on a heavy, heavy plate. It almost became more of a Joe Viskocil gag when he was a flamethrower. The technical aspects of making him into a flamethrower were Joe Viskocil, but mostly Mark Rappaport doing that work. On set, it just meant bringing a fire marshal there and setting up so it was safe. We never puppeteered him as a flamethrower, except for the R/C head a couple of times. It was certainly much more difficult to do a Six-Shooter shot as a puppeteer than it would be a Torch shot. When he was a flamethrower, he was just a prop that shot flame out of one of his hands. It really wasn't—as a puppeteer gag—that difficult."

While *Puppet Master* proved to be the result of an ever-changing script with none of its writers ultimately receiving credit, *Puppet Master II* proved to be a healthy opposite situation. Full Moon was apparently very happy with Pabian's script, for the most part. While changes were naturally made here and there, Pabian wound up being stunned at just how closely the finished film stuck to his script, down to even following when he noted flashbacks should be black and white and when they shouldn't. In an interview with *Cult Films and the People Who Make Them*, Pabian said, "Charlie said that he wanted a sequel, but not to worry about anything that happened in the first one except for in the vaguest of ways." His approach was an extremely intentional throwback to the Universal heyday of the 1930s and '40s, which Full Moon apparently loved. The Egyptian mythology hinted at in the original *Puppet Master* was embraced by Pabian, who clearly saw it as the potential to turn the film into a love letter to his favorite classic horror, 1932's *The Mummy*. In that same interview, Pabian confirmed this was intentional. "It was heavily influenced by the Karl Freund *Mummy* from 1932. I did that on purpose. I love that film so much."[2]

According to an interview in *Cinefantastique*, David Allen and Pabian held many story conferences before the script was actually written, which may explain some of the smoothness when compared to the more chaotic scripting of the original. Allen even noted in this interview that he did some touching up on the script himself. "Not that what I did made the original script unrecognizable by any means, but the success of any script is in having a clear understanding of what the story is about and being able to defend, point for point, why things are happening at a particular juncture at a particular time. It's the difference between a script that's writing itself by unconscious intuition and one that has precision and understanding of why the characters behave the way they do."[3]

The sequel appears to be far more aware and embracive of the fact that it is a horror film, not only embracing a distinctive gothic atmosphere, but also delivering on all of the gore and mayhem expected from a straight-to-video horror effort of the era. *Puppet Master II* ups the game in terms of the puppet effects and the overall practical makeup FX as well. On the original, *all* of the makeup FX were created and applied by Patrick Simmons, who essentially served as his own department. For *Puppet Master II*, David P. Barton brought his Modus EFX crew in to create all of the ambitious makeup FX work the script required. Barton had gotten his start in makeup as a part of the KNB FX crew, working with that team on *Phantasm II*, *The Horror Show* (aka *House III*) and *Leatherface: The Texas Chainsaw Massacre III*, among others. After *Puppet Master II* he would go on to work on such movies as *Bram Stoker's Dracula*, *Face/Off* and *Starship Troopers*.

While the original's makeup effects were mostly limited to the aftermath of the puppets' individual murders, the sequel would require a large range of different kinds of effects. The murders would be a part of it, for sure, but they'd be bloodier—from Tunneler's running start into Patrick's forehead to Lance's slit throat. But it would also include something not seen in the first film, but that would certainly wind up appearing in later sequels: creature effects. Toulon is, of course, a zombie in this entry. While he is bandaged for the bulk of the feature, hiding every inch of his body from view, those bandages are removed toward the end to reveal the hideously decomposed face underneath. According to Barton in an article he wrote for *Gorezone* on this film's FX, "Toulon was to have been buried in the soil for ages, so I referred to a photo of a corpse called the Borre Fen man. He was part of a group of bodies discovered in Denmark that were drowned in bogs centuries ago."[4] This is yet another moment that showcases *Puppet Master II*'s classic horror inspirations, as it heavily echoes both the unraveling in *The Invisible Man* as well as the mask being knocked off Lon Chaney's face toward the finale of *The Phantom of the Opera*. Because of the familiarity of the scene, the reveal of Toulon's decomposing face is *not* the film's major reveal. Instead, the biggest shock as well as the biggest feat for the practical FX team would be the unveiling of two full-size bride and groom puppet bodies for Toulon to transfer his own soul into, as well as that of the unwitting heroine, Carolyn. As both puppet bodies would come to life in the feature's final few minutes, it was up to the makeup department to figure out a way to animate them through full facial prosthetics, limiting the actor's visibility to tiny pinholes in the eyes.

The puppets also have more prey this time around than just a handful of psychics. That aspect of the original is instead reinterpreted in the form of the paranormal research team, but the puppets would also be padding out their kill count by targeting the locals outside the hotel for the first—and only—time. It makes sense for the story purposes, given that this time the puppets are killing for their own survival, allowing for a narrative purpose for the "bigger is better" approach typically inherent in sequels.

Leading the crew of humans is Elizabeth Maclellan as Carolyn Bramwell. Maclellan had previously worked with Band and Full Moon in her role as a prostitute in the previous year's *Crash and Burn*. As Carolyn, Maclellan would bring an earnestness and inherent strength to the role. She would still be playing a character very similar to the previous entry's Megan Gallagher, in that she is trying to make sense of the mystery unfolding around her and that she becomes as defined by her brother's death as Megan was by her husband's suicide. Maclellan also has the distinction of being the first person to portray Elsa Toulon in the franchise, during a flashback dream sequence to Toulon's time in Cairo. The decision to have her play both roles is somewhat necessary to the plot, as Toulon believes Carolyn to believe the reincarnation of his long-lost wife. All further films in the series would portray Elsa with a similar, dark-haired and fair-skinned appearance, despite the fact that she did not actually turn out to be a reincarnation of Elsa, and that that only existed in Toulon's own decaying mind.

Maclellan plays a much more strong-willed and determined heroine than we were treated to the first time around. This is largely due to the fact that the female lead is actually the protagonist of *Puppet Master II* with the male lead serving a supportive role, which is a distinct role-reversal from Alex Whittaker being the protagonist of the original. Carolyn is a scientist and though she is hopeful to find some evidence of the supernatural, she treats every potential incident with a healthy dose of skepticism. Even her desire to have some kind of paranormal encounter only seems to come from the fact that it's her job to find results. While Carolyn doesn't tend to get too much of the credit for *Puppet Master II*'s success, it's no coincidence that one of the series' most beloved entries also happens to provide easily one of its most well-defined and three-dimensional heroines.

Unfortunately, Maclellan never appeared in another movie after *Puppet Master II*, giving up her acting career altogether. Her career was short-lived, lasting only a single year in total, with her only other appearances being TV credits in *Santa Barbara* and *Friday the 13th: The Series,* in addition of course to her appearance in *Crash & Burn*. It's a shame, as she showed a clear talent and strong will that managed to shine through in even a film as small as this one. By all accounts she appeared to take the role seriously and earnestly—a task that would likely have proven insurmountable to any lesser actor.

Greg Webb, meanwhile, portrayed Carolyn's brother Patrick in the film. While he had significantly less screen time, it proved not to mean any smaller amount of work. For most of the film's first act, Patrick is Carolyn's only support system as well as her biggest heel. He's sharp-witted, but he's also a raging alcoholic and turns confrontational after having too much to drink. This is hammered home during the dinner scene, in which Patrick ridicules palm reader Camille, mocking the predictions made in her newspaper column. His alcoholic rant is hardly the worst thing his character suffers, however, as not too long after that he awakens in the middle of the night to find Tunneler taking a running start into his forehead. Patrick provides the film with its second death after Camille, although hers is not shown onscreen.

Once again, there's a bit of a bait-and-switch in terms of the movie's approach to gore. The opening scene in the cemetery promises a more sinister atmosphere than the way the puppets are depicted at the beginning of the first film, but even still the prologue shows them to be just as non-violent as the first few minutes of the original. With Camille's death being hardly violent, it almost leads the viewer to wonder if this sequel would possibly be even less gory than the—despite a few squeamish moments—relatively tame original. Patrick's death pulls the rug out from under the viewer in this respect. Not only is it gory, but it's shown in close-up, in great detail, even letting the camera linger on Patrick's dying convulsions after the puppet has been pulled off of him. It's a bit of a shock to the system after the almost playful way Pinhead and Jester take care of Camille, simply gagging her and dragging her off down the hall, and there's a reason that this death in particular has stuck with fans of the series for so long.

Webb also had to play his own corpse during the franchise's one and only funeral sequence, a unique scene that appears to take place in the hotel's walk-in freezer, while a funerary slowed-down version of Richard Band's iconic theme plays. It showcases the hardened strength of Carolyn in her determination to keep moving forward with the research despite this tragedy, her decision not to leave the hotel until she figures out exactly what killed her brother, in the form of a haphazard and makeshift wake.

As the eccentric Camille, Nita Talbot steals every scene she appears in, even though those scenes are few and far between. While the series largely forgets about her, fans certainly have not, and the fate of her character has gone on to become one of the franchise's biggest unanswered questions. Talbot began her career in the late '40s with small roles as models and showgirls in things like *It's a Great Feeling* and *Always Leave Them Laughing*. She began making more and more TV appearances in the '50s in shows like *Suspense, Perry Mason* and *The Thin Man*. Prior to her role in *Puppet Master II* she was best known for her recurring guest appearances in *Hogan's Heroes* and *General Hospital*. For the most part, Camille is portrayed as a mystic whose egotism occasionally gets in the way of the group's investigation, particularly because she is at odds with their scientific nature. In each of her scenes, though, she is portrayed as well meaning, as misguided as she might be. When comparing the sequel to the original, Camille definitely appears to be the Dana of the group, although she is less outright bitchy and simply more self-involved. It's interesting and probably unintentional that she dies first whereas Dana, in the previous film, died last.

Portraying her son, Michael, the film's male lead who happens to show up almost halfway through the runtime, is Collin Bernsen. He should be recognizable to horror fans for his last name, at least, as he is the brother of *The Dentist* himself, Corbin Bernsen. Collin Bernsen was relatively new to the acting scene at the time he got cast in *Puppet Master II*, having previously appeared in *The Young and the Restless* as well as the films *Dangerous Love* and *Mr. Destiny*. Even though Michael shows up rather late, he is a somewhat classical hero type while also being the most good-natured rebel without a cause to ever cruise up on a motorcycle in a movie of this type. Even though Michael is a relatively bland character—and somewhat hard to take seriously as a self-described author—he's interesting for the role he serves to the film as a whole. This is a guy who would typically be the hero calling all of the shots in the Universal pictures of the '40s. Yet here, portrayed exactly the same as those characters were in those features, he's a supporting role. Even if he rescues Carolyn from being turned into a human puppet at the end, fighting his way through Torch, Blade and Pinhead as if they were trials in the most minuscule Herculean test ever put to film, she still controls the narrative from beginning to end. Carolyn is the one investigating the mysterious happenings at the hotel, while Michael simply serves as her support system, and that is an interesting and refreshing dynamic between two leads that could easily have been stock characters.

Rounding out the team of parapsychologists are Jeff Celentano as Lance and Charlie Spradling as Wanda. Both of these actors were practically Full Moon day players at the time. Jeff Celentano would regularly appear under the name "Jeff Weston" in films such as *Alien from L.A.* and *The Revenger*. He would go on to appear in *Demonic Toys* after shooting *Puppet Master II*. Interestingly, that movie would also feature *Puppet Master II* playing on a TV in the background for a large chunk of its runtime. Lance and Wanda appear to be the respective Frank and Clarissa of *Puppet Master II*, with the exception that they don't actually have any kind of psychosexual abilities. Instead, they're just horny, something no doubt meant to cater to the already-established Full Moon demographic of young male viewers.

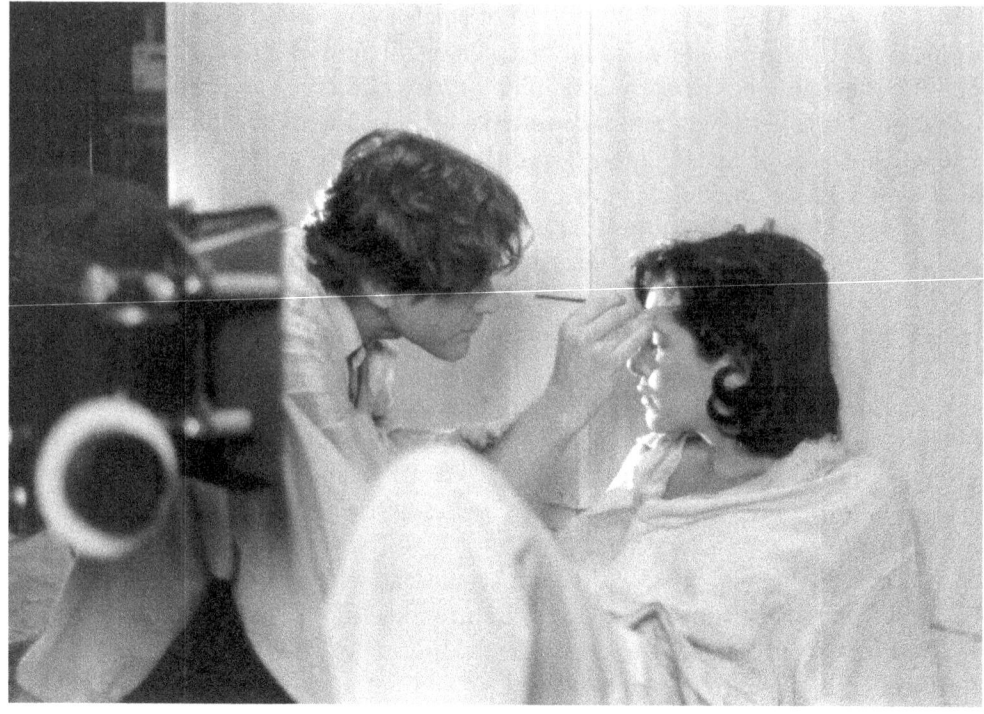

David Allen touches up Charlie Spradling's make-up (courtesy Chris Endicott).

In those early Full Moon years, Charlie Spradling was seen as a star to boys around the world. Charming, sexy, and refreshingly witty, she appeared in Full Moon feature after Full Moon feature and viewers quickly started to pay attention. So did Band, evidently, as he made Spradling the host of the Full Moon Fan Club and official spokesperson for the company. The Fan Club was something that helped the burgeoning company build its audience as it continued to find its footing. People knew what they were getting into with a Full Moon movie because Band went out of his way to appear in behind-the-scenes features to tell them exactly what they were going to be making and the sorts of films that would define their brand. With the Fan Club, he made the wise choice of hiring the captivating Spradling to let viewers in on the all the upcoming Full Moon merchandise they should pick up to show their appreciation for the company—as well as start building word of mouth, as Full Moon was still only a year old at the time. While Spradling seems to have fond memories of Full Moon in general, she did not seem to fondly recall her time on *Puppet Master II* in an interview with *Fangoria*. Though she praised the effects, saying it provided "some insight into how these special effects actually work," she said of Allen. "He simply does not know how to work with actors.... He worked much better with the puppets. As a matter of fact, the puppets were treated better than the actors on that film."[5]

Lance and Wanda are both brutally picked off by Blade, only moments apart from one another. He dies just after she leaves the room, and when she turns the light on she finds Blade standing over her boyfriend's corpse. In this moment, all of the details of Lance's death become clear even though the audience doesn't get to see a moment of the kill itself. His throat is slashed and the side of his head has been drilled into by the puppet's small knife. The discovery of his body leads the viewer into what might very well be the best, most complicated stop-motion shot in the franchise's entire history.

Blade spins around and grins widely at Wanda as she walks in on him, outstretching his arm as if to proudly display his work. He then runs to the end of the bed and leaps off, landing on the floor and continuing to rush toward Wanda with his knife slashing through the air in a single continuous shot. As challenging as this was to pull off for David Allen and his team, particularly because Allen was directing the movie as a whole and unable to devote all of his time to the feature's effects, the results are well worth the effort. It's one of the most memorable sequences in *Puppet Master* history, to the point that it was even recycled for the recent sequel, *Axis Termination*.

Chris Endicott recalls the filming of that standout shot: "It was storyboarded and unlike the first film, most of the interiors—especially the hotel rooms—were built on a stage." He adds, "So these were sets that were built first on Full Moon stages near Culver City and later they were moved to Rukus, which was an insert stage that Randy Cook had, that we shot a lot of the effects and some of the pickups for, but that set was also moved to David Allen Productions. Just a couple of walls, the bed, so that set was built at David's studio for that shot. If you look at that behind-the-scenes DVD, Paul Gentry had filmed David working on that sequence and you can see David animate it. So you can see it was impressive. I don't know if it was designed to be a standout shot, but of course, yeah, it certainly came out really nice. David was animating that at the same time Randy was doing one of the shots next door, one of the shots of the puppets going into the trunk, so they were actually animating that at the same time. It's a neat shot, but whether he knew it was going to be as cool going in as it turned out to be, I don't know."

The quintet of parapsychologists are not the film's only victims, though, as viewers are introduced to a hillbilly husband and wife who appear to live only just down the road from the hotel. In this respect, it's shocking that the hotel was ever as popular as it was boasted to be in the original, given its by all accounts extremely rural location. As mentioned, Martha and her husband Mathew are responsible for the tragic loss of Leech Woman, as well as serving the purpose of introducing the newest puppet, Torch. Sage Allen had only appeared in the TV series *1st & Ten: The Championship* before landing her role in *Puppet Master II*. After that, though, she went on to a lucrative film and television career, making appearances in such films as *Conspiracy Theory* and *Armageddon*, as well as shows like *The X-Files* and *ER*.

Mathew, meanwhile, was portrayed by the late great George "Buck" Flower, a character actor who should be familiar to almost all horror fans. Flower was a frequent collaborator of John Carpenter, appearing in several of the director's films including *The Fog, Escape from New York, Starman, They Live* and *Village of the Damned*. He also had roles in everything ranging from *Wishmaster* to *Back to the Future* to *Waxwork II*. He sadly passed away from cancer in 2004 at the age of 66.

The other, perhaps most controversial puppet victim outside the hotel would be the young boy who wanders away from a campground only to come face to face

David Allen animating Blade (courtesy Chris Endicott).

with Torch. Given that the franchise revolves around a cast of living toys with different personalities, *Puppet Master* has naturally been mentioned in comparison with *Toy Story* throughout the years. The differences between the two are obvious, but the parallels are never clearer than in this scene, in which young Billy seems to serve in every respect as a precursor to *Toy Story*'s sadistic child antagonist, Sid. Billy has left the camper to go play outside, which is a perfectly natural thing for a child to do. He then goes to a tree, strips his G.I. Joe half naked and proceeds to start whipping it, interrogating the toy as though it were a Nazi spy. As awkward and bizarre as the scene might be, it's also one of the first moments to explicitly mention Nazis in *Puppet Master* lore and further establish the connection that would eventually form the backbone of the franchise. Interestingly, Billy plays puppet master in this scene even before a puppet makes itself known, in a very meta way. He announces himself as the director, and gestures to the woods surrounding him as "the set." It's not a stretch to wonder if this depiction of weird torture is meant to replicate the often grueling work inherent to making a low-budget movie of this size.

After accidentally tossing his G.I. Joe into a nearby bush, Billy encounters Torch—although what the puppet was doing so far from the hotel is never made clear—and immediately forgets his doll in favor of this cooler, walking toy. He pokes and prods and clearly annoys the puppet. It's interesting to note that Torch almost appears to be friendly at first. It's not until Billy pokes at and belittles the puppet, annoying both Torch and the audience in equal doses, that the hotheaded puppet decides to take matters into his own hands. While the scene is shocking

RC controlled Torch in the David Allen Productions office (courtesy Chris Endicott).

and noteworthy for being one of the rare child deaths in a Full Moon production, it's almost even more mean-spirited simply because of the fact that the audience is meant to cheer it on.

Rounding out the cast, of course, would be Steve Wells as Toulon. As mentioned, this Toulon would be as different as could be from the seemingly harmless old man depicted in the original prologue. But *Puppet Master II* does a good job of effectively playing its villainous puppet master as both sinister and tragic, a move that is once again not too far off from the original Universal monsters that fundamentally inspired the script. Wells would only show his face during the film's Cairo flashback, which would at least hint at how Andre Toulon came to possess this magic in the first place. This sequence is also notable for featuring Charles Band's two young children in the crowd. Alex and Taryn Band would both be credited as "Cairo Child." Taryn made her one and only film appearance in that quick cameo, while Alex would go onto his own independent stardom as a musician, becoming the front man for the successful early 2000s rock band The Calling. The flashback scene depicts Toulon as a colder man than the first (and all subsequent films) portrayed him to be, but by no means an evil or sadistic one. The core of *Puppet Master II*'s Toulon is formed in the idea of a man who was passionate once, who loved and loved deeply, but whose years in the grave have deformed his spirit as well as his body. It's a classical antagonistic trope, a tragic through line that defines classic monsters from Dracula to The Mummy.

Toulon certainly echoes both The Mummy and the Invisible Man in appearance. Even the actor's eyes are not visible behind the character's dark goggles. Aside from his voice—which is appropriately menacing despite the fact that Wells inexplicably plays the clearly French Toulon with a German accent—he has only his physical mannerisms to convey the character's rage and melancholy. In a behind-the-scenes interview for the movie's *Video Zone*, Wells compared the role to Grecian Theatre, an apt and intriguing comparison, as those Ancient Greek actors would always play their roles behind masks.[6] In addition to being bandaged and disguised from head to toe, Wells also had to face another rare challenge for an actor: almost all of his scenes are spent monologuing to puppets. There are several scenes, some of them largely to explain the plot as it moves forward, in which Toulon is hidden away in his attic workshop, addressing (and even scolding) the puppets as they return from that night's hunt. He speaks not only to props being animated by puppeteers from below, but ones that also cannot even speak in the context of the story. Wells has to sell the strength and savagery of his character in those scenes, as well as sell the fact that the puppets even exist at all, as a misstep in any of that dialogue would only take viewers out of the moment to remind them that Toulon is speaking to characters that aren't actually there. Wells luckily sells these scenes, especially with his fluid, mime-like physical gestures. He makes for a unique and imposing Toulon, even if his portrayal is far more vengeful and sadistic than anything fans had seen in the character before or would ever see again, especially since this incarnation is willing to screw over the puppets he has fought so hard to protect just so he can continue to cling to his fantasy of reincarnation.

This of course leads him to be betrayed by the puppets in the same fashion

Chapter Four. Puppet Master II 51

John Teska sets up a shot with Tunneler (courtesy Chris Endicott).

that Neil Gallagher was betrayed in the original. There's a bit more weight to it this time, though, as we have the first movie to fall back on and have clearly seen the good-natured relationship between the man and his puppets. To see that sweet, old man from the original prologue scene fall so far in such a short time is as sad as it is jarring. Even in this movie, he had spent the bulk of the runtime talking to the puppets as if they were his own children. The puppets' motivations are also much easier to gauge in their takedown of Toulon than they had been for their attack on Gallagher. Here, it's extremely evident that Toulon has directed them to kill so that they can recreate the formula that keeps them alive, when in fact he's planning to fuel bodies for himself and Carolyn—believing her to be Elsa—while they wither and die. It's a leap, but one that leaves viewers to wonder what had happened in the man's life to lead him to such a tragic turn in the first place. Given the direction that the franchise would immediately take with the next entry, that was hopefully intentional.

The puppets' takedown of Toulon, as he falls from the attic window on fire, was also the very last thing shot as the production tried to adhere to Full Moon's schedule of 27 days of principal photography. In the *Cinefantastique* interview, Allen explained, "We were running late on the last day, and we were supposed to shoot a scene of the villain on fire. The stunt coordinator was understandably reluctant to try it with a tired crew, so we shot the scene a week or two later."[7]

At the end of the film, once Toulon has been defeated and Carolyn and Michael apparently go off to start their life together, the film wraps up its biggest loose end only to introduce another one that is much bigger and looser. Camille returns with

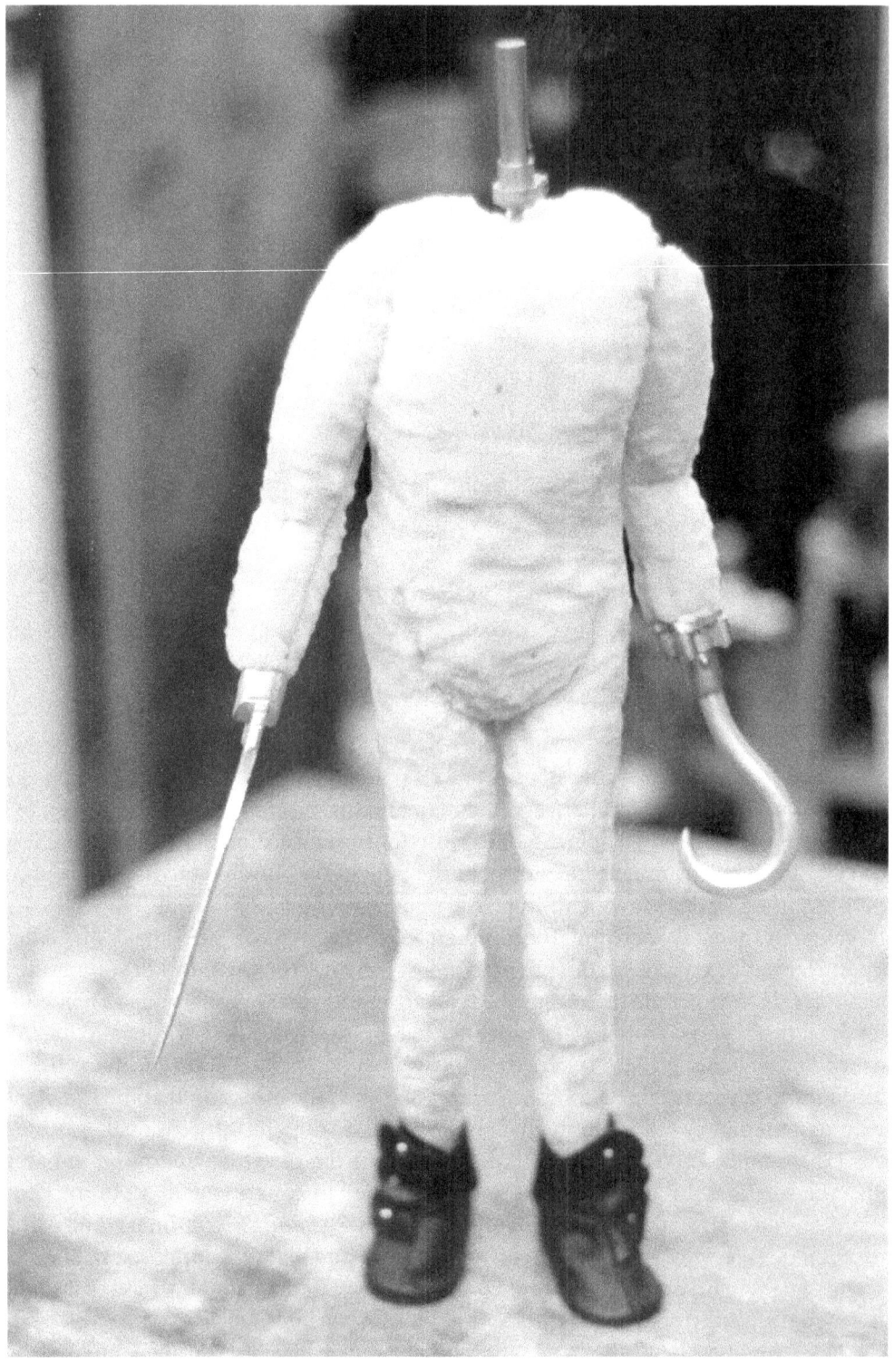

The making of a new Blade stop-motion puppet (courtesy Chris Endicott).

the puppets in tow, having been reborn into the puppet body that had been meant for Carolyn. She appears to be much more evil than she had been in life, suggesting they take their traveling puppet show to the Bouldeston Institute for Mentally Troubled Tots and Teens (a great name, that) so that they can set up camp in a place where nobody will believe rumors of living puppets roaming the halls.

It's a terrific cliffhanger that appears to set up an utterly bizarre third entry, one that could only be imagined as a cross between *Tourist Trap* and *A Nightmare on Elm Street 3*. Unfortunately, it would only continue the trend set by the original of ending on a baffling, enticing cliffhanger that would never be brought up again for the duration of the franchise, at least on screen. Luckily, fans wouldn't have a reason to be too terribly bothered by the fact that *Puppet Master III* would completely ignore the ending, as the next sequel would be an almost universally acknowledged high point for the series.

And the third entry, at this point, would be a guarantee. Rentals for *Puppet Master II* proved even higher than the first one, with much of that success undoubtedly coming from the fact that more people had seen the original and that word of mouth had spread. *Puppet Master II* saw release in January of 1991 to generally favorable response. That's not to say that *every* review was positive, of course, as *Fangoria*'s review ended by saying, "The only disturbing moment comes not within the movie but afterwards, during a making-of–*Puppet Master II* postscript when Charlie Band grinningly promises us a *III, IV* and *V*. Talk about scary!"[8] Even still, the message was clear among horror fans and rental figures: people loved these puppets and they wanted to see more of them. While Band had never overseen a franchise past its second entry, he made *Puppet Master III* a priority. It would not pick up after the sequel's cliffhanger but would instead pick up on the many, subtler references that had been made in *Puppet Master II* to Toulon's backstory. Seeing the puppeteer take such a tragic turn, viewers were left trying to fill in the blanks for themselves, wondering what exactly had happened to the puppet master's wife, not to mention the original's loose end of what exactly drew the Nazis to Toulon's puppets in the first place. With so many teases to a larger backstory scattered throughout the second film, the only direction for the franchise to take was abundantly clear. The series would have to address these dangling threads before moving on to more modern stories. If *Puppet Master* was going to continue, it would be in the form of a prequel.

Chapter Five

Puppet Master III: Toulon's Revenge

By the time *Puppet Master II* hit video stores, people had already begun to gravitate toward its diminutive stars. The designs of the puppets stood out and fans could not help but be intrigued by the series' ever-expanding roster. If *Puppet Master II* had introduced a new puppet in the form of Torch, there was every indication that the third would do the same and would introduce another new member to the little family. The puppets had significantly more screen time in the second than the first, with entire scenes devoted to them *not* killing people, but just spending time in the workshop with their master. Despite their evil deeds, the sequel showed an even softer side to the characters than the original had, leaning harder into their individual personalities and unique, specific quirks. Whether they killed people or not, the puppets were what people rented these movies to see. They had, without a doubt, become the heroes. With this in mind, the heroic turn of the characters in the films should not appear so dramatic. From the first few minutes of the original movie, they had been shown to be relatively harmless. But if that were the case, why would they be so deadly? Why carve a puppet with a drill in its head if it is not meant to perform some sort of lethal function? This was a fair question, and one that would be readily addressed in *Puppet Master III: Toulon's Revenge*.

The third movie in the saga would take a dramatic shift from the previous two. It would be the first *Puppet Master* feature to *not* center around puppets stalking around a hotel and killing psychics off one by one. Instead, it would abandon that extremely specific style to instead change the genre completely. Whereas the original had been an Italian-themed thriller and the second had been a classic, Universal throwback, *Puppet Master III* became a war movie.

David Allen once again took a backseat to focus on overseeing the special effects, while *Puppet Master II*'s producer David DeCoteau stepped in as director, continuing the uniquely specific trend of *Puppet Master* films directed by men named David. DeCoteau had already directed several cult classics for Band, including *Dreamaniac*, *Creepozoids* and *Sorority Babes in the Slimeball Bowl-o-Rama*. Just from the titles of his previous features as director, one would almost expect DeCoteau to bring a much campier sensibility to *Puppet Master III*. But there was a definite interest in doing something genuinely earnest and heartfelt with this film, which DeCoteau clearly understood. The very concept of this entry would incite no shortage of challenges, though. This is a prequel set during World War II, a *Puppet Master* movie that doubled as a war movie, that would have to appear bigger than the first two despite still being produced on an incredibly low budget. On the concept alone, there's almost no way it should have worked.

Luckily, screenwriter C. Courtney Joyner proved more than up to the challenge. The basic concept had already been laid out by Charles Band himself. He wanted the story to be set during World War II. It would take place before Toulon's escape to America and would center around the death of his wife, her resurrection as Leech Woman, and Toulon's titular revenge on the Nazis who had taken everything from him.

That is not to say that Joyner would not have his work cut out for him as a writer. He needed to make this story cinematic, emotional and believable, three things that weren't always required for a Full Moon feature. Joyner had first stepped into the world of independent film alongside director Jeff Burr with the horror anthology *From a Whisper to a Scream*. Featuring veteran actors like Clu Gulager and Vincent Price, the anthology definitely put their names on the map. Burr went on to direct *The Stepfather II* while Joyner went on to write *Prison* for Empire Pictures. Band had been so impressed with Joyner that he continued bringing him on as a writer after the end of Empire and into the rise of Full Moon. Joyner had some familiarity with the first two *Puppet Master* features when asked to write *Puppet Master III*. While he had enjoyed them, he had always been a die-hard fan of old Westerns and classic Hollywood war movies and saw the potential to bring both of those interests to the prequel. As Joyner himself has often put it, he set out to make the *Where Eagles Dare* of *Puppet Master* movies.[1] But, as I think most fans would attest, he wound up writing the *Citizen Kane* of *Puppet Master* movies instead.

Joyner remembers how he came to be a writer for Empire and Full Moon: "*Prison* … was kind of an interesting situation because with Irwin [Yablans] at one point we were going to do the movie at Cannon and the project was around a little bit, it had been developed with Irwin when he and Bruce Curtis were partners at a company called Voyager and then they split up. So he ended up with some properties and Irwin ended up with some properties. And of course Irwin had the history with Charlie because of *Tourist Trap* and all that stuff, so we ended up at Empire. I don't know how much financial involvement Charlie had with the project at that time. I don't know that it was a great deal. I believe Irwin Yablans was responsible for gathering the cast, because the thing was, like with *Re-Animator*, the thing had already been developed, we had a director, it didn't start with Charlie and Empire. So it turned out well and that's when Charlie started to say, 'Hey, would you be interested in writing this one and that one,' then I started working away on other projects at Empire, most of which were never made. Or one or two were actually made, but after the company folded and the properties were sold to somebody else. I think *Subterraneans* was rewritten into something, I can't remember. But I loved Albert and I got along with Charlie well and they were very supportive, and all that stuff. But then the company became Bandcompany, Irwin went to TWE and I went with him and did *Class of 1999* and all these other things. So I was away from Charlie and that group for a while before I came back to do *Puppet Master*."

As for how Joyner actually came to write *Puppet Master III*, it was a true case of simply being in the write place at the right time. "I went with a friend of mine who

Chapter Five. Puppet Master III: Toulon's Revenge

was an actor who was auditioning for a movie at Full Moon," he says. "And this was when they had their office down on Sunset Boulevard. And I hadn't seen any of those people in a while and I said, 'Can I just tag along with you?' and he said, 'Sure.' So he went to his reading and I walked into his office and the first person I saw was Albert. We stood there talking and having a great chat and Charlie came out of his office and heard our voices and we had a great time, we were all yakking away and then of course Charlie went off to do his business and Albert went off to look at some footage, my friend finished his audition and that was it. It was a lovely reunion.

"A little while later, I got a phone call from Charlie asking if I would mind coming down to the set of *Trancers II*. I was going to go down anyway because of Tim [Thomerson], we had become good friends by that point because of *Vietnam, Texas*. So I decided I would go down to the set and that was the first time Charlie said, 'Would you be interested in writing *Puppet Master?* I want to do a prequel to the first movie.' And I said, 'Oh, well, we know he kills himself and all that stuff...' But he said, 'No, let's do something about the war,' and all that stuff, the Nazi agent, we were just throwing stuff around while Charlie was filming and then he and I would have these little concepts. Dave DeCoteau was producing *Trancers II*, as I remember. They were actually shooting out here in the valley for a little while. They were doing the scenes with Helen Hunt and Megan Ward and I would go out there and talk to Charlie a little bit about things. David was always going to direct it, with John Schouweiler producing, of course. That's where I came up with my famous—or infamous, I should say— '*Where Eagles Dare* with Nazis' approach to a *Puppet Master* movie. I loaded Dave DeCoteau down with VHS copies of *Night of the Generals* and *Operation Crossbow* and *Where Eagles Dare*, of course. We just took off from there. But if I hadn't gone with my buddy on that acting audition, it never would have happened."

As was often the case with Full Moon, Joyner did not have a ton of time to work on the script. "Here's the thing," he says. "I sat down with Charlie. I'd done *Class of 1999*, I'd been doing movies that had been released in the theaters for a little while afterwards. *Class of 1999* had gotten a little bit of a buildup from Vestron, there were billboards all over town and stuff, it got a pretty big theatrical release. Charlie was very good. He actually offered me three movies. And so I signed to write three films with the caveat that I would direct one of them. Now, there was nothing specific but obviously it turned out very well for me, because they were *Puppet Master III, Doctor Mordrid* and *Trancers III*. That was the deal and it was okay, the money was okay. Coming from Charlie, the money was pretty good. Charlie, as far as I recall from the Full Moon stuff, a first draft was expected in like three to four weeks. I would say this: even though I'd gone through this process many times over at Empire, of course whenever you were writing a script you were working very closely with Debbie Dion, who I just adored. They trusted me and I would kind of check in and tell them what progress I was making, or what progress I wasn't making, and start.

"But with *Puppet Master III*, it kind of was building its own framework, really. Everything was supposed to be before the first movie. It wasn't like the *Trancers* situation, where you're trying to sequelize story elements that had come before it. Since I

Opposite: Puppet Master III magazine ad.

was before everything else, I could kind of do what I wanted. They were pretty hands off and would let me hand in my first draft, and then we would go from there."

The story would smartly not take viewers all the way back to the beginning—although that would be saved for a later sequel—but would instead drop them in only a short time before the original's prologue sequence. The prequel would accidentally date the film in 1941, despite the original opening in 1939, because of a misprint on Toulon's tombstone in *Puppet Master II*. Here, Toulon is depicted in a much closer fashion to the sweet old man shown in the original's opening few minutes. He loves entertaining children, he loves making them laugh, loves the craftsmanship of his puppetry and even the puppets themselves—already living at this point in time—and above all, he loves his wife, Elsa. Their relationship is lived-in and sweet. Not overbearing, but just a natural bond that the viewer can easily believe was built up over the course of decades. Unbeknownst to Toulon and his wife, a Nazi puppeteer attends the show and takes notice of both the mysterious way in which the puppets appear to be animated as well as the show's subject matter, which makes fun of the Reich and of Hitler in particular.

This is ultimately what catches the Nazis' attention. Toulon is initially warned to shut down his theater on the grounds of political satire, and in that respect he might as well consider himself one of the lucky ones. Political satire in and of itself was no laughing matter in Nazi Germany, to say the least. In some instances, people were executed publicly—via the guillotine, no less—for jokes they hadn't even come up with themselves but had told secondhand. The idea that Toulon would be targeted by the Reich for the subject matter of his children's puppet show makes every kind of sense.

The opening puppet show also introduces viewers to the newest puppet, a breakout star that the production clearly felt confident in: Six-Shooter. This character had been around since the earliest draft of the original *Puppet Master* but got cut alongside other puppets that would also go on to influence later characters in the franchise. This puppet in particular, though, had even predated the original Kenneth J. Hall script. Six-Shooter had been a character left over from Band's Empire-era production *Eliminators*. In that, he had meant to appear as a six-armed robot, but the idea had been scrapped. At some point, the robotic idea was abandoned in favor of a ninja puppet that would hardly make sense for the setting and era of *Puppet Master III*.

Joyner himself came up with the idea of making Six-Shooter into a cowboy instead of a ninja. Not only would it appeal to his own interests as a lifelong fan of Westerns, but it would also simply make much more sense given the character's already given name. Six-Shooter is apparently meant to convey Toulon's idea of an American, however tongue-in-cheek that is. Which one would take to mean a grinning, cocksure Cary Grant-esque cowboy type. In the opening puppet show, Six-Shooter is a, well, real American hero. He steps in and riddles Hitler with bullets to put the dictator in his place and singlehandedly win the war. It's a satirical exaggeration, but it's a noteworthy introduction to the first puppet in the franchise to completely miss out on being a villain. Joyner remembers being given a very different version of Six-Shooter at the start and the character's gradual transformation into the familiar cowboy. "The image that I was given of Six-Shooter may have been on one

Chapter Five. Puppet Master III: Toulon's Revenge

David Allen animating Six-Shooter for unused *Puppet Master III* title sequence (courtesy Chris Endicott).

of the old Empire Calendars," he says. "But it was that metallic, black, steel robot. In my mind, Six-Shooter immediately goes to the West. And I thought that was great. I've got to give Charlie full points, because when I said, 'listen, I think this is the way I want to do it,' he jumped at it. It seemed obvious. Why that character wasn't designed that way in the first place, I don't know. But he completely embraced it and he let me go for it."

Chris Endicott also recalls the creation of the Six-Shooter puppet: "Mark Rappaport had the idea that for Six-Shooter, maybe instead of the rod controlled puppet we could have some kind of cable telemetry puppet with a sophisticated Waldo. He had some people who had been doing that kind of work on other films, some big films, so that was a project that really tickled Mark. And Mark was really involved at David Allen Productions in developing this puppet and making sure it was ready to go. It kind of came late, so we did some shots with the rod puppet that we might not have done. For example, when you see the puppet in the hallway and he meets the general and they have that shootout, that would have definitely been Mark's cable control puppet if it was available at the time. It wasn't, so we did that on the set with lots of strings and stuff, kind of like that original shot of Blade in the hallway, but with more arms."

Puppet Master III would take a much bolder, deeper approach by not just digging into the backstory of Toulon and his wife, Elsa, but the puppets themselves. The prequel would harbor a major reveal that would prove to add a significant dramatic weight to the franchise's diminutive stars, something that would cement their place at the forefront of the series: these puppets were not simply carved and magically brought to life by their creator, they had been human once. Their souls were transferred into wooden bodies, so that they could continue on with some semblance of life after death. This idea had first been introduced in the Eternity comic series, with Elsa's transformation into Leech Woman, which this film would largely retain, but *Puppet Master III* took it one step further. Here, every single character became someone that Toulon was close to in life. On top of that, fittingly appropriate for the film's setting and time period, they were all either Jewish friends who had been executed by the Nazis or—in the case of Pinhead in particular—goyim who had been executed for aiding the Jewish people during their time of struggle.

This opening of the mythology would concretely state *Puppet Master*'s budding place as a surprising sort of modern-day Jewish folklore. The decision to turn the puppets into the souls of Toulon's oppressed loved ones would not be out of place at all. In fact, the very idea of toys coming to life—something frequent in horror fiction and films, particularly those produced by Charles Band—stems from the Jewish myth of the golem. Among the most prevalent golem myths is that of the golem of Prague, centered on a figure that was sculpted out of clay to protect the inhabitants of the city from Anti-Semitic attacks.[2] One can clearly draw a distinct line from that tale to the living puppets of *Puppet Master III*.

Charles Band himself is of Jewish descent and his father, Albert Band, who served as an uncredited producer on *Puppet Master III*, had actually escaped Europe during Hitler's rise to power, just before the start of the Nazi occupation.[3] Albert Band also provided the now iconic laugh of the puppet Six-Shooter, which means that every time Six-Shooter cackles as he's blasting away Nazi soldiers during the film, it is in a way the laugh of an actual Nazi survivor. The subtext of *Puppet Master III*, of a Jewish survivor literally carrying his dead friends on his back wherever he goes is not at all lost on Joyner, who notes that the filmmakers themselves caught onto it during production, at least to an extent. "That was actually something that again just kind of evolved out of what we were doing," he says. "It was something that we noticed. Because it does remind you of those photographs of people who were escaping. And I just thought, 'that's a wonderful thing.' And I think Dave really captured that in the movie with Toulon at night trying to get away from the patrols, and all of that stuff. We were actually aware of that. It's just something that grew out of what we were already doing. These nuances just kept popping up, which is nice. One creative spark leads to the next. That was a wonderful side benefit of it all."

With much of the plot hinging on Elsa's death and her resurrection as a puppet, Courtney Joyner and David DeCoteau found themselves not only facing the

Chapter Five. Puppet Master III: Toulon's Revenge

Chris Endicott animates Tunneler and Pinhead (courtesy Chris Endicott).

opportunity, but also the necessity to bring back the puppet that Band himself had apparently killed off in the previous entry. Even though the producer had thought Leech Woman to be too gross, she would *need* to come back if the movie was going to work, or at least have the same impact. For a puppet so often relegated to the sidelines, it was refreshing to see a movie in which she would be placed front and center, if not for both the first and last time. All of the other puppets from the previous two entries would appear as well, with the exception of Torch, which only makes sense given the fact that viewers saw him get created during the events of *Puppet Master II*, which was set decades after this entry.

There would be one other incredibly noticeable absence for the bulk of *Puppet Master III*: Blade, who is nowhere to be found until the film's final few minutes. This was not out of neglect for the character, but rather out of acknowledgment for his ever-growing popularity. His extended absence in *Puppet Master III* would only, in some ways, cement his place as the rock star of the group. The script takes a very clear "save the best for last" approach, and in a story that revealed the puppets had once been human, it even explores the most famous puppet's origin story. Blade is sculpted after the film's chief villain, the despicable Major Kraus. From the hat to the hair to the outfit, the visual similarities between the two are uncanny. But given that the prequel explains that the puppets were all good, decent people in their previous lives, it would not make any sense for Kraus to be the soul inhabiting the puppet. Instead, that honor would go to Dr. Hess, a scientist forced to work under the Nazis, kept under Kraus' thumb for the bulk of the movie. He is in awe of what Toulon has done and wants only to speak with him about his work, to perhaps work together and help people—a dream he never sees completed as he is killed for turning traitor and helping Toulon escape.

The dynamic between Hess and Kraus best explores why the puppets look the way that they do if they are not meant to be evil. Blade is sculpted in a ghastly facsimile of Kraus so that Hess' chief oppressor would be forced to look into a grotesque mirror image of his own face as he died. Puppets like Tunneler serve the same purpose, to force the Nazis to watch a vague and horrific version of their own images bear down on them as they died. It only makes sense as Toulon was, after all, a satirist. Even in the context of *Puppet Master III,* his satirization of the Reich was what caught their attention in the first place. He carved the puppets as caricatures to exaggerate the most nightmarish qualities of the things he sought to combat—first through his shows and then literally through the puppets themselves.

In addition to being the most story-driven *Puppet Master* yet, *Toulon's Revenge* is also the biggest, simply in its distinction of being the first film in the franchise not confined to the single location of an abandoned hotel. Originally, it was planned to shoot in Romania at Full Moon's newly erected studio there. DeCoteau has even claimed that he initially got the job as director on *Puppet Master III* because he was the only person who was willing to shoot there.[4] However, the recent experiment of *Subspecies* had at the time proven to be a very trying shoot on both the cast and crew. Romania was undergoing a civil overhaul at the time and the Full Moon crew had apparently not been treated with an overwhelmingly friendly response. It was also the dead of winter over there when they planned to start shooting *Puppet Master III,* which would not fit with the planned look and style of the production at all. It was DeCoteau himself who suggested a different option, one much more expensive than shooting halfway around the world even if it was in their own backyard. If they could pull it off, getting as much as they could out of as little time as possible, it would bring a studio aesthetic to *Puppet Master III* that had been missing from the previous two and would not even be recaptured in almost any Full Moon features that followed. Once DeCoteau managed to convince Band of his plan, it was finalized and official: *Puppet Master III* shot at the back lot of Universal Pictures.

This was, of course, limited to the exterior shots, and those consisted of only four days of shooting. That's still a lot of time for an independent film—for perspective's sake, that's about as many days as Donald Pleasence appeared on set in the original *Halloween*—and would take up a huge chunk of the movie's budget. But the sense of scope and (shockingly) prestige would not end with the shooting location, as *Puppet Master III* would also pull together an impressive cast of character actors.

The first of them would be Guy Rolfe as Andre Toulon who would, finally, become the protagonist of one of these movies. Despite impressive turns from both William Hickey and Steve Wells, Rolfe would without a doubt become the actor most identified with the role of Toulon. Rolfe was no stranger to killer toys when he was cast, especially those produced by Charles Band, as he had already starred in the producer's earlier Empire production, *Dolls*. In that film, his character felt ripped straight out of a Grimm fairy tale. He was kind and polite with a sinister undertone that he played perfectly throughout every scene. This character was more archetypal,

Chapter Five. Puppet Master III: Toulon's Revenge

David Allen animating Jester (courtesy Chris Endicott).

certainly not meant to be taken as anything bordering on realistic, particularly given the fact that everything in *Dolls* is heightened as it is essentially being processed through the mind of a child. Although as a toymaker whose creations come to life, Rolfe's character in *Dolls* might have a lot in common with Andre Toulon on paper, the similarities begin and end there.

Rolfe's portrayal of Andre Toulon is a soft-hearted, good-natured, genuine human being. He's everyone's sweet old grandpa, but a man who has clearly already seen some loss in his life. This is of course evidenced by his four puppets already active at the beginning of the picture and is something that would be further explored in 1999's *Retro Puppet Master*. Rolfe was a longtime veteran of stage and screen, with his most prominent role in 1961's *Mr. Sardonicus*. There's a quiet kindness to Rolfe's portrayal of Toulon that is so important to the early portion of the movie. When things take a turn, Rolfe seamlessly transitions into an almost graceful rage. There's an emotional resonance he brings to every scene that is completely unexpected but inherently refreshing for a movie of this size. Luckily, that same caliber of acting that Rolfe brought to Toulon would be adopted across the board.

"That was fun," Joyner recalls of the chance to finally write Toulon as the central protagonist. "The thing is, the background of the character was so murky from the first movie. You've got an old man who is being chased by these S.S. guys and you don't really know why. And of course, the focus of the first movie is Paul Le Mat and Irene Miracle, it's the other cast members. Not the guy who created it. To me it was like doing a *Frankenstein* movie without mentioning Dr. Frankenstein. So I wanted to write about Dr. Frankenstein. And having that background of Germany, Nazi experimentation and all of that stuff, I had this idea in my head of maybe going even a little bit further, because as we know, the S.S. obsession with Satanism and that stuff, they were exploring all kinds of crazy things. But that didn't really find its way into the script. It would have been appropriate, I thought, but that was a little too much. The concentration was really going to be just on the puppets and the idea of whatever made the puppets move could also make soldiers move after they'd been killed. That was really where I took off from."

Chris Endicott remembers both the benefits and the challenges of making the puppet master the lead for the first time, and as a result, having the puppets share much more screen time with the actors than they ever had before. "I don't know if it was a conscious decision. Certainly, Dave DeCoteau is really good at making sure he can get his day. Puppeteering shots tend to take time, so those two things don't necessarily work together well. We did have a huge second unit shoot session over at a place called Movie Tech in Hollywood. We got a giant meat locker and turned it into a stage and we did weeks of insert shots, not with just the puppeteers and Paul Gentry, as we did on the previous films. Dave DeCoteau was there and his D.P. was there, we had A.D.s, it was a much more regimented thing. Normally we'd rush to do these puppet effects but DeCoteau was really willing to make sure each shot got enough time. He still made us move fast, but not in the case where we felt like we had to wrap a shot up without feeling like we got it in the can. Not every director could do that. Not every director had the patience to sit down and direct puppet shots. It's a lot of painting out wires, it's a lot of slow stuff, but it worked."

Sarah Douglas was cast as Toulon's beloved wife, Elsa, allowing viewers to truly be introduced to a character that had really only been kept alive in Toulon's head in *Puppet Master II*. Douglas was and still is best known for her role as the villainess Ursa in *Superman II*. Before that, she had made an impressive turn in the sequel *The People That Time Forgot*. In the decade between *Superman II* and *Puppet Master III*, Douglas made guest appearances in numerous hit TV shows such as *V*, *Magnum P.I.* and *Remington Steele*. She made for an interesting choice as the kindhearted Elsa, as she had become so well known for playing such a cold and dispassionate villain. Elsa Toulon is anything but. This is a character that anchors her husband, having faith in him but worrying when his show might push its satire a little too far. The chemistry between Douglas and Rolfe is truly what sells the core relationship of *Puppet Master III*. Even though there appears to be a significant age difference between them, the viewer can easily buy that these two people have been married for decades. It's not done in a bickering way, either. There is a clearly defined impenetrable bond between them, and the success of that bond is important as it is severed only a half hour into the film. Even though Douglas' scenes are relatively few, hers is the character that forms the backbone of the movie and everything its protagonist is fighting for.

After Elsa's transformation into Leech Woman, the puppet received a more drastic new look than any of the others, with her satin pink dress replaced by a much more conservative purple gown. As Chris Endicott recalls, this was made mostly for story purposes. "I think that's from the script, right? Because suddenly she comes from his wife. So her old outfit doesn't quite work anymore does it? I think that's

Chapter Five. Puppet Master III: Toulon's Revenge

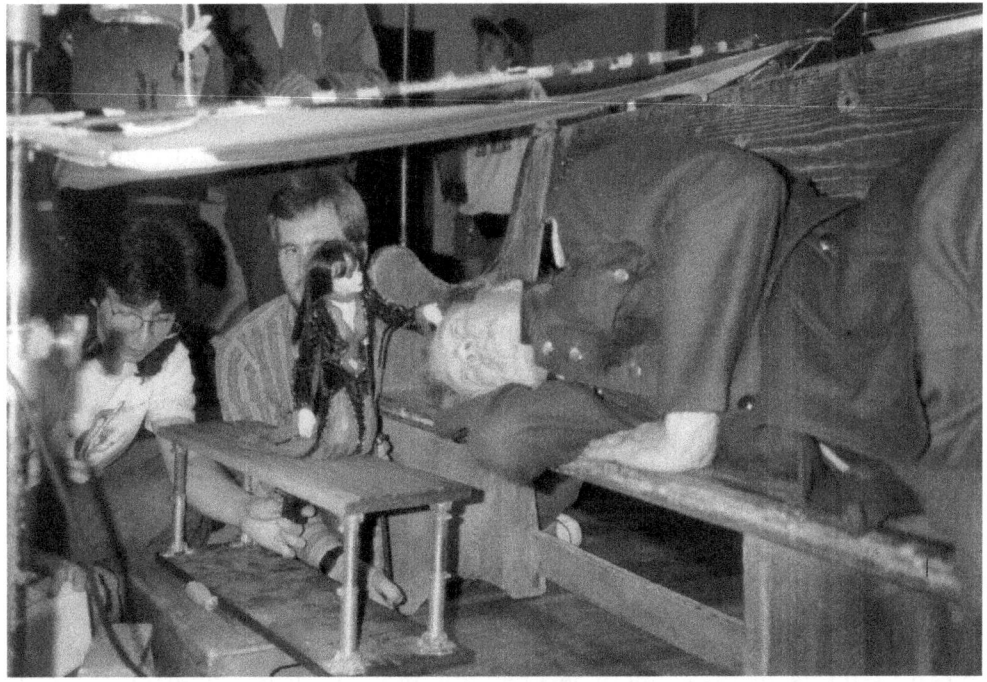

John Teska and Chris Endicott puppeteer Leech Woman (courtesy Chris Endicott).

what it is. And also Joanne Bloomsfield is an incredible seamstress. That was one of her strongest interests around the time we were making the film. She would make the costumes for the other puppets, we needed additional costumes for more puppets. Every film, we made more puppets and more puppets allowed us to change over quickly and also allowed us to shoot on different stages. I think she designed that purple outfit, that really nice dress that she has. And she also made that dress from that other puppet from *Puppet Master II,* the little Mephistopheles sequence, the little woman in the teal dress, she made that one as well. So that was her design and I guess it was out of the idea to make her a more attractive character."

Leading the group of evil Nazis and serving as the chief antagonist of the movie would be bad guy extraordinaire Richard Lynch as Major Kraus—though casting Kraus turned out to be something of a difficult process. Both DeCoteau and Joyner had agreed that with *Puppet Master III* being set in Europe, they wanted a predominantly European cast. For the most part, this proved easy, with actors like Guy Rolfe, Sarah Douglas, Ian Abercrombie and Walter Gotell all being well-known and respected English character actors. When it came time to cast the villainous S.S. Officer Kraus, both the director and writer wanted to keep that trend of European actors going and had both even settled on the same name: Ralph Bates. "When we were thinking about Major Kraus, David and I were talking and we were of course huge Hammer Film fans," explains Joyner. "And I said, 'look, why don't we try for Ralph Bates?' We actually went ahead, and our casting guys—it was Harry and Bob—they got ahold of his agent and we of course did not know that he was terminally ill. We went ahead and made the offer to him to come over and be in the film. I actually asked, well, I knew Herbert Lom and I'd also asked Herbert if he would be in the film. It was a wonderful reaction, because we started talking about the cost and the rest of it. He'd say, 'Your budget is what I was paid for my last film.' He was a great guy. When I told him we had Guy Rolfe he said, 'Oh my God, is he still *living*?'

"But we all thought the Ralph Bates situation would be just terrific," Joyner says. "Then he died. I remember we were seeing Ann Turkel. She came in to talk about being in the film, and of course we cast Sarah Douglas, and we got the message that Ralph had died. But he knew that he had been offered the movie before he passed, so we felt very good about that.

"The actor Christopher Neame came in that day. And he's a big guy! It really surprised me how physically large he was. He couldn't have been nicer and he knew about this situation. He sat down with us, and I'll never forget this, he told David DeCoteau and myself that if he played Major Kraus, he was going to donate his salary to Virginia Wetherall-Bates, who was Ralph's widow, because he and Ralph were best friends."

Despite the incredible gesture, the casting was not in the cards. As Joyner notes: "When we discussed it with Charlie, he had a very legitimate concern. He said, 'Look, guys, we've got all these European actors, we've got Guy Rolfe, Sarah Douglas, Ian Abercrombie and everybody, it does not appear to be an American production now. When I sell this, that is going to be a liability.' It was Charlie's company, you can't really argue with that. But he felt that if we cast one more European actor, that it really would be a problem in terms of what the advances would be and everything else. He had just had Richard [Lynch] in *Trancers II*, and so that was how Richard ended up playing the part. I thought he did great, and the thing is, even more than Christopher Neame, Richard Lynch *really* looks like the Blade puppet."

Bates had been an actor from the classic Hammer tradition which would have suited his involvement with *Puppet Master III* perfectly. He had appeared in so many classics throughout the '60s and '70s, most notably *Taste the Blood of Dracula, Dr. Jekyll and Sister Hyde, Lust for a Vampire* and *The Horror of Frankenstein*. From his credentials to his cold and consistently endearing screen presence, it's easy to see why DeCoteau and Joyner had both landed on his name. There was a very sinister grace to his Hammer performances in particular that would have made him a natural fit for the S.S. Officer who becomes the visual template for Blade.

Nonetheless, Richard Lynch proved to be iconic casting, as his portrayal of Kraus has become maybe *the* most celebrated villain of the franchise in the eyes of the fans. With early roles ranging from *God Told Me To* to *Battlestar Galactica*, Lynch had begun to earn a name for himself in horror and science fiction from the moment he emerged onto the scene. Prior to his Full Moon tenure, Lynch had begun to appear in Cannon Films productions like *Invasion U.S.A., Savage Dawn* and *The Barbarians*. With *Puppet Master III*, he truly looked just like the puppet he was serving as the basis for. In *Puppet Master III*, he is even dressed exactly like Blade, wearing the same hat and trench coat. Although, going back to the Nazis from the opening of the first *Puppet Master*, this could also simply have been traditional Nazi garb in the *Puppet Master* universe. Even if he had not initially been the first choice by either the director or the writer, Lynch's character has gone on to become without a doubt the most remembered, highly regarded villain of the entire franchise to date. Even though fans have noticed that his German accent tends to slip in and out, he plays the character with such sleazy menace that it's hard to peel your eyes away any time he's on screen, even though you're led to hate him so much. As tied-to-the-tracks evil as Kraus is, though, there's a respect for Toulon that at least makes this antagonistic relationship somewhat endearing beyond a simple surface level. Kraus has done his research on Toulon, even knowing the man's history in medicine before his career turn to puppetry, musing and thinking aloud to himself about why the puppet master had made some of the decisions he had made in his life. Kraus is a character who has, without a doubt, killed no small amount of people. Perhaps the most tragic thing about Elsa's death in the film is that Kraus had not even *planned* to kill her. She is an afterthought. Even though he shoots her for spitting on his shoe, he does it almost reflexively and without any hint of either malice or joy in his face.

This is a man for whom death is as natural as breathing and despite his commitment to the order of his job as well as to his superiors and their cause, he's a hunter who seems incredibly bored with his prey. Toulon is a character that, as Kraus admits, he does not understand. And while he never speaks of it to his only companion, Hess—a man that he hates—this lack of understanding of Toulon is exactly what fuels his obsession. Like any great dynamic in a film of this type, Toulon and Kraus are polar opposite characters and that is what makes their dynamic work so well.

As Kraus' superior officer, General Mueller, the production cast Bond villain extraordinaire Walter Gotell. First appearing as a SPECTRE henchman in *From Russia with Love,* Gotell was later cast as General Gogol for *A View to a Kill, Moonraker* and *Octopussy.* He plays a Nazi so well in *Puppet Master III* that it's easy to forget that he could ever play anything else, making things like his role as a eccentric old camp owner in *Sleepaway Camp II* that much more surprising. Gotell is also given the most uncomfortable sex scene in one of these films, as we are forced to watch a romantic interlude between an elderly Nazi general and a German prostitute. He also gets the distinction of being the standout kill for Six-Shooter, truly showcasing the new puppet's deadly capabilities. In the stop-motion sequence leading up to the kill, fans are also treated to a rare bit of improv from David Allen. When Six-Shooter is scaling the wall, he spots two Nazi officers walking below and shakes his fist at them, a decision that was apparently made while they were prepping to animate the sequence. It's a small moment that sells the overall tone and mood of the film, as well as giving an extra bit of personality to the new puppet.

General Mueller is also worth noting for being the aspect of the story most directly lifted from the 1990 Eternity comic book, aside from Elsa's transformation into Leech Woman. In the first issue, which is the prequel set during World War II, Mueller appears as the general who orders the theater to be shut down and who is assassinated by Toulon's puppets sometime afterwards. All of these things make it into the film intact, although it would obviously be Six-Shooter to kill him in the film instead of Blade as it had been in the comic book.[5]

Kraus has a much more directly antagonistic relationship in the film with Dr. Hess, played by the late, great Ian Abercrombie. The actor had been working non-stop since the early 1960s prior to his role in *Puppet Master III*. Abercrombie was best known at the time for appearances in shows like *Columbo, Fantasy Island* and *Alfred Hitchcock Presents*. Just before getting cast in the film, Abercrombie appeared in the *Tales from the Crypt* episode "The Switch" directed by Arnold Schwarzenegger, playing the butler to William Hickey, the original puppet master. Just after his *Puppet Master III* appearance, Abercrombie hit a whole new level of recognition as the recurring character Mr. Pitt in *Seinfeld*. He is still perhaps best known to horror audiences as the Wise Man in *Army of Darkness*. Hess and Kraus share almost every scene together, with Kraus tasked with supervising the project that Hess is overseeing—a project that, if successful, would see the Nazis reanimating their own fallen soldiers on the battlefield. With the plot revolving around the reanimation of dead bodies, it's interesting to note that the serum that gives Toulon's puppets life looks almost identical to the formula in an earlier film that Band helped to produce: *Re-Animator*. In both that visual aesthetic and its subject matter, *Puppet Master III* could almost be seen as a loose prequel to that movie as well.

Hess is a far more sympathetic character than the sadistic Kraus from the opening scene, despite the fact that they both apparently work for the same division. Hess is always speaking from a medical, scientific standpoint. He never seems to agree with the ideals held by Kraus and their commanding officer, General Mueller. Instead, Hess openly disagrees with the Nazi ideals, even casually noting that Hitler's quest for world domination was doomed to fail. It's easy to imagine that Hess was simply a doctor who had been working and making a living in Berlin when the Nazi occupation started and was simply forced to continue his work under the Nazis. It's even very easy to think that Hess was likely a Jewish doctor forced to work on this project until he would likely be executed later on, as Kraus repeatedly informs Hess that he'll likely be killed as soon as he finishes his work.

As soon as Hess begins to try and replicate Toulon's work, he becomes enamored with the man's genius to the point of turning coat in order to help keep Toulon alive—even, eventually, giving his life so that the puppet master can escape. The friendship (kinship, even) between Toulon and Hess comes in late, but it's a high mark for the film. As soon as they're sharing the screen, Rolfe and Abercrombie appear to have a natural respect and admiration for one another. In their few minutes together, the viewer is quickly led to root for their friendship. Once the mythology has been laid bare, it's easy to watch as a first-time viewer and quickly understand that Hess' friendship with Toulon will more than likely last beyond his own death. This transformation into Blade is explicitly hinted at two times: first, when Hess says to Toulon, "Perhaps some other time we could have worked together, and done great things" and the *Puppet Master* theme begins to play faintly, and a second time after their conversation when Toulon looks to Six-Shooter as if seeking his approval and the puppet gives a satisfied nod. Kraus may be hunting Toulon throughout the movie, but it's his constant belittling of Hess throughout their scenes together that make the ending feel so justified.

Kraus not only serves as the inspiration for the puppet that is now standing in front of him, ushering in his death, but is even literally turned into a puppet as the group work together to hook ropes through his arms and legs, stringing him up like an actual marionette. It is easily the most involved and complicated kill in the entire franchise but is delivered to the villain who unquestionably most deserves it. In that manner, it feels incredibly cathartic. "I loved the idea of really concentrating on the scientist, the doctor who is kind of imprisoned by the Nazis, if you will," says Joyner. "He's expected to come through with these experiments and Andre Toulon actually has the key to making all of this stuff work, but he's certainly not going to turn it over to the Third Reich. That was a lot of fun."

Providing a minimal glimpse of comic relief is the late Aron Eisenberg as the young Peter Hertz. The child appears at the opening puppet show, simply a fan boy for Toulon and his puppets—and, in that respect, a surrogate for the audience—before appearing later on as a fugitive hiding in the same abandoned building where Toulon takes root. There's a tragedy to Peter in that he does not understand the stakes of the events unfolding around him, that literally every moment is a matter of life or death. One even has to wonder if he was meant to be written for a younger actor, as the Peter we see in the film seems a little old to lean so heavily into the child's fantasy of seeing his hiding as an adventure, or even being as enamored with the puppets as he appears to be. Of course, it's just as easy to suggest that Peter may have been fully aware of the reality of his situation—that he and his father were wanted fugitives or that his mother had been taken and likely killed—and simply decided to retreat into a kind of escapism that he could hardly be blamed for. By the end of the film, he has lost his parents and Toulon has lost everything. There could be the suggestion that Toulon sees Peter as a kind of surrogate son, but their relationship is more distant than that. By the end of the movie, Peter has come to understand the horror of what they have been through and Toulon has lost both his beloved wife and his newfound friend. There is a definite indication that he might not want to take this child on this journey with him, as he loses everyone that he grows to love. It's one thing to stomach turning someone like Hess into a puppet, but another thing altogether to subject a child like Peter to the same fate. Toulon even gives non-committal answers when Peter asks him where they might be headed. At the end, there's a suggestion that they might continue on their adventures together, but that never happens.

In that respect, *Puppet Master III* continues the tradition of setting up a sequel that is never explored. Although later entries would try to pick up directly from the end of this movie, and later sequels would return to the same World War II setting, none of those entries ever sought to further explore the relationship between Toulon and Peter. It's interesting to note the impact that *Puppet Master III* has had on the franchise as a whole. While so many franchises seek to recapture the magic of the original, *Puppet Master III* is the well that the series keeps going back to, especially in more recent years. Over time, as this entry's audience grew and it became the critical highlight of the brand, Full Moon took notice and began to capitalize on that potential. When Full Moon returned in its Full Moon Features incarnation, they began to sell t-shirts and posters from the first and third entries, specifically. They released new resin statues depicting a crumbled, war-torn background that would be a clear reference to *Puppet Master III*. In 2005, cementing the movie's legacy in the franchise's eyes, Band announced that Full Moon would be producing a new trilogy set during World War II in order to try and recapture the magic of the series' most beloved sequel. It took them from 2010 to 2017 to deliver on that promise, but they

Puppeteers help Leech Woman do her thing (courtesy Chris Endicott).

did. If imitation is truly the sincerest form of flattery, then the *Axis* movies may be the brightest indicator to the lasting impact of *Toulon's Revenge*.

With a closing shot centering on Six-Shooter (assuring fans that he would be here to stay no matter what continuity errors may arise from it) the film ends with the promise of "*Puppet Master 4:* When Bad Puppets Turn Good!" This would be the first *Puppet Master* movie to not only end on a vague cliffhanger, but actually end on the concrete promise that the franchise would continue—and soon.

By the time *Puppet Master III* was released, Full Moon was already moving into new merchandising ventures with the first model kits based on the puppets. A longtime fan of classic horror, Band was no doubt inspired by beloved Aurora Universal monsters models when he made this business decision. For the puppet kits, Band hired sculptor and FX artist Greg Aronowitz to design the very first *Puppet Master* collectables ever. In some ways, this was as important a move for the franchise's longevity as the films themselves. With these model kits, Band and Full Moon had begun to realize the potential of the puppets as iconic figures that could be marketed directly to the fans.[6] Although he likely did not realize it at the time, this idea sparked the kernel of the collectable game that would wind up defining the *Puppet Master* franchise.

As there were very few produced and they didn't tend to last incredibly long, the original model kits are now incredibly sought-after items by the fans. Depicting Blade, Tunneler, Pinhead, Torch and Six-Shooter, the model kits were released quickly and did not stay available for long. If anything, this might be a surprising instance in which Full Moon underestimated just how big its audience was getting and how popular the franchise was starting to become. While they knew that the series would continue as promised at the end of *Puppet Master III*, they had no way of knowing just what that promise would mean.

Puppet Master III: Toulon's Revenge hit video stores on October 17, 1991, almost exactly two years after the original. It quickly garnered the best reviews in the franchise and continues to be the most beloved and respected to this day. While Full Moon had already won over its demographic with the first two, *Puppet Master III* brought in critical attention that the previous entries had mostly lacked, such as horror writers, critics and magazines like *Fangoria* that had been largely dismissive of the series up to that point.[7] *Toulon's Revenge* proved that not only was the franchise here to stay, but that it could also have something to say. While the original had taken the material more seriously than people had expected from the producer of *Ghoulies* and *Dolls,* the third movie had pushed things even further into that direction—and with great results, to boot. *Puppet Master III* had burst the franchise wide open in several ways: in terms of the mythology, in terms of the quality, and in creative terms of where the series could potentially go from here. Nobody seeing *Puppet Master III* when it came out could have possibly predicted where it would go next. Would it continue on in the past? Would it return to the present and follow up from the Camille cliffhanger of *Puppet Master II?* Or would it take an entirely different approach? What did the "When Bad Puppets Turn Good" tagline even mean? Could they really get *better* than killing Nazis? These were questions that needed to be answered.

But the truth was, Full Moon didn't even have those answers in place before they made the promise of *Puppet Master 4* in the closing credits of the third film. The title was a placeholder if anything. It presented a more complicated riddle than had been anticipated, and answering that riddle proved to be a longer and stranger journey than anyone involved had probably anticipated.

Chapter Six

Puppet Master 4 and *5*

With *Puppet Master III* promising a bold new direction, Band and Full Moon got to work on figuring out how to figure out how to make good on that promise. Band had talked in the very first *Video Zone* about seeing these films as his own cinematic equivalents of comic books. He obviously wanted these characters to keep going, to face new challenges and, eventually, to cross over. There had been talks of exactly how to do that, and for Full Moon, 1993 could basically be seen as "the crossover year." He had ambitiously begun to assemble his own team of Avengers long before the days of the Marvel Cinematic Universe. Originally conceived as a *Doctor Strange* adaptation according to the 2012 *Full Moon Catalogue*, Full Moon eventually let the rights lapse before the movie's production and thus had to evolve into becoming a different story altogether while retaining that classic *Doctor Strange* influence, as well as changing the title to *Doctor Mordrid*.[1] Instead of being the "Master of the Mystic Arts," Combs' Doctor Mordrid would be the "Master of the Unknown." He was the first of Full Moon's off-brand superheroes, which is only fitting being that he was actually meant to be a Marvel character in the first place. Losing those rights only made the company more ambitious, however. *Mordrid* was followed by *Mandroid*, which would introduce another low-budget hero that—even though he was original and cheesy as a cheddar hell—could have easily fit right into the Lee and Kirby Marvel era of the early '60s. Except for the fact that Band's superhero movies leaned heavily into exploitation, as one would only expect from the company at this point.

The Mandroid would make a return appearance as a main character in *Invisible: The Chronicles of Benjamin Knight,* which would for all intents and purposes introduce Full Moon's version of S.H.I.E.L.D. This was a high-tech spy team with supernatural monsters, science experiments gone wrong and robots at their disposal. It was not only a deliberate and direct crossover, but it was a crossover extremely similar to those later seen in the Marvel Cinematic Universe. Characters wouldn't just wait for the huge team up, they would move casually in and out of each other's films. After *Invisible* came the harder-edged female antihero of *Dark Angel: The Ascent.* The intent was to eventually cross these characters over into their own mega-event movie, assembling a Full Moon super group and allowing for individual franchises as well as bigger crossovers. It is exactly the same model that would wind up being adopted by Marvel Studios, with the major difference (other than the drastic difference in budget) being that Full Moon never actually got to see their crossover team-up through to completion, even if they did wind up releasing each of the individual solo films.[2]

Chapter Six. Puppet Master 4 *and* 5

While the new, super-heroic direction of Full Moon would not affect *Puppet Master* in terms of actually using any of its characters, it would clearly define the direction the next movie would take, and therefore deserves mention for at least that reason. Band was influenced by his crossover plans, though, when at the end of 1992 he announced the upcoming *Puppet Master 4* with a teaser poster, even if there was no set script or story yet, in pure Band tradition. The idea and intent were clear and sold themselves just by the poster art alone, which depicted the puppets locked in battle against the Demonic Toys.[3] This would not be an ambitious Marvel superhero team-up, but instead a horror crossover in a long tradition of classics ranging back to *Frankenstein Meets the Wolf Man*. It made perfect sense in context with the teaser at the end of *Puppet Master III* as well. With the puppets now re-established as heroes, the Demonic Toys would serve as the perfect foils. In some ways, the Demonic Toys felt like successors to the throne, taking over the "killer toy" slot after the puppets had concretely rebranded themselves as forces for good. Ultimately, this *Puppet Master vs. Demonic Toys* idea would not come to pass in the next installment, perhaps seen as too expensive a concept to pull off at the time. But the idea would absolutely not go away. With the crossover now out of the question Band elected to pit the Demonic Toys against a different Full Moon hero: Dollman in a feature that he wound up directing himself.

Band appeared dead set on doing something ambitious with *Puppet Master 4*, even though it took some time to figure out exactly what that would be. Full Moon was only growing bigger, embracing its fans through the Fan Club and bringing in many new fans through the movies themselves, which always had box art enticing enough to lure in the most curious horror fans. Even though Band had created Full Moon specifically to target video retailers and rentals that had made Empire such a success, there seemed to be the potential for something bigger. At this point, Full Moon could do more and—as he always did—Band sought to capitalize on its newfound success. *Puppet Master* was, without a doubt, Full Moon's flagship franchise. It had become so successful on video store aisles that most people who rented the movies by this point simply assumed that the original must have gone to theaters, and that maybe they had just missed it during its short run. In fact, that's a misconception that many fans *still* have to this day.

It's also a misconception that Full Moon sought to turn into a reality at the time. As the series continued to generate hype and following the rare critical notice of *Puppet Master III,* Band decided that the next *Puppet Master* would be a theatrical motion picture. Getting *Puppet Master* into theaters would not be easy and would be the company's most ambitious move yet, but the producer was dead set on the idea. Band decided to move forward with this high-flying heroic puppet adventure with himself at the helm. If it was going to be the biggest and riskiest move yet, it was only fitting that the creator finally step behind the camera to oversee it. After three entries in the franchise so far, Band elected to bafflingly call this theatrical venture *Puppet Master: The Movie.*

For the script, several writers wound up receiving final credit and it's tough to say who contributed the most. Unfortunately, while the script was clearly written, *Puppet Master: The Movie* would never come to pass. The dreamed-of theatrical Full

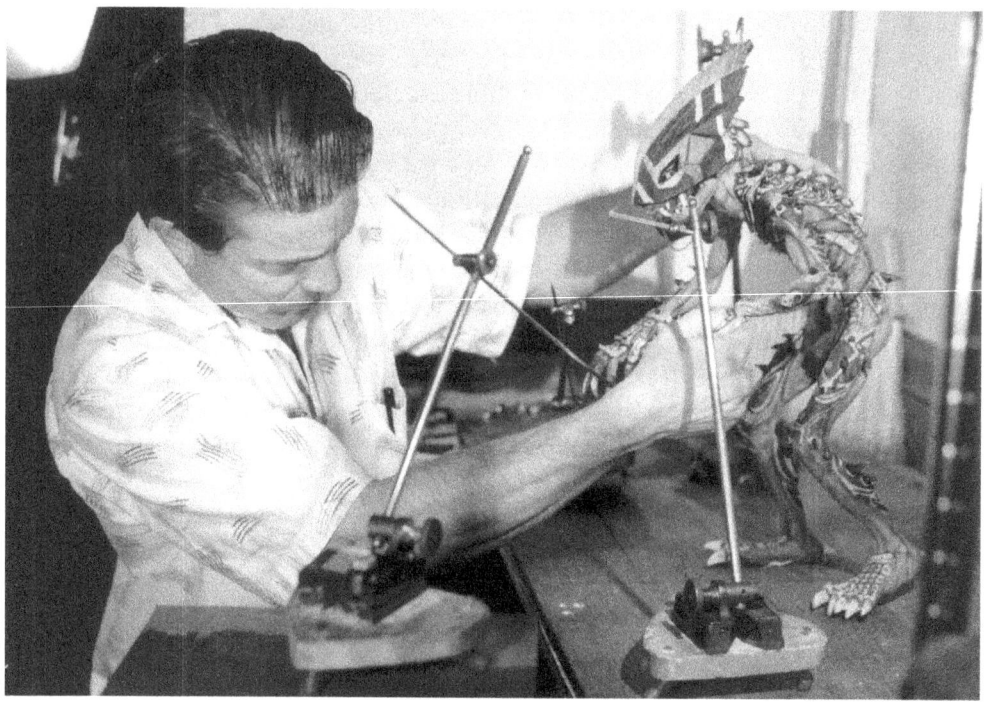

David Allen animates a Totem for *Puppet Master 4* (courtesy Chris Endicott).

Moon movie could not quite become a reality just yet, and it seemed a big screen *Puppet Master* just wasn't meant to be. Instead, the fabled theatrical Full Moon flick would happen only a year later, with the much more surprising choice of *Shrunken Heads*.

The script for *Puppet Master: The Movie* was cut in half and underwent a great deal of padding in order to be turned into two separate films that Full Moon would once again distribute direct to video. This bold new direction included the concept of the puppets being targeted by a malevolent demon as well as the idea of the puppets having to face off against creatures of their own size. While no less ambitious in principle, this concept posed a lot of challenges for what would eventually become *Puppet Master 4* and *Puppet Master 5*. Although it wouldn't be theatrical, the next story would in some ways be the biggest yet, as it would be told over the course of two separate films. In a tradition Band was beginning to embrace in hopes of saving money, *Puppet Master 4* and *5* would be shot simultaneously. The very same year, Band would repeat that trick for the productions of not only *Subspecies II* and *III*, but *Trancers 4* and *5* as well.

The frustration of the original *Puppet Master*'s ever evolving script would pale in comparison to the screenplays for *4* and *5*, which were never finalized even as the two movies were filming. The compound script for the two features wound up boasting five screenwriters in total. For four out of the five, these would be their only writing credits ever. The lucky fifth, Doug Aarniokowsi, was primarily an assistant director at Full Moon—in fact, he was the assistant director on these two movies, as well—and would go on to write only one more feature many years later in 2013's infamous *Nurse*

Chapter Six. Puppet Master 4 *and* 5

3D starring Paz de la Huerta, which he also directed. With this in mind, it's a miracle that the story is even half as comprehensible as it turned out to be.

Jeff Burr took on the challenge of directing this *Puppet Master* double feature. Having gotten his start directing the Vincent Price anthology *From a Whisper to a Scream* (aka *The Offspring*)—which had been written by none other than *Puppet Master III*'s Courtney Joyner—Burr had then gone on to direct some major horror sequels including *The Stepfather II* and *Leatherface: The Texas Chainsaw Massacre III*. So he was no stranger to jumping into an established franchise. Burr also had a familiarity with the *Puppet Master* series itself, as he explains.

"One of the movies I was supposed to do at Empire was going to be produced by David Schmoeller, so we had known each other a long time. We got to know each other in 1987, working on various projects, so I knew him and got to be friendly with him. And as a matter of fact, he called me and said 'Hey, do you want to come to this screening of this new movie I'm doing for the Bandcompany called *Puppet Master*.' So I went into a small screening room with him and a few other people at the Deluxe Lab in Hollywood. So I got to see the original *Puppet Master* on a big, nice film laboratory screen. So I was familiar with that. I was always a fan of David Allen, so I did see *Puppet Master II,* because he directed it. And that, to me, still has the single best stop-motion shot of the series: Blade leaping off of the bed. It's stunning. I was friends with DeCoteau and Courtney Joyner, so I had seen and actually been on the set of *Puppet Master III*. So I would say I was fairly well versed in the *Puppet Master* universe."

As to how he wound up becoming director of the next two installments, Burr says, "In terms of the process, I came in fairly late in the game. I think Charlie was originally going to direct the movie himself and it was going to be *Puppet Master: The Movie*, the first theatrical feature for Full Moon. That was the basic idea. Then they decided to make two movies out of it. What story there was, they put it into kind of two parts. But it was really one movie, in terms of making it, for me. I think the only reason Charlie thought of me for these movies was that I had seen him, I think the Christmas before. It had been a long time and I saw him at a Full Moon Christmas Party, hosted by Courtney Joyner or somebody. I think that put me back in his mind to direct the movie."

From the opening moments, *Puppet Master 4* clearly embraces Full Moon's new comic book-themed direction to its core. It is in stark contrast to anything seen in the previous three movies, opening inside of the lair of the demon Sutekh, a character crucial to the mythology despite having never been mentioned up to this point. As his exposition suggests, the magic Toulon uses to bring his puppets to life was originally stolen from his people, and he simply wants it back. He will kill anyone it takes to get his hands on the magic that brings these puppets to life, even if Toulon is not necessarily at fault, having not been the person to have stolen it in the first place.

Once again, the new sequel would bring a change in sub-genre, although this would be the most extreme tonal shift yet. Following *Puppet Master III*'s earnest war movie, *Puppet Master 4* would leap into campy sci-fi horror headfirst. While a jarring departure for the series, it would follow organically not only from the puppets' heroic turn in the previous movie but would be perfectly suited to the new climate of Full

Uncovering the trunk (and Torch) in *Puppet Master 4* (courtesy Chris Endicott).

Moon at the time. In the era of *Dollman, Doctor Mordrid, Mandroid* and other Full Moon superheroes, puppets defending their master from evil demons only makes total sense. The story begins with the introduction of a demonic overlord that had never been referred to in any of the films up to this point yet would become crucial to the overall lore. The demon Sutekh sits surrounded by skulls and robed minions in a lair in his home dimension that feels like it could have been directly lifted from an early *Doctor Strange* comic. It turns out that the magic Toulon uses to bring his puppets to life, which was (at this point in time) given to him by a sorcerer in Cairo, actually belongs to Sutekh, and despite never having made an apparent move up to this point, the demon will now stop at nothing to kill the puppets and their new master and get their secrets back.

The Totems make for interesting villains across both sequels as they give the puppets something to fight, something to play hero against, allowing viewers to see what the puppets can do in very different ways than had been seen in the first three features, where the puppets had always been pitted against people. The skinny, slender little demons posed some FX challenges as well, as Chris Endicott notes: "Well, of course, Sutekh and the Totems were the same puppet. The mechanics of the telemetry version of the puppet were really nice." He also adds, "When it worked it was really great, the way it could move its fingers and gesture was great. Like the shot with Torch where it kind of reacts to the flame and covers himself a little bit, it was just fun to do that stuff. That was neat. It would be a lot harder to do that with a rod puppet. It definitely suits the rod puppeteering that those puppets weren't supposed to be puppets. They had that kind of artificiality about them. Sutekh is supposed to

Chapter Six. Puppet Master 4 *and* 5

be a living creature and he definitely benefited from having that telemetry to come to life."

The new puppet master in question is scientific wunderkind Rick Myers, who is completely different from any person to serve that role up to this point. For one thing, he's young. Rick's college age but has already gotten his masters and is working for a huge scientific firm attempting to develop artificial intelligence. Despite his best efforts, Rick has not come anywhere approaching the capacity for independent thought in the robots he has been designing. Unlike previous leads, Rick is not after the puppets for any kind of personal gain. He's not looking to find the secrets to immortality and he does not want to overrun the earth with an army of self-aware robots. He just wants the discovery and the puppets happen to be exactly what he's looking for. These new elements push the story into a much more science-fiction based direction than had been seen in previous *Puppet Master* movies.

While this was a new direction for the franchise to take, the niche combination of sci-fi and technology was making a comeback at the time. The early '90s saw several technologically themed horror films, from *The Lawnmower Man* to *Ghost in the Machine* to *Man's Best Friend* and even *Project: Metalbeast*. The 1990s had often been referred to as the computer age and this is something that both *Puppet Master 4* and 5 fundamentally embrace. In both movies—which, collectively, are one story—computers serve as an all-purpose Deus Ex Machina. Throughout the two films, computers are in their own way almost magical. They represent the threat to Sutekh's magic that causes the action to kick off in the first place. The demons have resurfaced because Rick Myers and the people he works for are on the verge of either replicating their magic or simply uncovering it, potentially predicting Rick eventually finding of the puppets themselves.

Perfectly blending these elements and infusing the franchise with fresh blood, so to speak, would be the newest addition to the ever-growing puppet ensemble, Decapitron. This puppet continues the tradition set by *Puppet Master III* of introducing a puppet character that would actually be a recycled idea from the Empire Pictures era, although this one would be an even more extreme example. While Six-Shooter was originally a character that had been attempted for use in the original *Puppet Master*, long planned to be included as a puppet before finally making his debut, Decapitron was originally meant to be the star of his own movie. Originally planned for release in 1989, the same year the original *Puppet Master* came out, *Decapitron* was an incredibly ambitious project from the onset, so it is easy to see why it did not pan out. Estimated for a $14 million budget, it would have been Empire's most expensive film ever. With a screenplay by Danny Bilson and Paul De Meo—the team behind *The Rocketeer*, not to mention the original *Trancers*—it would have been directed by Peter Manoogian, who went on to direct the first installment of *Puppet Master*'s sister franchise, *Demonic Toys*. Like almost every Charles Band project, a poster was created for the movie even though it eventually fell through.[4]

Despite what you might think, *Decapitron* would still have been an incredibly different entity from the character that eventually made its way into the film itself. The Empire movie was planned to revolve around a destructive robot (similar to what we eventually saw with Full Moon's *Mandroid*) with the ability to take off its head and replace it with any variety of different weaponized heads, each with their own function. The character was written to carry the heads in a sort of briefcase, which would no doubt have proven impractical for action sequences. And with the budget in mind, it sounds as if the movie was going to have no shortage of action. But, obviously, it did not come to pass.

Like many other projects, the collapse of Empire Pictures spelled the end of *Decapitron.* Band's other attempts to venture into larger budget filmmaking hadn't worked, either. Stuart Gordon's *Robot Jox,* Empire's highest budgeted movie, had won over the same audience that the Empire flicks generally appealed to, but failed to reach beyond that. Box office reception was relatively lukewarm on that feature, so *Decapitron* became less of a priority for the studio even before it went under. In this instance, though, the character was likely retooled for the better. The idea of multiple, interchangeable heads is something that just fundamentally makes more sense for a puppet than a life-sized human robot.

Tossing out the full-blown robot idea, *Puppet Master 4*'s Decapitron instead elected for a design that would cater much more to the World War II elements of the other puppets, so that the character would easily fit in with the rest of the group. The clothing is almost identical to Torch, but with a leather jacket instead of the tan one that the other puppet wears. This helps the puppet to feel in place with the others, which is important, as virtually everything else about the character, from its abilities to its execution and place in the story, make it stand out.

Chris Endicott recalls the creation of the Decapitron puppet: "By the time it came to us, the fact that it had a backstory from the Empire days had no bearing on us. Obviously David knew about those designs because he was part of the Empire fold at the time, but that just became pre-production artwork from another movie incorporated into suggestions. 'Here's a picture of how it was going to be in that movie, make it more like that.' The design and those things were definitely the purview of Dennis Gordon and his people. He was the one who gave that almost sort of steam punk appearance. The Frankenstein kind of lab, that purple table that he came with, I don't know where that came from, but the whole look definitely came from Dennis Gordon."

The most important thing about Decapitron as a puppet hinges on the success of *Puppet Master III.* Because that movie had revealed that each of these characters had once been human, fans following the story would have to wonder who would be occupying the new puppet. It's something that fundamentally changed the series, as each new puppet's origin would have to be explained in the franchise moving forward. People had also reacted well to Guy Rolfe's incarnation of Andre Toulon, with good reason, and Rolfe had even stated during the *Video Zone* for *Puppet Master III* that he hoped that people couldn't wait to see him in *Puppet Master 4.*[5] Of course, that would be easier said than done as the sequel is set in present day and Toulon had been dead for several decades before that, in addition to getting killed off once again in *Puppet Master II.* As ridiculous as it would sound, though, Decapitron's featureless morphing head would allow Rolfe to return to play the character once again, albeit as a puppet. According to director Jeff Burr, Rolfe was on set for a single day and understood nothing of the role and what it required of him.[6] Acting against a blue screen

Chapter Six. Puppet Master 4 *and* 5

Randy Cook animates Blade and Pinhead in *Puppet Master 4* (courtesy Chris Endicott).

was totally alien to him, as were the close-ups in which he technically portrayed the puppet. It's a testament to Rolfe's acting ability, though. Virtually all of the lines the character has in both *Puppet Master 4* and *Puppet Master 5* are exposition, yet he sells it well.

"I can say, on a literal level, I worked with Guy Rolfe," Burr says of his brief time working with the actor on set. "It is very true. In reality, it was just hilarious. He flew in and he barricaded himself in his hotel suite in the Holiday Inn on Highland, and would not come out until Charlie put his salary under the door in cash. He was supposed to work *that day*. I got reports every hour like, 'Okay, they're up to his hotel room, they are putting the hundred dollar bills under his door. They hear movement! They hear movement! It sounds like cash is being put in an envelope. I think he's coming.' I would get hourly reports like that and then lo and behold the soundstage door opens and there's Guy Rolfe looking incredibly jet-lagged going, 'Where the hell am I?' We were so pressed for time that I literally shook his hand and said, 'Okay, get on the slab.' This slab that he was strapped to like Frankenstein's Monster, which you could raise up and lower down. I am sure that to his death he had no memory of any of it. He was completely jet-lagged, but very happy that his pockets were full. If you mention Guy Rolfe to me, all I can think about is him strapped to a sheet of plywood, moving up and down with a look on his face like, 'What country am I in? Where am I? Why am I here?' I can never watch *Mr. Sardonicus* again."

It's a bizarre turn to watch the puppet master actually become one of his puppets, especially watching an actor have to attempt to pull that off, but it's a narratively fitting one for this franchise. As much as both movies are about taking things in extremely bold new directions, both *Puppet Master 4* and especially *Puppet Master 5* are about bringing things full circle as well. Returning to play Andre Toulon as the Decapitron puppet, Rolfe also had the distinction of being the very first returning actor in any *Puppet Master* film up to that point. Watching the master become the puppet set things up for an easy passing of the torch—so to speak—to the younger Rick Myers.

Gordon Currie took on the lead role of Myers for both sequels. Like many actors who eventually moved to Los Angeles, Currie originally hailed from Vancouver, British Columbia. While he was born there, though, both of his parents were American citizens, likely making the transition to the States an easy one. When he first moved to Los Angeles, Currie lived in a small apartment taking whatever acting jobs he could find, alongside his roommate who was also a struggling actor by the name of Brad Pitt. One of the first jobs that Currie landed in Los Angeles was as Ronald McDonald for local appearances and events at the restaurant. In 1987 he landed a role in *21 Jump Street,* then he went on to make a few appearances in *Beverly Hills 90210* before landing his big-screen debut in *Friday the 13th Part VIII: Jason Takes Manhattan.*

Without a doubt, Currie is most well known for his eventual role in the *Left Behind* films. Not to be confused with the Nicholas Cage reboot, Currie starred in all of the original movies featuring Kirk Cameron, based on the series of popular Christian-themed young adult novels. In these films, Currie played the ominously named Nikolai Carpathia, a character who turns out to be the Antichrist and who is focused on rallying forces against the remaining Christian followers. Faith aside, it's interesting to note that Currie would become best known for playing an utterly evil villain when he provided possibly the best, most inherently good character in the entire *Puppet Master* franchise. Rick is the only protagonist who doesn't have to venture into too much gray area or get blood on his hands, as he's completely out of his element and not at all at fault for the things that are happening to him. The bond he forms with the puppets feels like genuine friendship. And since they're just puppets, that's really a testament to Currie's ability and inherent likability as an actor.

Chandra West plays Rick's girlfriend, Susie, who serves as the character's support system, is surprisingly able to adjust to his newfound leadership of a group of living puppets, and who even gets to fight back a bit by dousing a little demonic Totem in acid. Also a Canadian native, West studied acting at Oxford when she was sixteen and eventually went on to appear alongside the likes of Val Kilmer and Josh Brolin in things like *The Salton Sea* and *Mister Sterling.* She also went on to feature prominently in *CSI, NYPD Blue* and *I Now Pronounce You Chuck and Larry,* as well as starring in the short-lived genre series *The Gates.* In the accompanying *Video Zone* for *Puppet Master 4,* West noted how refreshing she found the good-natured and wholesome character of Susie after playing a long stretch of bitchy characters in other roles at the time.[7]

In *Puppet Master 4,* what Rick expects to be a weekend with his girlfriend turns out to be an unexpected reunion as Susie brings along her psychic friend Lauren (again, a psychic to tie everything back to the original) and Lauren's boyfriend, Cameron. It turns out that Cameron and Rick happen to have a history, as they studied together before Rick went on to extreme success and Cameron got stuck, jealous of Rick's genius and success. This character is the sequel's embodiment of the long-running trope of a person so abrasive and obnoxious that the audience cannot wait for them to die. He is antagonistic, even going as far as attempting to steal the formula and puppets from Rick so that he can sell them to a rival company, The Phoenix Division. While the early entries hadn't seen this trope, it was introduced with the extremely antagonistic Major Kraus in *Puppet Master III*. By comparison, Cameron is obviously not that bad. He's not a Nazi, he's not out to kill anybody, but he does make things worse for the heroes and eventually meets his end at the hands of the Totems.

Taking on the role of Cameron fell to Ash Adams, who was credited as Jason Adams in the film. A Los Angeles native, Adams made a name for himself in the TV series *Ryan's Hope* as the titular character of John Ryan. He then made numerous guest star appearances in series like *Beverly Hills, 90210, The Young Riders* and *Renegade*. He also made an appearance in the Jean-Claude Van Damme vehicle *Lionheart*. For horror fans, however, Adams' most intriguing credit is also his very first, as he appeared as Surfer #2 in Wes Craven's *A Nightmare on Elm Street*. Adams brought everything needed to make Cameron work, from the college bro attitude to the self-obsession and cutthroat ambition that made the character's death that much more exciting.

His girlfriend Lauren is a polar opposite character, genuinely nice and sweet, serious about her craft even when no one else—including our hero, Rick—takes her

Randy Cook animation in *Puppet Master 4* (courtesy Chris Endicott).

remotely seriously. Unlike Cameron, Lauren carries over into *Puppet Master 5* as well, though she might as well not, given that her scenes in that sequel are solely comprised of squirming in a hospital bed and eventually waking up screaming. Although a little rough around the edges, there's a genuine innocence to Lauren that had been almost entirely absent from the psychic characters presented in the previous movies. Most of the other psychics had either been out for themselves, using their gifts to exploit others or otherwise use them for their own purposes, but Lauren never does that. In many ways, she's the character that most closely resembles the franchise's original protagonist, Alex Whittaker.

Impressively, actress Teresa Hill actually made her debut as Lauren in *Puppet Master 4* and *5*. Prior to these two movies, she had only appeared in a TV short titled *Battle in the Erogenous Zone,* in which she was uncredited. Since her *Puppet Master* breakout, however, Hill has gone on to appear in several big-name movies and TV shows including *Hercules: The Legendary Journeys, Bio-Dome* and *National Lampoon's Van Wilder. Puppet Master 4* and *5* wouldn't be her only foray into direct-to-video sequels, either, as she also appeared in *Cruel Intentions 2* opposite Amy Adams, which was itself actually comprised of episodes that had been shot for a failed *Cruel Intentions* TV series.

Director Jeff Burr made casting a priority for his two *Puppet Master* films. He somewhat criticized the earlier entries in the series for not really caring who filled out the cast—with the notable exception of *Puppet Master III*—and elected to hire an impressive collection of known character actors for his back-to-back sequels. For *Puppet Master 4,* he brought in Felton Perry and Stacie Randall as the scientists (Dr. Baker and Dr. Piper, respectively) overseeing Rick's ongoing experiments with artificial intelligence. Perry is without a doubt best known for the *RoboCop* franchise, appearing in all three entries of the original trilogy, a distinction he shares with only Nancy Allen. Prior to *Puppet Master 4,* he also made recurring appearances in *The Fresh Prince of Bel-Air* as the unlikable Uncle Lester. Randall, meanwhile, was a staple of Full Moon at the time, appearing in back-to-back entries in the *Trancers* franchise at virtually the same time as *Puppet Master 4.*

After the defeat of the Totems at the end of *Puppet Master 4,* Sutekh crafts a new creation, a sort of ultimate Totem (simply, itself, referred to as Sutekh during production) to send after the puppets and their master as his final stand. Sometime between the two films, Rick is arrested and charged with the murders committed by the Totems in *Puppet Master 4.* The police captain who informs Rick of his dire situation is played by veteran actor Ron O'Neal, star of hits like *Super Fly* and *Red Dawn.* Diane McBain plays an attorney in the same scene, notable for her inability as a seasoned professional actor to hide how utterly ridiculous all of the exposition around her sounds. It completely works for her character, though, as she clearly does not believe a word of Rick's story which adds the incentive for Rick to try and prove his innocence on his own, given that even his own lawyer isn't really confident in the fact that he's telling the truth.

While *Puppet Master 4* had some character actors to its credit, *Puppet Master 5 is* absolutely full of them in an admittedly delightful way. Burr notes that this was intentional. "That was certainly a mission, as it is on every movie I make. I wanted

Totem on the repair bench (courtesy Chris Endicott).

actors that had influenced me growing up. I have a reverence for character actors. It's one of the great joys, to me, of filmmaking, to be able to cast someone who's a person you admire and have a good working relationship with them. Guys like Ian Ogilvy, Willard Pugh—a wonderful, underrated actor, he's been in tons of stuff—and 99% of people wouldn't know Diane McBain, who plays the lawyer in *Puppet Master 5*, she was a contract star at Warner Bros in the '60s. Ron O'Neal, it was a delight to put some dough in his pocket and work with him even just for a day. Duane Whitaker, who I've gotten to know over the years, Clu Gulager had a little part. I love glowing up these small parts with real, seasoned actors. There's a professionalism, too, that they have that is not necessarily in the next generation."

Doubling down on the self-serving narcissist role previously filled by Cameron would be Ian Ogilvy as professor Laurence Jennings. In a nice touch—though an easy one, as they were filmed at the same time—Jennings is mentioned in *4* before showing up in *5*. Although he fills the same basic role as Cameron, he's much more closely tied to the plot as a genuine secondary antagonist. He's so out for himself and willing to screw over both humans and puppets to get what he wants that he also winds up having the distinction of being the only human being killed by the puppets over the course of both movies instead of being another victim of the Totems. Jennings has it all: he's ambitious, he's cunning, but he's also a coward, so he can't truly be respected as a villain, which is great because liking this guy would be a disservice to how well Ogilvy conveys the character's utter sleaziness.

Even if Sutekh is the main villain (despite the puppets never actually sharing a scene with him in his true form) Jennings is the character who best embodies why

Decapitron comes to life in *Puppet Master 5* (courtesy Chris Endicott).

these puppets cannot fall into the wrong hands. Not only is this rival scientific firm absolutely ruthless in its approach, it's also completely ignorant of anything it's gotten involved in. If there's a theme to *Puppet Master 4* and *5* as a collective entity, it's that knowledge is literally power. The secret of life, the formula and how it works, these are not tangible things. But they're what drive the plot. Knowing these things is what puts these characters in harm's way and some of them, like Cameron and Jennings, are ultimately burned in their attempts to steal this knowledge for themselves. In Jennings' case, that's literal too, as he is dropped down an elevator shaft after being shot by a burst from Torch's flamethrower.

In his pursuit of the puppets, Jennings recruits a crew of thugs to help him break into the Bodega Bay Inn, which is now a crime scene. Portraying the group are Duane Whitaker as Scott, Nicholas Guest as Hendy, and Willard Pugh as Jason. Whitaker should be fairly well known to horror fans, with roles in everything from *From Dusk Till Dawn 2* to *Feast* to *Rob Zombie's Halloween II*. In *Feast*, he appears alongside the great Clu Gulager, who also makes a brief appearance in *Puppet Master 5*. Whitaker is without a doubt best known for his role in *Pulp Fiction*, as he plays the accomplice to the sadistic rapist, Zed. Nicholas Guest, meanwhile, had appeared in *Christmas Vacation* and Full Moon's *Dollman* alongside dozens of TV appearances prior to his role in *Puppet Master 5*. He has since gone on to an extremely successful career as a voice actor. Willard Pugh had appeared in *RoboCop 2* as Mayor Kuzak and had also been seen in things like *The Guyver* and *The Hills Have Eyes Part II* prior to being cast.

Puppet Master 5 clearly suffers from the decision to split the films into two, as the entire movie is a glorified third act. And yet, almost accidentally, it feels closest to the original in some ways. Even if the puppets don't kill people, even if they are the heroes and are protecting people from otherworldly monsters and the plot could not be more different, there are deep and fundamental connections. Like *Puppet Master,* much of *Puppet Master 5* is focused on characters wandering around the hotel, searching to uncover the same secrets that the psychics searched for in the original. Like the first, there's very little puppet action until just over halfway through. There's even an opening sequence involving Blade exploring the police station that sees the return of the POV puppet-cam. Even if the action is stockpiled in the back half of the movie, there's more of it and said action delivers in spades. Appropriate for a final chapter, *Puppet Master 5* is the closest we have ever come to seeing all eight of the main puppets on screen at the same time, in the same film. Only Leech Woman is absent, as the filmmakers and Band were committed to the idea that they had killed her off in *Puppet Master II*. In addition to that, her inclusion could have been out of place in what are largely considered two more kid-friendly sequels, even though they retain the R rating. This also means that Torch sees his first and only return since *Puppet Master II,* as well. Many fans have found this baffling over time, pointing out that if 4 and 5 were shot at the same time, there would be no reason for one puppet to be in one movie and not the other. Torch even appears on the poster and VHS/DVD/Blu-ray cover for *Puppet Master 4*. He can even be glimpsed inside the puppet trunk in *Puppet Master 4,* even though he is never taken out of it alongside the other puppets.

Burr remembers the decision to leave Torch out of *Puppet Master 4* as both intentional and practical. "That wasn't a case where the puppet was in the script and we had to cut it out. It was designed not to be in the script because that was the most expensive puppet. They knew Charlie wanted it in at least one of the movies, so they decided 5 not 4, which makes very little sense. But for obvious reasons, Torch was the most expensive puppet. Every time he shot fire, there had to be more fire marshals there, more emergency stuff, etc. So it was a big deal to shoot fire, and it took longer, so that's why you don't see too much of him. But in my recollection, it wasn't like we cut him out of 4."

With Torch rejoining the group for *Puppet Master 5,* though, the sequel delivers perhaps the best effects the franchise has ever seen. And it does that in spades. As great as the stop-motion effects had been in the previous films, the work done in the fifth entry might top them all. There are combinations of stop-motion and special effects that harken back to Old Hollywood in the best way possible. This is the *Jason and the Argonauts* of the *Puppet Master* franchise. Back to back, the two movies are even structured like a good, old-fashioned adventure serial. The showdown at the end of *Puppet Master 5* is perhaps the high point of puppet FX work during the Paramount era of Full Moon Pictures. Blade, Decapitron, Six-Shooter and Jester each take on the Totem, in the lobby outside the elevator. That's the same elevator where the puppets took out Neil Gallagher in the first movie, to once again bring back some of the original's flavor, at least in some small way. The climactic sequences features the most fluid puppet animation to date and it is still dazzling to watch.

"We tried our best," says Chris Endicott, recalling the FX challenges of *Puppet Master 4* and *5,* particularly that final lobby showdown. "One thing that's interesting

Pinhead and The Totem battle in *Puppet Master 5* (courtesy Chris Endicott).

about that film is that once principal photography was done, I don't recall how the original number 5 ended in the script, I have it, but I haven't looked at it. But I know that as part of principal photography, we shot the two leads reacting to Sutekh on the table, screaming and crying as the puppet was gesturing at them, and then them running out of the Castle Green Hotel, but everything else was kind of a question mark as to how it was going to be done. At one point, David sat down with the storyboard artist—not Pete von Sholly this time, Robin Bielefeld, and she blocked out this elaborate sequence that ends the picture, like a puppet battle royale. So we reconstructed the Castle Green lobby set on the stages at Full Moon. It was quite a very elaborate set, it was using a lot of the same props that were meant from the movie. That set sat at Full Moon for maybe a year and whenever we could, we would just knock off a few shots."

Despite being shot at the same time, there was nearly a year between the release of *Puppet Master 4* and *Puppet Master 5*. As Jeff Burr recalls, "It sat. It wasn't like it took longer, it just sat. Part of that was finishing the Full Moon slate, getting Paramount to sign off on stuff, the shit had hit the fan between *4* and *5*'s release. *Puppet Master 5* just sat on a shelf for a long time and then we had done a rough cut of it—or a fine cut, if you will—and then nothing happened. Then we get a phone call saying 'Oh, we need it.' It's very typical professional filmmaking, the 'hurry up and wait' and then 'Oh, shit, we need it right now.' That's how it happened. To me, there wasn't enough time to really finesse it, but then again there was the running time issue too, where it had to be longer than everyone else wanted. The editors and I wanted it shorter and we had to conform to a pre-arranged running time, unfortunately."

Chapter Six. Puppet Master 4 and 5

Joel Fletcher animates Decapitron for *Puppet Master 5* (courtesy Chris Endicott).

The director also mentions, "I've always said—and I certainly don't have any patience to do it in my advanced age—but if someone could do a fan edit of the two movies together, make it like 95 minutes, it would be a blast."

Puppet Master 5 would, of course, not be the final chapter it was promised to be. Not by a long shot. But in some ways, that tagline feels somewhat prophetic. This is a final chapter, even if it's not in the way one would expect. It's the last *Puppet Master* from the original era of Full Moon, the Paramount era that put the company on the map and defined its best years. It's the last *Puppet Master* to see FX work from David Allen Productions, the team that had been and continues to be almost solely responsible for so much of the franchise's success. David Allen lost his battle with cancer in 1999. *Puppet Master 5* still stands as the end of an era. It's a bittersweet ending, but not a sad one, as the David Allen Productions team ended their *Puppet Master* tenure on top, delivering effects that still stand as the best of the franchise today, and will never be outdone.

The film was not touted as a true finale at the time. In pure Full Moon fashion, Charles Band announced the end of the franchise during the *Video Zone* for *Puppet Master 5* while also immediately explaining where fans could expect to see the puppets next.[8] The story would not end. Even then, there seemed to be an understanding—at least on Band's part—that it never truly *would* end. Instead, the diminutive heroes would only move on to bigger and better things. They'd upgrade from their back-to-back finale to star in their own trilogy of movies picking up off of the end of *Puppet Master III*. Yes, an era of the series was over. But if Band had anything to say about it, a new era was just beginning.

Chapter Seven

Puppet Wars:
The Unmade Trilogy

Despite being filmed back to back, there was a bizarre length of time between the home video releases of *Puppet Master 4* and *Puppet Master 5.* One came out almost a full year after the other, whereas *Puppet Master II* and *III* had wound up being released in the same year despite being conceived and shot entirely separate. This created a more immediate need than would otherwise have been expected to continue the franchise past its touted final chapter. On the *Video Zone* for *Puppet Master 5,* Band explained that while the series was over, as he put it, Full Moon would launch a brand-new trilogy called *Puppet Wars*.[1] The new series would pick up directly from the ending of *Puppet Master III*, which saw Toulon and Peter board a train bound for Switzerland. There was no clear idea as to what the story would be, only that it needed to tell the story of what happened next, finally bridging the gap between the old man who escaped the Nazis in *Toulon's Revenge* and the old man who committed suicide in the original *Puppet Master.* But first, as with any story, they would need to start with a writer.

Enter Jay Woelfel and Dave Parker. Both of them had been making a living as editors at the time. Woelfel had moved to Los Angeles in 1990 and had edited a short called *Bronx Cheers* as well as the film *Eddie Presley: A Tribute to the King* for director Jeff Burr. Woelfel had met Dave Parker on that same project and, being likeminded horror fans, the two had hit it off. Woelfel had conceived the story for a film that he thought could be easily tweaked to become a sequel to Full Moon's *Seedpeople* and so the two of them wrote it completely on spec. Woelfel remembers how the would-be *Seedpeople 2* led to *Puppet Wars.* "I had a short story that I had written called 'Tree of Screams,' he was like, 'Hey, we could turn "Tree of Screams" into *Seedpeople 2*' and that's what we did. We wrote a whole, not just a treatment, we wrote a whole script. So Parker was working there already. Charlie, in a year or less, his office would move. So we started at one office and go to another. Parker was working full time there in what today we'd call special features, something that Full Moon kind of invented," he says. "So he would hear about stuff around the office and we would get together and I would write up, usually, whatever the general idea was. After the *Seedpeople 2* thing, which they loved, but they were like, 'this is the one movie we're never going to make a sequel to' we were at least on their radar for 'these guys can write.'"

That led to more and more writing for Full Moon, primarily rewriting and script doctoring, as Woelfel notes. "We wrote a couple treatments for *Ragdoll*. That was after they hired Matthew Bright and he was fired, and we turned in some treatments

Chapter Seven. Puppet Wars: The Unmade Trilogy

for that, and we didn't ultimately write the script for the movie that never really got made—in that form, anyway—but some of our elements did end up in that thing." He adds: "Then they were going to do *Puppet Master,* and again, we wrote treatments and went in to pitch our ideas and then we actually got hired to write those three scripts. And then we'd get to direct. Either I'd direct one and then he'd direct one and we'd co-direct the other, whatever, at least we'd have a shot. But there was no contract for that part of it, we were just hired as writers."

Both of them would go on to have lengthy and lucrative working relationships with Full Moon as well. Woelfel, beginning as an editor and writer with the studio, wound up directing the sixth and (to date) final entry in the *Trancers* franchise. Parker, meanwhile, also served as a writer and editor on numerous projects—including directing sequences of Full Moon's kaiju/*Power Rangers* riff *Kraa! The Sea Monster*—before directing his first feature film for the company in 1999, titled *The Dead Hate the Living*. The movie is similar to Stuart Gordon's *Castle Freak* in two ways: it is completely unlike anything else in the Full Moon catalogue, and it was one of the rare Full Moon entries to garner widespread praise from genre critics, particularly *Fangoria*, which had almost always dismissed the bulk of the company's output. A standout of the post–*Scream* era, *Dead Hate the Living* is a film for die-hard horror fans, by die-hard horror fans. While *Scream* makes references to mainstream slashers like *Friday the 13th* and *A Nightmare on Elm Street,* as well as directors like John Carpenter and Wes Craven, *Dead Hate the Living* goes far left of mainstream in its genre references. The movie borrows most heavily from Lucio Fulci and Dario Argento, freely dropping the names of their stars, cinematographers and composers as well. It's possibly the least Full Moon movie that Full Moon ever made and as such remains one of the most fascinating entries in the studio's entire history.

Before Parker and Woelfel carved their own paths to success as directors for Full Moon, though, they were hired to write a massive project just after their initial pitch for *Seedpeople 2*. It was a commitment, but by the end of it they would revitalize a currently dead franchise and launch their own careers as directors. That was, of course, Full Moon's planned *Puppet Wars* trilogy. When Band announced the films at the end of *Puppet Master 5,* he gave viewers nothing to go on except for a piece of key art—which was natural for the time. The artwork depicted the puppets going toe to toe with the green Humunculi creatures that had first appeared in the flashback sequence in *Puppet Master II*. Perhaps even more interestingly, the artwork depicted the pyramids in the background. It suggested that this franchise, which had been entrenched in Egyptian mythology from day one, would finally be traveling there. Which, while exciting for a poster, would not be the case for the script itself.

Knowing that this first incarnation would feature elaborate special effects work, possibly outdoing the ones that had come before, the decision was made to set the entire first film in the trilogy on a train so that production costs could more easily be put into the effects. It only made sense, as *Puppet Master III* had ended with Toulon boarding a train and *Puppet Wars* planned to continue that journey. But the two writers had broader, even more ambitious plans for three features aside form just doing three period movies at once. Together, Woelfel and Parker conceived the idea that each entry in the planned trilogy would pit the puppets against a different classic monster.

Woelfel remembers the decision to include the classic monsters as a fairly natural one. "It was set during that era anyway. We figured it was the '40s, that was when those classic monster movies were coming out. Weirdly, we took the Hammer titles, but yeah, it just seemed appropriate for the era. The other thing was that it hadn't really been done in Romania, yet. They would go all the way to Romania to shoot movies that were supposed to be set in, like, Cleveland, you know? We were like, 'This really needs to be set in Romania. Let's not pretend it's not Romania.' That was Dave and I, too. That way we're not limited on what we can show and it won't have that funky feel that other movies have, where you see an American street that's kind of correct, but isn't quite right. We thought we'd make a relatable movie. It was all about seeing what was being done there and trying to make more out of the opportunity. We all, including Courtney, we all loved those Universal monster movies anyway. Charlie, presumably, did—although I never discussed that at great lengths with him or anything."

A clearly well-documented fan of the old Universal movies, Band signed off on the concept. The first film, titled *Curse of the Puppet Master,* would dive deep into the franchise's Egyptian mythology roots by pitting the puppets against The Mummy. The second would then see Dracula enter the mix, while the third would see them go up against a Frankenstein Monster. As a fan of both the *Puppet Master* series and the classic Universal Monsters, it's hard not to get excited at the prospect. With those iconic characters being in the public domain, and therefore free to use, it just seemed like a no brainer to combine those elements together. The *Puppet Master* movies had already been deeply entrenched in references to the Universal classics, especially in *Puppet Master II,* so actually introducing those characters and their respective mythos felt like a no-brainer.

The initial *Curse of the Puppet Master* script is interesting right out of the gate for how different a story it is for Toulon. In *Puppet Master III,* Andre Toulon was a wanted man. He was forced into hiding, into the shadows, where he was forced to take out Nazi officers without being seen. With all of Berlin to hide in and puppets that could sneak in anywhere, Toulon's revenge actually felt relatively easy. He had the upper hand and never really lost it. *Curse of the Puppet Master* reverses this concept. This time, Toulon is on a train with nowhere to hide, nowhere to disappear to. More than that, the end of *Puppet Master III* saw Toulon assume the identity of Major Kraus in order to escape Germany as he boarded the train at the end of the film. Here, he continues to be forced to use that identity. This time, Toulon can't pick off Nazis from the shadows, he's actually forced to mingle, to play nice with them so that he does not blow his cover. It's entirely new ground for the character, which makes it a fascinating new direction for the story. On a more emotional level, it also means that Toulon doesn't just have to pretend to be a Nazi, he has to pretend to be the Nazi that killed his wife.

On board the train, Toulon has to stay out of the crosshairs of four main Nazi officers. First, there's the psychopathic Colonel Kron, who is introduced as a legendary killer who publicly executed his own mother. Then, nymphomaniac Claire who bears a striking resemblance a character we'd meet much later in *Axis Rising* and shares the same fate. Then we have the Nazi scientist Mehner and the subordinate

Carl. Also on board is Egyptian Ahmed Bey, a scholar who the Nazis turn to for help on their hidden cargo, a statue that is supposedly able to resurrect the god of death Anubis. Bey has a secret similar to Toulon's, as he is the current master of the Humunculi first seen in the Cairo flashbacks of *Puppet Master II*. At first, he attacks Toulon believing him to be exactly who he says he is: a Nazi. Once they realize they are on the same side, however, Toulon's puppets and Bey's Humunculi are forced to work together toward a common goal. They need to stop the Nazis from completing their ritual and awakening Anubis, or else the Reich will gain power over death itself.

Bey himself is hiding many secrets, though, including the fact that he is actually a living mummy. He knows a great deal about the religion of his ancestors because it is, in actuality, his religion. He was there. This clever twist is not really a surprise, especially considering that Bey's name alone is a reference to Boris Karloff's Ardeth Bey in Universal's *The Mummy*—which would, at that point, make *The Mummy* a film that the *Puppet Master* franchise just could not stop referencing. But these references and pastiches actually work in the script's favor. Overall, the script for *Puppet Wars: Curse of the Puppet Master* evokes a puppet-infused combination of *Murder on the Orient Express* and *Raiders of the Lost Ark*. It's an ambitious combination but not by any means an uninteresting one. While the film is entirely confined to a train, the scope does not feel small. There's plenty of action contained within its pages that would have made for riveting viewing for longtime fans of the franchise.

The script also gives the puppets plenty to do. Pinhead is killed and resurrected within the first half, Blade gets a great sequence in which he smashes out a light so he can take out several Nazi soldiers in a darkened hallway and also gets himself a new weapon. Early on in the *Curse* script, Blade's knife is broken so he replaces it with a carving knife that's described as being just as tall as he is. Impractical as that might be—even just in terms of the poor puppet having to lug it around—it would have made for interesting viewing. There's even, for the first time in *Puppet Master* history, a moment when one puppet is picked up by a victim and used to fight off another. Baffling as it sounds, a scene in which Tunneler is grabbed while his drill is still spinning and used to grind away Blade's knife is actually one of the moments that would have been most delightful to witness on screen.

As strong as the train gimmick works in the first script, Woelfel and Parker definitely made the right decision to abandon that premise for the next two installments of the trilogy. This would have helped *Curse of the Puppet Master* to stand alone as an individual entry of the overarching story. It would have felt like its own movie.

The Romanian setting would work wonders for the story as well, as it factored heavily into both the second and third scripts. With their mummy tale out of the way, the second installment would have introduced Dracula. The Lord of Vampires already shared an interesting connection with Full Moon's established vampire lore, as the historical Vlad Dracula—best known worldwide as Vlad the Impaler—had a younger brother named Radu, which is of course also the name of the vampire at the center of Full Moon's second most popular franchise, *Subspecies*.

The Vlad that appears in *Puppet Wars,* however, is in many ways a more faithful version of *both* the historical Vlad Dracula and the character of Stoker's novel in that he is utterly devoid of romance or remorse. This is a warlord. He was a cold and calculating ruler in life and proves to be just as ruthless after death. He is vicious and that makes sense for the story. By this point in time, more and more *Dracula* tales had begun to interpret the vampire as a sort of fallen antihero. But the *Puppet Wars* scripts see Vlad forming an alliance with the Nazis, so the story would only work if this version of the character was truly depicted as the worst of the worst. In that, they certainly succeeded.

The script for the second installment, which would likely have been titled *Tomb of the Puppet Master*—although *Vault of the Puppet Master* was also tossed around—would have continued to push the story in new directions. It would have been a departure in terms of tone and style but would have gone back to basics for the puppet master himself. Having his cover blown and escaping *Curse* by the skin of his teeth, Andre Toulon would be back on the run in the second *Puppet Wars* feature, hiding out with a group of refugees. While each of the three scripts have their own strengths, I'll admit that the very notion of a *Puppet Master* vampire movie is endlessly exciting.

Initially, plans for that second script had been very different. "The middle script was I think originally supposed to be a concentration camp, where Toulon gets captured and they all get put in a camp. With the original treatment, they had already said they didn't want to do a concentration camp so that idea never really got off the ground. So that one became the graveyard, so we wound up not having as distinct a location as we wanted to," Woelfel notes.

After having to play nice with Nazis in the first installment, Toulon is much more in his element in the second. After his escape, he makes his way to a small village occupied by a group of rebellious Nazi hunters. The opening puppet attack even includes a brief but intriguing cameo by the Demonic Toys, years before the film was eventually set. It's not just the Nazis that these villagers—led by the fiery, spirited Jeanne—are afraid of, however. They make sure to get themselves indoors by sundown each evening. These people are protecting themselves from vampires.

Surviving the first installment, Kron and Claire are hard at work on tracking down Toulon and bringing him to their sadistic brand of justice now that they know the truth and have seen what both he and his puppets can do. Both of them now understand the raw power of Toulon's secret and how valuable it could be to the Reich. Roaming the forests outside the village, the puppet master and his newfound friends also have to protect themselves from the Vampire Korps, a group of vampires in a militarized fashion similar to the Nazis. They don't wear uniforms and shoot rifles, however, instead they remain faithful to the concept of war as it existed in Vlad's own time. They are dressed like crusading knights and carry the weapons that Vlad's forces would have used during their reign in the 1400s.

The script also sees the introduction of the demon Baal, Blade and Pinhead operating a machine gun (Pinhead aims while Blade works the trigger) as well as Blade getting captured and experimented on by Kron and his forces and—perhaps the best part—the puppets getting equipped with new weapons designed for killing vampires. Blade even temporarily has a hand, taken from the remnants of the previous movie's Humunculi. There's even an action scene that would have made for a jaw-dropping stop-motion sequence with Pinhead picking Tunneler up and throwing him toward a hungry vampire. There are so many more exciting elements to the script. Even though it sounds sillier in concept, the second *Puppet Wars* would certainly have been much darker in tone than the first. It would also have had a totally different flavor, thanks to its different monsters.

This vampire themed entry has much more of a Hammer feel than the previous. Set in a small, foggy village plagued by the undead, it's hard not to make gothic comparisons. But it certainly would have stood on its own. The script even takes care to make its unique vampires stand apart from those seen in the *Subspecies* franchise. One of the interesting things about the monsters in this script is that they raise the stakes, so to speak, for Leech Woman and truly give that puppet something to do. For creatures driven by blood, another being that sucks it out of them would prove to be a great threat and so Leech Woman is actually able to do quite a bit of damage to the Vampire Korps, at least on the page.

Of the three scripts, this one also has the most shocking and darkest ending, firmly establishing its place as the *Empire Strikes Back* of this would-be trilogy. Not only does Dracula return to ravage the earth and command his Vampire Korps soldiers, but Andre Toulon is flat-out killed in the finale. For fans with even the most remote knowledge of the franchise, that would have been both a gut punch and an endlessly puzzling cliffhanger. By this point in time, everyone had seen Toulon shoot himself in the opening of the original film. It's the very first scene in the franchise. For a trilogy that builds to Toulon's travels to the Bodega Bay Inn and sets the stage for his inevitable suicide, it is incredibly shocking to actually kill him in the middle and let that linger as an ending until the next installment would have been released.

Yet the very notion of killing Toulon at the end of the second script perfectly sets the stage for the third, which would have been the *Frankenstein* story of this trilogy even though it never actually introduces that character, nor his monster. Instead, it's a thematic *Frankenstein* tale with the theme of resurrection running throughout. One the most obvious level, there's a Nazi soldier resurrected as a very obvious new incarnation of a Frankenstein monster. But Toulon himself is resurrected as well.

While the first installment easily stands on its own, the second two scripts are much more reminiscent of *Puppet Master 4* and *5*. They have many differences but are more or less one story broken up into two halves. While the first script is the only one to deal with mummies and the Anubis statue, Vlad Dracula and his vampires carry over from the second script into the third. Vlad is even introduced toward the end of the second, causing his role in the final installment to be much bigger.

In the third script, Toulon is actively tracking Kron and his Nazi cohorts rather than hiding from them. The end of the second installment saw them take the young Jeanne as a hostage, so Toulon and the vampire hunting monk decide to travel after them and end things once and for all. Both Toulon and Kron find themselves resurrected, but Kron is distorted by it and scarred by it, becoming at least a visual stand-in for the Frankenstein creature.

For die-hard *Puppet Master* fans, the real highlight of the third *Puppet Wars* feature would have been the re-introduction of Torch. Given that he was brought in during *Puppet Master II*, so long after Toulon's suicide, *Puppet Wars* would have completely retooled the puppet's origin, making the version we see in the first sequel something that Toulon was rebuilding rather than designing for the very first time.

This script's retooled origin for Torch reveals that the puppet was created by Kron and his soldiers as a countermeasure to Toulon's puppets. This Nazi origin makes sense given the puppet's more overtly Nazi-themed design as well as its hugely destructive capabilities. There's even a scene later on in the script in which the puppets face off against an army of Torches, revealing that the Nazis have built four of the puppets instead of just one.

The third script also kills of Six-Shooter as an attempt to explain the puppet's absence in *Puppet Master I* and *II* despite being an already established member of the gang in *Toulon's Revenge*. It only creates bigger plot holes, though, as Six-Shooter appears in *Puppet Master 4* and *5* through the rest of the franchise, which would have been pretty impossible had his remains been left somewhere in Romania in the '40s.

Things cultivate in an appropriately old-school Universal Monster showdown between Vlad Dracula and the mutated and malformed Kron. Toulon escapes while his new assistant CJ attempts to destroy the monsters by bombing the castle. As Vlad and Kron are closing in on each other, they hear a voice from above telling them that their time is up and that there's nothing left to do but die. In the script's most shocking reveal, they both look up to see that the voice is coming from none other than Blade.

While this probably would have been the most hotly debated moment in any of the *Puppet Wars* scripts, it's actually something that's set up way back in the first installment. In that, Blade tugs at Toulon's leg and basically goes through a game of charades in attempt to explain something and Toulon notes, "I suppose it's my fault for not making you able to talk" and suggests that he's planning on remedying that when they get to America. This small aside would have been fantastic, as it would have suggested that the puppets were in some ways unfinished and that Toulon's time with them was truly cut short, making his suicide in the opening of the original movie all the more tragic.

Woelfel sheds some light on that scene, which would no doubt have been hotly debated among fans had it made it to the screen. "That's what, you know, we knew those movies and we knew what they hadn't done with them yet. That was kind of our whole point: 'let's not do the same old thing. What else can you do with these?' Not 'How do you reinvent them?' because that's not really what we wanted to do, but give them new and different things, like in the final script when Blade speaks briefly, that kind of thing. And again, just a lot more puppet action."

He further elaborates on why the decision to give Blade a line, if anything, felt natural. "The idea was that he kind of gets destroyed there, so then afterwards, he doesn't talk right away, and he got all screwed up. We saved it to the end where it was kind of a payoff, and wanted to do it in such a way that you wouldn't just be expecting the puppets to speak all the time. In this case, we were hired to do three things all at once and then you're dealing with individual movies, but it's almost like a three act structure, like a script would be. My approach is just to make the greatest one you possibly can and not worry about leaving something on the table for the next time. You don't want to make it someone else's problem to top what you've done or

Chapter Seven. Puppet Wars: *The Unmade Trilogy*

whatever, so to not hold back. Having him speak and everything, that was kind of our out. It just seemed like something the puppets had never done and if you're going to do it with one of them, that would be the one. That would be the moment. Kind of like Frankenstein pulling the switch with, 'We belong dead.' If that had been the only thing he said in *Bride,* it would probably be even more powerful. I mean, you know, the whole story with *The Wolf Man* where they had him speaking and they took all that out in post. Anyway, it was all about trying to give the puppets new stuff to do that fans would hopefully love or hopefully hadn't seen a bunch. If you're genuinely a fan and you're into it, then you just have to trust your own sense of, 'Well, I think it would be great if *this* happened.'"

Looking back, Dave Parker reflects on how ambitious the three scripts truly were. "Initially, we weren't given many ideas except that [Band] wanted, you know, he wanted three movies. This was still in the days when Paramount was funding things. So we weren't told to write for a budget, which, funny enough, when you look back at these scripts, now I look at them and go, 'Oh my God, these things would have cost five million bucks.' I mean, the amount of stuff that we put in. We came from a real pure place of just wanting to make a great puppet to be included, having the puppets do a lot of stuff. And it's funny, looking back, just quickly, at some of the scripts and the stuff that we had them do. It was pretty elaborate. David Allen probably would have had a nervous breakdown, trying to do all these effects because we made all the cardinal sins of having these things run around and leap, I mean, stuff that would have taken months and months and months to actually pull off."

In addition to all of that, and keeping in tradition with all of the *Puppet Master* films up to that point, the planned *Puppet Wars* features would have introduced a new major puppet called Bombshell.[2] Only the second female puppet ever, Bombshell would have essentially been a Jessica Rabbit–esque lounge singer puppet with bombs for breasts, created by Parker himself. "Every *Puppet Master* movie up to that point had a new puppet," he says. "It was all about taking inspiration from American bomber planes where they would paint a bombshell on the nose of the plane, right? And then, of course, how great, she's got rocket launchers or bombs for breasts, because I knew Charlie would like that. And I thought it was interesting, because it was like, 'Okay, we haven't had another female character.' So I thought that might be interesting. And I do remember they made my vision of Bombshell originally. It was there, it was a puppet that was made. It hung around the office for a long time, I don't know whatever happened to it, it was probably auctioned off with a lot of other things when Charlie downsized."

Once the overall story of the trilogy was in place and Parker and Woelfel began writing the scripts, they also consulted an expert on the franchise to oversee what they were doing and provide notes if necessary, said expert being *Puppet Master III* scribe C. Courtney Joyner. While the stories of the three *Puppet Wars* scripts have their own distinct flavor, the input from Joyner is clear just in how smoothly—for the most part—the three stories handle the overall continuity of the franchise. Band was happy with the scripts and it appeared that everything was set to go, with plans being made to film the first installment in Romania.

Joyner recalls his brief time consulting on *Puppet Wars,* "Charlie asked me to do that, and I was fine with it, but Jay and Dave, I thought they did very well with what they were given. Here's the thing, though, about what happened with *Puppet Wars*. Those scripts were designed around a production situation that was pre-existing. They kind of had their hands cuffed a little bit because they were like 'OK, we're going to be filming in Bucharest' or wherever it was going to be, with these limitations and everything else. So they kind of had to write their script according to those limitations. Fortunately for us, when I was writing *Puppet Master III*, we were still under the Paramount umbrella. In fact we were kind of new under Paramount. So we had a little bit more wiggle room. I mean, still Full Moon budgets, but Jay and Dave took on a very difficult task. But I remember they did very, very well. And of course I was reading the pages as they were creating them. In fact, I thought they did a terrific job. I was just sorry that whole thing didn't go the way it was supposed to, because I think it would have been very good."

David DeCoteau was naturally the first name thrown around to helm the first installment of the *Puppet Wars* series and there was even talk of bringing in a huge, classic genre name to take over the role of Andre Toulon. For fans of *Puppet Master III* especially, this would be shocking given that Guy Rolfe had played the character so well and—at this point in time—had now played the character in three consecutive movies. But there was some concern that at his age, Rolfe would not be able to handle the substantial amount of action that the new trilogy would require from him. Instead, DeCoteau was rumored to reach out to horror legend Christopher Lee to take over the role of the puppet master. While the notion of seeing Lee in a *Puppet Master* film is undeniably appealing, it would have been jarring to see someone else take over the role of Toulon, especially for a direct follow-up to *Puppet Master III*. Eventually, Guy Rolfe was cast to return as the puppet master instead.

After the end of Full Moon's relationship with Paramount, *Puppet Wars* did not completely disappear. Energy appeared to be refocused on just making the first feature, rather than making all three. According to Jay Woelfel, his original script was rewritten both by himself and Parker as well as by Full Moon's in-house writer at the time, Neal Marshall Stevens, independently of one another. "We went to Charlie's office. And Charlie said, 'We want to make *Curse of the Puppet Master*,' which, as far as I know was one of the scripts that Charlie had read a couple years ago, at that point. At some point they had Neal Stevens rewrite it, I think to try and make it cheaper. But then nothing really came of that," says Woelfel. "But when Charlie called Dave and I into his office, at that point, they were over in the Broadway building of Hollywood, he said, 'You know, I like the *Curse of the Puppet Master* script, but we have to change it so we can get away with making it. You can interpret that however you want,' I didn't ask. So what we did was, Dave and I came up with the idea of setting it on a boat instead of a train. So I think I did most of the rewriting on that, although Dave wrote some of it, but basically we kept as much of the action as we could and we did a whole draft setting it on a boat."

Things didn't stop there, though. Even after Full Moon abandoned the *Puppet Wars* ideas for the more affordable *Curse of the Puppet Master* that was eventually released, the project still didn't quite die. "At that point," says Woelfel, "they were like, well, we need to make a movie called *Curse of the Puppet Master*, but we can't afford the one you wrote. So we're going to use that title on this other movie we're going to make, but don't worry, we still like that movie and we're going to make it. So they did go off and make *Curse of the Puppet Master*. But after that, they came back again and said, 'Okay, now we want to make your script, but we don't need the boat thing. We don't need to do that. It was really better on a train, let's just make the train version.' We went back to the train version. And then they were at that point like a 'We're just going to make one movie at a time' kind of deal."

Amazingly, things only grew more ambitious at that point as talk started of potentially making a *Puppet Master* PC game, thanks to a deal with DVD and computer giant Philips. But just before that happened, the film came some close to happening that it even cast its lead star. "Before Philips, they actually hired Guy Rolfe. They were like, 'We're going to make this, we're going to make this,' and I said, 'Shouldn't you hire Guy Rolfe? We're supposed to shoot this in less than a month.' And they did, they did book him." In addition to Rolfe's casting in the unmade movie, footage of the train had been shot and would actually later be used in *Retro Puppet Master*, which would itself wind up being Rolfe's last film. Woelfel notes that he "got a job at Philips by landing a deal with Philips and Full Moon, to make games out of Full Moon titles. And Full Moon was kind of running out of money at that point. It would help make the movies the way they were originally supposed to be made, because Philips would pay for half of them. So they struck a deal and the first thing they would do, because Philips liked me and apparently Full Moon liked me, so I met with Charlie and I came up with this whole production schedule, which I had done with *Titanic* [*An Interactive History*], for when Full Moon would turn things in and what Philips would do. I met with this game company that was going to do the gaming elements, and we were going to do all three again.

"We would shoot some material for the game, separately, but it was really telling the same story," Woelfel adds. It's worth noting that a similar approach of shooting footage for the video game while simultaneously shooting back-to-back sequels would be used years later in *Enter the Matrix*. "There would be some slightly different alterations. And then there would be the shoot-'em-up elements and things like that, which would be unique to the game. They're a lot more sophisticated now, but at the time they were already starting to get that way, where there were items that you would amass, and weapons and all that stuff. The idea of the game was that you couldn't just kill puppets all the time, eventually you would lose. You had to really play the game aside from making it just a *Doom*-like game. You had to make decisions. We never got to the stage of the script where I or anybody else was rewriting the alternate versions of scenes or adding anything new, it was still just like, 'Here's the three scripts.' I actually showed the third script to the game company at that point. I never got paid for the third script, Full Moon never saw it, but I gave it to the game company so they would understand what the arc of the whole thing was."

Parker also remembers having some involvement with the game. "I remember working on that. Charlie had me pull up every bit of footage of the puppets from all of the movies and then do a reel, like, every scene with every scene shot with a puppet. I did pull for that game that never came to be."

It's worth mentioning that while the game never came to pass, a CD-ROM demo titled *Origins of the Puppet Master* was released in 1996 alongside the also unfinished first-person shooter *Subterraneans*.[3] This is no doubt the result of the same deal with Philips that would have led to the much larger *Puppet Master* PC game, had it happened. While only a glimpse of what the final project could have been, *Origins of the Puppet Master* is effectively a comic book adaptation of *Puppet Master III* with the ability to click on certain panels and play clips from the film at various points. The demo promised a 1996 release for the full *Origins of the Puppet Master,* but that obviously never came to pass.

As for why this incredibly ambitious project never came together, it's not too different a story from any other in the history of *Puppet Master*. "Philips paid Full Moon their first deposit shortly before Christmas of that year," explains Woelfel. "And then really what happened was that Philips went belly up, not as a whole company but … DVD was now a thing and they no longer needed to support production on the films. They had product to sell and other people were making things, so Philips was bought by another company…. That was sort of the final nail in the coffin, to date, anyway, for *Puppet Wars.*"

Puppet Wars would have been ambitious for Full Moon in its prime, and that is entirely part of its appeal. It's also—just in terms of its scope and the amount of puppet action—not something that should have been attempted after the loss of David Allen, nor could it have been. In some ways, the franchise can be broken down not just by the pre- and post–Paramount eras, but in terms of before and after *Puppet Wars.* Even if these three scripts never materialized into the films they could have been, they've been influential on every single entry in the franchise that has followed in their wake. We are still feeling the ripples of *Puppet Wars* in the series to this day. Ideas, titles and even characters have been lifted from these three stories and re-used in later *Puppet Master* films.

In this franchise, there are many, many things that never made it to the screen. There are so many concepts that never came to fruition and original drafts that could have been entirely different, dating all the way back to Kenneth J. Hall's original script for the first feature. Yet, if you ask any *Puppet Master* fan the one thing they wished they could have ultimately seen, they would say *Puppet Wars.* For fans of this franchise, it's the white whale. That's a testament not only to the concept, the very idea of carrying on with Toulon after the events of *Puppet Master III,* but to the sheer scope and ambition of the project as a whole. While so many things never materialized, *Puppet Wars* will always be the one that got away in the eyes of the fans.

Chapter Eight

Puppet Master:
The Action Figure Series

In 1997, the future of *Puppet Master* was uncertain. There had always been plans to keep going, to keep these characters alive, especially as they had in many ways become the face of Full Moon as a whole. With the Paramount deal dissolving, the clear presence of *Puppet Master* would be the perfect way to let fans known that the series was not going anywhere. But several attempts to get *Puppet Wars* off the ground had gone nowhere. Their attempts to produce a new movie weren't going as planned. Band made an international partnership with the Kushner-Locke company to distribute Full Moon's features moving forward, but that didn't help these franchises with long-gestating entries. So Band, ever the entrepreneur, needed to look at the situation from a different angle. While the movies were sorting themselves out and rebranding themselves, Full Moon would need to look at different business ventures in order to keep both the company and its iconic characters alive. Full Moon, and it seemed *Puppet Master* especially, needed merchandising more than it ever had before.

With the studio undergoing so many changes and drastically shrinking in size, it didn't make any sense on paper for Charles Band to elect to start a new company. But it proved to be the best choice he could have possibly made at the time. This new company would be costly, but it would allow Full Moon's characters to reach a bigger audience than it had ever seen before. And thus, Full Moon Toys was born.

To head the new company, Full Moon appointed Rick Phares. While Band served as President/CEO, Phares managed the day-to-day running of the company and was the major creative force behind it. As always, Full Moon liked to keep things in house when it came to hirings and promotion. Phares had already begun working with the company through its new distributor, Kushner-Locke, handling distribution services for much of the new releases. Already very familiar with the toy industry, Phares happily took over the new job, heading up a toy company designed specifically to revolve around Full Moon and its related characters. Anything the studio owned could be brought to life and immortalized in plastic. "I've always been a collector," says Phares. "I came aboard Full Moon as a sales representative for the video distribution. That was when video was in its heyday with things like Blockbuster and so I was actually working in the sales department with a couple other people, bringing Full Moon video to different retailers. I had an office set up and in my office I had a lot of action figures on blister cards hanging up on my wall. And Charlie Band came into my office one day to discuss something to do with our video sales, and when he was in my office he looked around and said, 'Wow, I've always wanted to do action figures based on some of our characters.' I looked at him and said, 'Charlie, that's a great idea.'"

The 1990s had also seen a boom in horror toys in general. The years of 1992 and '93 saw the releases of horror-themed play sets like Monster Face and Creepy Crawlers, which were not only mass-marketed to kids but even encouraged them to indulge their weirder, grosser interests. Cartoons based on adult-oriented material like *Toxic Crusaders* and *Tales from the Cryptkeeper* had begun seeing their own action figures. The mid-nineties saw a major anniversary for the Universal Monsters as well, allowing those characters to make appearances in everything from coloring books to Burger King Happy Meal toys. Those major classic icons were back and were being sold to kids, truly being introduced to a new generation. At the same time, McFarlane Toys got off the ground and became *the* biggest independent toy company of the decade, completely changing the game. Their figures were still action-oriented and designed to be played with, but the embraced a level of detail completely unseen in any company that had ever existed before them. *Spawn* and toy lines based on R-rated fare like *Aliens, Predator, Blade* and *Virus* only continued to prove that there was a place for horror figures on the market.

For Full Moon, *Puppet Master* was the perfect place to start. Not only was it the company's flagship franchise, but the characters made the most sense to get the toy treatment, given that they themselves were toys. Considering Charles Band's obsession with childhood playthings coming to life, it's amazing that Full Moon had not attempted something like this sooner. They had of course released the Greg Aronowitz model kits in 1991. Those were sold through the Full Moon Fan Club and their reach was not all that wide, which is why they remain such highly sought collectibles to this day. The idea was completely different this time. Full Moon wanted to be a full-blown toy company, and that meant their toys would be sold in specialty shops, comic stores and wherever else they could manage. After years without a *Puppet Master* film, they just wanted the figures to be seen.

Blade, being the clear icon of the series at this point, was the perfect character to launch the toy line. By the time the franchise was three movies deep, he had already become the figurehead. He was the one that people recognized, the one that stood out and the one that had become the face to Full Moon's overall brand. An action figure based on Blade could have sold well enough on its own without Full Moon ever even needing to dip into the full-blown action figure series. But they clearly knew that their characters would reach an audience if treated right. Because of that, they became the best merchandising enterprise in Full Moon's entire history. "Basically, when you launch a new product line, in anything, particularly with entertainment licenses, you want to lead with your strongest character," says Phares. "So we basically started with Blade because he's the most iconic *Puppet Master* figure and I think as far as Full Moon characters go, whether it be *Dollman, Trancers,* any of them, Blade is still the most iconic. When you think of Blade, you think of Full Moon."

The figures were detailed and clearly representative of the characters on the screen. Blade was clothed in a cloth overcoat with a felt hat in order to effectively evoke the puppet's appearance in the films, even though the action figure would only be about six inches tall. Blade was also packaged with an accessory never seen in the films, something that would be repeated throughout the line as a whole. The toy featured the ability to switch out Blade's weapons, either reversing the knife and hook, or replacing either one with a new hatchet accessory. While Blade would never actually switch out weapons until 2017's *Puppet Master: Axis Termination,* there was at least groundwork laid for the concept in the *Puppet Wars* scripts which saw Blade switch out his knife for both a longer knife and a hand at various points.

Joining Blade in the debut series was Six-Shooter. Since making his debut in *Puppet Master III,* Six-Shooter had quickly become a fan-favorite puppet., though Phares notes that that was not quite the reason for his inclusion in the first series. "Six-Shooter was chosen because I felt it was a good second-tier character. He wasn't in the first film, he was introduced a little bit later, I think in the third. Tunneler was right there in the first film. I wanted to save some of the other, higher profile figures like Tunneler and Leech Woman and Jester, so for each group there would be a strong lead-in, at least."

More importantly, he is one of the most visually striking of the group, which allowed the figure to reach beyond just the fans toward potentially more mainstream appeal. Anyone who sees a six-armed cowboy with the name Six-Shooter is bound to be immediately intrigued. Unfortunately, Six-Shooter didn't come with anything near the bells and whistles of Blade and would wind up being the most featureless figure of the original series lineup. Six-Shooter has no cloth clothing outside his red bandana, instead opting for a pure plastic approach. The character is well detailed and the likeness is virtually perfect, but the toy doesn't actually do anything, nor does it come with any other accessories other than the chrome-coated guns in its six hands, but its likeness to the puppet of the films is thankfully terrific.

Appropriately, series one of *Puppet Master: The Action Figure Series* saw release in October of 1997. There was no question that the company had created two extremely worthwhile figures that fans would be thrilled to have, but whether or not they could truly sell the toys and market those characters on a wider scale remained uncertain until the first sales figures came back. The numbers were high. And as they kept coming in, they kept getting higher. Series one, it turned out, had sold out over night. The toy series was an instant success. And that meant that not only did they have to quickly get more Blades and Six-Shooters out to retailers, they also had to get to work on series two as well.

Series two focuses on Tunneler and The Totem. While Tunneler is a beloved puppet that had appeared in every movie up to that point in time, The Totem was a different story. It made sense, though. *Puppet Master 5* was the most recent feature in the franchise at that point, so it was worth it to capitalize on the entry that people had most recently seen. With so many features, the toys were designed to be played with and that could be tricky for young fans who knew the puppets as a collective unit. They worked together. Adding Totem to the mix would actually give young fans something to let their imaginations run wild and give the puppets an enemy to fight. In terms of quality and effectiveness, both figures reflect the first series in many ways. In an interview with *Lee's Action Figure News & Toy Review* at the time, Phares smartly noted that Totem's inclusion catered to young fans of the movies, to potentially provide a villain for Blade to fight and allow for imaginative play.[1]

Tunneler is a great likeness of the character and his spinning drill—which works by a dial on the toy's back—is the perfect action feature for that character. The Totem was a different story. Once again, the character was a strong likeness—none of the figures would have a problem in this area—but would be utterly featureless. Totem was only packaged with a small accessory dubbed the "power gem," which did nothing and couldn't really be used for anything. Even though these were action figures, Phares noted that with Tunneler especially, it was important to find ways to adhere as closely to the movie as possible. That didn't simply translate to the various action features, but even articulation and mobility of the individual figures. "Tunneler if you notice, I added the rotating drill top. And the articulation that he had would allow him to move forward into the running drill pose."

While not a fan-favorite character, Totem marked, as Phares points out, potentially the most undervalued figure of the entire line-up. "With Totem, a lot of people probably didn't realize it at the time, but that was a very detailed figure. If you look at the paint applications, there's a lot of very detailed paint applications for Totem. McFarlane was doing a lot, but a lot of McFarlane's paint applications were dry brushing, washes, things that didn't take a lot of very detailed hand painting. This one had a lot of very detailed hand painting and it was an expensive figure to produce. That actually cost more money to make than a Pinhead or a Leech Woman."

Series three saw the release of Pinhead and Leech Woman. Both are among the best in the series and, for once, both were packaged with their share of extra features. Leech Woman is, one would only assume, the most controversial figure in the lineup. Give the fact that she had already been deemed too gross to appear on screen and absent from *Puppet Master 4* and *5,* it's a little surprising that she was even included in the toy series at all. The character is almost always the puppet that gets the most visceral reaction out of people as soon as they look at her. But Leech Woman is a great puppet, a core member of the group, and it's a small miracle that her action figure ever even came to exist in the first place. Not only does the figure feature a leech coming out of her mouth, but the toy plays directly into her squeamish nature by including a button on her back that makes the leech wriggle in her mouth. The Leech Woman figure also came with four extra leeches, in case she needed spares. Unlike every single one of the other puppets, her accessory actually *is* something she used in the films: her knife from *Puppet Master II*. On a more controversial level, while each of the other puppets is fully clothed under their cloth clothing accessories, Leech Woman is not.

It makes a degree of sense, as Leech Woman has bare arms and legs in the films and is slightly more exposed but undoing the Velcro on the front of her dress reveals a character clad only in a skimpy pink thong. "When I was designing the figures, I had access to a lot of the puppets used in the very first *Puppet Master* movie. These were the ones that we had in our display case in our office lobby. Some of them were Charlie's personal collection. So I was able to base these not only on the movie but also the actual puppets and have them in hand. So, for Leech Woman, her nipples were added because they were there on the original prop," says Phares.

Puppet Master: The Action Figure Series, series 2: *Tunneler & Totem* magazine ad.

Rounding out the main line of original puppets, series four contained Torch and Jester. Once again, both figures would have features and accessories of their own. Both would have a degree of "real" clothing in the form of Torch's jacket and Jester's tunic. Like all the others, both Torch and Jester were strong likenesses of their movie counterparts. The only exception to is perhaps Jester's highly debated unibrow. While early sales art and prototypes for the figure saw the character boast two eyebrows similar to the films, the final product bears a solid, three-dimensional eyebrow instead. It's possible that, due to the thinness of Jester's eyebrows in the first place, the early painted designs didn't work. They could have worn off or been lost in translation during mass-production, allowing for the 3D, molded unibrow to be the best alternative. "Yes," says Phares, "it was a production issue and came down to what would translate well. Because with Jester, we had three pieces that had to rotate independently and some of the real fine edges were prone to breakage and things like that."

Each of the figures is an incredible rendition of the respective characters. Each one is dynamic and stands on its own. There's no debating that, as great as this series can be, the puppets are and have always been the selling point. Those designs are striking and when they're able to be put out into the world, people always notice. "I looked around and noticed that there weren't a lot of action figures coming out with cloth accessories," Phares says. "And I wanted to add that little bit of realism in our action figures. That's why Blade had the trench coat, that's why Pinhead had the sweater." He also adds that this decision to convey some sense of realism with the movies even extended to the figures in the packaging. "Basically, knowing that these were puppets, I didn't want to do them already posing in an action stance. I knew going forward that they should just be puppets in their natural pose, as if they were in Toulon's trunk or on Toulon's workshop shelf. So that was a given that just in the neutral position in the blister package, it would be just a natural pose. Then I had the challenge of figuring out where the articulation should go in, in terms of what the action features should be and what the actual character puppet did in the films."

This was incredibly true in 1998, when the figures were released on the heels of the already-successful Blade and Six-Shooter. Fans were delighted by the toys and they instantly became the most sought-after *Puppet Master* collectibles and still remain so to this day. The best decision made by Full Moon in terms of collector mentality, though, was the decision to embrace the then-new market of variant figures. The concept of variants had only really been introduced in the early '90s. The idea was that a certain number of toys would be made and most would be the regular versions of each character, but certain retailers would get exclusive versions that would all look slightly different. McFarlane's first *Spawn* toys were among the earliest figures to embrace the concept. KB Toys carried gold-painted exclusive figures of the original characters, while FAO Schwartz carried an exclusive unmasked version of Spawn.

Puppet Master: The Action Figure Series elected to do the same in what proved to be a genius marketing move. Each character would get no less than four variants for different retailers. In addition to their original versions, the characters would be available in Troll & Toad, Previews, Gold Edition and Japanese Exclusives. The differences in each character ranged from ideas that were visually striking—like a red-coated Blade echoing the masquerade sequence of *Phantom of the Opera* or Torch in a camouflaged jacket—to those that actually struck a little closer to the movies themselves—like Blade with the more movie-accurate cone-eyes instead of glowing eyes, or Jester dressed in the new outfit from the then-upcoming *Curse of the Puppet Master*.

"When I was doing sales and marketing for the toy line," says Phares, "I would contact retailers directly. I had a very good relationship and still do to this day with Medicom toy company in Japan. And I would actually fly to Japan a few times a year and just have meetings with them. The Japanese market is very creative. They said, 'Rick, we would like to do exclusive versions,' and I said, 'Sure,' because that's more sales." The variant possibilities, to everyone's surprise it seems, only grew from there. "We'd be bringing them into the fold to come up with their own ideas and concepts. They were happy with it, they'd come back for the next release, and it was a very successful venture that way. That's why there's so many variants. They would come up with their own concepts and I would look at it, Charlie would look at it, and most of the time we were okay with it. As long as it wasn't too off the map. There were a few instances where I came up with the concept." Still, Phares notes that most of the time, "it was the accounts who bought it that knew what they wanted to do."

Because of the variants, a line-up that originally consisted of only eight toys became dozens of unique figures. With some variants being incredibly rare, with a few only produced in quantities of the low thousands, they each became highly sought-after by the fans. People still continue to hunt for them at conventions, comic shops, flea markets and, of course, eBay. In many ways, after over twenty years, *Puppet Master: The Action Figure Series* is still flourishing.

Full Moon Toys was a burgeoning company, though, and there were no plans to stop with the release of the major puppet characters. The last remaining of the main puppets to go without a figure, Decapitron, would be the first character to get the deluxe edition treatment with the release of a fully clothed, 12-inch, strikingly movie accurate figure featuring (naturally) multiple different heads. Decapitron was a perfect character for the deluxe treatment, given his placement as de facto leader of the puppets in *Puppet Master 4* and *5*.

The packaging for the *Puppet Master* figure series was standard figure packaging with the puppets standing in front of the Full Moon logo. The back of each box would conveniently list which figures were currently available and which figures were on their way. By the time Torch and Jester were coming out, the packaging began announcing the arrival of other Full Moon characters as well. On the heels of *Puppet Master: The Action Figure Series,* Full Moon Toys launched *Legends of Horror,* which would see figures based on *Subspecies* villain Radu, Stuart Gordon's Castle Freak and the Shrieker from the then-new film of the same title. Despite this new focus, there were plans to continue on with the *Puppet Master* action figures.

The problem was that they had already released all of the main puppets from the films at that point. After Decapitron, the first figure released through the series was Mephisto, a character that had only appeared for one scene in *Puppet Master II*. A series that had been highly successful to this point already seemed to be running

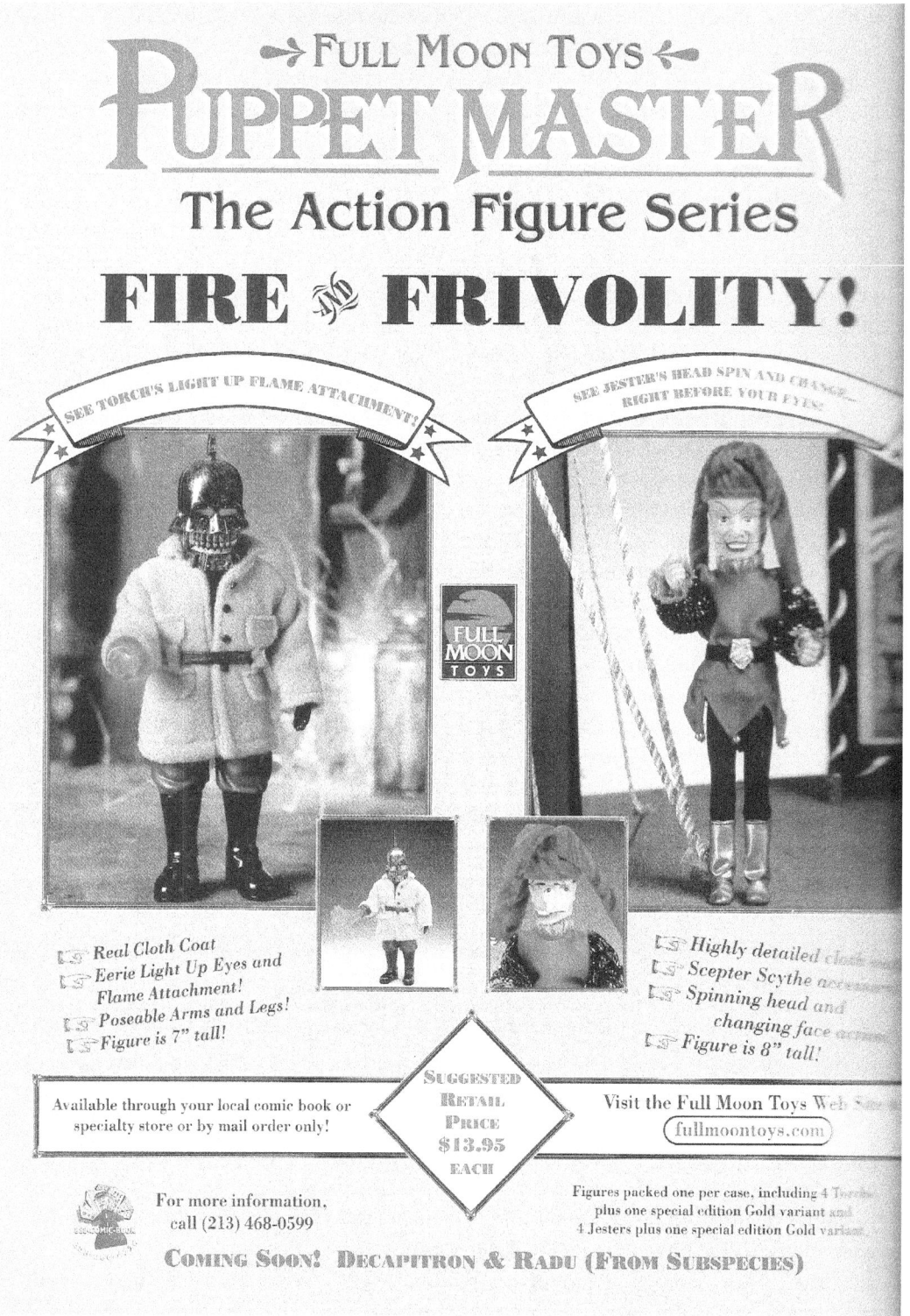

Puppet Master: The Action Figure Series, series 4: *Torch & Jester* magazine ad.

out of ideas. Luckily, that problem would soon be solved. In 1999, Full Moon planned to release its second prequel in the franchise, this time going all the way back to the beginning for *Retro Puppet Master*. This would see all-new early incarnations of the original puppets, as well as a couple of new characters. This would not only provide the movies with a fresh direction but would allow for the action figure series to continue almost seamlessly.

Phares found the solution to keep the *Puppet Master* toy line going simply by stumbling onto an old piece of artwork in Full Moon's warehouse one day. It was Lee MacLeod's original *Puppet Master* art. "I used to love going into our storage facility, because there was just hundreds of pieces of artwork that were made for films that were never released," says Rick Phares. "And I remember finding the really old original painting for *Puppet Master,* before *Puppet Master* was even written. I think you've probably seen that by now. That artwork was in his office and at that point we had kind of exhausted all of the mainstream puppets and I was trying to come up with a way to keep the *Puppet Master* line alive, because honestly Radu and Castle Freak sold, but they didn't sell as well as *Puppet Master*."

The toy line was rebranded as *Retro Puppet Master,* with the gimmick being that the new figures would be based on the original concept designs for the puppets fans had come to know and love. The first two, Retro-Blade and Cyclops, were clearly based on the artwork, specifically. After the release of that first series, the toy line changed to reflect the designs of the newly released *Retro Puppet Master* feature film. Retro-Pinhead, Dr. Death, Retro-Six-Shooter and Retro-Tunneler all look almost identical to the puppets that wound up appearing in the movie. These figures came with plenty of accessories but had much less in the way of action features. Retro Tunneler forgoes the rotating drill of the first Tunneler figure and instead features a wind-up drill that proved to be a little less functional.

The Retro figures also featured fewer variants, at least after Retro-Blade and Cyclops. These new figures were also available in more stores than the previous ones, due to the success of those toys with retailers. In addition to comic and specialty shops, the *Retro Puppet Master* figures and other related Full Moon Toys of the time were available in Suncoast Video, FYE, Electronics Boutique, Spencer's Gifts and more big-name stores of the era. Full Moon Toys was an ever-expanding, proven success. More retailers allowed more exclusive variants and even exclusive new toys to be made, though, so the company was still gaining popularity and rising in the toy world. *Puppet Master: The Action Figure Series* even made the cover of *Lee's Action Figure News and Toy Review* twice.

Given the fact that the *Retro Puppet Master* line did not match the previous figures' popularity, the decision was made that—one way or another—new toys based on the classic characters were designed to hit larger retail shelves. Because of this, Full Moon Toys rebranded itself in 2000 with a whole slew of figures available in more stores than ever before. The classic puppets returned in the form of new "Movie Edition" figures, adding new touches to the original designs to better reflect the films.

"I literally ran the toy division more or less by myself," says Phares. "Basically, I was not only doing the toys, I was also selling the toys. It was my responsibility to talk to Diamond Comics and the top retailers at the time. I was also trying to get into

Toys "R" Us and the mass markets. So I had many different hats to wear during that period. I had started trying to increase our sales from the very first release. So when you started seeing more product at the time it was simply because I was having more success and opening more doors. At the same time, the retailers that had picked up the earlier releases had sold out, and they saw how successful Full Moon Toys was for them, so when new products came out, they increased their orders. We were able to pick up more retailers for our product and the current retailers were starting to increase their orders for product."

Blade saw a new paint job on the face, reflecting the more cream color of the original film instead of the plain white face of the first figure. Instead of the glowing red eyes, the new Movie Edition Blade had black-painted cone eyes, as had previously been seen in the Troll & Toad exclusive figure. Tunneler had a more grayish repaint than the general forest green that had been seen the first time. While he came with the same accessories, he also had another nice touch in the addition of a white rag that had been used to wipe the blood from his drill in *Puppet Master 4*. Pinhead received a new orange-colored sweater that felt a little closer to the sweater of the original feature, especially the scene by the fireplace. His pants were changed from blue to brown to more closely reflect the films as well. Six-Shooter, like Blade, would no longer have chrome weapons, instead featuring painted and removable weapons. Torch's new orange jacket featured the star emblem that Torch wore on his jacket in the films and Jester featured a removable hat, so as to reflect his appearance in the original. His spinning head would now be wind-up, the same decision that had been made with Retro-Tunneler's spinning drill. The Movie Edition figures saw new versions of Blade, Tunneler, Pinhead, Six-Shooter, Jester and Torch, with plans for others at the time. There would be no new Movie Edition figures based on either Leech Woman or Totem. However, Phares noted in an interview with *Lee's Action Figure News and Toy Review* at the time of release just what an interesting prospect the Leech Woman figure would have been, as he mentioned that the Movie Edition Leech Woman would not only have removable leeches, rather than the leech glued into the mouth of the original figure but would have been clothed in the long white gown she had briefly worn in *Puppet Master III*.[2]

Alongside the Movie Editions, Full Moon Toys also released a new version of Pinhead. The most sinister *Puppet Master* toy yet, Halloween Pinhead saw the burly puppet wearing a blood-splattered orange sweater and a black domino mask with accessories that included a large carving knife and a bag of severed limbs. The toy also had a new hand sculpt in order to hold his brand-new knife. Phares notes: "At the time, we were doing Full Moon Toys, Charlie came to me and said, 'Rick, I'd like to do an exclusive. Some kind of Halloween exclusive.' And that figure was Charlie's idea. He said, 'I don't know, why not come up with something like Pinhead with a severed head or something?' And when he said that, I said, 'Okay, I'll do exactly that.' Because when he said that, it did kind of make sense. We could do a bloody trick-or-treat bag that the head could go in or something like that. So that whole concept was kind of Charlie's idea, and I took it and kind of expanded upon it. That was the only figure in my opinion that maybe pushed the envelope a little bit more. It's a little bit gorier with the severed head."

Chapter Eight. Puppet Master: The Action Figure Series

Puppet Master: Movie Editions magazine ad.

Two more variants were created based on the Retro Puppets in order to be sold exclusively through Full Moon Direct. The first, Bullet Tunneler, would be a repainted Retro Tunneler with silver clothes and body and a gold drill. The second figure, The Mortician, would be a darker, grayscale variant of Doctor Death. Alongside the Movie Editions, these toys were more highly marketed than ever, advertised in magazines ranging from *Fangoria* to *Wizard* and *ToyFare*.

These wouldn't be the only figures based on the iconic puppets to see release in 2000, though. Based on the success of 12 Decapitron, even though that had been one of the lesser popular characters in the series, Full Moon decided to move ahead with a whole line of 12 figures based on the main puppets. Having had decent success with a less beloved character, the company was confident that a larger, fully clothed and highly detailed figure based on their flagship character would do incredibly well. Thus, they produced the 12 Blade, the mostly highly detailed figure Full Moon Toys had released up to that point. The doll was released in many different stores, with Spencer's offering an exclusive blood-splattered version. The rusty, highly detailed knife and hook accessories also proved to be impressive highlights of an overall stellar design.

The 12 Blade doll was only meant to be the beginning, however. Following on the puppet's heels, Full Moon meant to follow the release order of the first figures, with Six-Shooter planned to be next. The 12 Six-Shooter saw a prototype sculpt, arming himself with a rifle as well as the lasso he used in both *Puppet Master 4* and *Curse of the Puppet Master*. "Six-Shooter, I loved it. That would have been the premiere 1/6 scale figure because it translates so well into that scale. His accessory was a rope, a lariat. The thing was almost a foot and a half long and had a wire armature inside, so you could actually pose it in the air like a lasso. It was a really cool figure and I really wanted to see that get released, but sadly it never happened." After that, Full Moon planned to go down through the list, making 12 figures of each one of the puppets, with the next one after Six-Shooter planned to be a 12 Torch. According to a release schedule in *Lee's Action Figure News and Toy Review,* those puppets would have been followed by Leech Woman and Totem.[3] Says Phares of the plans for continuing the 12 line: "After I had left Full Moon and the company kind of resurrected itself several years later, another small company came in to help Charlie do some product and they re-released Blade and the Pimp doll. The original Pimp doll was done by myself, and Blade was done. Those were the first two. And they had done very well. My thought was to continue. I had a ⅙ scale Torch, as well." There were plenty of other new figures announced during that time as well. Each of the Movie Edition figures came packaged with a trading card that showed off concept designs for the long-gestating *Puppet Master vs. Demonic Toys*. The back of the box promised that the brand-new Cyber Puppets would be making their way to toy store shelves in the coming year.

Taking a more comical approach, Full Moon Toys also showed off artwork of a new series called Tiny Terrors, which capitalized on the burgeoning bobblehead craze of the time. These were planned to take the head sculpts of the full-sized figures and attach them to tiny bodies for figurines displaying more humorous situations and takes on the puppets' abilities, such as Torch

Chapter Eight. Puppet Master: The Action Figure Series

using his flamethrower to light a cigar and Pinhead showing off his buff body in a speedo.

Full Moon Toys also announced one of their most genius marketing ploys yet, something that went all the way back to the early days of *Star Wars* toys. They planned to release a collector's case in order to house the *Puppet Master* action figures as so many had been released at that point. The case would, of course, be the classic trunk seen in the movies. Whether it was planned or not, Toulon's trunk became one of the most iconic images in the entire franchise. After all, the original *Puppet Master* poster displayed the puppets inside the trunk, so most people associated it with the puppets from the very first time that they laid eyes on the characters. Making a version of the trunk that could be used to house the toys was such an obvious idea that it's amazing they hadn't attempted it sooner. Given that collector's cases had been a successful marketing tool for years and the puppets already had one within the franchise itself, it was a perfect opportunity for the action figure series.

Another promised prototype has had fans guessing for decades. Under the title *Japanese Puppet Master* an image has circulated for years of a prototype character named Comb Queen, not seen in any of the films. This, perhaps unsurprisingly, stems from Full Moon Toys' positive relationship with Japanese company Medicom. "We ran a contest for fans to send us their ideas and original artwork for a brand new puppet. We asked the fans to create their own puppet. I believe it ran in a magazine, it may have been *Lee's*. We ran the contest and asked people to submit their ideas, and we would have them all sent in and Charlie and I would look at the top three. The second runner-up, third runner-up would win some kind of prize. But the winner of the contest, their prize would be that we would make a prototype for them, they would receive their prototype and it would be an actual toy release for our future toy line. Charlie chose Comb Queen, he liked that one. This has been so many years, I don't even remember the winner of that. But I do know the artwork was really cool, I believe at the time, Charlie just loved the concept. He always wanted to introduce another female puppet."

The topper of Full Moon's announcements in 2000, without a doubt, would have been the much talked about collection of Cyber Puppets, planned to coincide with the release of *Puppet Master vs. Demonic Toys*. These figures would have been sold on their own and in a box set, with figures based on the Demonic Toys sold in another box set. Prototypes were made of the highly detailed and impressive Demonic Toys, which fans would have eagerly bought given that it was one of Full Moon's more popular franchises. The most intriguing thing about these new figures would be a more experimental angle. The Cyber Puppets would have some degree of animatronic capabilities, so that collectors could get a somewhat authenticated feel of the puppets actually moving on their own. That prospect is endlessly intriguing, but, like so many of those things announced in 2000, they never saw the light of day. To this day, they have never been released and there is no doubt that they never will be as most prototypes were sold off, lost or destroyed. "There was this drive to come up with new ideas, so I came up with another line called Cyber Puppets. I always loved the *Terminator* films and I thought it would be really cool if I could take the *Terminator* concept and mash it with the *Puppet Master* puppets. So basically I had the idea of doing

Cyber Puppets, and we had the artist Lee MacLeod take these concepts and do artwork for the Cyber Puppets, and then I actually had prototypes made up. And again, that was another line that never saw release because of the demise of Full Moon at the time. I believe what wound up happening, it's been a few years since I've seen *Puppet Master vs. Demonic Toys,* but they made the puppets a little cybertronic. Those were my designs."

Full Moon Toys had gained a lot of traction in 1998 with the first *Puppet Master* figures and continued to build momentum after that, starting in specialty stores and eventually winding up in the mass market. The toys that were available at more and more retailers were—aside from maybe the Movie Editions—not what people had wanted to see. The toys had sold when they were a little harder to find, only making their way into comic and specialty shops, and they had sold incredibly well. If anything, it's possible that those original figures could have sold even better had they seen the same widescale release that the *Retro Puppet Master* figures eventually saw. The Movie Editions were not only successful, they were finally a mainstream release. By the end of 2000, *Puppet Master* figures were in toy stores all across the country, and Full Moon Toys had countless, promising projects on the horizon. The ending, therefore, came as a surprise to everyone.

On the demise of Full Moon Toys, Phares says, "we finally got into Toys 'R' Us and I'll never forget, I traveled to Japan at the time and I actually walked into a Japanese Toys 'R' Us and saw *Puppet Master* up on the shelf. That was actually a dream come true, to see that happen. Unfortunately, after that happened, Full Moon as a company—and I don't really know the details—ran into some financial difficulty. The whole company shut down. And Full Moon Toys was not independently run, it was a part of Full Moon, the whole film studio. So when one part falls, the whole empire falls. So when they shut down Full Moon it shut down the toy division as well. And it was a shame, after all those years of trying to break into the mass market, we finally had success, and it was an accomplishment for not only myself but Full Moon as a company as well, to get product into the mass market like that."

Since then, Full Moon has continued their own marketing ventures with barely a breather. In 2007, they began releasing their own line of full-size replicas based on the puppets, but the price was high and the quality of the work wasn't up to what fans had been used to during the Full Moon Toys era. Shortly before that, in 2005, Full Moon released a series of resin statues that actually were very detailed and well-designed, but just like the toys before them, they were cut short. Only four were released of a planned six.

Full Moon has branched out into more resin statues of late, including *Ghoulies* and *Demonic Toys,* and even ventured into Halloween costumes. Given the success of the Blade mask in 2000, the company put out their own Blade costume and followed it up with Jester, Tunneler and Pinhead. Other Full Moon characters such as Radu, Killjoy and the Castle Freak also saw masks and costumes. Over the years, Full Moon's merchandising ventures have grown more and more eccentric, with the most extreme examples including a line of horror-themed bras dubbed "Monster Bras" and a very short-lived line of edible Gingerdead Man cookies.

The best of the more recent era of *Puppet Master* merchandise, though, are easily

Chapter Eight. Puppet Master: The Action Figure Series

the Plush Buddies. Although only Blade and Torch were made, these *Puppet Master* plushies allowed for genuinely adorable updates on the designs of the classic puppets. Torch even came with a smiling sidekick flame stemming from his flamethrower hand, which the toy's tag dubbed "Smoulder." While some of the hardcore fans might have snubbed their nose at the idea of "cute" versions of their favorite characters, the Plush Buddies were a hit and continue to be a highlight of conventions, with Full Moon famously selling a Plush Buddy Blade to Guillermo Del Toro at San Diego Comic Con.

In 2017, Full Moon relaunched *Puppet Master: The Action Figure Series* in name only. Only one figure, Blade, was produced, with Jester and Torch finally promised to follow up in the fall of 2020. Before that, Full Moon abandoned their brief step back into action figures to jump right back into the more comfortable replica business they had already been in for so long. In 2018, the replica line relaunched with a brand-new attitude and a focus toward accuracy to at least the versions of the puppets seen in the *Axis* trilogy. The new replicas were hand-made by Tom Devlin, who had created the puppets for both *Puppet Master: Axis Rising* and *Puppet Master: Axis Termination*.

Even though *Puppet Master* merchandise continues on, the days of Full Moon Toys are long behind us now. In the overall scope of the franchise's thirty plus year history, the toy company was barely a blip on the radar. Yet, it was one of the most revolutionary and influential things that had ever happened to this series. The very concept of taking established horror movie characters and giving them high quality figures could very easily have inspired McFarlane Toys in getting the now iconic Movie Maniacs line. The *Puppet Master* toys were also not afraid to be action figures in an era when everything was shifting and gearing toward a new focus on collectors. Actual action was being replaced by intricate detail, but the *Puppet Master* toys focused on both. They were R-rated toys based on R-rated characters that were still designed for kids to play with. That's a concept that, on its own, simply shouldn't work. But it's also a concept that has come to define the success of the franchise as a whole.

More importantly than that, than anything, really, is the fact that the toys introduced a whole new audience to *Puppet Master*. People who had never heard of it before, who had skipped over it on the video store shelf, could not help but notice the toys in their local comic shop or Spencer's. The designs of the puppets are and always will be the best advertisements for the movies and this proved to be no exception. Just as I had done as a child, many young people—and even older ones—saw those toys and those designs and could not help but be immediately intrigued. In some ways, despite the loss of the Paramount deal, Full Moon as a brand was bigger than ever. Their toys had come as close to breaking into the mainstream as these characters and films were ever likely to be.

The problem, of course, was that the film studio behind the toys was smaller than ever. And, moving forward, it would find itself in the unexpected position of fighting to keep up with its own merchandising empire.

Chapter Nine

Curse of the Puppet Master

From 1991 to 1994, Full Moon Entertainment had released four *Puppet Master* movies. That's an output of over one movie a year. Each time out, the films had proven to be a video store success and the studio had always treated the franchise as an ever-growing brand throughout the early 1990s. Even though *Puppet Master 5* had been billed as the final chapter, it had never been planned as an actual ending. Before it even hit shelves, there were plans for follow-ups. But year after year, the planned *Puppet Wars* trilogy failed to get off the ground. Behind the scenes, there were even larger problems that prevented the franchise from continuing, at least in a way that would be recognizably similar to what had come before. In 1995, only a year after the release of the so-called final chapter, Paramount cut its distribution deal with Full Moon Entertainment, threatening to turn the aforementioned tantalizing tagline into a somber, blunt reality.

There are conflicting rumors as to what exactly caused the end of the Paramount deal. According to some, the delayed production of *Ragdoll* went noticed by Viacom execs who had just purchased Paramount in 1995. The fact that one of their companies had had a film on the slate since 1992 that still had yet to be made soured their opinion of Full Moon, as to them it looked like a liability that was not delivering on everything that it promised. *Ragdoll,* which was in pre-production at the time, was affected by this and shut down immediately.[1] There are also reports that Stuart Gordon's *Castle Freak* had an accidental hand in causing the split. During the golden era of the early 1990s, Paramount never seemed to care what Full Moon produced as long as they produced it on time. The studio, especially around 1993 and '94, had gained a reputation for being tame in comparison to many other contemporary horror efforts, thanks largely to Band's apprehension toward gore and favoritism toward excitement and fantasy.

Castle Freak was entirely off-brand for Full Moon at the time, which won it a lot of praise in horror circles of the day. The movie even won a coveted *Fangoria* Chainsaw Award for Best Limited Release Film, which was made even more exciting by the fact that the magazine had been lukewarm on the company up to that point. Whereas most Full Moon efforts preceding it were more tongue-in-cheek and almost optimistic, *Castle Freak* is an extremely violent and borderline nihilistic movie. It almost seems that the movie was green-lit simply because Paramount let Full Moon make whatever they wanted to make. But as fate would have it, Paramount higher-ups happened to visit the editing bay on a day when *Castle Freak* was being cut together and were thoroughly disgusted by what they had seen.² This could certainly be one factor as to why Paramount cut its ties with Full Moon. Realistically, there are probably dozens of factors that went into the decision, but however it happened, the end of the Paramount era changed the course of Full Moon forever.

Scrambling for ideas, Band looked at some of the other offshoot brands that had blossomed during Full Moon's success in order to keep some studio backing. He had seen a lot of success with the Moonbeam line, through which he made family-friendly fare like *Dragon World, Beanstalk* and the *Prehysteria* films. With Paramount no longer standing behind those efforts, Band made the decision to take Moonbeam and its respective properties to Disney in order to hopefully make a deal that would allow things to continue with at least some level of studio distribution. While many might scoff at the notion of Full Moon working under the Disney banner, Band had ties to the company through his father, Albert, who had served as an executive producer on *Honey, I Shrunk the Kids*. That feature had also been co-written and produced by longtime Band collaborators Stuart Gordon and Brian Yuzna. The idea of taking Moonbeam to Disney was not, by any means, unfounded. All the same, they promptly turned Band down on his offer.

Instead, Band made a deal with Donald Kushner and Peter Locke's Kushner/Locke company to finance Full Moon's further endeavors. The restructuring to a smaller company did not decrease Full Moon's output. If anything, Band somehow put out *more* movies a year than he had done before. Rather than making a few features for roughly the same cost, the new model would see Full Moon productions with drastically reduced budgets, made for half the time of the already incredibly tight schedules that each of the Paramount-distributed features had seen.

Admittedly, Band came out of the gate swinging with one of the most bizarre films Full Moon had ever made up to that point. The year of 1996 saw the release of *Head of the Family,* directed by Band himself, which has gone on to become one of the biggest cult favorites in the studio's history. It was an incredibly important film for the company, as it proved to potential retailers that despite their set backs, Full Moon had not lost a step. It was still focused on putting out the same bizarre, off-the-wall content it had always been known for. At the same time, Band also began to make new deals, looking into new merchandising ventures, the biggest of which would be Full Moon Toys. At the same time, he began setting up new partnerships for different sub-sets of movies, producing everything from children and family features through the PulsePounders line, to late-night softcore material via the Surrender Erotica line.

Full Moon Toys was an experiment that proved to be a bigger success at first than anyone had really anticipated. *Puppet Master: The Action Figure Series* put the studio's flagship franchise back on the map. People were either rediscovering these characters all over again or discovering them for the first time. Either way, there was a hunger for *Puppet Master,* but there had not been a feature in the franchise in four years. Given the output the series had seen through the early '90s, that four-year gap felt like a decade. After several years, the *Puppet Wars* features were no closer to becoming a reality. Given that they were three ambitious scripts, the loss of Paramount backing basically assured that those movies would never see the light of day.

Even if it meant going back on the supposed finality of *Puppet Master 5,* Band made the decision to scrap the spinoffs and keep going with a much more economically feasible entry in the series. The sixth entry would, however, retain one of the most important aspects of the *Puppet Wars* trilogy: a title. Despite having nothing to do with those three scripts whatsoever, the next film in the series would bear the same name as the trilogy's intended opener, *Curse of the Puppet Master*.

Obviously, Band did not want the franchise to be forgotten, especially as he had just begun his biggest merchandising venture to date. After four years, with Full Moon rebuilding itself and its output, the timing was right for another *Puppet Master*. But more than that, it needed to be ensured that a new film would hit video stores, just to keep the *Puppet Master* brand alive. The question of what exactly that new *Puppet Master* would be was a different question altogether. The past two attempts to be ambitious with the series, in both *Puppet Master: The Movie* and *Puppet Wars* had only led to delayed productions and simply hadn't worked out in either case. The new approach would be entirely different. The company just wanted something to release bearing the franchise's name. *Curse of the Puppet Master* would, in some ways, be the most low-risk entry up to that point.

But technically speaking, *Curse of the Puppet Master* was already being developed at the same time *Curse of the Puppet Master* was just about to enter production, as confusing as that might sound. At this point in time, Full Moon was *still* attempting to produce *Puppet Wars I: Curse of the Puppet Master* at their own Castel Studios in Romania. In an incredibly enlightening 1997 interview with *Lee's Action Figure News and Toy Review,* Rick Phares had this to say: "*Curse of the Puppet Master* is being filmed right now over in Romania. We're sort of stuck in the middle of that one right now. It's an expensive film. We're doing a lot of location shooting, and right now the weather is really brutal over there—a lot of snow and a lot of cold. We're using an old train and a section of railroad track that are also being used for another film, and everything's taking a lot longer than we expected. So we shot *another* film here in Los Angeles over the last few weeks, in order to satiate the need out there for another *Puppet Master* film. We're not sure if it will be called *Puppet Master VII* or what. We're in a position where one film is completed and the other, *Curse of the Puppet Master,* is still in production and we may just end up calling the first release *Curse of the Puppet Master* and the one we're still shooting *Puppet Master VII* or whatever."[3]

This is absolutely fascinating on a lot of levels. The train sequence Phares talks about being filmed is no doubt the footage that was eventually reused for *Retro Puppet Master,* the only thing from the filming of the original *Curse of Puppet Master* that is believed to have ever been shot. The nameless, completed sequel he refers to is of course the *Curse of the Puppet Master* we now know. This confirms that that movie was made, to some extent, as an afterthought, that there were circumstances dictating that film from the very beginning that were completely beyond its director's control. *Curse* as we know it was clearly dictated by two things: one, obviously, that the original *Curse of the Puppet Master*—formerly of *Puppet Wars*—had been taking years to get off the ground without any real momentum. The other was that there had not been a *Puppet Master* film in four years, the longest period ever without one in Full Moon's history. The action figures had already hit shelves, but there was no new movie to accompany them. That's naturally why Full Moon shot this movie in Los

Chapter Nine. Curse of the Puppet Master

Angeles simply to keep the brand alive. To accompany the release of the toys, something needed to hit video stores to remind viewers and potential collectors who these characters were. That something was 1998's *Curse of the Puppet Master*.

Even still, it had a whole lot to live up to. Not only would the next movie in the series be the first from Full Moon's self-distributed era, it would also be the first one without David Allen providing the puppet FX. There was no question at this point that Allen was too sick to continue on providing the effects for these or any other movies, no matter how small a responsibility they would be. But that didn't mean that the original puppets and the FX for the new film were not in good hands. Mark Rappaport, who had played an integral role in developing the puppet creations on the original film, would take over the puppet effects for *Curse of the Puppet Master*. He designed the new puppets himself, using the original molds and staying incredibly faithful to the designs of the previous five movies, with only one exception. Jester, this time out, would get a total makeover. While the face mold remained the same, the puppet's lips and overall appearance were darkened and he was given an entirely new outfit. While a new toy variant was made to capitalize on the character's new design, it's uncertain if that was why the decision to change Jester's appearance was made.

In some ways, though, many David Allen effects would make it into the finished film regardless. Because the *Puppet Master* films had always been so technical, there simply wouldn't be time for *Curse* to have anywhere near the same amount of attention put into its special effects. Gone were the days of filming weeks of second unit puppet inserts after principal photography had wrapped. This meant Full Moon would have to embrace something they had never had to resort to before: stock footage. Many scenes in *Curse of the Puppet Master* are directly lifted from earlier movies and, in most cases, they're extremely noticeable. Some work better than others. A close-up of Blade on a shelf that's actually taken from *Puppet Master 4* is almost seamless, but also completely unnecessary because it's a static shot. The puppet's not moving at all during the scene, so the decision to use stock footage is sort of baffling. For other uses, like Jester's spinning head, it makes a lot more sense. But given that Jester has a completely new outfit in *Curse,* those moments of stock footage become incredibly noticeable. There are some scenes lifted out of previous entries that are so obvious that the background completely changes. It's hard to miss Pinhead getting off a bed in one shot and then suddenly being in World War II in a shot lifted from *Puppet Master III*.

Rappaport would not be the only returning thread from the earlier films, either. With the new film coming after a four-year gap and being made by a totally new Full Moon in many ways, Band made the smart decision to bring back David DeCoteau to direct the new installment. DeCoteau's *Puppet Master III* had already become a fan-favorite as well as the most praised entry. While DeCoteau had directed some films prior to *Puppet Master III, Curse* would be directed by a more seasoned DeCoteau. Having returned to Full Moon for the dawn of this new era, DeCoteau was coming back as a true professional in the world of B-Movies, a director notorious for getting virtually anything done on time and under budget. That, more than anything, was what Full Moon needed to ensure *Curse of the Puppet Master* was a success.

In 1998 alone, Decoteau directed four features for Full Moon. In addition to

Curse of the Puppet Master magazine ad.

Curse, he helmed *Shrieker*, *Talisman* and *Frankenstein Reborn*. In many ways, *Curse* would prove to be the trickiest. Even though one was a new spin on one of the most iconic stories ever told, there was a preconception to a new *Puppet Master* that the other features didn't have. *Shrieker* and *Talisman*, in particular, were entirely new and there had been dozens if not hundreds of *Frankenstein* tales on screen before DeCoteau directed his. *Frankenstein* was only meant to kick off Full Moon's *Filmonsters* series, which aimed to be a sort of straight-to-video television series which saw *Goosebumps* style adaptations of classic horror stories with the new angle of catering them to children. By that point, it only made sense. There were tons of different junior novelizations of those horror tales aimed at children already, and the classic monsters had become Burger King toys. Full Moon had a plan, but the two episodes—DeCoteau's *Frankenstein Reborn* and Jeff Burr's *Werewolf Reborn* failed to launch anything memorable.

But *Curse of the Puppet Master* was the sixth installment of the series that put Full Moon on the map, from the director of the most popular entry in the franchise. The pressure to create something new and exciting was definitely there. The only problem was that Full Moon didn't really have the time to think about exactly what that would be. They were rolling a different movie into production every two weeks. In order to keep the brand consistent, Full Moon needed to turn out features systematically, like clockwork. The problem was that they only had a handful of writers at the time for a fairly large output. There really wasn't time for anything to go beyond a first or second draft. So far, that luckily hadn't been a problem, both Band and directors like DeCoteau had been relatively happy with everything.

Until *Curse*.

DeCoteau, according to the Blu-ray commentary, received the screenplay for *Curse of the Puppet Master* over the weekend before filming began, read it that night and thought—by his own admission—that it was absolutely unusable.[4] He couldn't decipher it, he didn't want to do it, and he didn't even think that he could save it. All of a sudden, only days before shooting, the movie didn't have a script. Full Moon passed the reigns along to one of their only other writers, Benjamin Carr (aka Neal Marshall Stevens), who spoke briefly with DeCoteau about the general vibe they wanted from the film. But they needed to come up with an entirely new story and were obviously incredibly pressed for time. There was really no way to conceive a workable script on the spot for the minimal locations they already had. So, instead, they opted to take another route.

Whether coincidentally or not, *Curse of the Puppet Master* wound up borrowing heavily from the cult eco-horror *Sssssss*, about a nefarious scientist who runs a reptile show and winds up transforming his newest assistant into a snake. Essentially, *Curse* simply swaps the concept of turning a human being into a snake for the concept of being turned into a puppet. While it might not be shot for shot, as DeCoteau certainly shot it in his own moody style, it is without a doubt a very close remake of the earlier film.

However the story came about, it does offer some interesting new things. The concept of a human being turned into a puppet and a doctor running a roadside sideshow would inevitably return to the tone of the first two *Puppet Master* films, something that many fans had been itching for after the characters' heroic turn in the third, fourth and fifth entries. Given the many attempts to make *Puppet Wars*, Full Moon clearly wanted something at that time that was more in line with *Puppet Master III*. But *Curse* wouldn't have the budget for that. It would need to be the most scaled-back, limited *Puppet Master* yet, so a return to full-blown horror made the most sense both from a fan perspective and a production standpoint.

Despite being rushed into production, *Curse of the Puppet Master* yields some strong performances from a few of its lead actors. Starring as the new puppet master would be George Peck, who had first appeared as Rick in the Fulci-influenced *Dawn of the Mummy*. He had appeared in a few other roles in movies like *Agent on Ice* and *Robot in the Family* before his turn as Magrew. Although not taking on the role of Andre Toulon, Peck's performance borrows heavily from both William Hickey and Guy Rolfe. The character is even dressed similarly to Hickey's portrayal especially, which cements the sort of back-to-the-original vibe that *Curse of the Puppet Master* tries to achieve. It works for Magrew as a character. In general, he's one of the more interesting things about the movie and what it adds to the overall mythology.

The first film established the threat of what could happen if the puppets were to ever fall into the wrong hands. But that feature revolved around a villain who had intimately studied Toulon's journals and planned to use them for his own purposes. At this point, especially after the introduction of a level-headed and heroic puppet master in the fourth and fifth entries, the series had begun focusing on the responsibility that comes with the magic, the formula and especially the ownership of the puppets. It's actually an admittedly fascinating take to explore someone who simply stumbled across the puppets, had no idea how they worked and no idea what they were in for and how they were affected because of that. Magrew recognizes the miracle in the same way that Dr. Hess had done in *Puppet Master III*, but he lacks the conscience to know how to use the magic and he doesn't have Toulon to explain it to him or walk him through it. Magrew knows nothing about the puppets or what makes them work, but he knows that he wants to create one exactly like them even if he has no idea how to do it.

Josh Green plays Robert Winsley, better known by his nickname, Tank. Somehow thoughtful and dim-witted in equal doses, Tank is the subject of Magrew's ongoing experiment to turn a human into a living puppet. A gas station attendant with an amazing gift for woodcarving, Tank is taken in by Magrew to work for his roadside oddity museum while also agreeing to carve his living puppet, even though Tank is given no details as to exactly how that is supposed to happen. Green is stiff at times but can be genuinely sympathetic during scenes like the one in which he explains how afraid he is of his own inner rage and where it might come from.

Emily Harrison provides the heart of the film as Jane Magrew, daughter to the sinister doctor who is completely unaware of what her father is doing. She's a genuinely sweet and nice girl next door and her relationship with Tank is surprisingly believable, at least to an extent. Regardless, Harrison anchors the character and gives one of the film's most naturalistic performances. There's also an interesting theme of education that's frequently related back to her character. The movie makes multiple references to the fact that Jane is just home from college on a break and that she is one of the first in her family to attend. Magrew himself never attended, and stresses at one point that the "Doctor" in his title is simply honorary. Tank has never had any education, which is something that is constantly addressed as the character is often referred to as "simple." Even Jane herself is critical of (seemingly) intelligence as a whole when reassuring Tank by telling him that the brain is the most overrated organ. Yet, for her educational background and apparent advantage, Jane is the most oblivious character in the entire movie. Even serving as caretaker for the puppets, even after one of her father's assistants has already gone missing, she never has an inkling of a realization as to what's actually going on.

As the bully, Joey, with his eyes on Jane, DeCoteau cast Michael Guerin, who had first appeared in a small role in Brian Yuzna's *The Dentist*. The same year he appeared in *Curse of the Puppet Master*, Guerin also appeared in Full Moon's *Power Rangers* riff *Kraa! The Sea Monster* as the villainous Lord Doom. Three years later, however, Guerin would actually join the *Power Rangers* franchise for a few episodes of *Time Force*. He returned to work with DeCoteau once more in 2000's *Prison of the Dead*. In some ways, Joey as a character is essentially Cameron 2.0. He's an arrogant, self-serving and pretty irredeemable guy designed to be the character that viewers can't wait to see get picked off. Traveling everywhere with his gang of pseudo-greasers, Joey bears a heavily resemblance to Stephen King antagonists like Ace Merrill of "The Body" and *Stand by Me*, as well as Henry Bowers of *It*. While Joey serves the same basic purpose that Cameron served in *Puppet Master 4* and Dr. Jennings in *Puppet Master 5*, this time it seems to go much further. Joey's not just a self-serving egomaniac and secondary antagonist, he's a genuine psychopath and even a would-be rapist. It's only appropriate that such an extremely unlikable character gets such a memorable end.

Joey's death is one of the more gruesome sequences in the entire franchise by far and is easily the highlight of *Curse of the Puppet Master*. After the attack on Jane that leads to the temporary death of Pinhead, Magrew sends Blade and Tunneler to take out Joey in his own home. There's a bizarre sequence in which Joey seems to imagine himself raping Jane while he's lifting weights. This is cut short when Blade and Tunneler make their move, with Blade slicing open Joey's forehead while Tunneler drills him right between the legs. Even now, this is one of the most talked about sequences in the series' entire history. It's possibly no coincidence that it's also the only death scene in the movie without the use of any stock footage.

Robert Donovan also stars as Sheriff Garvey, a character who seems heavily antagonistic, but it's of course only because he's right about everything. He knows that Magrew is up to something and frustratingly just can't seem to prove it. Donovan had just appeared in the TV series *Click* prior to his turn in *Curse of the Puppet Master*. His character is a classic bad cop, suspicious of Magrew from the first time he steps onto the screen. He understands that the man is up to something but, reasonably, cannot even fathom what it actually is that Magrew is working on. The character is interesting because he's a hero played as a villain. Everything he does is to stop another person from disappearing, but because the viewer is seeing things largely from Magrew's perspective, Garvey comes off as cruel and intimidating. He's killed alongside his partner only moments before he could arrived to save Tank in the nick of time. Garvey's death marks something of a milestone for the series, though. As he's forced down to the floor, he's killed by both Blade and Jester as they take turns carving up his face. This marks the only thing close to a kill for Jester in the entire franchise.

The head scratching ending of *Curse of the Puppet Master* is something that fans have pointed out for years, ever since the movie was first released. As Tank's soul is being transferred into the new puppet, said new puppet is revealed for the first time. Up to this point, there have been multiple scenes of Tank sitting and carving the puppet alone in his studio. All of those scenes clearly show Tank carving something out of wood. In most of those scenes, it appears that he's carving a leg. So it is naturally a surprise for the audience when the puppet is revealed to be legless and made entirely out of metal.

The reason for this ties into the not-so-subtle approach to the character's name. Robert has wound up carving a literal tank, which is now going to be his new body. With a cannon for an arm and a TV screen for a head, Tank the puppet would be the least memorable new puppet that had appeared in the franchise yet. It also marked the first time that the new puppet introduced in a sequel never wound up appearing again.

After seeing the horrific creation that Magrew has accomplished, the puppets turn on him. This very directly references the endings of both *Puppet Master* and *Puppet Master II*. With *Curse* marking a return to the style and tone of the early movies, it was a wise choice to end this new sequel in classic tradition. The puppets turning on their master defined the climaxes of those first two features. This time, Magrew was clearly a villain from the beginning and while it's a little jarring to see the puppets turn so quickly even though they're aware of what he's doing, it's a great homage to the first two entries that's delightful for long-time fans. The highlight of the *Curse* finale is definitely the fact that it truly unleashes Blade and showcases a rage that the puppet hadn't really demonstrated in the series before.

The finale also features the movie's one true standout FX moment. Just before Jane arrives at the house to discover what has happened to Tank, she returns to the spot in the woods where Tank found a burnt, puppet-sized hand. Magrew had been shown burning something in the woods in the opening of the film, but we couldn't see what it was. Finally, just before the end of the movie, Jane finds exactly what it was by revealing a burnt, human/puppet hybrid, the answer to what happened to Magrew's previous assistant Matt and the result of an earlier, failed experiment. A true cable-controlled animatronic, the Matt Puppet is the closest thing to the effects showcased in the earlier features. Creepy, twitching and inhuman, it is the standout effect of a movie that's otherwise heavily reliant on stock footage to get the job done.

Curse of the Puppet Master also marked the first time that an entry in the series would not be scored by Richard Band. The movie takes great care to make sure viewers don't notice that fact, though. Much as many of the puppet sequences resort to stock footage, the *Curse* score is comprised almost entirely of re-used cues from the earlier features, with the main theme playing no less than five times throughout the film. Interestingly enough, that may have proved to be too much for viewers, as it was the last time the original version of the theme would ever appear in the series. Jeff Walton composed the new music, with the most memorable new piece being a love theme for Jane and Tank. Walton had previously scored features like *Dark Universe* and *Jack-O* for Fred Olen Rey and scored *Shrieker* (again for Full Moon and DeCoteau) the same year as *Curse*.

The film was edited by J.R. Bookwalter, who also had a brief cameo in the feature as the voice of Magrew's associate Tommy Burke. Bookwalter was a notable independent filmmaker in his own right, having already helmed the well-regarded no-budget zombie feature *The Dead Next Door*. He was founding Tempe Entertainment at the time, which would partner on many projects with Full Moon, especially as the latter began to once again experience financial troubles. Bookwalter had his work cut out for him, editing not only the feature as a whole but inserting stock footage throughout the film. His biggest achievement, though, was an opening credits montage that quickly recapped everything people had loved about the previous movies and their small-scale stars.

When *Curse of the Puppet Master* finally hit video store shelves, fans of the franchise were divided, to say the least. Many criticized the lack of budget and the re-use of so many puppet FX sequences, while others appreciated the return to form after *Puppet Master 4* and *5* had been such a departure from where the franchise had initially begun.

Quality aside, the feature would spawn an entirely different and altogether more baffling debate: When the hell was the movie set? While the previous entries had had their share of continuity errors, they followed a mostly clear through line in terms of the overall story. But *Curse of the Puppet Master* abandons continuity entirely. It is the first present day sequel not to be set at the Bodega Bay Inn. Not only does it separate itself from the central location of the earlier features, but it is the only *Puppet Master* movie in which the name Andre Toulon is never uttered once. The film also looks as though it is somehow set out of time, it could be modern, but so much of it feels as though it's set in the '50s or early '60s, from the locations to some of the cars. There's a Southern Gothic flair to *Curse of the Puppet Master* that is definitely one of its more interesting qualities, and that touch is almost otherworldly.

Adding to the confusion about when the feature could possibly be set, *Curse of the Puppet Master* reintroduces the character of Leech Woman. Even though she had returned for the prequel, *Puppet Master 4* and *5* honored the decision to kill the character off in *Puppet Master II*. There's no explanation given, no focus on how Leech Woman has returned, she's simply just there. So why just suddenly bring her back in this new sequel? The answer might actually be very simple.

Even though Full Moon wanted to put another film to keep the *Puppet Master* brand alive, *Curse* was made for one reason above all others, and that was the fact that they had an action figure series to come out. The primary function of *Curse of the Puppet Master* was to keep the franchise alive in the public consciousness and to coincide with the release of the action figure series. If Leech Woman had not gotten her own action figure, it is entirely possible that she never would have returned in the films at all. Still, her presence in *Curse* has always raised questions for continuity-conscious fans. The sequel could very well be set after the fifth entry, but Leech Woman's presence is hard to explain. Because of that, many fans assume that *Curse* is set either between *Puppet Master* and *Puppet Master II* or even between the prologue and present-day sequences of the original film. Either of those would be a satisfactory explanation, though one could always simply assume that the puppet was rebuilt or remodeled sometime after the events of *Puppet Master 5*.

Curse of the Puppet Master does have its merits. Even though its structure is lifted from another feature, it is a very clear tonal return to the style of the first two films in the franchise, which was welcoming after the departure of the fourth and fifth entries. It contains some of the franchise's most memorable kills, and that's worth noting because it's no small victory it was able to even pull those off given the amount of time and money DeCoteau had to work with. But the drop in quality was clear in the eyes of most fans. This was a staunch departure from the David Allen days and nothing could really cover up that fact. The use of stock footage was entirely noticeable, and, above all, it was just jarring after what people had been used to in the first five films. Still, *Curse of the Puppet Master* has its admirers. The movie hit video on May 26, 1998, and certainly did its job in reminding viewers of the franchise and its characters. It reminded people that *Puppet Master* was still alive and kicking, that the franchise hadn't gone anywhere and, above all, it helped to sell some toys.

The videocassette was bookended by toy ads. In between, there's a movie that's neither the best nor worst in the series but is easily digestible once one gets over the overall drop in production value. It is certainly the only feature not bogged down by backstory, by the now-lengthy Toulon lore, as the puppet master's name is never even uttered once. Most importantly, thanks to Mark Rappaport's slight reworking of the

David Allen takes a break from filming atop his studio (courtesy Chris Endicott).

David Allen designs, the puppets still look good. They're very recognizable as the characters fans had grown to love and given the absence of David Allen, that's nothing short of a minor miracle. The film hit video with the full title *Curse of the Puppet Master: The Human Experiment*, and the subtitle went a lot further than the original title in explaining what the movie was actually about.

Most importantly, *Puppet Master* had returned after a four-year absence and Full Moon had made it clear that they never wanted to experience that kind of gap again. So the question remained of where to take the franchise next. A direct sequel to *Curse* was out of the question. None of those characters save Jane survived and it's unlikely she would have had the same playful relationship with them after watching them murder her father. The film was also shot in Los Angeles, but all Full Moon movies at that point were gearing up to be shot at the company's new studio in Romania where even this one had technically planned to film. There wasn't really anywhere left to take the puppets in the present day. They had returned to the horror roots of the first two and anything following on the heels of that would just feel like *Curse* rehashed. And there was no way they had the FX power to carry on from the cliffhanger ending of *Puppet Master 5*. This latest sequel, despite its lack of continuity, had focused on a great deal of repetition. Full Moon wanted to avoid that moving forward, and with nowhere left to go in the present, the answer to the future of *Puppet Master* would be found in its distant past. *Puppet Master III* had been a prequel set toward the end of the puppet master's life. To truly take the series to new heights, Full Moon would be going back to the very beginning.

Chapter Ten

Retro Puppet Master

Regardless of the lukewarm reaction toward *Curse of the Puppet Master,* Full Moon still had every intention of moving forward with the franchise. The toys were still selling well and, more than anything else, this was Full Moon's flagship series and they wanted to keep it going. While the rebranded company had much smaller budgets to deal with, that did not stop them from producing more and more content. The year of 1998 had seen the return of both the *Puppet Master* and *Subspecies* franchises and even if they weren't universally beloved, there was an inkling of a return to form for the studio that still excited most fans. With some small-scale favorites like *Shrieker* and *Hideous* under their belts, Full Moon set out to prove that even if they were smaller now, they could still be ambitious. 1999 would be, in many ways, the year that defined that for them. By the end of that year, Full Moon would release two of its most wildly unique and refreshing movies to date, *Blood Dolls* and Dave Parker's *The Dead Hate the Living*. They were taking risks. If a feature could be pulled off on time and on budget, then Charles Band gave the go-ahead to make it.

The late '90s were still booming for Full Moon, though, largely thanks to the action figure series. Full Moon Toys had begun to dominate the specialty collector market, with figures in more and more stores and locations. The toy company had been proven to be a success, with the *Puppet Master* line having proven to be far and away the most successful. The only problem was that, having now covered all of the major characters, it was running out of toys to produce. That was when Full Moon Toys Executive Vice President Rick Phares stumbled onto a new idea, one that would keep the figures going and then some.

"I was in Charlie's office quite often to discuss different concepts and we'd talk about the sales and things like that, and in his office there was some original artwork," says Phares. "He was a big art collector. He always had a really great artist, Lee McLeod, he did a lot of really cool artwork, would just come in and Charlie would say 'Hey, here's the concept, do this' and he would go off and do the artwork, and then the film would be made around that artwork. I used to love going into our storage facility, because there was just hundreds of pieces of artwork that were made for films that were never released. And I remember finding the really old original painting for *Puppet Master,* before *Puppet Master* was even written." Phares is referring to the original concept painting by Lee McLeod, before David Allen Productions designed and created the puppets we all know today.

Phares goes on to say, "That artwork was in his office and at that point we had kind of exhausted all of the mainstream puppets and I was trying to come up with a way to keep the *Puppet Master* line alive, because honestly Radu and Castle Freak sold, but they didn't sell as well as *Puppet Master*. Charlie and I agreed that we needed to figure out a way to keep the line going. I saw that artwork, and at the time there was kind of a resurgence in 'Retro' items. So I said to Charlie, 'Why don't I do figures based on the concept art? A lot of Full Moon fans probably haven't seen this artwork and they would get a kick out of knowing what Tunneler or Blade looked like before the figures they actually know.' So I took that artwork and I went ahead and did the first two figures based on the artwork. And then once that was done, Charlie was looking at it and we were talking about it and he said, 'You know, maybe we should go ahead and make a new *Puppet Master* film and call it *Retro Puppet Master*.'"

With that, they not only had a new toy line, they had the next movie in the franchise. After so many tie-in products, the next *Puppet Master* film would be *based* on a concurrent toy series, and not the other way around. Still, *Retro Puppet Master* only had the characters and designs lined up at this point. There was a lot of work to be done creating the actual film itself. Even though *Retro Puppet Master* would be made for a similar amount as *Curse,* the film would be far more ambitious. Everything about that sequel had been borrowed, in some way or another. But *Retro Puppet Master* would offer viewers a glimpse into the early years of Andre Toulon. This time, they would be going back to the very beginning to explain just how the puppet master came to discover the magic that brought his puppets to life. The inherent problem with doing a prequel, though, is the fact that one had already been done and had been done incredibly well. Fans embraced *Puppet Master III* when it came out and seemed to be embracing it more and more each year. It may have focused on a much older Andre Toulon, but it explained enough about the mythology and how it worked and introduced many new concepts. Fans were definitely hesitant as to whether or not a second prequel would even be warranted.

There had even been a sequence in *Puppet Master II* that, if taken at face value, should have given all the information viewers needed as to when and how Toulon had come across the magic and why he agreed to practice it. Given the franchise's track record for continuity at this point, it was easy to assume that any origin set forth in *Puppet Master II* would be completely undone by the new prequel. Neal Marshall Stevens returned to write the screenplay for the follow-up to *Curse,* which would be a completely different movie in everything from look and style to the overall tone.

After seeing the same puppets throughout six movies with almost no variation in terms of design, it was decided that the franchise could use a little fresh blood, so to speak. With this new installment going back to the very beginning, it would forego the classic puppets people had been used to seeing, relegating them to a wraparound sequence. The main puppets of this entry are essentially rough draft versions of the ones that fans knew and loved. These designs took loose inspiration from the original concept art to the very first *Puppet Master.* And even though they look much closer to those sketches than the puppets in the finished movie, the new Retro Puppets wound up being their own individual characters with their own unique designs.

The job of designing a movie's worth of brand-new (yet old) puppets fell to Jeff Farley and Christopher Bergschneider. Even though this was the seventh, low-budget

Retro Puppet Master magazine ad.

installment in a long-running series, the job came with no shortage of responsibility. This would mark the first time that the puppet effects would not be handled by a member of the original David Allen team. Both men were raised in the world of independent horror, though. Farley had cut his teeth on movies like *Demon Wind* and *Jack-O*, while Bergschneider had served on Kevin Yagher's crew for *Tales from the Crypt*

Chapter Ten. Retro Puppet Master

Presents Demon Knight. By this point, both were practically in-house at Full Moon. Bergschneider had just worked on *Vampire Journals, Kraa! The Sea Monster* and *The Killer Eye.* In 1999, in addition to *Retro Puppet Master,* Farley also provided effects for *Totem, Murdercycle, Witchouse* and *Blood Dolls.* Farley explains how he came to work with Band and Full Moon, saying, "Like many others, I caught Charlie's early films in theaters and somehow, I knew that I'd end up working for him. While John Buechler was running MMI, Empire's effects house, I began to call and interview there and after stints working with James Cummins, Makeup Effects Lab and Lance Anderson, I was hired at MMI during the productions of *Prison* and *The Garbage Pail Kids Movie.* John actually was going to bring me onto *Cellar Dweller,* but due to budget cuts, had to inform me otherwise, though I did end up on the insert crew for that film." He nearly got the chance to work on the franchise at a much earlier point. "I was very familiar with the series," he says. "My friend, Pat Simmons, had done the makeup effects for the first film and by the second film I was called by Dave DeCoteau to bid on the makeup effects, which Dave Barton received and did an amazing job."

In truth, the fact that the puppets would be entirely new made the absence of the David Allen crew much easier to swallow. These would be never-before-seen creations, so it stood to reason that they would need someone new to the franchise to bring them to life, at least on camera. The resulting puppets are very believably the work of a much younger and more inexperienced Toulon. Just about everyone refines their talents throughout their life. Most writers get better as they get older and gain more experience, and it's the same with painters, musicians and certainly puppeteers. The intricately designed puppets of the previous features were created by a much older man. The Retro Puppets, as they are collectively known, are the work of a man who is great at his craft, but still learning. The designs reflect that. There's much more of an emphasis on their wooden features, whereas the earlier puppets could be—and often are—mistaken for dolls. "The designs in this film are almost accurate to the artwork developed for the original. After I sculpted the heads, Chris Bergschneider added lips to Dr. Death, which ended up being a nice touch. Otherwise, they were pretty much the same."

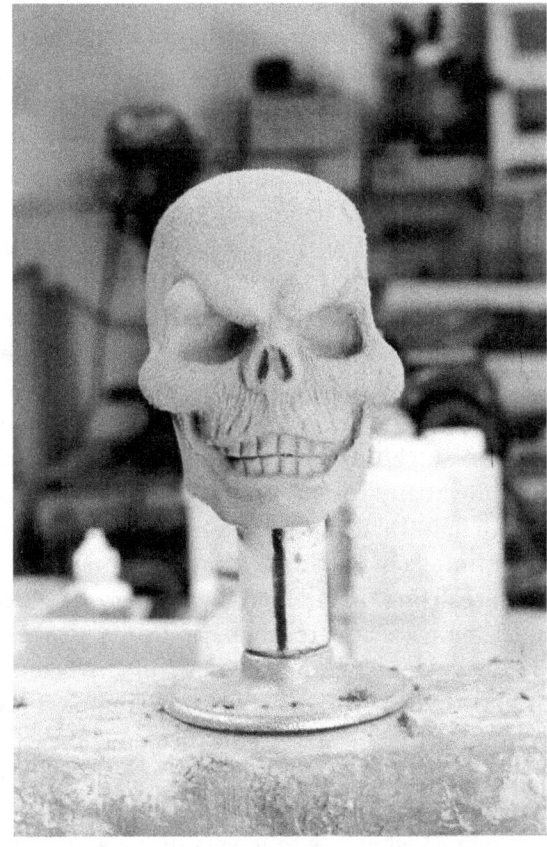

Constructing Dr. Death (courtesy Jeff Farley).

Whereas the original puppets had very distinguished features, each with an individual style, there's something almost uniform about the Retro Puppets. They largely all share similar design elements, with similar clothing and body designs. Retro Pinhead and Retro Six-Shooter even have basically the same face, with Doctor Death being the only real standout. Apart from any of the others, that character in particular feels as though he could easily have been introduced into the main cast of puppets without anyone batting an eye. He is by far the closest stylistically to the original David Allen puppets. The rest of the Retro crew, however, share distinct stylistic similarities. These are great because they bond the characters together as almost a single entity and are also interesting from a story perspective as they represent a certain stylistic period in Toulon's development as an artist.

To tie everything together, the Mark Rappaport puppets from *Curse of the Puppet Master* make an appearance in the opening and closing sequences of *Retro*, which are set sometime after the events of *Puppet Master III*. All of the puppets that appeared in *Curse* are present, with the notable exception of Six-Shooter. It's possible that this was done on purpose, to acknowledge the fact that Six-Shooter disappeared sometime between the events of the third and first movies, though it is far more likely that that puppet was not close enough on hand to fit in the scene in the amount of time that they had to shoot it.

Although *Retro Puppet Master* proved to be different from *Curse* in almost every way, David DeCoteau returned to helm the prequel, making his third round in the franchise. This would be his second prequel but would also allow the director to go to uncharted territory in a series that had already been pretty well mined by this point in time. Ironically, years after getting the job on a *Puppet Master* prequel for being the only one willing to shoot in Romania—only to film on the Universal back lot instead—DeCoteau would actually get to do his Romania-filmed prequel in *Retro Puppet Master*. This time, however, the country would be a stand in for 1902 Paris.

Retro had the job of effectively introducing the mythos and the key characters of the franchise for the very first time. In doing so, it had the opportunity to reference the previous entries while also taking the series to completely unexplored territory. But that did not mean that nothing in *Retro Puppet Master* would be familiar. The film opens in Cairo with the sorcerer Afzel being hunted by the minions of the demon Sutekh. His followers on Earth are devoted to protecting the secrets of the afterlife at any cost. We're dropped into the middle of their attempt on Afzel's life, which fails. He winds up meeting a young Andre Toulon at his theater in Paris, where the minions of Sutekh continue to pursue him. Toulon takes in Afzel and cares for him, realizing that the old man is dying. Sutekh's followers are revealed to be mummies, who are apparently periodically awakened by their master to do his bidding and have done so since he first ruled Ancient Egypt as the evil god Seth. Toulon's friends and co-workers at his small puppet theater are killed when Sutekh's followers follow the trail of Afzel to the theater. During the preceding chaos, Toulon meets Elsa (mistakenly dubbed Ilsa in promotional material), the daughter of a Swiss ambassador. Energetic and willful, she is immediately captivated by the driven Toulon, but is kidnapped when the followers discover Toulon's weakness for her. They take her on board a train, where Toulon and the puppets follow for a third-act confrontation.

Much of that is new and a natural extension of the mythology. But it's all worth pointing out because much of it is also clearly lifted from the original *Puppet Wars: Curse of the Puppet Master* script. Not only does Egypt and overall Egyptian mythology come back into play, but so does the presence of mummies, which were an initial selling point for that first *Puppet Wars* feature. Sutekh can even be seen as a stand-in for Anubis. *Retro Puppet Master* basically trades one Egyptian god for another, stepping around the fact that Anubis was not inherently evil by embracing the literal god of evil instead, and one that had already been firmly established in the *Puppet Master* canon. The entire third act of *Retro,* everything set aboard the train, is heavily—and in some cases, directly—lifted from *Puppet Wars I: Curse of the Puppet Master.* The train footage that was shot for *Puppet Wars* before it was cancelled is actually used in *Retro* as the exterior of the train in which the movie's finale takes place. In some ways, this was as close as Full Moon could come to fulfilling the promise of the *Puppet Wars* prequels on the budgets they had to work with. Much like the first installment of the unmade trilogy, *Retro Puppet Master* also ends with the promise of new adventures. Sadly, those never wound up coming to fruition as well.[1]

Although the train-set finale is entirely lifted from *Puppet Wars,* it showcases the budgetary shortcomings of *Retro Puppet Master* better than anything. Even though the train-bound story was always confined, the original script was bursting with puppet action and never ran out of anything for the little guys to do. In *Retro Puppet Master,* the confinement is much, much clearer. Instead of a full train, there are two cars and a showdown between Toulon, his puppets and the three henchmen of Sutekh. There is barely anything for the new puppets to do. For all of their exciting new features, they don't necessarily get to do anything except slash at sandbags, which can be seen as one of the unfortunate side-effects of the movie's rating. Even in the fight scenes, which are brief, the puppets are barely a presence and the film's finale truly drives that home, perhaps in an unfortunate way. It's not the fault of the director, the FX artists or truly anyone involved with the production. But the puppet sequences in *Retro* shine a strong light on just how different an experience viewers were going to get in the new Full Moon era than they had been used to seeing only five years prior. Scenes like this finale truly drive it home just how rapidly and drastically the series had taken a scaled-back, budgetary turn.

Farley notes the difficulties of pulling off the puppet effects on the time and budget provided: "While you are shooting, especially with the complicated scenes we were setting up, you end up praying that any of it works. Dave (DeCoteau) had infinite trust in us and asked Chris to direct the puppet scenes, which ended up being a good idea as he did a great job. My favorite shot was a tough set-up. Mainly one puppet on the shoulders of another, while nailing on a rune painted on a panel into a wall. Of course, that shot was cut from the US release, though I believe it may be in the European cut. Some of the shots, though, were inserts done at Full Moon's stage in Hollywood a few months after we returned."

With a script and director in place, the hunt was on for the most daunting task: who would play the young Andre Toulon? By this point, things were very different from the early days of the series, where a different actor played the character in each of the first three films. Guy Rolfe had immediately proved himself as the definitive

Retro Puppets in the workshop (courtesy Jeff Farley).

Andre Toulon and, at this point, fans had seen him three times in a row, with the character being entirely absent in *Curse of the Puppet Master*. Even for a series as small as this one, anyone taking on the role of Toulon had big shoes to fill. Given that the casting window was incredibly small, the pressure to find a new Toulon was even greater than it had been in the past.

Dozens of young men auditioned for the part. While the production saw many people, none of them were really living up to what they imagined for the character. Whoever landed the role of Toulon needed to embody traits of dignity, intelligence and, above all, confidence. Nobody seemed to be what they needed, at least until a young actor by the name of Greg Sestero walked in.

Sestero had just moved to LA to pursue his dream of becoming an actor and, so far, things were looking very promising. He had moved to the city with his friend, the enigmatic Tommy Wiseau, who offered him a free place to live. Sestero had landed an agent on his very first day in the city, at the first agency he had walked into. And now here he was, auditioning for the lead in a feature film. His luck was skyrocketing. According to Sestero's memoir, *The Disaster Artist*, the audition itself went fairly standard, the producers offered some simple sides, but asked Sestero if he could audition with an English accent, as that was what they were looking for.[2]

The only trouble was that Sestero couldn't actually do an English accent.

When they asked, nervous that he'd be disqualified for the part, Sestero made sure to mention that even if he couldn't do the English accent they were looking for, he could do other European accents. One of the accents he listed happened to be French. On one level, it's somewhat surprising that the production wasn't looking for French accents to begin with. After all, Andre Toulon is a very French name and a French character in origin, not to mention the fact that the film itself is set in Paris. On the other hand, it's not a surprise by any means, as most of the characters in *Puppet Master III* spoke with English accents, despite that particular entry being set in Berlin. In the film, Sestero is capable if not always confident, with the accent that got him the role often proving to be more distracting than anything else. It's only in the scenes with the puppets that the young Toulon shines as a believably younger version of the character we know and love from the earlier movies, though it's still hard to take him for a young Guy Rolfe. In an interview with *HorrorHound*, Sestero recalled his time on *Retro Puppet Master*. "I auditioned for a few horror movies, like *Jeepers Creepers*, and I'm definitely a fan of them.... I think *Retro Puppet Master* is, in its own way, a pretty good horror movie. I definitely tried harder on this film than, say, what I did in *The Room*. I approached the film respectfully and gave it my all. I had reasonable expectations for *Retro Puppet Master* and wanted to be able to practice my craft. I'm still grateful for that opportunity."[3] Jeff Farley has positive memories of working with Sestero, saying, "Greg and I spent some time having dinner together before the shoot and he never brought Tommy up once, though there was a rumor I heard later that he had shown up in Bucharest. But I believe it was only a rumor. I have met Tommy since and he is a funny and pretty nice guy." Sestero also admitted in the same *HorrorHound* interview to being totally unfamiliar with *Puppet Master* or any Full Moon production prior to getting the role, though he did his homework getting up to speed on the series. "I did some research and watched *Curse of the Puppet Master* and I had also been briefed before filming. I loved indie, quirky horror movies, and the fact that we were shooting the film in Romania made it even more exciting. I was definitely excited to take part in the film, especially as it was my first speaking part ever in a movie, and I was thrown in as the lead." In his book *The Disaster Artist*, Sestero recalled his time on the movie, particularly getting cast. Being a *Star Wars* fan, he elected to play it kind of like Anakin Skywalker, a young hero years before his eventual turn to darkness.[4]

At its heart, *Retro Puppet Master* is the origin of a romance almost as much if not more than it is the origin of the puppets themselves. With that in mind, the other character anchoring this movie would obviously be Elsa, Toulon's future wife. Brigitta Dau was cast as the character, looking much more believably like a young Sarah Douglas than Sestero's young Guy Rolfe. From the moment we're introduced to her, Elsa is a shining light in this movie. She's arguably a more interesting character than even Andre himself. She's curious, adventurous, she wants to see the sights of Paris without being restricted by a guide. It's revealed that Elsa is the daughter of a Swiss ambassador and practically lives like royalty. She starts out not unlike a Disney princess, cooped up inside a lavish but empty lifestyle and dreaming of embarking on some larger, undefined adventure.

Brigitta Dau gives a genuine, realistic and lively performance as Elsa. She might have an English accent for no particular reason, but that was what the production team was looking for during casting, and it's common for most period pieces as well. Her performance is easily one of the best in the movie. Her scenes with Sestero are awkward and fumbling, but in that sense, feel almost perfect for a budding, sweet—if ultimately tragic—romance. There's very little of the eventual Leech Woman in this version of Elsa, but she bears a look and spirit that fit the character well. There's a sweet sincerity to her that makes her so endearing every time she's on the screen, even though she has almost nothing to do with the overall plot until the final few minutes. Dau did very few films after *Retro Puppet Master* which is unfortunate as she's without a doubt one of the best things about it.

The brief scenes with Elsa's father are interesting as they essentially wind up bookending this relationship with extreme political distance. Her father, an ambassador with many men at his disposal and a daughter firmly under his thumb, pays his men to beat the living hell out of Andre solely for the audacity of speaking to Elsa and perhaps keeping her out past her curfew. While he's by no stretch described as a Nazi, there are some very clear parallels between the Ambassador and a figure like Major Kraus. In *Puppet Master III,* it's Kraus and the Nazis targeting the couple and ultimately killing Elsa in the process. The scene in which Toulon gets beaten and left in the snow is a nice inversion of the tragic loss of Elsa in *Puppet Master III*. In that movie, the Nazis were after Toulon, focused on obtaining the formula and shutting down his show that dared to mock the Reich. Elsa was just collateral damage. Here, that is completely reversed. This time, it's Andre that's the collateral damage while the father's resentment seems to perpetually be targeted toward Elsa herself.

Much of the main cast consists of Andre's co-workers at the theater, but unfortunately, there's barely any time to get to know them. The most exciting element about their inclusion is actually getting a chance to see Toulon in his element, to see him as a young theater owner working alongside people who are in it for the art, just as much as he is. There are a few brief interactions with the other puppeteers, but they're just that—brief. Because these characters are just there to provide souls for the Retro Puppets to inhabit, they have much less distinct personalities and are more defined by readily noticeable characteristics. It's an efficient, quick way to get the point across as to who each one is and who matches up with each puppet.

Cyclops, for example, actually has an eye patch before becoming a one-eyed puppet. Dr. Death is the medical expert and impromptu doctor of the group. Blade has hair that matches the puppet's, Drill Sergeant is very neat, strict and orderly, and so on. Each character also operates the puppet they later become, suggesting that their individual puppets were based on their likenesses and personalities even before they died. For characters like Retro Pinhead and Six-Shooter, the puppet personalities don't match up as well with a specific character, putting them in a situation more similar to *Puppet Master III,* where they are characters we get to spend a bit of time with individually before they actually meet their tragic end and find new life as a living puppet. In the case of Retro Pinhead, it's especially interesting, as this is the first time Toulon ever brings a puppet to life and it goes horribly. Even if there's not much time devoted to it, the first-generation Pinhead is actually terrified of what has happened to him and it takes a long time for him to adjust. It's only when the threat arises and Toulon's life is clearly put in danger that Retro Pinhead truly steps up to the plate.

Leading the crew of Sutekh's servants is Stephen Blackehart. Prior to taking on the role of the film's primary villain, Blackehart had begun his acting career in Troma's cult classic *Tromeo & Juliet*. He then appeared in huge blockbuster action vehicles such as *Lethal Weapon 4* and *Rush Hour,* both in 1998. Although the caked-on death makeup is incredibly obvious and the characters don't have much of a chance to prove how menacing they actually are, these servants of Sutekh are nonetheless interesting as they all bear a sleek design reminiscent of *Dark City.* There's a surprising element of continuity to them as well, which is shocking at this point in the series. In *Puppet Master 4,* there's only the briefest glimpse of a human servant of Sutekh, but in those scenes he is dressed exactly as the three villains in this movie are dressed. However, the servants' transformation into the traditional *Puppet Master* trench coat and hat wearing villains were an addition that came very late in the game.

Stephen Blackehart as Sutekh's evil servant (courtesy Jeff Farley).

Jeff Farley confirms that the classic mummy appearance that the servants sport when first awakened were the designs meant to be much more detailed and feature more prominently in the film. He explains, "The mummies were a bit of a disappointment for me as Charlie, if I recall correctly, he told Chris the scene where the mummies rise was cut out and we wouldn't have to worry about it. My plan was to utilize prosthetic masks and have sculpted, exposed ribs and even possibly the suits pre-made. The scene entailed the mummies to rise from the sands and shuffle off into the desert … but Romania suffered the worst snow storm in 50 years. Snow mummies weren't an option. Chris and I ended up taking an afternoon to head into Bucharest to find every roll of gauze bandage we could. Ionel Popa assisted me and we did the best we could with our limited resources to create those characters. There was another small creature the lead mummy (Stephen Blackehart) was to have swallowed before turning into a super mummy. It would have been fun, but alas, it too was cut."

Aside from the return of Guy Rolfe, the biggest draw of the *Retro Puppet Master* cast is Jack Donner, who plays the sorcerer Afzel. He's certainly one of the best actors in the movie and has one of the biggest filmographies to bring to the table, especially as this appearance came only a few years after his blockbuster turn in *The Fifth Element.* Aside from appearing in so many features over the course of decades, Donner was also a co-founder of the Oxford Theater, alongside his fellow actor Lee Delano. Their students have included the likes of Don Johnson, Craig T. Nelson and

Barry Levinson, and Donner was once even an acting teacher to Jack Nicholson. As Afzel, Donner brings a welcome aloofness. He doesn't take a single one of his scenes too seriously, which is refreshingly unexpected for a character who could easily have been weighted down by exposition. The man was a serious actor and he brought his talent to the table, even for a low budget affair like this one. There's not a great amount of dramatic build up to Afzel's decision to bestow his knowledge onto the younger Toulon and, like many things in *Retro,* those scenes pass by rather quickly. But there's still a wry sense of humor that makes his teasing of Toulon enduring to watch.

Looking at Afzel as a teacher, he has to be compared to the Toulon we know from later films, especially with Guy Rolfe already in the same movie as well as the fact that Afzel is the only master of this magic that we ever see prior to Toulon himself. It's pretty clear that Afzel did not use the magic to animate puppets, that's a trademark entirely belonging to Toulon, but whatever he did use it for is ultimately never answered. The only clear application of the magic Afzel uses is in reference to his age, as he notes that he's over 3,000 years old. Ultimately, that's one thing that holds *Retro* back from reaching its full potential in general. It has an ambitious concept and definitely feels as though it is catered to go in the opposite direction from what *Curse of the Puppet Master* had done. It's a new story with new puppets, no stock footage and the idea itself is wholly admirable. But the budgetary realities of Full Moon at the time were still what they were. Any time magic is used, it's a very blurry digital effect that gets the job done, but hardly feels like the spectacle of even the magical blasts the Totem was using in *Puppet Master 5.* The ambition of the script is outmatched by the limited budget, but the attempt at doing something this creative during this period in Full Moon's history is extremely admirable and makes the movie's standout moments worth it.

Drill Sergeant close-up (courtesy Jeff Farley).

Perhaps the most jarring thing about *Retro Puppet Master* is its PG-13 rating. This is an overlooked aspect of the movie, but an important one. *Retro* is the first in the franchise to not be rated R by the MPAA. The most interesting thing about the film's rating, though, is that it would not have been any kind of shock at all had this come right after *Puppet*

Master 5. People often tend to forget that the fourth and fifth entries even are rated R because even if there's an element of gore, they're far tamer than the preceding entries and do feel more explicitly geared toward children. But *Retro* was coming right after the series had essentially reclaimed its R-rated horror roots with *Curse of the Puppet Master*. That entry was far more violent, possibly even the most violent of the series up to that point. The decision to immediately undo this is surprising, but not unexpected. Given that so much of the purpose behind *Curse of the Puppet Master* lied in promoting the toy series, the decision to make the film so explicitly adult-oriented feels at odds with the overall intent of putting together another film in the series in the first place.

The unexpected rating of *Retro Puppet Master* does at least allow it to feel like its own entity, entirely separate from *Curse*. Looking at these two films together, there's very little connective tissue between them, even though they were made only a year apart by the same director. The *Puppet Master* sequels were beginning to feel like anthology movies, abandoning long-running plot threads for more self-contained stories. *Curse of the Puppet Master* is entirely continuity free, its only connection to the other features being the fact that the puppets are in it. *Retro Puppet Master*, on the other hand, relies heavily on continuity, but it is set so far before the other entries that it is certainly able to stand on its own as a solo entry. Ultimately, twenty years after its release, that is still the most endearing thing about it. When *Retro Puppet Master* succeeds, it is because it is a completely different beast. Much of that of course comes down to the fact that this is the first and to date only movie in the saga to focus on an entirely different cast of puppets than the ones we are used to. After six features centered on a varying roster of the same characters, it's jarring to be introduced to an entire crew of new ones. But that's a large part of the movie's charm as well, even if these new puppets don't prove to be as memorable, save perhaps for Dr. Death. In its approach, *Retro Puppet Master* echoes movies like *Halloween III* and *Friday the 13th: A New Beginning*, which dared to take risks and explore new ideas and characters. They were both chastised at the time and both have grown an audience as time has gone on.

It's visually very different from the other films in the series, too. The locations almost make it feel more at home in the *Subspecies* and *Vampire Journals* realm, but those are all things that help it to stand on its own. It does suffer from a pacing that promises a much more action-packed and exciting movie than *Retro Puppet Master* could ever actually be. Because of this, movies like this one and even *Subspecies 4* best represent this period in Full Moon's history. The stories were no less ambitious even if the budgets were drastically reduced. This was a time when Full Moon was trying to make movies exactly the way they had done them in the past. In some ways it was working, in others not so much. In this instance, though, one can look at two movies side by side and see a clear difference between the Full Moon of the Paramount era and the Full Moon of the Kushner-Locke era. *Puppet Master III* and *Retro Puppet Master* are both period piece origin stories that both largely set out to achieve the same things, even if their internal stories are very different, and one of them certainly succeeds more than the other.

Farley confirms that the schedule led to a lot of material not making it into the finished film. "The script was very well written," he says. "There was a lot more action with the puppets that time and budget wouldn't allow. One scene I can recall is the puppets were encased in bricks when a wall collapses on them and they dig themselves out." But he notes that the overall experience was a positive one. "I wish we would have had more budget and time, but there's not much else I would have changed. The cast and crew were wonderful."

Retro Puppet Master hit video in late 1999. For basically the first time in the franchise's history, there wound up being two different cuts of the film. It's not unheard of for the low budget horror world, but it's nonetheless incredibly surprising for the first entry in the series to not be rated R. The U.S. and European cut don't differ in terms of one having more adult content than the other at all. It's simply a little longer and almost everything in the European version seems cut for time. While all DVD and Blu-ray

Cyclops close-up (courtesy Jeff Farley).

releases have featured the U.S. cut, the European cut is available on the *RiffTrax* version of the movie.[5] That, if anything, speaks to the movie's long-term success. More than possibly any other *Puppet Master* movie, *Retro Puppet Master* has found more and more of an audience as time has gone on, thanks largely to its leading actor. Greg Sestero wound up becoming a cult icon for his role in *The Room* as well as his friendship with its director/star/producer/writer Tommy Wiseau, and even detailed some of his time working on *Retro* in his memoir, *The Disaster Artist,* which was of course turned into a phenomenally successful film of its own. There was even a scene shot for that movie but unfortunately cut that even featured the filming of *Retro Puppet Master,* rebuilding the set and the puppets, as well as even featuring a cameo from DeCoteau himself.[6]

Retro Puppet Master, at the very least, has a story that tries to take the mythology seriously and handle the franchise with care. It's no doubt a story that would have been incredibly successful during the Paramount era. All of the elements are there, especially because so many of them are borrowed from the previous *Puppet Wars* scripts, to the point that a showdown with Anubis could have made it into *Retro* had the budget permitted anything that bold. But the budgetary realities, especially in terms of the production time, didn't allow *Retro* to succeed as well as it should have for as ambitious a story as it was trying to tell. Full Moon showed no signs of stopping, though. As soon as the movie hit video stores, the company was already trying to get an even *more* ambitious project off the ground. Following on the heels of *Retro,* Full Moon showed clear signs of wanting to leap headfirst into the long-awaited *Puppet Master vs. Demonic Toys.* Just as they had done with *Retro,* Full Moon announced a toy line ahead of the movie and wanted to make sure fan anticipation was high even before the film's release. But their toy plans were bigger and better. They announced lines for both the puppets and the Demonic Toys. The toys were announced in 2000 with the movie slated to hit in 2001 or 2002, but nothing happened. Full Moon announced the feature, even planned to produce it through their new partnership with Tempe Entertainment. Fans waited. The company's plan to build anticipation had worked.

But a few years passed and still *Puppet Master vs. Demonic Toys* came no closer to happening. *Retro Puppet Master* was the freshest in everyone's mind, but the memory was already beginning to fade. Full Moon had done whatever it could to get new movies out to coincide with the toy series. After a four-year absence, they returned with brand-new back-to-back *Puppet Master* films between *Curse* and *Retro.* But it would ironically be another four years between *Retro Puppet Master* and the franchise's next entry. The new stories, the anthology format of self-contained features under the *Puppet Master* banner hadn't ultimately worked. Even though *Retro* suffered from its budget, Band had an unshakable need to go bigger with the next movie. Fans had waited long enough for *Puppet Master vs. Demonic Toys* and he felt a genuine need to do right by them in making that a reality. But the longer that took to happen, the franchise sat stagnant. Full Moon Toys went out of business, the DVD box set went out of print due to a licensing issue with the older titles. *Puppet Master* seemed to be disappearing. There was a very real question of whether or not the franchise could be sustainable in the new Full Moon era.

The Kushner-Locke years had seen a good deal of success for Full Moon, even resulting in some of their weirdest and most celebrated movies from *Castle Freak* to *Head of the Family* and *Blood Dolls.* But the budgets were getting smaller and smaller all the time. The new model was not self-sustaining and the larger franchises leftover from the Paramount years, like *Puppet Master* and *Subspecies,* were floundering because of it. For a series that had never really left the spotlight, at least in the horror video world, the future was looking dimmer and dimmer. It became more and more apparent that some kind of new entry would need to be made in the interim before *Puppet Master vs. Demonic Toys* could finally see release, if it ever would. And so the standalone, solo story method of *Curse of the Puppet Master* and *Retro Puppet Master* would be abandoned for a sequel that would instead attempt to wield each and every single one of the franchise's many dangling plot threads together, for better or worse.

Chapter Eleven

Puppet Master: The Legacy

By 2003, things were looking grim for the franchise. Only two years before, there had been a licensed Blade Halloween mask, the toys had been widely available with new variants catered to larger retailers, and a DVD box set was released that contained every movie in the series up to that point. Within the span of just over a year, *everything* changed. The toy line had gone under with numerous prospective releases getting completely canned in the process. The DVD box set had gone out of print after a licensing dispute with Paramount. Full Moon had found new life with Kushner-Locke after the end of the Paramount deal, but Kushner-Locke found itself facing bankruptcy by the time *Retro Puppet Master* was even released. Through 2000 and 2001, while licensing deals kept their characters in the public consciousness, Full Moon made a deal with another indie company, Tempe Entertainment, to make movies that were as small if not smaller than anything they had done previously. Most of the Full Moon releases through the late '90s were shot at Band's studio in Romania, but even that had become a problem. By the early 2000s, mainstream Hollywood had discovered Romania and was looking to take advantage of its affordable production costs. This would allow for much more cost-effective Hollywood blockbusters, allowing them to keep costs down in some areas to make up for the massive costs of effects and, generally, the stars and other above the line crew members.

Full Moon's Romanian reign, which had begun with *Subspecies* in 1992, had come to an end. They had to drastically rethink what they were going to do moving forward. Band partnered with J.R. Bookwalter's Tempe Entertainment, a smart move for their new business model if the company hoped to keep the lights on. An editor at Full Moon during the Kushner-Locke era, having edited *Curse of the Puppet Master* and even doing a voice cameo for that movie, Bookwalter had also pioneered micro-budget filmmaking years earlier with his essentially homemade movie *The Dead Next Door*.

A zombie film produced on a budget of just a few thousand dollars, *The Dead Next Door* caught the eyes of genre legend Sam Raimi, who saw much of the indie spirit and passion of his original microbudget *Evil Dead* in the film, helping to produce it and helping it to land distribution. Through the partnership with Tempe, Bookwalter helped Band to discover how to make incredibly cost-effective films right in Full Moon's own backyard. Tempe entered a multi-picture deal with Full Moon to produce films for the company as a sub-contractor, the first of which was 2001's *Horrorvision*. Despite being made on a shoestring budget, that film found a degree of success thanks to the surprisingly confident style of first-time director Danny Draven. The next feature to result from the Tempe deal was *Stitches,* while Band worked on another microbudget partnership with David S. Sterling, beginning with the no-budget evil gladiator movie *Demonicus.* The Tempe Era continued to produce movies like Danny Draven's *Hell Asylum* before trying to recapture some of the old-school Full Moon flavor with Jay Woelfel's *Trancers 6* and a new series of "Stuart Gordon Presents" features in which the iconic director of so many of Full Moon's best served as executive producer.

But the partnership between Tempe and Full Moon grew more and more strenuous as time went on. Full Moon's financial status proved too restrictive for even the micro-budgeted Bookwalter. Producing these movies seemed to appear more like an impossibility each time. Bookwalter's last collaboration with Band would be the killer scorpion movie *Deadly Stingers,* which is also known under the title of *Mega Scorpions.* Shortly after that film and the end of the Full Moon/Tempe partnership, Bookwalter left Los Angeles altogether, moving his production company back to Ohio, where it remains to this day.

Band, meanwhile, was more determined than ever to return to the roots of Full Moon. As he had always stated, he had never been interested in making other people's movies, but in the financial strain of the previous few years, that was exactly what he had wound up doing. Since 1999, Full Moon had stumbled. They had lost the best licensing and merchandising deals in the company's history, they had lost their production offices in Romania, they had lost the rights to distribute the original, classic Paramount-era titles. All Full Moon had left was its name, which in itself had become an iconic staple of the horror video world.

And then it lost that, too.

With the company in serious financial straits, Band entered into a deal with 20th Century–Fox Home Video. In the early '90s, the prospect of a deal with a major studio like that could have been as big as the Paramount era. But here, there was no real money in it. Band would continue to produce micro-budget features through a new partnership company, shedding the Full Moon title completely in favor of a new company: Shadow Entertainment.[1] Shadow, of course, derived its name from the classic pulp antihero of the thirties, even bearing that character's trademark font and logo. The first Shadow release was, appropriately, the last feature to be produced through the Band/Tempe deal, *Deadly Stingers.*

The Shadow Entertainment releases lacked the mainstream movie flair of even 20th Century–Fox's in-house straight-to-video releases. The budget of something like *Deadly Stingers* made *Wrong Turn 2* look like *The Avengers.* Conversations about the financial reality of the home video world of the time led Band to make another loose partnership, one that it was kind of astounding he hadn't thought to make yet. Full Moon had been created to cater to the world of video retailers and at this point in the early 2000s, the video store market was still flourishing. It had undergone changes, of course, the biggest of them being the advent of DVD and the takeover of chains like Hollywood Video and Blockbuster. Band's titles had always been successful rentals. No matter the budget, he knew how to produce features that people would spot on the shelf and immediately want to see. It only made sense for Band to sit down and talk with Blockbuster representatives about the kinds of movies people wanted to see. Those conversations led Band to doing a kind of film that he had long stated he had never wanted to do: a slasher. True, Band had a hand in distributing the cult classic *Intruder,* but he had never made one of his own. Yet the Blockbuster talks revealed that people were still hungry for dry-witted, meta slashers in the vein of *Scream,* even though that franchise had already come to a highly publicized close with the apparent finale of *Scream 3.*

So Band set out to produce his first original slasher movie, *Bleed,* a Shadow Entertainment release. With cameos including Brinke Stevens, Julie Strain and Lloyd Kaufman, *Bleed* hit video in December of 2002. While not officially, it was essentially the result of a conversation with Blockbuster to release the kind of movie that the customers still wanted to see. Because of that, *Bleed,* more than anything else, paved the way for the next entry in the *Puppet Master* saga, as minuscule as it would eventually turn out to be. Given that *Bleed* had wound up being a successful rental, Blockbuster entered a more formal agreement with Band to possibly produce a movie catered to Blockbuster retailers. It turned out that the *Puppet Master* series had always been greatly successful for the chain, so the question turned to whether or not it would be possible to produce a new movie in the series exclusively for Blockbuster.

The prospect of a new *Puppet Master* was exciting. The series was the most popular in Full Moon's library and it had already been four years since the release of *Retro Puppet Master.* But the financial situation made it tough to put together any kind of new story. After losing both the Kushner/Locke and Tempe partnerships, they simply didn't have the money for a new *Puppet Master* film, at least not anything that would approach feature length. That was how the idea began to form of what *Puppet Master: The Legacy* would eventually become.

There was no money to shoot an entire feature's worth of material, no matter how small-scale. But since *Curse of the Puppet Master,* Full Moon had gotten more and more used to the idea of stock footage. Even *Puppet Master 5* had had a lengthy recap sequence bringing people up to date from *Puppet Master 4.* Could it be possible, then, to put together a sequel that would be comprised primarily of stock footage, this time using new footage only to fill in the gaps? The question was more or less redundant. Whether or not the idea could work, it didn't matter. It had to. Shadow Entertainment needed to put together another *Puppet Master* movie and this was all that they had. But that didn't mean that, in spite of the financial situation, Band couldn't attempt to get the most out of this new entry. There was a way to spin this into something the fans would want, something they could even get excited for. Band had heard all of the fan complaints over the years, as so many other filmmakers involved with the series had heard. There were numerous timeline inconsistencies, unresolved plot threads and general continuity errors that had racked up over the course of the previous seven movies.

Puppet Master: The Legacy was never without potential. There was an opportunity here to course correct, to address some of the issues with the timeline, for Full Moon to treat this as a breather and get their affairs in order, clearing up some of the biggest unresolved issues before moving on to the next entry, whatever it would be.

The intention seemed to be just that. Knowing that the movie would consist of

Chapter Eleven. Puppet Master: The Legacy

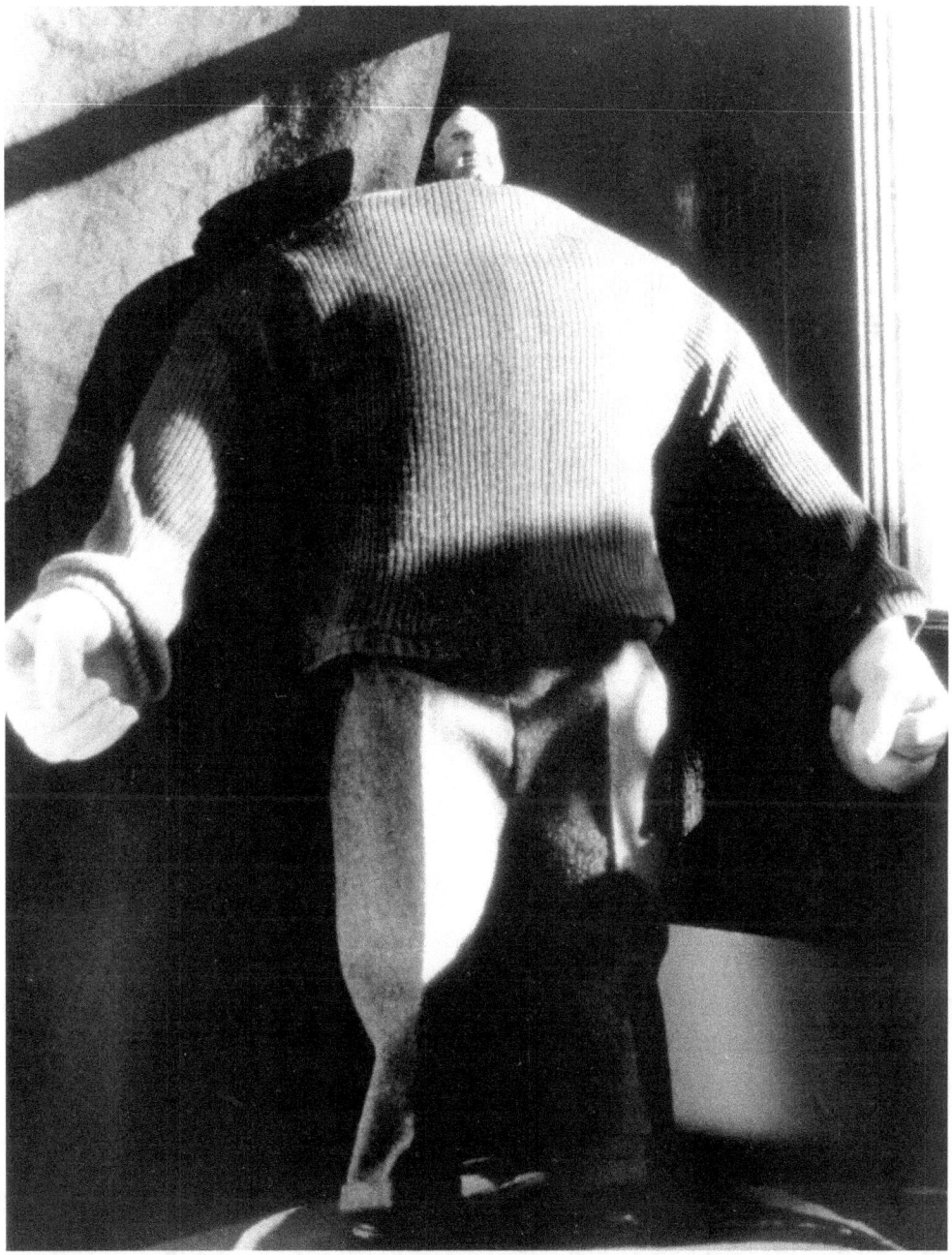

Pinhead on the set of the original (courtesy Chris Endicott).

only a half hour of new material, Band nonetheless wanted to hire someone intimately familiar with the series to write the new scenes. Having cemented so much of the overall mythology in *Puppet Master III*, Courtney Joyner certainly fit the bill. He had long been considered to be a pillar of knowledge when it came to the franchise and had served as a consultant on the defunct *Puppet Wars* scripts, since those picked up directly from the end of the third entry. The intention was to lay the timeline clear for fans so that they could finally put their debates to rest. Joyner even smartly elected to do one exciting thing to get fans interested in *The Legacy* by bringing back a character from *Puppet Master III*. The new puppet master of this new entry would be none other than Peter Hertz, the young assistant of Toulon's in the third movie, now an old man. Though largely confined to one room, the story would even be a long-awaited return to the Bodega Bay Inn. "Yeah, that was just something where Charlie called me up and told me what he wanted to do, we did it in a day," says Joyner. "In fact, if I recall, I was even there while they were filming some of it. That was just something where he either had to deliver a *Puppet Master* title or what have you. The idea was to try and organize the clips into some sort of fashion, I think, so he could then launch from that movie into any direction he wanted to go. That was really all that one was about. That was really like dashing something off so they could have something, it was helping the editors putting the clips together in some fashion to have bridging material between those clips."

Joyner also notes that the clips used in the film were pre-chosen, so that he would have to write his script around specific flashbacks that had already been selected. "As I recall, they were. There were a lot of them and they were trying to get some sort of chronology or reference point for them. That was kind of what I was supposed to supply, which I guess I did. But that's really what that was about. I recall sitting around with the guys while they were putting it all together, but that was basically like a week's job."

Jacob Witkin was cast as the older Hertz. Primarily a television actor, Witkin had been acting since the '70s, with appearances in shows ranging from *Tales of the Unexpected* to *Hammer House of Horror* and several episodes of *Swamp Thing: The Series*. He also appeared in a memorable role as Dr. Diablo in Joe Dante's *Matinee*. *Puppet Master: The Legacy* would be the beginning of a long series of collaborations between Witkin and Band. After starring in this film, Witkin would go on to appear in *Dr. Moreau's House of Pain*, *Evil Bong*, *Gingerdead Man 2*, *Evil Bong 3* and *Evil Bong High-5*.

The story finds Hertz in control of the puppets with no explanation given as to how he came to be reunited with them—which, at this point, was not at all surprising. The puppets appear to be completely inanimate, and though it's referenced that they are running low on serum, it's impossible to tell which ones are even alive or if he's simply speaking to puppets that have run out of fluid and are simply lifeless wood. He is also pursued by a rogue agent named Maclain. A tough-as-nails young woman, Maclain will stop at nothing to get her hands on Toulon's diary and the secret of bringing these puppets to life. She's constantly on the phone with whoever has hired her to get the formula and the diary, but there's some mystery there as to exactly who she's speaking to. She corners Hertz in his workshop and, essentially, forces him to play Toulon's voice recordings, haphazardly introducing the flashbacks that take up the bulk of the running time.

Kate Orsini stars as Maclain, who is also the film's only other character. Prior to being cast in *Legacy*, she had been a steady TV actor and had made brief appearances in shows such as *Grounded for Life*, *Gilmore Girls* and *Buffy the Vampire Slayer*. She brings a surprising amount of intensity to the role of Maclain, who could have been a very interesting character had she been given the chance to really develop. As it stands, there's too much left unrevealed. She's a very intense person, but we never know why, or even what exactly it is that she does. One could argue that this is to preserve a sense of mystery, and perhaps it is, but there's no real reason for it, no feeling of anything intentionally unrevealed except for the obvious question of who she's working for, which is teased often throughout the film's incredibly brief running time.

The use of stock footage attempts to patch up one of the larger series loopholes created by *Retro*, but it only winds up making it that much more noticeable. There's a flashback shown in *Puppet Master II* that seems to sum up in one scene exactly how Andre Toulon came about his magic, and it's completely different from anything that we eventually see in *Retro Puppet Master*. Aware of this mix-up going into the flashbacks, *The Legacy* attempts to cover this gap by blending the two together. Instead of simply accepting *Retro*'s origin as the new canon, the movie keeps the lead-in of Toulon's narration "it all began … with old Afzel, in Cairo." The flashback from *Puppet Master II* does contain an old man and is set in Cairo, so it's technically in keeping with everything Toulon says there, but it only works at all if one hasn't actually seen *Retro Puppet Master*. The flashback is cut down quite a bit, but still includes a Toulon much older than Greg Sestero's incarnation, already married to Elsa, before cutting right into the *Retro Puppet Master* recap, showing those characters looking younger and completely different while also clearly depicting Andre and Elsa meeting for the very first time.

Helping to bridge us from flashback to flashback is the narration of Andre Toulon himself in the form of an old voice recording left for Peter by the puppet master, presumably when he was a boy. Which is also baffling, because the narration extends into the present well beyond Toulon's death. He talks about things he definitely wasn't a part of and speaks of them authoritatively. One could just imagine that it was Toulon as the Decapitron puppet, recounting his story, but that's just as silly as not being given any explanation at all. The truly interesting thing is that, even if it's just a voice-over role, this essentially makes *Puppet Master: The Legacy* the last movie in the franchise to feature Andre Toulon. Even more interesting is that the man who would lend his voice to the puppet master is none other than J.R. Bookwalter. After playing the voice cameo of Tommy Burke in *Curse of the Puppet Master*, this would be Bookwalter's second voice-only role in the series, though this one is a little more expanded than the first.

From *Retro* we naturally move into the flashbacks for *Puppet Master III: Toulon's Revenge*, as this appears at first to be an attempt to put the franchise timeline in order. Because of the decision to make the older Peter Hertz into the protagonist, the *Puppet Master III* sequence is easily the best of the entire film. Not only does it effectively give us the bullet points of that prequel, naturally sacrificing some of the emotion in offering up a condensed version, but it also allows us to see Hertz' reflection on that time in his life. As a child in that film he understood almost nothing of what was going on, at least of the weight of it. Explaining that he was left with relatives in Switzerland when Toulon made the decision to flee to America, Hertz notes that he hated the puppet master for a long time after that, having wanted to serve as his assistant and continue to fight the good fight, even though he eventually came to understand that Toulon knew that his time was up and simply wanted to keep the boy safe.

The marginal effectiveness of this moment, I think, has everything to do with the fact that *Puppet Master III* was the only other film in the franchise that Courtney Joyner had written. Even under the severe time constraints of this script, he knew that movie inside and out because it was a story he had crafted. He understood those characters and those motivations in a clear and well-defined way. This whole sequence is completely believable because of Joyner's total understanding of the material. And it segues nicely into the prologue of the original film and Toulon's suicide.

The most surprising thing about *Puppet Master: The Legacy* is that the shot of Toulon shooting himself is the *only* flashback taken from the original movie. There's no reference to the events of that feature whatsoever. There's not even an extended clip of that prologue sequence, just the moment of Toulon pulling the trigger. It's not only baffling in the sense that one would think the first feature would get the most focus, not the least, but also incredibly blunt. After seeing so much of Toulon's heart and his loss in the *Retro* and *Puppet Master III* flashbacks, we're flung into a quick shot before the story moves onto discussing the events of *Puppet Master II*.

There are a couple of reasons why the original film might not have had any kind of presence of its own. First, there's a matter of runtime, although the film is barely feature length and one would think that some of the sequels could have been condensed before cutting out the events of the original entirely. It's probably more of a structural matter. As discussed in their respective chapters, *Puppet Master* and *Puppet Master II* are almost identical movies from a structural standpoint. If this is truly the story of the puppet master and his legacy, he has much more to do with the second than he does the first, as he's out of that feature after the opening scene. *Puppet Master II* also has way more death sequences to draw from, some of them being among the most memorable of the entire franchise. Still, it's undeniably surprising that the original feature would be almost completely absent from a film that existed only to serve the purpose of honoring the series and tying everything together.

One can't help but wonder if it speaks to the fact that by this point, *Puppet Master* was thought of as a collective entity and not so much as a single cult classic film that spawned several sequels. Franchises have always tended to divide themselves that way. When fans think of Jason, they don't always think of the original *Friday the 13th*. Classic as it is, the same is even true for *A Nightmare on Elm Street;* fans think of Freddy first. Other franchises like *Halloween* and *Texas Chainsaw Massacre* are more concretely defined by the impact of the original feature. And then there are some, like *The Exorcist* and *Jaws* that are almost never thought of as franchises first even though they spawned several sequels. *Puppet Master* was a huge success for Full Moon upon release, but by 2003, even within the series it almost appeared as though it was being forgotten while the second and third movies were becoming more celebrated than ever.

Puppet Master II even has two whole separate flashback sequences devoted to it in the movie, which makes it unique and even jarring, considering the way *The Legacy* is generally structured. The first clip reel for the sequel is focused on condensing

Chapter Eleven. Puppet Master: The Legacy 147

Jester, with rarely glimpsed hat, on the set of the original (courtesy Chris Endicott).

the film's kills, making it just a sizzle reel for puppet carnage. The second flashback compilation, coming toward the end of the film, is devoted much more to the undead Toulon of *Puppet Master II* and is focused on breaking down the major plot points. This is an interesting way to go about the flashbacks in a movie that is typically much more straightforward in its use of stock footage. It's possible that the *Puppet Master II* segment was simply too long at first and had to be broken down into two pieces.

Narratively, bringing it back around to Toulon's evil actions in *Puppet Master II* suggests that the film is closing on the reminder that while Toulon did a lot of good things, he did some terrible things as well, with *Puppet Master II* being the most extreme example of them.

While *Puppet Master* would only be given a three second clip, one sequel is actually entirely absent from *The Legacy*—sort of. There is no footage from *Puppet Master 5* in the movie whatsoever, electing to instead use the recap of *Puppet Master 4* which had been used at the beginning of 5. This makes a lot of practical sense as it was already at their disposal. They didn't have to cut anything new. With both *4* and *5* essentially being one long movie, it's not surprising to sacrifice one for the other when—by using this pre-cut flashback—they would not need to edit together any new footage from either. Toulon's intro to this segment is completely baffling. First and foremost, he gets the new puppet master's name wrong, calling him Rick Gordon, no doubt an accidental splicing of the character's name, Rick Myers, with the actor's name, Gordon Currie. Toulon then introduces the *Puppet Master 4* flashback as though he selected Rick to carry on his legacy and handed the secrets of his formula down to him, when the flashback itself shows this is not the case, explicitly rehashing how Rick discovered the puppets and the formula accidentally. Given that this sequence is narrated by Rick himself, it's jarring to hear in context after the voiceover from Toulon that introduces it. It seems as though it would have been easier simply for Peter to have announced that he had obtained a recording left by Rick inside the hotel, as that would have provided an easy explanation for why the sequence is narrated.

Without a doubt, though, the worst offender of the *Puppet Master 4* sequence is Maclain's casual reveal that she killed Rick off screen just before the movie began. Even though the puppets themselves are the stars, there are certain characters in the franchise that have been strong enough for fans to latch onto. Rick was absolutely one of those characters. Young fans especially took to a cool, hip new puppet master who basically felt like a big kid. Gordon Currie brought a refreshing energy to the role as well. Even if he never appeared again, most fans would probably agree that the character really didn't deserve to go out like that. The moment was likely there to be a shock for longtime fans of the series, but it's so quick that there's certainly no time to feel the gravity of it. Fans at the time often talked about the possibility of Rick returning to the series one day, given how open-ended the end of *Puppet Master 5* had been. There was never any reason given as to why Rick had given the puppets up, when he seemed to accept the responsibility of taking them on long term. *The Legacy* could easily have conceived of some explanation, however haphazard, for Rick's absence in the later sequels instead of letting those questions go unanswered in addition to adding the reveal of his death.

After the recap of *Puppet Master 4,* the film then moves onto recapping *Curse of the Puppet Master* in what might be one of its better sequences. Hertz and Maclain talk about the ramifications of Toulon's formula and what could happen if it fell into the wrong hands, if it were to be used by misguided people who didn't understand its power or how to harness it. That's a fairly seamless introduction into the events of *Curse* and allows one to look at that movie as an anecdote about what happens when

Chapter Eleven. Puppet Master: The Legacy

people who don't understand this magic seek to embrace or recreate it. It's also *Curse* condensed down to its best moments, focusing heavily on Magrew's unraveling mental state as he seeks to make a living puppet by any means necessary, as well as the intense kill sequences.

The downside to the *Curse* flashback sequence is that, in a movie comprised mostly of stock footage, the stock shots in this sequel are more noticeable than ever. Some fans do miss them while watching *Curse* the first time around, but there's no way to miss those moments when watching them at the same time you're watching flashbacks to all of the other movies that this one borrowed its puppet shots from. In some ways, this was the epitome of the fan complaints against late-era Full Moon, almost bordering on self-parody. After the criticisms that had already been launched against *Curse,* here was *Puppet Master: The Legacy* delivering stock footage *within* stock footage.

From there, *Legacy* launches into its final flashback, recapping the ending of *Puppet Master II.* Because this is a film that in every other aspect attempts to go chronologically, some fans have actually wondered if the final flashback here was meant to imply that the other movies somehow happen during the events of *Puppet Master II,* but that is definitely not the case. One of the best things about *Puppet Master II* is that it is self-contained and clearly takes place over the span of just a few days. The way the finale of that sequel is used also seems to explain why Toulon was evil in that movie—something fans have debated for decades, at this point—by simply suggesting that perhaps he had always been evil and that his good deeds were a kind of façade. Which effectively negates the entire series, from the original movie's opening to the puppet master's heroic and tragic arcs throughout *Retro Puppet Master* and *Puppet Master III.* That is especially ironic for a sequel with the sole mission statement of tying the whole series together.

As this unfolds, Hertz himself seems to turn to the dark side in an instant, declaring that Maclain would never get her hands on the puppets—which he refers to unceremoniously as "creatures"—because they belong to him. It's a rabid obsessiveness that he must have been holding back very well throughout the earlier scenes, as it truly comes out of nowhere.

Finally the puppets spring to life, so to speak. Pinhead throws a wrench at Maclain to know her to the floor and Blade raises his knife at her in a threatening way. While the puppets are shown on the desk throughout the entirety of *Legacy*'s non flashback scenes, these are the only times that any of them move, and these are the only movements we get from them. Jeff Farley and Christopher Bergschneider returned from *Retro Puppet Master* to provide these very minimal puppet effects, once again using the puppets designed by Mark Rappaport's for the previous two movies. Here, they have even less to do than they had in *Retro*'s wraparound sequence. There, each puppet was shown slightly moving its arms within the trunk. Here, we're still reduced to arm movement, but its only coming from two puppets. Still, this marks an interesting moment in Farley's *Puppet Master* career, as it is the only film in which he provides the puppet FX without drastically redesigning the puppets from the ground up. In *Retro,* he designed the brand-new first generation puppets and in *Puppet Master vs. Demonic Toys,* he would redesign both sets of characters for the Sci-Fi Channel, who wished to take things in a newer and fresher direction. Farley notes that on *The Legacy* he had "the shortest amount of time we could possibly have. One day. The wraparound was shot in two days."

Still, despite the effects being put together in only a day, Farley remembers the minimal puppet work that *Legacy* required. "Since the puppets were the display copies from Charlie's office and the same ones utilized in *Retro*," says Farley, "We just wiggled them in front of the camera, so I can't recall much more than how heavy they were. What I do recall is my car broke down and my stepmother visiting the set and gushing on how handsome Charlie was. I had never seen him blush before."

In the final moments of *Puppet Master: The Legacy,* Hertz turns the gun on Maclain who reveals as she is dying that she was sent by the "ones Toulon left behind, human souls trapped in wooden bodies." After all, she was speaking to a mysterious benefactor at the beginning and noted that she had been sent to receive the formula by somebody. There's at least some degree of clever misdirect, as virtually every movie has involved someone trying to use the formula for their own nefarious means. One immediately assumes that that's what Maclain is up to, even though she never really makes it clear one way or the other. The truth, it turns out, is that she wants to destroy the formula and the puppets permanently. It's actually a strong twist at face value.

There are many motivations that her character could have for wanting to destroy the formula, though, and *The Legacy* definitely settles on the most head-scratching of all of them. While Maclain could easily have been someone who's loved ones had been killed by the puppets in the past, or someone who sought to recreate the formula only for it to blow up in her face, Maclain is instead revealed to be working for what we can basically assume to be the surviving Retro Puppets. Ending on the prospect of a potential fight between the puppets and the Retro puppets is no doubt something that got fans excited at the time, but it's also terribly confusing, especially when one considers the scenes of Maclain speaking to her employers on the phone—not to mention how they planned on paying her. Even the crossover potential is immediately negated, though.

Considering the fact that everyone involved in the movie had been listed in the opening credits, *Puppet Master: The Legacy* does not actually have ending credits. Instead, it ends with a message thanking the casts and crews of every *Puppet Master* feature for their hard work over the years. It's a message that reads wholeheartedly like an epitaph and given Full Moon's situation at the time, one has to wonder if that was intentional. For fans, it definitely raised concern, with some websites even posting R.I.P. images for their beloved franchise at the time. This was as low as it had ever gotten, financially. People were already nervous that the franchise had become so scaled-back and this final "thank you" message sounded very much like a goodbye.

After all, while Full Moon had been so dead set on promising *Puppet Master vs. Demonic Toys,* fans had no way of knowing if the crossover would ever come to pass. The budgets were lower than ever. *Puppet Master: The Legacy* hardly made a dent in rental figures, given that it was a blockbuster exclusive and the fact that it contained so little footage that fans hadn't already seen before. It's a tough sell when the other *Puppet Master* movies are right there beside it on the shelf, immediately available for rent. Ultimately, even though *The Legacy* might be the least exciting entry in the franchise, it does have a few interesting ideas. There are moments that are hard not to like, even if they come from other movies. And if one has gone some time without seeing the series and needs a short refresher course, *The Legacy* is a totally serviceable solution.

While other entries in the series had left the future uncertain, *Puppet Master: The Legacy* managed to take things one step further. There was no concrete word on *Puppet Master vs. Demonic Toys,* nor was there news of any other sequel or spinoff in development. Given the sheer smallness of it, not to mention its downbeat ending message and the fact that the movie did not even feature the classic Full Moon logo in favor of the new Shadow Entertainment logo, fans were beyond concerned for the fate of the series. It seemed that *Puppet Master* had given up its attempts to stay afloat after the end of the Paramount deal and the Kushner/Locke bankruptcy. Here, fans found themselves in a place beyond worry and doubt, and merely of acceptance. Acceptance that the merchandising boom of the few previous years would not return, acceptance that the series would never be what it was, and overall acceptance of its loss. After that message solemnly thanking all those who had supported the series, fans could do nothing but accept the apparent reality that their beloved franchise was dead, as was Full Moon along with it.

Chapter Twelve

Puppet Master vs. Demonic Toys

Puppet Master vs. Demonic Toys began with a piece of promotional art in 1992, used in both a calendar and to tease the upcoming movie during the *Video Zone* of *Seedpeople*.[1] The artwork depicted Blade, Pinhead, Six-Shooter and Torch going up against evil toys by the names of Jack Attack, Baby Oopsy and Robot. In the classic font, the artwork promised this as *Puppet Master IV*. But the two franchises had been entwined even before that. In *Demonic Toys*, during the scenes in the security office, *Puppet Master II* could be seen constantly playing on the television. This served as a frequent reminder to the fact that Full Moon was leaning into creating another killer toy franchise so soon after *Puppet Master*. It's true that Band has always been known for films about various sorts of toys coming to life, but after *Puppet Master* Full Moon had truly started branching off into completely different areas. *Shadowzone, Meridian, Crash and Burn* and *Subspecies* were not only all movies with a different focus, but all movies that even felt like they belonged to different genres. That was the point, at the time: to create a wide and varied brand of features that all still felt like they were crafted by the same hands. *Demonic Toys* was the first to really feel like it was retreading old ground for the studio. Originally titled *Dangerous Toys,* the film was promised to be one of the first post–*Puppet Master* features from the studio, though it didn't actually see release until 1992.[2]

Demonic Toys' biggest claim to fame might be its screenwriter, David S. Goyer. Kicking off his career writing this film as well as *Arcade* for Full Moon, Goyer has gone on to become a major Hollywood talent. He has written numerous hit films such as the *Blade* trilogy, *Dark City, Man of Steel, Batman v. Superman,* but his biggest claim to fame will likely always be co-writing the *Dark Knight* trilogy. There's not much of that future A-list writing talent present in the *Demonic Toys* script, which he had only days to write. There are a few moments, however, in which those character quirks come through, especially with the in-over-his-head fried chicken delivery man. Perhaps most ironically, *Puppet Master II*'s Jeff Celantano (Lance) makes an appearance in the film.

Compared to earlier Full Moon features, especially the original *Puppet Master, Demonic Toys* is almost aggressively simple. It's about a group of people trapped in an abandoned toy warehouse with toys that have sprung to life to obey the will of their demonic master, who is trying to be reborn in the flesh through the unborn child of our heroine, Judith. While there are a few stop-motion shots, the effects are much more scaled back. For the most part, these are hand puppets, though it's easy to overlook that thanks to the impressive creature designs by the late John Carl Buechler. While each toy has its own personality, the highlight of this film would have to be the rabid teddy bear, which grows in size the more it feeds—something previously seen in *Critters,* though abandoned for its sequels—until it becomes a monstrous, man-sized bear monster. In fact, that in and of itself harkens back to a similar scene in Stuart Gordon's *Dolls.*

Instead of a proper sequel, Full Moon delivered *Dollman vs. Demonic Toys* in 1993. When the planned *Puppet Master* crossover had been scrapped, the evil figurines found themselves facing off against another contender of their own size, space cop Brick Bardo. The shortest film of the Paramount era, *Dollman vs. Demonic Toys* clocks in at only 65 minutes including credits and features almost fifteen minutes of footage recapping not only *Dollman* and *Demonic Toys,* but *Bad Channels* as well as the movie adds a character from that as the Dollman's love interest. It's interesting that Full Moon at least thought of a *Puppet Master* crossover before ever even entertaining the idea of a solo sequel for the characters. With one true sequel and two versus movies, *Demonic Toys* is a franchise defined by crossovers, which few if any other horror series could say.

Considering the fact that Charles Band, from the very first *Video Zone* segment, mentioned the idea of his films being like comic book characters that would interact and crossover at various points, it almost seems as though the *Demonic Toys* could have been designed as nemeses of sorts for the Toulon puppets.[3] Whatever the case, it was actually smart of Full Moon to immediately attempt to bring the two groups of toys together in a crossover piece. Instead of simply noticing the similarities or blaming one for aping the other, fans looked at *Puppet Master* and *Demonic Toys* as somewhat entwined right from the very beginning. It was a promise fans were made aware of early on, but unfortunately it would take years to actually *deliver* on that promise.

After *Dollman vs. Demonic Toys,* the toys sat dormant for several years while the *Puppet Master* franchise continued to flourish, at least by Full Moon standards. After *Retro Puppet Master,* while Full Moon Toys was in the height of its retail accessibility, the company recognized that there was no better time to make good on its promise of a new at combining the characters. After all, the premise of two groups of toys colliding with one another is inherently perfect material for an action figure series. And both the original *Puppet Master* and *Retro Puppet Master* toy lines were wrapping up by that point. *Puppet Master vs. Demonic Toys* would be a win-win in almost every respect. It would deliver on a crossover that had been promised a decade earlier, it would keep the franchise running and would allow the toy line to continue.

Full Moon Toys kicked off the *Puppet Master vs. Demonic Toys* promotional train in 2000, showing off not only prototypes of the new puppet and toy figures, but concept art of the new drastically redesigned puppets. While the Cyber Puppets were initially created as a separate toy line, they were used in all of the promotion that Full Moon did for *Puppet Master vs. Demonic Toys* at the time. And even though the film would not be seen for another few years, that was quite a bit. In 1999, Full Moon even ran a contest in *Tomart's Action Figure Digest* for a lucky fan to win a walk on role in *Puppet Master vs. Demonic Toys,* which (according to the contest) Full Moon had initially planned to shoot in Los Angeles that year.[4] It's hard to say if, after Band

Puppet Master vs. Demonic Toys Magazine contest ad.

saw their designs, the Cyber Puppets had always been meant to appear in the movie itself. But it would certainly track, given the origins of *Retro Puppet Master*. From a toy marketing standpoint, the new designs made sense, as they had already not only done figures of all the classic puppets, but dozens of variants of those puppets at all. If they had exhausted the old designs and looked forward to some kind of change, that would make sense as it was similar to what had been done with *Retro Puppet Master*.

There were the characters everyone knew and loved, just presented in a very different way. Of course it's worth pointing out that these designs were being promoted in magazines at the same time that Jason Voorhees was receiving an almost identical treatment in the tenth *Friday the 13th* entry, *Jason X*.

The Kushner/Locke deal had ended and Full Moon was establishing its partnership with Tempe Entertainment. This partnership would initially have a major influence on *Puppet Master vs. Demonic Toys,* as it's been long-rumored that Band courted Tempe head J.R. Bookwalter to direct the feature. By the time they were promoting the potential toy series, Full Moon had a script in place and to their credit, clearly planned to shoot the installment as their next movie. Not too much is known about the draft or drafts of the script at this time. The most persistent rumor is that in this incarnation, the film would have supposedly seen the puppets being bought on eBay and stored in a warehouse that also housed the evil Demonic Toys, naturally resulting in a fight between the two. Traci Lords, who had gotten her start in the adult entertainment industry before moving on to a lucrative and successful career in film and television, was rumored to be cast as the new puppet master. This is worth noting if true, as it would have made for the first female puppet master in the franchise's history, something we would only finally see in 2020's *Blade: The Iron Cross*. According to Jeff Farley, "I knew the project had been around awhile, but the first script I had seen was in 2002, while we were shooting the Sci-Fi Channel show with William Shatner. The final version we received in 2004 had some changes. The character of Bael, though, was not present until we were in pre-production. Chris [Bergschneider] ended up playing the part to his usual high standards. I thought he did a very good job in the role."

Ultimately, though, *Puppet Master vs. Demonic Toys* simply wasn't in the cards for Full Moon at the time. The studio barely had the budget for a solo *Puppet Master* movie, let alone an ambitious crossover. There really wasn't a way to feasibly pull it off, as Bookwalter was quick to point out to Band. As much as they wanted to bring this together for the sake of the fans, Full Moon was far from financially stable enough to make it happen on their own. Band recognized this, leading him to consider something he had never had to attempt in any previous film: a co-production with another major company.

By the early 2000s, the Sci-Fi Channel had begun producing its own movies on a weekly basis. They showed many Full Moon efforts, especially the *Puppet Master* films, regularly. It only made sense that if Full Moon needed to establish a partnership that they would go to Sci-Fi first. After all, especially in the beginning, those branded Sci-Fi Originals were incredibly similar to the features that Full Moon had been making for over a decade, on budgets that better resembled the early *Puppet Master* entries. With Band's noted pride in his universe of in-house entertainment, it was unheard of for him to let other people handle characters that he had played such a significant part in creating. But Band, to his credit, recognized that this was a movie that fans were dying to see and that his company was not in a remotely proper state to pull it off on their own. The decision was made solely for the sake of the fans, in the hopes that they would get the movie they had always wanted to see. In fact, at the point in the early 2000s when *Puppet Master vs. Demonic Toys* began its initial development, Full Moon was producing a television series for the network. *William Shatner's Full Moon Fright Night* centered on Shatner acting as a classic horror host, showing and riffing on some of Full Moon's more recent features at the time, as well as interviewing celebrity guests such as Roger Corman and Stan Lee.

The partnership, from the beginning, was fraught with problems. Sci-Fi had no problem putting up their half of the money, but Full Moon struggled to present theirs. While they continued to not be able to pay the agreed amount, the film sat dormant without entering production. It had been big of Band to recognize the need for help and attempt a co-production with the Sci-Fi Channel, but at this point a harsher reality was setting in, as it became clear that Full Moon didn't even have the money for that. If *Puppet Master vs. Demonic Toys* was going to happen, Band would have to sell Sci-Fi the film outright and abandon creative control. It was something he had never done in Full Moon's history and especially never something that had been considered for the company's flagship franchise.

But the fans had been dying to see this movie.

And so a new deal was made. The Sci-Fi Channel was given the go-ahead to produce *Puppet Master vs. Demonic Toys* on their own, without the involvement of Full Moon. In some ways, this was a tragic progression from the previous year's *Puppet Master: The Legacy*. That film had been the first not to feature the Full Moon logo, paving the way for the next entry not to feature the involvement of the company whatsoever. Band sold off his involvement and gave Sci-Fi free reign to produce and distribute the film on their own.

Even still, while *Puppet Master vs. Demonic Toys* is not a Full Moon production, it's really only not a Full Moon production on the most technical level. During the Tempe era, *Puppet Master vs. Demonic Toys* underwent a few rewrites, but with new management—so to speak—the story would need to be rewritten from the ground up. Luckily, the job went to someone intimately familiar with the franchise. C. Courtney Joyner was brought back to write a very different *Puppet Master* story than he had written in the past. Having given the series its most emotionally strong entry in *Puppet Master III: Toulon's Revenge*, Joyner took an extremely different direction with *Puppet Master vs. Demonic Toys*. This time, it was decided that the movie should be—for the most part—an irreverent family comedy. Given the almost family-friendly direction of *Puppet Master 4, 5* and *Retro Puppet Master* it hardly came as a shock, especially considering the fact that this new movie would first broadcast on television, which would have to censor any gore or adult language if they had bothered to add it anyway.

Joyner reflects on how he came to write the film: "Now I had been around a little bit on the *Dollman vs. Demonic Toys* thing, just because I was there and I think I'm listed as one of the producers or something, I can't remember. But the idea behind *Puppet Master vs. Demonic Toys*, the idea had been around forever. Charlie had announced it many times. But I never saw like a treatment or anything as I recall. And when the whole thing went over to Jeff Franklin and the Sci-Fi Channel, it was kind of a situation of where it had been separated from Full Moon and the idea, at least as it was approached to me, was that it was going to be the pilot to a television show. I wrote it, and they really wanted it to be very much in the tone of something like *Gremlins*."

For those who had been anticipating the movie for years, the decision to push the

Chapter Twelve. Puppet Master vs. Demonic Toys

film in a more overtly comedic direction was jarring, as was the decision to set the movie around Christmas. But these ideas by themselves showed enormous potential. With a comedic tone and Christmas setting, the movie had the prospect of being the *Gremlins* of the two franchises. A full-blown over-the-top creature comedy, pushing the brand back toward the Empire heyday of *Ghoulies*—which had also been a PG-13 franchise, for the most part. This new story was designed to center on a father and daughter who come into possession of the puppets. The father, Robert Toulon, is the great grand-nephew of Andre Toulon. He's a sort of absent-minded professor figure, a bumbling mad scientist played largely for comedic effect.

The plot as a whole revolves around the evil Sharpe Toys, led

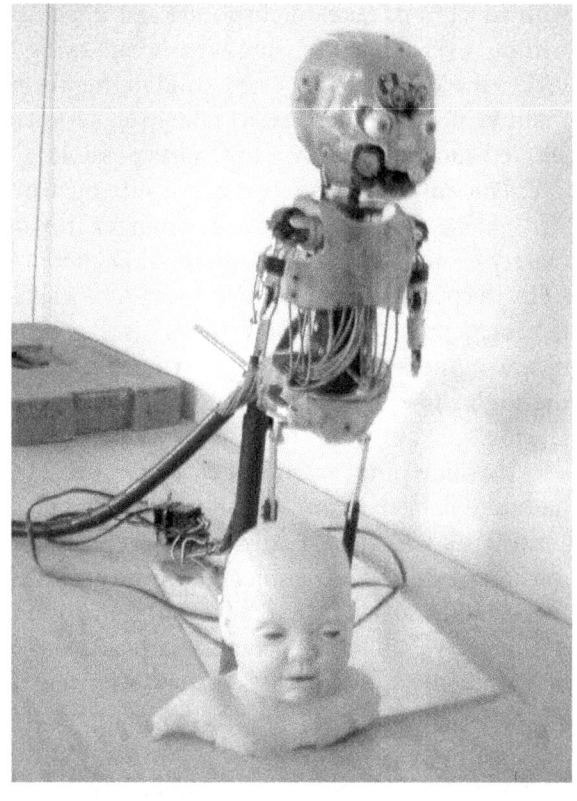

Constructing Baby Oopsy (courtesy Jeff Farley).

by Erica Sharpe. At some point in time, she came into the possession of the Demonic Toys, as an apparent part of a deal her father—the previous head of the company—had made with the demon Bael. A completely evil woman down to her core without an ounce of humanity to her, Sharpe wanted toys that would do her bidding and enact her will. But the Demonic Toys turned out to be terrible at their jobs, killing with no rhyme or reason and engaging in all sorts of antics simply for their own amusement. Sharpe wants toys that will do what she tells them to do, that are disciplined, so she sets her eyes on the Toulon puppets. This is the reason for the puppets and the Demonic Toys co-existing in the same feature, but it's almost irrelevant to the plot as a whole. Sharpe's overall plan is to mass-produce the Demonic Toys as the much more appealingly renamed "Christmas Pals." With a huge ad campaign including commercials and in-store appearances, Sharpe distributes the Christmas Pals worldwide with the intention of killing every child in the world by awakening the toys when the children watch the commercial on Christmas morning. While *Curse of the Puppet Master* gets a great deal of heat for its similarities to *Sssssss*, it's important to point out just how similar this plot is to that of *Halloween III: Season of the Witch*.

The major difference between the two, of course, lies in tone. *Halloween III* is a much darker movie, more straightforward in its take on consumerism, allowing for a bleak and uncomfortable ending, one that offers no real answers as to whether or not the larger threat is even stopped. *Puppet Master vs. Demonic Toys* is much more whimsical in its take on corporate satire, painting with a cartoonishly broad brush without ever really focusing on any one thing in specific. As silly as it is, it almost makes the idea of killing every child in the world somewhat easier to digest, knowing that the movie simply doesn't take itself seriously and that every aspect of it is exaggerated and played as over the top as possible.

The ending is much more uplifting when compared to that of *Halloween III*. Instead of an ambiguous cliffhanger in which the world's children may legitimately have died, *Puppet Master vs. Demonic Toys* leaves no room for interpretation. The puppets have a clean victory and walk away as the winners, with the human heroes merrily singing "Jingle Bells" as they head off to Christmas dinner. It's a good, old-fashioned (perhaps *extremely* old-fashioned, even) story of good vs. evil. This highlights one of the common problems of crossover films that *Puppet Master vs. Demonic Toys* manages to avoid: who are we supposed to root for?

It's something that's plagued every film of this type. Usually, the filmmakers have had to look deep within the franchises and characters to find some kind of answer, sometimes without actually finding one at all. In *Freddy vs. Jason,* both men have massacred dozens of people, but in the grand scheme of things Jason is a lesser evil than Freddy, so he is given more of the empathetic focus. Conversely, in *Frankenstein Meets the Wolf Man,* both creatures are deeply sympathetic, but Larry Talbot becomes our protagonist, so the Frankenstein Monster shifts into the villain role by default. In *Alien vs. Predator,* both species massacre much of the principal cast, but the Predators are more conscious and cognizant and thus more capable of teaming up with a human survivor if necessary. 2003's *Underworld,* depicting a race war between vampires and werewolves, might have the most inspired twist on this trope, as it points out that history is written by the victors. After being told for most of the feature that vampires are heroes and werewolves are evil, it turns out that the racist and aristocratic vampires were the ones who had forced werewolves into slavery and led to a just (if ultimately failed) revolution.

Puppet Master vs. Demonic Toys is one of the few "versus" movies to provide an easily digestible answer. For years, at this point, the puppets had been well established as heroes. They had fought alongside humans and saved human lives in *Puppet Master III, 4, 5* and *Retro Puppet Master.* The Demonic Toys, on the other hand, had never been depicted as anything but evil. Their horrific nature is right there in their name. It's easy to see which group the audience is supposed to root for from the moment the film begins. At the same time, that eliminates part of the fun of these movies. *Freddy vs. Jason* was a huge blockbuster not just because it combined the characters, but because so many fans fell into different camps as to which slasher was their favorite. With *Puppet Master vs. Demonic Toys,* there's no wiggle room on who to root for, which fizzles out some of the energy and fun that stems from making a crossover movie in the first place. It might not have been anything to worry about, though, because even though *Demonic Toys* had its fans, the number of *Puppet Master* fans certainly eclipsed them.

With a story in place, another major Full Moon alumni came aboard to direct the project, no doubt putting fans at ease who had been worried about the movie's departure from the franchise's parent company: Ted Nicolau, who had directed the four *Subspecies* films and *Vampire Journals* for Full Moon, as well as the Empire cult classic *Terrorvision*. One of Full Moon's regular rotating directors during the Paramount era, it was somewhat shocking that Nicolau had actually gone this long without directing a *Puppet Master* movie. With his involvement and Joyner's script, fans were given every reason to rest easy when worrying whether or not this would feel like a Full Moon production. Jeff Farley reflects on his fellow Full Moon alums working on the film: "Courtney's job had already been completed and unfortunately he wasn't present during the shoot in Bulgaria. I loved working with Ted, though we butted heads a few times. There wasn't much different. You're working with the same parameters on every show, so that is a commonality. The one difference was the shift in location from Romania to Bulgaria."

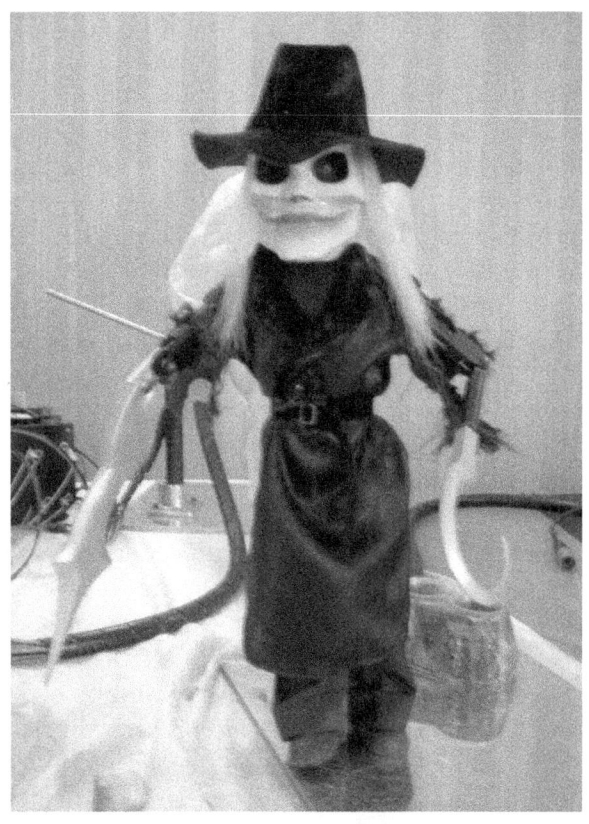

Blade in the workshop (courtesy Jeff Farley).

Not only was Sci-Fi enthusiastic about the project, they were ambitious as well. They saw *Puppet Master vs. Demonic Toys* not simply as a movie of the week that would capitalize on a successful title; they saw a long-term investment. The network planned for *Puppet Master vs. Demonic Toys* to serve as a pilot to launch a *Puppet Master* television series. With eight films behind it, *Puppet Master* had already become somewhat episodic in nature. It was long-term storytelling, already as convoluted as any soap opera by this point. It only made sense for *Puppet Master* to transition into an actual episodic television series. This had been their goal since first making the deal to produce the feature: to create continuous content based on the *Puppet Master* brand in the form of an original series. They were testing the same waters at this time with *Tremors: The Series*, based obviously on the film franchise of the same name.

Unfortunately, there was a catch. While the Sci-Fi Channel had planned for a TV series following the premiere of *Puppet Master vs. Demonic Toys,* it was either not apparently allowed by their contract with Full Moon, which only gave them the rights to produce a single picture, or the series was scrapped to do the lower viewership or eventual lack of interest from viewers in *Puppet Master vs. Demonic Toys* when it eventually aired. Either way, the television series—as exciting a prospect as it may have been—never came to be.[5]

Fred Willard was being circled to star as Robert Toulon, but that too did not come to pass. "The idea was that Toulon was going to be Fred Willard–esque," says Joyner. "It was gonna be the grandson or something. He would be a single parent with his own kids and everybody would be on these little adventures, whether it would be the kids or what have you. It was definitely lighter in tone even though we had some torture and I think even a topless girl or two. When they cast Corey Feldman, I actually went 'Oh, really?' I had no idea that's what was going on. I had worked very closely at that time with Tom Vitaly who was at the Sci-Fi Channel and he was great. This was really one of the first things that the Sci-Fi Channel did on their own. They were gearing up to start producing their own movies but when they got Corey Feldman I said 'Oh, OK,' and I was really just waiting for the opportunity to go in and rewrite so that at least the character would be age-appropriate. It could still be Andre Toulon's nephew, but at least make it right for the actor. Then this bizarre choice was made and I don't know really that Ted endorses that."

Throughout the late 1980s and early 1990s, Feldman had been a teen heartthrob. He had seen massive success with young roles in movies such as *Friday the 13th: The Final Chapter*, *Gremlins*, *Stand by Me*, *The Goonies*, *The Lost Boys*, *Teenage Mutant Ninja Turtles* and more. Coming into his own as a leading man with friend and co-star Corey Haim, he headlined the likes of *License to Drive* and *Dream a Little Dream*. In the early 2000s, Feldman was just coming off of the success of his reality series—again with Haim—*The Two Coreys*. In his early thirties at the time, he was the last person anyone would expect to fit the role of this Doc Brown–esque mad scientist character, which had so clearly been written for a grandfatherly older actor. Though Feldman was perhaps the biggest headliner the series had seen up to this point, his casting by the network definitely signaled a message that things were off to a rocky start.

Still, for a movie designed to shoot for irreverence from the get-go, casting someone decades younger than originally planned didn't necessarily mean the end of the world. Everything about *Puppet Master vs. Demonic Toys* is over the top and tongue-in-cheek, so it's hard not truly single out Feldman's performance as something that is distracting or even something that feels out of place. Feldman definitely gets what kind of feature he's in and hams it up wildly, never toning it down for a single solitary second. He even puts on an old man voice that he uses to deliver every line, pretends to have a bad back and a bum knee and be completely blind without his glasses, many of which had to have been little improvisational touches that he brought to the role.

Jeff Farley echoes Joyner's mention of the early TV series possibilities, as well as Feldman's casting and working with him on the set: "Early on, before we were even given a chance to begin, I received a call from the film's executive producer, Jeff Franklin, that we should prepare to stay quite a while in the film's original location, Romania, where we would have ben shooting on the sets left over from *Seed of Chucky*. I had heard that Fred Willard was to portray Robert Toulon and I was thrilled. Unfortunately, he wasn't able to join us. I actually was in Jeff Franklin's office when the deal was made to bring Corey Feldman aboard and though he seemed like an odd choice, he couldn't have been nicer and kinder to work with. He, too, was very professional."

Vanessa Angel was cast as the evil Erica Sharpe, head of Sharpe Toys. Angel was best known at the time for starring in the *Weird Science* TV series, in which she played the role originated by Kelly LeBrock, as well as the Farrelly Brothers comedy *Kingpin*. Like Feldman, she plays her role completely over the top. Angel is not physically what someone would think of when they imagine this evil businesswoman, especially as she's largely playing a female version of *Halloween III*'s Conal Cochran. Luckily, it's this casting that allows this character to stand apart on her own. Instead of being an old witch, Erica Sharpe feels much more like a stuck-up brat who's been handed everything her entire life, including her own country. This is no doubt the person that Veruca Salt would have grown up to become. She is a narcissistic, privileged evil devoid of empathy, but at the same time, impossible to take seriously. This is intentional, of course, as *Puppet Master vs. Demonic Toys* is first and foremost a farce. Angel's vain and pouty villain hardly feels like a great threat, but she's playing more of a classic foil, just there to comment on things and be antagonistic, rather than represent fully realized stakes. If anything, she makes it easy to forget that the entire world is hanging in the balance should her plan succeed. At the very least, one can recognize the snobbish privilege of the central villain and understand why she would want to sacrifice the world's children, even if that reason solely boils down to just proving that she's capable of doing it.

Danielle Keaton plays Alex Toulon, daughter of Corey Feldman's Robert. Ironically, with his aged-up appearance, Feldman's cranky old scientist is portrayed to actually be far older than the father of a teenager. Even though he was in his thirties, Feldman plays Toulon as though he's in his sixties.

While necessary, the exposition moments are the flattest and most baffling of the entire movie. Toulon goes over the finer points of the plot a few times, which is unavoidable, but there are other moments that only make *Puppet Master vs. Demonic Toys* stand out that much more from the rest of the franchise before it. There's a moment early on in the movie where Robert refers back to the events of *Puppet Master III*, which is a nice reference to the fact that Joyner also wrote that entry. This moment suggests that even though this is a different studio and a new set of characters, that the movie can still take place within the franchise and the larger Full Moon universe. By the end of the movie, this is a total impossibility. Even in the opening scene, the callback to previous adventures immediately clashes with a new version of the formula. Instead of running on human souls and brain tissue, the new formula simply needs a drop of Toulon blood in order to work. These little moments that feel at odds with the rest of the series work up to the greater revelation of a completely new origin for the puppets.

Whether the decision was made because Nicolau had no interest in the established Egyptian mythology ingrained in the franchise or the decision was meant to keep the franchise from feeling stale, he and Joyner conceived of a new origin. This time, the puppets are said to be hundreds of years old, rather than simply decades old. The concept of human souls occupying their small bodies seemingly disappears as well. Instead, the new origin revealed them to be carved of a mystical oak by an ancestor of Toulon's in the middle ages. This oak, imbued with magical abilities, brought the puppets to life on its own.

Much more noticeable than the briefly mentioned new backstories of the puppets and Demonic Toys, however, would be their new designs. Once again, Jeff Farley returned to provide the puppet and toy FX as he had done for both *Retro Puppet Master* and *Puppet Master: The Legacy*. This would be a much more exciting and challenging creative endeavor than *Legacy* had been, as Farley would once again be tasked with redesigning the puppets from scratch. This time, however, he would not be completely overhauling and reinterpreting the puppets, but rather updating the classic designs. And, of course, he would be applying the same treatment to the Demonic Toys.

Given the new focus of the film, both as a comedic movie and as a feature geared toward kids and pre-teens, the designs of the classic characters are significantly toned down. Blade, Six-Shooter, Pinhead and Jester look like toys you would actually let a kid play with. Blade, out of all of them, remains the most untouched which only makes sense as the character had become something of an iconic in his own right by this point in time. Each of the others would lose any of their meaner looking character traits. Pinhead no longer has one squinting eye, but rather two open and alert eyes. Jester's mean, downturned eyebrows are replaced with perpetually surprised and delighted upturned brows. Six-Shooter's wild-eyed sneer is gone, making for a much more normal looking cowboy, six arms notwithstanding. Despite these toned-down changes, the puppets are still extremely recognizable as the puppets.

The Demonic Toys, on the other hand, suffer more from the less explicitly frightening designs, but in a way that is unavoidable as their toning down is crucial to the plot. In this film, the Demonic Toys are mass-produced and rebranded as "Christmas Pals." They're a toy craze and something every kid wants to play with, which on its own sort of requires them to lose their edge.

The John Carl Buechler designs were, well, meant to be horrifying. These were nightmarish versions of classic children's toys and that was their appeal to begin with. But that doesn't necessarily fly for a more kid-friendly version. *Puppet Master vs. Demonic Toys* is definitely not a movie designed to give children nightmares about their own teddy bear. Because of that, the new Demonic Toys are mostly underwhelming. While Jack Attack looks closest to the original movies, his features are exaggerated to still be cartoonish and clown-like. Baby Oopsy Daisy looks grumpy and his green irises reflect the solid green of the original toy's eyes, but otherwise he looks like a baby doll. Grizzly, with the exception of his very small teeth and almost unnoticeable claws, looks exactly like a normal teddy bear. None of this should be blamed on Jeff Farley, who was simply operating under the parameters of what the movie needed to be. Sinister, even ghoulish, designs simply wouldn't make sense for a more comedic and kid-friendly movie. Considering the story requirements and the time he had to bring them to life, Farley's FX work for *Puppet Master vs. Demonic Toys* is pretty great.

"We were promised seven weeks to prepare in Los Angeles," Farley remembers, "and quickly realized that with shipping and customs, that knocked a couple weeks off. We prepared as much as possible and finished at our lab in Sofia. The puppet crew, again, were wonderful, especially the fact that I was able to hire living legend Mark Shostrom to sculpt some of the characters alongside myself. Again, the process was the same as *Retro*. We were even forced to re-use the molds for the bodies from *Retro* due to the time crunch. Again, Bud McGrew was involved on the animatronic end and outdid himself."

As with any redesigns of recognizable characters, it proved to be a delicate balance to determine what elements needed to be included and what could be open to a new interpretation, as Farley notes. "The most difficult decision was: how far removed can we get, yet retain the essence of the characters? We knew, even though the puppets were completely new sculptures, there had to be familiarity. Originally, we wanted to utilize the original molds when we were involved in 2002, but we found out that, in a move, Full Moon had tossed the molds in the trash. We were forced to redo everything and do the work from photos supplied to us.

"As far as the 'toys,' I had worked on the first *Demonic Toys* film over at John Buechler's for a few days, and though I loved everything they were doing, I didn't want to step on John's toes and copy verbatim. I had always seen Baby Oopsy as a thuggish character and in some sort of boxers-hoodie type of wardrobe rather than the dress the original had. Also, since the toys had to appear as though they were manufactured, we gave them that sort of look. Jack's box was redesigned mainly because we just couldn't get the artwork from the original and Chris came up with a novel solution. Hence, the red box with silver spots, similar to the fabric we located. The wardrobe changes came about as I had several puppet costume crew located in Sofia. We made up foam copies of the puppets and shipped them early so they would have time to prepare and when I saw them, despite slight differences and color changes, I was very pleased. They were very professionally made."

The biggest new design elements of the movie lay in a promise that had been by Full Moon years before. In a truly shocking turn of events, the feature honored the promise of the Cyber Puppets. Farley and Bergschneider helped to finally make them in to a reality. Blade, Pinhead, Six-Shooter and Jester each got a cybernetic upgrade just as promised in the concept art, even sticking pretty close to those designs. In some ways, the Cyber Puppets are a reminder that no idea is ever really dead at Full Moon. Something that has been abandoned, or a promise that seemingly went forgotten, might show up in some wholly surprising way, shape or form at any point down the line. That was definitely the case with the Cyber Puppets.

Unfortunately, fans don't get to see a great deal of the newly upgraded puppets in the movie. While many speculated that the team would need to be upgraded following a fight with the Demonic Toys, the film reveals that the puppets actually get damaged in a completely random accidental fire. Because of that damage, they sit out a large chunk of the feature that is instead devoted to Robert's investigation of Sharpe Toys and his steps toward uncovering their evil plan. The body count is, as expected, relatively low. In order to bring the Christmas Pals to life and murder the world's children, Erica Sharpe needs to honor her bargain with Baal by regularly sacrificing him virgins, which she does by simply going up to young women and asking them whether they're virgins or not. These disposable virgins provide the cannon fodder for the Demonic Toys.

Given the fact that it is set during the days leading up to Christmas, it only makes sense that *Puppet Master vs. Demonic Toys* would aim for a December release.

The movie made its premiere the week before Christmas of 2004 and actually brought in strong ratings. The brief teasers shown on the network had promised a fight between two minor powerhouses of the straight-to-video age. Unfortunately, it's another promise that *Puppet Master vs. Demonic Toys* never really makes good on. There are only two scenes in which the puppets and Demonic Toys face off with one another. One is a confrontation in the office as the puppets break out of their box to save Robert from Jack Attack, the other is the promised titular showdown. Blade faces off against Grizzly, while Pinhead takes on Baby Oopsy and Jester battles Jack Attack. Six-Shooter, meanwhile, helps the humans to fight off Erica Sharpe's many armed guards.

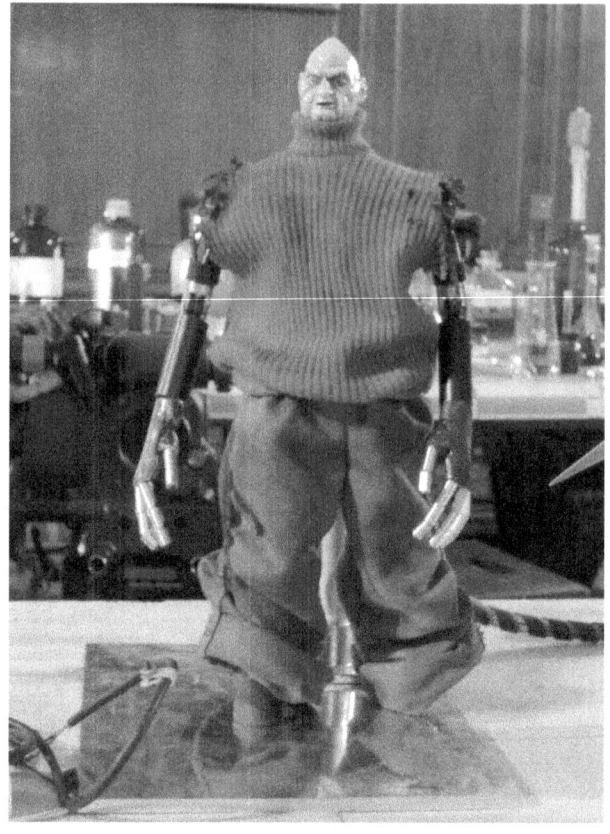

Cyber Pinhead (courtesy Jeff Farley).

For the most part, it seems that the puppets and Demonic Toys are squared off visually, with those with the most visual similarities going up against one another. That way, we have two sharp-handed figures battling it out, as well as two burly bald toys, topping it off with a clown fighting a Jester. It's an easy way to divide the characters The larger problem with the scene and the resulting fight is that it is all over within three minutes.

Those who just showed up to see the battle between the two groups of toys no doubt felt disappointed after viewing *Puppet Master vs. Demonic Toys* for the first time. Not only did they need to sit through the longest entry in either franchise to date—clocking in at ninety-five minutes—but less than five minutes of that running time was devoted to any kind of fight between the two sets of toys. Many dismissed this as another black mark on the series and Full Moon's legacy, many loyal fans ignored it entirely due to the lack of Full Moon involvement, while others found the humorous take to be a much-needed breath of fresh air. Jeff Farley confirms that there were larger plans for the showdown between the two groups of toys that just couldn't be realized on the budget.

"Everything was shot pretty much as is seen," he says. "But yes, there was a scaling back on how complicated we could get as the sets were not built to accommodate the puppets and we had a lot of practical locations, also. We had to demand a second

Chapter Twelve. Puppet Master vs. Demonic Toys

unit for the puppet shots as, originally, production felt we could get everything in three weeks. They relented and we got not only a second unit, but an extra week to shoot, otherwise this might have been the first *Puppet Master* film with no puppets. Even then, it just wasn't enough time, though our second unit director, Gary Jones, and makeup artist, Melanie Tooker, helped us immensely along with my local crew, Yana (Stoyanova) Miro and Miglena Bogdanava."

Farley also had a brief personal scare during the hectic filming of the movie, as he explains. "My birthday was during the shoot and that is when I was informed that the local custom was that whoever's birthday it is, they have to purchase the chocolate and distribute it. I thought they were pulling my leg until I started to hand out the candy. I was given three cakes that day, two on set and one from the hotel. It was a very special day. The worst was it appeared as though I was exhibiting signs of colon cancer and ended up having to stay an extra week for hospital tests. Luckily, the results came back negative."

Baby Oopsy mugs for the camera (courtesy Jeff Farley).

It's hard not to wonder how things could have turned out had Sci-Fi actually been given the rights to the franchise. Fans would almost certainly have gotten a *Puppet Master* TV series following the movie, though whether that would have differed in tone from the feature or not is anyone's guess. When making that initial deal, Band made sure that he would retain the rights to both franchises. By this point, he had lost every partnership he had made to keep Full Moon afloat, even lost the company's name, but he made sure that no matter what, he would not lose the franchise that put Full Moon on the map. However it turned out, there *is* something admirable about that. Farley reflects on the film's hectic and troubled production: "It was the only production I have been on that was rushed through from one end to the other and that was due to an iron-clad airdate on the Sci-Fi Channel before Christmas 2004. They required the final finished product one month ahead of the air date to create the advertisements. We began pre-production in late June (2004) and I had to travel early in August prior to that shoot, with Chris and Bud following shortly after. The shoot went into September. This meant that post-production was going on while

Six-Shooter burned (courtesy Jeff Farley).

we were shooting and they were going 24/7 to get finished." As for the experience as a whole, he says, "It was all a blur. There just wasn't much time for enjoyment, but the experience was tempered by such wonderful people involved."

It doesn't change the fact that it was a hugely risky move for Full Moon, as Band did not have the money to make another solo *Puppet Master* film by himself at that point in time. There was no clear sign that he would ever be able to produce another *Puppet Master* feature on his own, which if true would have meant that he had signed away the only chance to keep the series going in any way whatsoever. The contract with the Sci-Fi Channel had to have been written on the unshakable faith that somehow Full Moon's luck would turn around, that it would be able to put itself back on top and that one day, without complicated partnerships or deals with brands like Sci-Fi or Blockbuster, Band would be able to make his movies his own way once more. And that, more importantly, he would find a way to not only continue the *Puppet Master* series without the involvement of an outside studio, but even to allow it to flourish.

As great a prospect as that could be, it was far from the reality of where Charles Band and Full Moon were by the time *Puppet Master vs. Demonic Toys* made its premiere. But there were new things on the horizon. With the crossover finally proving to be underwhelming for fans, December of 2004 felt like simply another passing hour in a very long, dark night for the franchise and especially for fans of its parent company.

But there was a new moon rising.

Chapter Thirteen

Puppet Master: Axis of Evil

The end of 2004 had delivered fans the long-awaited crossover movie *Puppet Master vs. Demonic Toys,* but not in a way that anyone had expected. The feature was too comedic for some, for others it didn't deliver enough on the carnage promised in its title. But more than anything, it felt much more like a Sci-Fi Channel movie and much less like a Full Moon production. At this time, Charles Band's movies were being made under the Shadow Entertainment moniker, per his deal with 20th Century–Fox. By the end of 2004, that deal had dissolved, and Band returned to a name familiar to anyone who had followed his career from the beginning: Wizard Video. Under the new Wizard Video label, Band promised a whole slate of new content, announcing six new movies a year. While this sounds much more doable than previous announcements Band had made in the past, the catch this time would be that he would direct every single film himself. He also promised that each new movie would be partnered with a doll or figure that would be sold in limited qualities through Wizard Toys.

Despite an output of much more tongue-in-cheek and comedic titles like *Gingerdead Man* and *Evil Bong,* Band still made the effort to be clear that even if Wizard Entertainment was the new studio title, the classic Full Moon franchises would not be going anywhere. He announced that they would make a sequel to *Subspecies,* as well as *Bride of the Head of the Family,* something that he had been promising since the release of the first film. He also announced surprising plans for sequels to *Castle Freak* and *Demonic Toys.* But most ambitiously of all, Band announced not just a new *Puppet Master* film, but a new *Puppet Master* trilogy set during World War II.[1] This news shocked fans who had almost entirely begun to believe that the franchise was dead and buried. After barely being able to afford to produce *Legacy* and selling the crossover film to another studio, finally Band was announcing new in-house *Puppet Master* features to further the series.

At the same time, fans had every reason to be skeptical. On one hand, while Wizard Entertainment was producing movies at a rapid rate, they weren't on the ambitious level of a *Puppet Master,* especially not a period piece. More than that, Band had announced this exact same news a decade earlier and it had gone nowhere. After all, *Puppet Wars* had been slated to be a trilogy of movies set during World War II. Like the new planned trilogy, that had been designed to capitalize on the success of *Puppet Master III.* But after so many years, *Toulon's Revenge* had only grown into a more and more beloved entry. Somehow, tackling new *Puppet Master* movies in that vein felt like it was treading more sacred ground than *Puppet Wars* ever had. Considering that *Puppet Wars* had been a huge point of fan excitement that eventually went nowhere, people were hesitant to jump on board getting excited for the promise of three new *Puppet Master* films, which felt impossible to pull off even if the company was getting back on its feet.

These were only three of several new sequels to classic Full Moon franchises that Band promised at the time. As Band's renaissance continued, there were plenty of new features, but no sign of the return of the older Full Moon properties. 2006 saw the release of *Evil Bong* and the alien/mummy creature flick *Petrified*. Band was setting up new franchises, providing sequels to the *Gingerdead Man* and *Evil Bong* titles that proved to be so successful with new viewers. The best of them, and one of the best of the late-era Band movies in general, was *Gingerdead Man 2: Passion of the Crust*. A self satire in the vein of an irreverent *Wes Craven's New Nightmare*, *Passion of the Crust* is essentially about the killer cookie crashing the production of a standard Full Moon movie. Directed by William Butler, who had sharpened his teeth working under Band both as an actor and as an FX artist in the Empire years, *Passion of the Crust* is one of the most fun Band-produced features in over a decade. But the movie would also hold another important distinction. Released in 2008, *Passion of the Crust* would be the first film to feature the return of an iconic logo.

Wizard Entertainment was no more. In 2008, the iconic blue moon and yellow lettering returned to the spine of each new DVD the company released, this time under the banner of Full Moon Features—which only makes sense, as Full Moon Entertainment and Full Moon Pictures were both defunct and could no longer be used.[2] Band made it clear that the return of the logo meant something important to the studio's direction as a whole. Under the Full Moon Features banner, he would make good on his promise to return to the classic franchises that fans had grown up with, and that were already at this point considered part of the "classic" Full Moon era. 2009 would see the first of them in the form of *Demonic Toys 2*.

While many were still skeptical as to whether or not the proposed *Puppet Master* trilogy would ever even happen, the release of *Demonic Toys 2* gave people hope. Finally, Full Moon was making good on its promise to revisit older titles. There was a question, though, of how *Puppet Master* would even fit into the newer Full Moon climate. The earlier Paramount movies had their tongue-in-cheek charms, but many of them attempted to be serious in nature. The *Puppet Master* movies certainly fell into that category. Even if they had their moments of humor and eccentric beats, they were story-driven features by Full Moon standards. It was hard to imagine them standing side by side with the likes of *Evil Bong*. The studio's return to the *Killjoy* franchise made much more sense as it felt completely in line with the irreverent absurdity that the new school of Full Moon seemed content to focus on. *Demonic Toys* had also been a little more intentionally goofy than other movies, but many fans thought the direct sequel pushed things too far in the direction of intentional camp.

Still, Band made good on his promise. *Demonic Toys 2* had only been the beginning, just as he had said. A new *Puppet Master* sequel would be following directly on its heels, the first of the proposed new trilogy set during World War II. Ever since the three new movies had been announced, fans had begun to wonder if the new prequel trilogy meant that they would finally get to see their *Puppet Wars* dreams realized. But even though Full Moon did own those scripts, they were written for a much more ambitious time in the studio's history. The new movies, whatever they would be, promised to be entirely different stories featuring the puppets as fans knew them and loved them. To further win back the trust of the fans, as well as to show how serious he was about making the new feature feel similar to *Puppet Master III*, he brought David DeCoteau back to direct the new entry. Titled *Puppet Master: Axis of Evil*, it promised to be a bold new chapter in the series' history.

The screenplay for the new film was written by the late Brian Muir, under the pseudonym August White. With a lengthy career as a screenwriter, Muir had written numerous recent Full Moon favorites, including both *Gingerdead Man* and *Evil Bong*, as well as *Petrified, Decadent Evil* and more. His biggest claim to fame, however, was (as Dominic Muir) writing the cult 1986 hit *Critters*. Spawning a successful little monster-themed franchise of its own, with a terrific second installment by Mick Garris, *Critters* managed to stand apart from other post–*Gremlins* movies at the time. It has a cult following that still continues to this day. It's also ironic that the producer of *Ghoulies* eventually brought the writer of *Critters* on board as an in-house screenwriter. Sadly, Brian Muir passed away before in September of 2010, just months after the release of *Axis of Evil*.

Muir clearly understood that a new *Puppet Master* had different requirements than *Evil Bong* or *Unlucky Charms* and the finished film reflects that. Even though it was made by most of the same people, this was a much more serious story than anything else Full Moon was working on at the time. The new story goes back to the roots of the series in an incredibly literal way. It kicks off during the events of the original film's prologue sequence, introducing us to an apprentice of Toulon who was working in the Bodega Bay Inn the same day that the puppet master shot himself to prevent his secrets from falling into the hands of the Nazis. While this relies on stock footage, it's actually a more inventive use of stock footage than had previously been attempted, as this edits new characters into the events of the original movie. This scene also sets up the entire feature, allowing it to go back to the biggest unanswered question of the original *Puppet Master:* who were the two Germans that followed Toulon to the hotel?

This question had first been explored in the original 1990 comic series. Like *Axis of Evil*, that picks up immediately after the original's prologue sequence, but unlike this film, it centers on Andre Toulon after his resurrection. *Axis of Evil* definitely takes a different direction and introduces us to young hero Danny Coogan. Afflicted with Polio, Danny is a classic 1940s all-American kid. All he wants to do is go over and fight in the war and serve his country, but his illness keeps him away from the battlefield. In retrospect, it's amazing that this movie actually came out *before* Marvel's *Captain America: The First Avenger,* as the two movies have almost identical arcs for their main characters. While the Eternity comics travel from the Bodega Bay Inn to the streets of Cairo, *Axis of Evil* is much more contained. This new story is set in Los Angeles. But there would be a twist due to the feature's shooting location.

Puppet Master: Axis of Evil is set in L.A.'s China Town, based on the fact that the movie would be shooting in China. Finding the prospect of shooting a movie set in

Los Angeles to be most expensive if it actually shot there, the notion of shooting in China seemed much cheaper. This would be the most that Full Moon had traveled in a long time, since the end of their Romanian studio. Judging by Band's announcements of *Axis of Evil* being the first of many Chinese-based productions, it seemed clear that Band was attempting to set up a new studio similar to the one he had had in Romania. It was a noble effort and a sensible one as well. Full Moon's latest movies were, with the exception of *Demonic Toys 2,* mostly filming around L.A. But the cost of shooting within the city has always been incredibly high and for a more ambitious project like *Puppet Master,* it only made sense to focus those energies on finding a cheaper location, even if it meant a great deal of travel. The story is set in China Town to attempt to cover up the fact that it's shot in China, but for the most part, it doesn't do a terrific job. The scenery, the fact that nearly every extra is Chinese and (especially) the dubbing of some of the major characters definitely makes the location feel noticeable.

For the most part, *Puppet Master: Axis of Evil* is confined to a factory and an abandoned opera house, where the two German assassins—now named Max and Klaus—meet with the Japanese Madame Ozu to bomb the weapons facility that Danny's girlfriend Beth happens to work at. To do this, Max goes undercover as a new employee at the factory, getting close to Beth in order to get his hands on the blueprints to the facility. Danny was the first one to discover the scene of Toulon's suicide and saw Max's face as he was walking away, so he is the only one who knows what's going on. This plot setup actually introduces an intriguing love triangle, one that the film almost explores, but stops just shy of truly diving into. Beth doesn't believe Danny when he first tells her about Max, even though it's not at all surprising to simply say that someone in one of the major U.S. cities at the time would be a Nazi spy, especially if he had witnessed him doing something terrible. The only reason Beth would have for not immediately believing Danny would *have* to be an unstated attraction to Max. While she plays it coy, however, Max is extremely open in his attraction to her. A character devoid of empathy—being a Nazi assassin and all—Max uses every aspect of his personality as a weapon. He is charming when he needs to be, using that charm to get the blueprints from Beth and to get Madame Ozu to agree to an alliance. When he can't be charming, he resorts to much more expected fear tactics. And with Danny, he weaponizes his attraction to Beth. Danny has been fairly overtly worried about the fact that this guy who he knows is terrible has eyes for his girlfriend, so Max intentionally crosses a line and cements himself as being a full-blown sadistic bastard when he announces that he's going to violate Beth while he makes Danny watch.

The misogyny of Max's character is made overtly clear, as is Klaus' to a lesser extent. These men are fascist villains and they behave like them, spouting off racist remarks as easily as breathing. Their constant reminders of the Reich's mission are ironically what separate them from the Nazi villains of *Puppet Master III*. There was a sense of subtlety to those characters that the antagonists of *Axis of Evil* definitely lack. From the moment we're introduced to Major Kraus in *Toulon's Revenge* we are completely aware that he is evil. He doesn't always need to say how evil he is or talk about how he is going to eliminate the Jews. It's all there in his delivery, in his voice.

The hatred seeps out of him without him needing to spell it out. The only time Kraus ever really speaks in this kind of manner is when he refers to Elsa as "the Jew woman" and that one phrase is enough of a reminder as to both who this man is and what he believes.

Max discusses the beliefs of the Reich much more freely, but this could easily come from being a younger and more arrogant character. While Max serves the same narrative purpose as Kraus and draws immediately relevant parallels to him, he is a different character. Much more cocksure and full of selfish pride, Max is a decidedly more vain villain than Kraus could have even been imagined to be. Luckily, Ozu is there to serve as a refreshing foil. Even though this woman is just as evil, she calls out Max on quite a few of his more annoying traits, particularly his ego and vanity. The open racism and bigotry spoken by the villains is not unique to them, however, as the rest of the characters engage in their fair share as well.

Watching *Axis of Evil* it's almost jarring how freely the characters speak of killing German and Japanese soldiers, often in slurs and almost always referring to them as shifty-eyed or sneaky. This is, without a doubt, clearly meant to be an honest reflection of the time. The amount of casual racism in the story could easily lead a viewer to construe the film as racist, but the intent certainly seems to be to create an accurate portrayal of America during the height of World War II. It showcases not just the malicious intent of the Nazis, but the everyday intolerance of the time. Madame Ozu even uses the American's racism toward Asians to her advantage, hiding in plain sight as a Chinese Dragon Lady simply because she knows that Americans can't even tell the two races apart.

As heroic as he is, Danny is definitely fierce to go overseas and kill both Germans and Japanese troops to defend his country. His brother Donny is about to ship out to do just that and Danny couldn't be happier for him, though there is an obvious jealousy toward Donny for being able to do the thing that Danny himself is incapable of doing. It's also easy to read a small degree of resentment in the character as well, given that all Danny wants to do is be a soldier and defend his country and his loved ones, yet Donny actually gets to do those things and doesn't seem to care. Donny is much more of a practical joker, going on dates and getting drunk and laughing throughout virtually all of his scenes. While it's easy to assume that Donny is simple getting everything he can out of home before he ships off to war, it's understandable that Danny could construe that as a lack of caring on his brother's part. If anything, this is what establishes the connection between the two of them that gives Donny's eventual death at least something of an emotional resonance.

One of the many ways *Puppet Master: Axis of Evil* attempts to return to the glory days of the franchise is by introducing a new puppet. During the early years of the series, this had been a standard practice. Each new sequel would add a new puppet to the ever-growing cast. In this case, that puppet is Ninja. While boasting an extremely simple design, solid black with glowing red eyes, Ninja still felt like a big deal. *Curse of the Puppet Master* had introduced the lackluster Tank in its final few minutes. Here, Ninja at the very least feels as though he's a part of the action. Even if he's not quite front and center like Torch and Six-Shooter were in their respective introductions, he comes into his own and has a larger part to play through the third act, similar to how Decapitron had been used in *Puppet Master 4* and *5*. At the very least, it looked as if Full Moon was making it clear that this was another permanent introduction to the group and a character that fans could expect to see again as the series continued.

Nonetheless, as is true of every *Puppet Master*, the biggest draw for returning fans would be the puppets themselves. With the addition of Ninja, the returning puppet cast is the same classic five as had featured in the original movie. Blade, Leech Woman, Jester, Tunneler and Pinhead are all present and accounted for. Given that *Curse of the Puppet Master, Retro Puppet Master* and *Puppet Master: The Legacy* each used the Mark Rapport character designs, *Axis of Evil* would be the first time that the puppets had been remodeled for a Full Moon sanctioned sequel—thus excluding *Puppet Master vs. Demonic Toys*—since 1998. Unfortunately, the new designs are fairly unceremonious. The benefit of the new puppets is that they were unable to use the Mark Rappaport designs because the new puppets would do much more than those designs had been capable of. Those puppets, good looking as they were, were created for features that relied more heavily on the use of stock footage to bring the characters to life. Thankfully, outside of the *Back to the Future II*-esque opening sequence, *Puppet Master: Axis of Evil* contains no stock footage whatsoever.

At least as far as Full Moon movies were concerned, the release of *Puppet Master: Axis of Evil* felt like an event. Fans had been burned for years by the series at this point. After the low point of *Legacy* and the outsourcing of *Puppet Master vs. Demonic Toys,* fans of this franchise desperately needed a win. *Axis of Evil* had everything it needed to be just that. The puppets, while not even approaching the levels of David Allen's wizardry, were able to do things that they hadn't been able to do in years. Fan-favorite David Decoteau was once again returning to helm a prequel—his third, by this point, and his fourth *Puppet Master* feature overall. And most surprisingly of all, Richard Band returned to compose the music, including a brand-new version of the classic *Puppet Master* theme.

Everything about *Puppet Master: Axis of Evil* as a movie seems to promote a mission statement of taking the franchise back to its roots. It literally opens *at* the beginning of the original movie. After a prologue setting up the main character's discovery of the puppets, it then segues into an opening credits sequence that moves over the details of the faces of the various puppets, reflecting the credits of the original film. This time, though, it's a little less dazzling because the sequence takes us into extreme details of designs that obviously don't hold a candle to those that David Allen designed for the original. Even still, the intent is clear and admirable. In general, that more or less sums up the film as a whole. It's not everything that it could be, and it's probably impossible for it to have done everything that it set out to achieve, but the intent is clear. *Puppet Master: Axis of Evil* is not a stellar movie by any stretch, but its heart is fundamentally in the right place.

While many fans were underwhelmed by the production value and even the effects, expecting some kind of return to the glory days of the Paramount era, others were just excited to see a movie that felt like it was *trying*. The flaws are obvious, chief among them being the absolutely atrocious dubbing of Madame Ozu. The bluntness of the dialogue can sometimes pull a viewer out of the movie and the puppets themselves don't foster excitement the way their predecessors did. But none of that necessarily changed the fact that fans were given a *Puppet Master* movie that took itself seriously again, especially after the intentional farce that was *Puppet Master vs. Demonic Toys.*

While it stood out compared to every other Full Moon feature being made at the time, the entire point of *Axis of Evil* appeared to be to bring back some of the original fans, many of whom had felt alienated by the more stoner-friendly slapstick approach of the recent Full Moon output. In that respect, the new sequel did exactly what it set out to do, making a film much more similar to what people had grown up watching during the early days when Full Moon was just making itself known on the video market. It was a serious movie for fans who *wanted* a more serious movie. Recognizing that the feature was designed to cater to those original fans, Charles Band made one more incredibly smart business decision when promoting the movie's release. *Axis of Evil* saw release on both on DVD and Blu-Ray, as that had become a popular format at the time. In addition to that, the original *Puppet Master* would make its debut on Blu-Ray around the same time. The two were even sold together in a small box set designed to look like the iconic trunk the puppets were carried in throughout the series. *Puppet Master*'s Blu-Ray debut marked a great new step forward for the fans of the early movies, as they would be able to finally see their franchise favorites the way that they were meant to be seen.

Even though the Paramount era movies were designed for release on videocassette, they were shot on film in widescreen and screened theatrically for the cast and crew. Restoring the transfer from the original negative and presenting the original movie in the proper aspect ratio for the very first time, the *Puppet Master* Blu-Ray kicked off a series of new Blu-Ray releases of the classic Full Moon titles. For fans burnt out on the newer releases, the Blu-Ray of *Puppet Master* allowed them to revisit a classic and finally see it with new eyes.

In many ways, *Axis of Evil* was as divisive as any of the sequels and prequels that had immediately preceded it. Yet it felt fresh and new and it was the first entry to get fans excited since *Retro,* if not before. Some viewers certainly felt underwhelmed, but others embraced and welcomed the new approach. There was at the very least no doubt that the movie was attempting to tell a sincere story and add something to the mythology by expanding on the mysterious assassins of the original feature, while also going back to the tried-and-true formula of *Puppet Master III* and reminding fans of everything they loved about the franchise's early years. While mileage varied in terms of entertainment value, fans at least agreed on one thing: it was a step in the right direction.

Chapter Fourteen

Puppet Master: Axis Rising

Since the early 2000s, Full Moon had undergone many changes, not the least of them being several new company names, from Shadow Entertainment to Wizard Entertainment to Full Moon Features. But the early 2010s brought about the biggest, most irrevocable change of all. From its inception, Full Moon had been designed to cater to the video market. Band's Empire Pictures releases had not been successful in theaters, for the most part, but had found enormous success on video so he restructured his vision and created a company to cater to the video retailers who actually seemed to care about the types of movies he was making. Throughout all of the ups and downs, Full Moon's movies were always made with that one vision in mind: to make a movie people would want to rent. In the late 2000s, Netflix had started picking up steam, eventually dominating the video rental marketplace and then, later, completely redefining it. *Axis of Evil* was the first *Puppet Master* movie to not be widely available at most video rental stores, because by this point, they were closing across the country. They just didn't exist anymore. This impacted not only the direction of the franchise, but everything Band was doing and everything Full Moon stood for as a company. At this time, just as Netflix was taking over and video stores were slowly dying out, there was a question of how Full Moon was going to stay afloat, but there weren't any clear answers.

The Blu-Ray releases of the early films, combined with the residual fan hype surrounding *Puppet Master: Axis of Evil* as well as the replicas—which, despite criticisms, continued to sell out—kept the franchise alive and, even more than that, kept fans hungry for more. There was a clear desire for a new *Puppet Master* sequel and *Axis of Evil* had ended on a cliffhanger promising new adventures. Unlike any of the sequels to do so before it, *Axis of Evil* would prove to have the first cliffhanger in the series that would actually be followed up. Band had promised a World War II trilogy and seemed intent to deliver on that promise.

Part of the success of *Puppet Master: Axis of Evil* had been that it was the first *Puppet Master* movie in years, following the first movie in the series that hadn't been produced by Full Moon. The new movie would need a new angle if it was going to recapture some of that success, other than simply catering to fans who were always willing to support a new *Puppet Master* entry. Whereas the early 1990s had produced a sequel every year—sometimes more than one—they were at this point starting to feel like event movies, made with the rarity of a *Star Wars* entry. It felt like a return to form for Full Moon to begin working on a new *Puppet Master* that would be released only two years after the previous one.

Announced via a vidcast from Charles Band himself, the new movie would be titled *Puppet Master X: Axis Rising*. As Band had referred to *Axis Rising* as the ninth entry, the "X" in *Axis Rising* officially confirmed that the Sci-Fi produced *Puppet Master vs. Demonic Toys* was officially not counted as part of the series canon. The first numbered entry since *Puppet Master 5*, *Axis Rising* would focus much of its marketing on being the tenth entry in the long-running series, despite actually being the eleventh in total. Even in an era when Full Moon's budgets were at their lowest, *Axis Rising* was meant to be something of an event movie, at least by this series' standards. Band even announced that he would be directing the movie himself, promoting it as his first time directing an entry of the franchise that had built Full Moon and that he had such a prominent role in creating—by this point, most of the merchandising had already begun to read *Charles Band's Puppet Master*. But this is also not entirely true. Albeit under a pseudonym, Band had helmed the present-day sequences in *Puppet Master: The Legacy*, which is an official entry in the series canon.[1] Nonetheless, it makes sense for Band to not have included that, as the new footage amounted to under twenty minutes. As it stands, *Puppet Master: Axis Rising* does mark his first time directing a full-length entry in the franchise.

In that respect, it's amazing that the series had lasted this long without a full-blown entry helmed by Band himself. This announcement also did exactly what it was supposed to do and sparked much speculation amongst longtime fans of both the franchise and Full Moon in general. What exactly would a Charles Band *Puppet Master* movie look like? After all, the *Puppet Master* films (alongside *Subspecies*) had always been the most serious Full Moon features, neither of which had ever had any entries directed by Band. Looking over most of his filmography, Band has always been a much more quirky filmmaker, with perhaps his most serious films being *Trancers* and *Doctor Mordrid*. His highlights as a director had always been in tongue-in-cheek exploitation showcases of the weird and bizarre, such as the successful *Head of the Family* and *Blood Dolls*. Those directorial trademarks made for so many eccentric and memorable Full Moon movies, but they didn't much match with what the *Puppet Master* series had been up to this point. Many fans began to wonder, as soon as Band made it known that he would be directing, whether he would adapt to the existing style of the franchise, or whether he would adapt the franchise to his own.

One thing became immediately clear, however. As promised years earlier, the second installment would be a direct continuation of the events of *Puppet Master: Axis of Evil*. This would mark only the second time in this franchise that a sequel would pick up immediately after the events of the previous, with the other being *Puppet Master 5*. In some ways, this would be even more of an accomplishment, as that was shot at the same time and *Axis Rising* would be following two years after the release of *Axis of Evil*. Since that film had been so recent, it would at least be easy to reel in fans without much of a lengthy recap. Writer Shane Bitterling was hired to write the script. Bitterling had previously written the film *Beneath Loch Ness* and the TV movie *Desperate Escape* and joined Full Moon to write *Axis Rising* alongside the company's attempt to capitalize on the then-current found footage craze, *Reel Evil*. Bitterling had been a friend of *Axis of Evil* scribe Brian Domonic Muir, who had passed away before that

Chapter Fourteen. Puppet Master: Axis Rising

film saw release. Familiar with the franchise and the general tone and style, Bitterling crafted a story that furthered the plot of the *Axis* trilogy while also—though likely accidentally—returning to some extremely familiar territory.

Bitterling recalls how he came to pen the project: "I knew Charlie for awhile. Courtney Joyner's one of my oldest friends out here, I've known him for twenty years. And Courtney was doing all that stuff, so I would always show up on set." He goes on to say, "another friend, Brian Muir, who was writing a lot for Charlie under a pseudonym—and again, I was always hanging out, so Charlie and I knew each other but we just hadn't worked for each other—and Brian died in 2010, and I kind of took it upon myself to hold what we called the Brian Muir-morial at the New Beverly Cinema, where we showed *Critters* and there's a whole story behind that. We all met at the bar and had a sendoff for him and Charlie was there. Somebody brought it up like 'Hey, why don't you have Shane?' Because Charlie was about to go into production on some stuff, so they said, 'Why don't you call Shane?' He called me and we talked and nothing really worked out for a little while, but then around the same time, Charlie had *Puppet Master X* that he wanted to do, and *Reel Evil*."

The feature begins with the death of Ozu, confirming that the villainess who had been met with relatively poor reception from fans would not be returning as the overarching antagonist of this new trilogy. In this respect, *Axis Rising* announces its differences right out of the gate. Ozu is killed before the opening credits to make room for a new Nazi villain: Commandant Moebius. Bitterling remembers the decision to take out Ozu so early on: "I would have liked to see her back, but I don't think we could have gotten the actress back. It was also a theme with Full Moon at the time where Charlie loved to see characters from the last movie set up in the new movie and killed immediately. And he did that in several Full Moon movies. He actually did it in the last *Puppet Master*. So that was just sort of a thing that he just *really* liked to do. That was kind of his idea. I would have liked to have brought her back, but it didn't really make sense for her to be in the script that I was doing, so it all worked out."

Moebius is a despicable S.S. Officer who has no redeeming qualities and has lost himself to the study of the occult, going mad in his search for ways to turn himself into some kind of god, pursuing a way to destroy the barrier between life and death. Joining him is his romantic partner and assistant, Uschi, a blond, buxom, sadistic nymphomaniac. The names may be different, but these characters match up almost directly with the antagonists of another World War II–set *Puppet Master* trilogy that had never materialized. They are almost identical to the villains Kron and Claire of the would-be *Puppet Wars* films. All we have to go by is how these characters are depicted on the page, of course, but as such they're astonishingly similar. Kron and Moebius share the same goals, the same obsessions and, above all, the same ruthlessness. Claire is identical to Uschi in terms of description, characterization, everything. With these two villains, the *Axis* movies almost become a self-fulfilling prophecy. Even though the *Puppet Wars* scripts were too ambitious to be made for what Full Moon could ever have afforded at the time—or could even afford now—the idea of a trilogy set during World War II was something Full Moon had never given up on. *Axis Rising* would prove that many key elements of those scripts would eventually make it to the screen, even if the ambitious stories themselves would not.

Scott King was cast as the villainous Moebius. Having done many small roles, featured extra work and short film appearances, Moebius would prove to be his big break in many ways. Not only was this a lead role, but it was also a role that allowed him to play a totally over-the-top scenery chewing madman. And there's no doubt that he brings all of those things to the role, pushing this Nazi antagonist into the realm of cartoonish satire. Yet, there are moments on the page that definitely feel as though they're meant to be shocking and probably would be, were it not for the incredibly scaled back production, which feels even smaller than *Axis of Evil*, even if it has a slightly larger scope. As his assistant Uschi, Stephanie Sanditz was cast. Like King, she had mostly done short film work at the time, as well as smaller roles in numerous TV series, but has gone on to appear in everything from *The Young and the Restless* to *It's Always Sunny in Philadelphia*.

Rounding out the main crew of bad guys would be Oto Brezina as Dr. Freuhoffer, a man held captive by the Nazis and forced to work on their experiments under the promise that if he cooperates he will be able to see his daughter once again. Brezina had appeared in numerous productions prior to *Axis Rising*, including the infamous *The Poughkeepsie Tapes*. He has also appeared in features such as *Rockin' Romeo & Juliet*, *Cry of the Mummy* and *Nude Nuns with Big Guns*. Freuhoffer's character is worth noting for several reasons. First and foremost, he is reflective of the earlier *Puppet Wars* scripts, as his motivations echo those of Ahmed Bey, the Egyptian scientist brought in to help the Nazis unlock the statue of Anubis in *Puppet Wars: Curse of the Puppet Master*. On a deeper level, though, this character bears a much stronger and much more obvious resemblance to a previous one: *Puppet Master III*'s Dr. Hess. Like Hess, Freuhoffer is forced to cooperate with a Nazi superior officer who will kill him if he does not deliver results. The differences here are numerous, though. For one, there's no banter between the two of them. Even though one of them was a looming, threatening presence over the other, there was an energy to the dynamic between Hess and Kraus in *Puppet Master III* that made it so engaging to watch. *Axis Rising* doesn't do much to recreate that, but there doesn't seem to be any attempt to. Ultimately, the two movies are aiming to achieve incredibly different things. *Toulon's Revenge* is incredibly earnest, aiming to reflect the horror of its setting while counterbalancing it with the heroic flair of golden age war movies. It's aiming to be about the time, whereas *Axis Rising*, like *Axis of Evil* before it, aims more to be *of* the time. While *Axis of Evil* seems to aim to reflect the reality of America in the '40s, *Axis Rising* feels much closer in tone and style to the wartime monster movies of that era.

This, if anything, is the premiere difference between *Toulon's Revenge* and the later prequels, even though they are on the surface very similar stories of the puppets battling Nazis in World War II. In style and tone, *Axis Rising* embraces the high camp absurdity of the monster movies of the 1940s. It's a movie about mad scientists and their bizarre creations. It seeks to recapture the magic of the '40s era of Universal, the less remembered time between classics such as *The Wolf Man* and *The Creature from the Black Lagoon,* when Dracula moved to Louisiana under an alias, Frankenstein's Monster and The Wolf Man went toe to toe and *The Mummy* became a glorified slasher franchise. It was an era for these characters where anything could happen, presuming it could happen on a limited number of sets. That almost perfectly sums up what Band sought to create with *Axis Rising* and the *Axis* trilogy in general. More than simply being a stylistic approach to the material, this is also probably the best and only approach Band could have taken given the current state of the studio. *Axis Rising* leans into its sheer cheapness by embracing the moneyless B-Movies that inspired it. Those same influences also make it much more of a Charles Band film than the preceding entries, not because of any budgetary reasons, but rather because the movie takes much more glee in the less realistic elements. Mad scientists and twisted creations are not only staples of '40s creature features, but also of Band's own filmography as director, particularly in the cases of *Blood Dolls, Hideous!* and *Head of the Family*.

Facing off against this trio of Nazi threats are the returning heroes Danny and Beth. While these are the protagonists of *Axis of Evil*, the actors do not carry over from that film. Instead, Danny Coogan is now portrayed by Kip Canyon and his girlfriend Beth is played by Jean Louise O'Sullivan. The change in actors is almost superficial, though, as they are both almost identical to the previous entry. Canyon still maintains Danny's limp, though his polio is much less of a focus in this film than its predecessor. He's just as good natured as Danny, just as naïve and carries that same willingness to throw himself into the fight without thinking twice, just to prove that he's *there*. In both movies, Danny is obsessed with his handicap, berating himself for being useless far more than anyone around him. By the start of this sequel, though, he's gotten a bit cockier since successfully bringing down a Nazi operation in *Axis of Evil*. In general, this movie almost plays as a sort of wish fulfillment for the character.

Jean Louise O'Sullivan, on the other hand, provides a slight reworking of the character of Beth. She remains a faithful and supportive girlfriend for the hero, but this new actress does her best to bring an untapped wit to the role. This is a much, much spunkier version of the character. By this point, having survived the events of the previous movie, she's as much a part of the fight as Danny and therefore has just as much of a say in what they should or should not do. She's not in agreement with him on everything, particularly when it comes to the latest addition to their group, Sarge. He's appointed to look after them following the events of *Axis of Evil*, in case the Nazis send another operative to take them out as they had attempted to do with Toulon. Sarge is a rough-and-tumble soldier of his era, a meathead and complete caveman. He and Beth see eye to eye on almost nothing.

Because of that, though, there's room for some interesting character work—and there are inklings of that in the feature, these two incredibly different people forced to work on the same side because they ultimately believe the same things—but developing that dynamic simply didn't prove to be a reality with the schedule and budget provided. If anything, Sarge mostly seems there to be the comic relief, which works because he takes himself almost completely seriously. Characters like this, macho, gritty soldier types almost always have louder, more colorful and obnoxious sidekicks to bounce off of. Here, Sarge is the sidekick, which at least allows the character to somewhat defy conventional genre trappings and tropes. It also allows for an egotistical hero similar to *Big Trouble in Little China*'s Jack Burton, only in this case, it's the puppets who continuously upstage Sarge—making that blow to the ego even more dramatic.

Of course, the stars of any *Puppet Master* movie are the puppets themselves, and this time the job fell to long-time franchise fan Tom Devlin to make them. "My first real experience with *Puppet Master*," says Devlin, "I was probably fifteen or sixteen years old, and I rented it from Movies on the Move in East Charlesworth, Pennsylvania, and actively fell in love with the series. I started rapidly collecting all the action figures, every variant of every figure there was, so my first experience was that I was just a huge fan. It was so punk rock because it was direct-to-video. Although I love *Child's Play,* this was like a killer doll movie for the outsiders. Growing up I found a lot of people shared the same experience, but for me it was like I thought I found something that nobody knew."

Devlin goes on to explain how he became involved with the film: "John Lechago and I had done a lot of films together. We kind of became really close friends as well as filmmaking soul mates. I get his vision and he trusts me to make it," and goes on to say: "He [John] was always working for Full Moon as a visual FX artist, on and off, and then he got offered to direct *Killjoy 3* in China. He went in and he had told Charlie that he wanted to bring his FX guy. Charlie said 'No, no, no, we have a whole FX team in China.' And John said, 'Well, I need my guy. We work well together and I really need him.' Charlie, for all of his pros, and maybe it is a pro, is cheap. He didn't want to bring another guy and fly another person and pay another person. But it just so happens to be that one of my better friends is Trent Haaga, who played Killjoy in *Part 2,* who they had no contact with. So John used that as leverage, said, 'Hey, my FX guy's buddies with Trent Haaga, we could have Killjoy back.' And Charlie was like, 'OK, let's talk to him.' All of a sudden, I was valuable."

For Devlin, the *Puppet Master* job was a long time coming: "I had been doing movies for Full Moon and Charlie for a good few years under a handshake agreement that I'll work for these peanuts because I'm doing the next *Puppet Master* movie. When it came to *Axis Rising,* I was working on *The Dead Want Women* and I found out that Chris Bergschneider was doing *Axis Rising.* And I got really upset about that. I just felt bummed out, man. I was like, 'I put all this work in, I'm trying to build a reputation.' Looking back, I totally get it. Chris was a veteran. He and Jeff together did a lot of great things. Chris is a great artist and he was a very good friend of mine, there's no bones. We used to teach together. But I got really mad and stormed off like a pouty little boy, and it wasn't until a couple of weeks later that Charlie called me and said, 'Dude, Chris can't handle all of this. There's more work to be done than one person can do. Chris is kind of stepping out of the production.' He made the Nazi puppets, which were Weremacht, Blitzkrieg, Bombshell and Kamikaze, and he said, 'But I need you to make me the traditional puppets.' Which was what I wanted to do anyway. Those were the puppets I grew up on."

Axis Rising also promises much more puppet action than the previous entry and, for the most part, it delivers. The puppets themselves are not as animated as they were in *Axis of Evil.* Blade's cone eyes and moving jaw are completely gone and Leech Woman's leeches and Tunneler's drill are both much more scaled back. Devlin's goal with *Axis Rising* seemed to be to bring the characters back to their glory days, feeling that *Axis of Evil* hadn't quite got the look right. "What I wanted to do to the puppets, in my mind, I was a little cockier back then and I hadn't done a full puppet feature, so I was like 'I'm gonna bring them back to their original look, I'm gonna bring back that *Part II* flair.' And I failed. I failed at it, and not for lack of trying," says Devlin. He explains, "It's just that a lot of those materials aren't available anymore. Every one puppet equals three puppets, at least. You have a stunt puppet, a rod puppet and an FX puppet. Doing five puppets is really doing it times three. I had three weeks to get them ready, I had never done a puppet movie, I had never used a sewing machine, my wife helped me with all the costumes, and it was really difficult."

By this point, Full Moon was deep in the swing of their replica sales. Along with the movies, these were the only things fans had to get excited about, even though many of them often complained about the sculpts of the puppets being so different from their film appearances. That wouldn't really be the case for long, though. Given that Full Moon had promised to only make 200 of each puppet, they came up with new versions and variants in order to keep the replica line going. In particular, they introduced Battle Damaged and Stealth puppets, making versions of Pinhead for both of those lines, and they are both looks that Pinhead wears in the movie in order to promote the replica sales. In an even more extreme example, Full Moon had just introduced a Stealth Six-Shooter replica before the release of *Axis Rising*. They had released their original Six-Shooter a few years after the others, as the puppet took so much longer to produce, given his build. In *Axis Rising*, Six-Shooter only appears toward the end, after a dramatic build-up to his reveal. His introduction plays out almost like a toy commercial. The heroes are in over their heads and they need back up, enter Stealth Six-Shooter to get the job done.

Bitterling remembers the origins of Stealth Six-Shooter as a replica first and foremost. "Yeah, that was Charlie. He's always thinking of the ancillary stuff on this. He wanted to bring back some of the puppets and said, 'We're going to basically sell a variant of the same thing. We're going to do Pinhead and we're going to do Six-Shooter.' But I had already written Six-Shooter in. So he was already in the script, and then he came up with the stealth thing."

Devlin also remembers the origins of Stealth Six-Shooter: "So, on *Axis Rising*, Stealth Six-Shooter and Stealth Pinhead literally came out like two weeks before *Axis Rising* started shooting. It was supposed to be the opposite from what I understood when I took the job, Stealth Six-Shooter and Stealth Pinhead were supposed to pop up at the end of the movie and then they were going to launch the replicas, so we would be establishing them in the movie rather than vise versa. Man, I was so excited to get to bring Six-Shooter back in black. He hadn't been in the last couple movies before that and I just was really excited and then it's like 'Oh, one shot of him and he's gone.' And Charlie didn't like my original sculpt on the head and we wound up using a replica head at one point. You can see both in the movie."

Without a doubt, though, the selling point of *Axis Rising* does not lie in the return of the Toulon puppets themselves. In the film's most ambitious move, the plot revolves around the heroic puppets facing off against a new team of Nazi puppets. They are Blitzkreig, a tank reminiscent of the toy robot from *Demonic Toys*, Weremacht, a werewolf puppet (worth noting, because a werewolf puppet had been included in the original concept artwork for the original film), Kamikaze, a '40s suicide bombing stereotype, and Bombshell, the puppet form of Uschi who shoots machine guns out of her breasts. The introduction of four new puppets proved to be the most ambitious decision made on this film, given its budget. Instead of returning to China, where they had shot *Axis of Evil,* Band elected to instead shoot the movie right in Los Angeles in just over a week. The new puppets in the mix bring at least some degree of low-end spectacle, something to lure in returning viewers with the promise of more puppet vs. puppet action than they'd seen before. And, of course, each of the new Nazi puppets would be receiving their own replica.

Of these new puppets, Bombshell is certainly the most noteworthy as she is the one thing most clearly, directly lifted from the abandoned *Puppet Wars* scripts. In *Puppet Wars,* Bombshell's name was an overt pun as she was planned to launch bombs out of her breasts. *Axis Rising* abandons that, giving the character the same S.S. uniform as that worn by her human counterpart. Instead of shooting bombs from her chest, the Bombshell of the movie shoots machine guns from her bosom in what seems to be a direct reference to the Fembots of *Austin Powers.* "This is just, forgetting how the movie turned out, the greatest thing you could ever do is create new puppets or a new puppet master," says Bitterling. "It's just awesome. So I came up with all the new Nazi puppets. And then I had written Bombshell, but her name was Barbie Wire. That character was basically the same, but she could extend her hands like and shoot them out like a grappling hook, and it was barbed wire. So she could strangle people that way, or repel, all that stuff. Then Charlie remembered, 'Oh, we have one that we never really used, Bombshell. Let's just change her to Bombshell.' That's really how that happened. It was before the script, I had to come up with little backgrounds and histories before I wrote the script, and it was in that stage that they changed her back to Bombshell."

Despite the new puppets, the action is back loaded to the final few minutes and plays out relatively quickly. While *Axis Rising* had an impressive number of puppeteers, including the returning Christopher Bergschneider, there was only so much that they could do with the amount of time provided. The showdown is, at the very least, longer than that seen in *Puppet Master vs. Demonic Toys.* The highlight of this battle is a catfight between Bombshell and Leech Woman. Having sat out *Puppet Master 4* and *5* as well as *Puppet Master vs. Demonic Toys,* this would be the first time Leech Woman had ever actually fought another puppet and even though the fight devolves into a comical slap-fest, it's still one of the major highlights.

Bitterling notes that the finale was originally meant to be much more involved. "The movie kind of turned out what it was, but the thing that's always really frustrating is that the scripts that I do, they always have, like … an ending," he says and goes on to add, "When I write these things I know how they're going to be shot, so I kind of write for that, and then it's always taken like a few steps down from there. Maybe it was five pages and we can maybe do this in three shots or four shots and then he'll do all of the kind of puppet pickup stuff after the shoot. 'Maybe we'll do the rest from there,' but then it winds up being one shot. The Nazi guy, Moebius, he gets thrown in the rejuvenation tank, he comes out like a super Nazi and he's all messed up, and that was going to be a big thing, but as it is now I think he trips and Blade sticks a knife in his neck. It would be off screen or cheated, someone would just stab something into somebody's neck, and I was kind of like, 'Oh, okay. That's pretty anti-climactic and not cool, but it's kind of expected.'"

Chapter Fourteen. Puppet Master: Axis Rising

Devlin's reflections on the film as a whole are also bittersweet. "There's elements of *Axis Rising* that I love, but so much that I would have changed if I had known what I was doing. Not that I was a newbie or anything, but it's a whole different world making puppets than making full, walk-around creatures. It's completely different. I had made little gargoyles and monsters before, but never a full cast of very important characters that aren't supposed to look stupid."

While the attempts to sell replicas are overt in *Axis Rising*, this is not the first time that Full Moon had done this, to be fair. The Medicom variant of the Jester action figure mirrored his appearance in the then-new *Curse of the Puppet Master* and *Retro Puppet Master* had had an entire action figure series to promote it. If there was any difference this time, it's that both the new movie and its tie-in merchandise were all being sold in the same place, as most fans were buying everything directly through the Full Moon Direct website at this point in time. The other noteworthy factor is that some of these replicas preceded the movie itself, they were simply things that Full Moon was selling at the time. Both the variant Jester and the *Retro* figures had been released to promote their respective movies, whereas *Axis Rising* in some places feels like a movie that was made to promote things already available on Full Moon's site at the time.

The promotional train ran both ways, though, as Full Moon tried harder than ever to promote this new entry in the saga. From the new puppets, to the fact that they were acknowledging it as the tenth entry in the series and the first one to be directed by creator Charles Band, Full Moon went harder than ever to promote this movie and make sure it was something fans both wanted and needed to see. *Axis of Evil* had brought some fans back into the fold, but not all of them. Full Moon no longer had video stores at its back to bring in curious viewers who were not necessarily familiar with the franchise. The only way this series was going to survive was to market itself directly to the longtime fans, so that's exactly what Full Moon did. From the tie-in replicas to all sorts of deals on the site, including signed copies of the screenplay and posters signed by the cast. This was Charles Band the showman, completely unrestrained, because he no longer had anyone else to promote these movies for him. There was no one at his back anymore. As in-your-face as the new puppets and their respective replicas were, these were the things that needed to be done to sell the movie and ensure that it made back its very low production cost. In many ways, *Axis Rising* marks the point when the production of a *Puppet Master* movie truly became a communal experience between Full Moon and its fan base.

To drive that point home, Full Moon even reintroduced the Executive Producer credit, something that they had previously done for the films *Petrified, Gingerdead Man 3: Saturday Night Cleaver* and *Killer Eye: Halloween Haunt*. For those movies, fans who spent a certain amount of money during a sale or event or purchased a special deal on the website—such as the Full Moon Evergreen Card, which had just been introduced at the time—would receive an executive producer credit on an upcoming Full Moon movie. Fans had been excited to have their name in the credits of one of the company's movies, but for *Puppet Master: Axis Rising* it meant even more. For some people, this was an opportunity to see their name in the credits of their favorite franchise. By that same token, however, people who had been promised their name in the credits of some of the previous offers hadn't actually wound up receiving their credit, largely due to the complicated process of writing hundreds of people's names into the credit scroll. There was bound to be some oversight, but for those diehard fans to whom *Puppet Master* meant more than any other Full Moon movie, their exclusion from the credits would be devastating. Even still, *Axis Rising* felt in some ways like a completely fan funded production. A *Puppet Master* movie made by fan money in order to do nothing more than ensure the franchise's future.

And it seemed as though that future looked brighter than ever. With the release of *Axis Rising* Bad also took to a Vidcast to announce *Puppet Master Forever*, a promotion that seemed to be nothing more than the promise on Full Moon's part to release a *Puppet Master* movie every two years, apparently for as long as they possibly could. More than anything, this seemed to be a way to assure the fans that the series was not going anywhere. *Axis Rising* had been the second part of a planned trilogy, but there had never been any news about where the series planned to go beyond that. With the announcement of *Puppet Master Forever,* though, fans knew that they'd be seeing as much of the puppets as they could possibly stand.[2]

Full Moon began to adjust to its almost impossibly low budgets by making its movies more slapstick, more akin to Lloyd Kaufman's Troma movies. In the past, they had never really done that. Full Moon's movies had always taken themselves somewhat seriously, embracing different tones and styles depending on the stories they were attempting to tell. This continued to be the case even after their first dramatic budgetary cutbacks during the Kushner/Locke era. But this era of the company's history marked a dramatic shift which *Axis Rising* best showcases, in which Full Moon began to change their model to reflect something a little more similar to Troma's. It made sense for the budgetary realities, but still couldn't help but be an extreme shift so late in the game for the studio. Full Moon had begun embracing their inherent campiness and low-budget, lowbrow antics in a much bigger way than they had ever done before. Rightfully, one could begin to wonder where *Puppet Master* fit into that, if it even fit into that model at all.

But it was not something fans would even have to worry about for long. *Puppet Master Forever* was the new moniker, a promise made by Full Moon that, for fans unimpressed with the recent entries, felt like a warning. Whether they wanted it or not, whether they were excited, prepared, or ready or not, more *Puppet Master* was coming their way. Potentially more than they had ever seen before. With the release of *Axis Rising* two years after *Axis of Evil,* this seemed like a foolproof business model. Full Moon had settled into a new rhythm and had figured out a way to sell straight-to-video movies in the internet age. They were now running directly off the money put into them by the fans, and therefore it only made sense to cater to what the fans wanted, so the promise of *Puppet Master Forever* was two-fold. No matter where Band went or who he met, no matter what new franchises Full Moon began to build, *Puppet Master* was always in high demand. And so it seemed fans would look forward to the franchise in perpetuity, just as the studio would look forward to delivering on that promise. Whether either of them truly wanted it didn't seem to matter, because the promise had been made, and *Puppet Master* was here to stay.

Chapter Fifteen

The Action Lab Comics

By early 2014, it became clear that Full Moon's *Puppet Master Forever* promise would already be broken and that they would not be producing an entry in the franchise every two years. This did nothing to slow their momentum, however, nor were most fans worried. Everyone knew that the concluding chapter in the *Axis* trilogy would be on its way eventually and the company continued to produce movies in that time, offering up new entries in the *Gingerdead Man* and *Evil Bong* franchises and even combining the two characters together in a crossover, harking back to the glory days of *Dollman vs. Demonic Toys*.

At a panel during the 2014 San Diego Comic Con, Charles Band surprised every *Puppet Master* fan by announcing a partnership with Action Lab Comics (specifically their adult-themed imprint, Action Lab Danger Zone) for an upcoming *Puppet Master* comic series.[1] From the get-go, this was an exciting prospect. There had not been any *Puppet Master* comics since the two Eternity miniseries in 1991. Those had, of course, hailed from a time before *Puppet Master II* had even been released. Because of that, from the ground up, this new comic series would be different in every way. It would not only be able to use characters like Six-Shooter and Decapitron, who had never made it into the Eternity books, but would also be able to tell stories in the present day, which the Full Moon entries in the franchise had not really done since *Curse of the Puppet Master*, as even *Puppet Master: The Legacy* was mostly flashback. The idea of returning to the present to carry on with the puppets in the modern era was, already, something that proved exciting for longtime fans. With the movies stuck in the past, so to speak, while also being hindered by all-time low budgets for the franchise, there was something extremely exciting about the notion of *Puppet Master* stories that would only be hindered by imagination and not by what the puppets could and could not do on a short schedule for a minimal amount of money.

Writer Shawn Gabborin was best known at the time for his indie horror comic *Fracture*. He had been a fan of *Puppet Master* and of Full Moon in general since childhood, and when revisiting the entire franchise and watching it in order, had begun to notice the numerous plot holes and inconsistencies that had come up several times over the course of ten movies. Rather than glossing over them, these inconsistencies or unresolved plot threads sparked ideas. Gabborin reached out to Charles Band just to see about obtaining the *Puppet Master* or even the Full Moon license for the sake of creating new comics. Band immediately agreed and the comics were up and running. The *Puppet Master* series would be the only monthly ongoing title, with other Full Moon properties being handled as miniseries under the *Full Moon Presents* banner. To draw the series, Gabborin brought on Italian artist Michela Da Sacco, an extremely promising rising talent. Even though she was unfamiliar with the series, Da Sacco showed that she could nail the likenesses of the classic puppets from the very first artwork showcased at the Comic Con announcement.

Gabborin remembers what led him to the decision to pitch the series to Full Moon. "Well, my wife bought me, I think it was *Puppet Master X* that she bought me for my birthday or Christmas, maybe. And I just, over the course of like a week or two, I sat down and watched through the whole franchise in order, because that's what we do as geeks. That's what I grew up with and everything, and watching all the movies, I'm seeing things that could be expanded on and the cool mythology and all that stuff like, 'Oh, yeah, I remember that from when I was younger and would watch these every weekend.' And just by the time I was done with those ten movies I had, in my head, a list of notes of stuff I'd want to do. And I was like, 'There's so much fun to be had with this.' So I just, you know, I've been writing comics for a number of years now. And this is a franchise I feel I know pretty well. So I just figured you know, what the hell, it couldn't hurt to reach out and ask."

The series kicks off with a three-issue arc called "The Offering" which is designed to essentially bring the reader up to speed on the concept of *Puppet Master* in general. This opening act is interesting as it almost plays out like the perfect template for a reboot. This is a modern story with modern characters, a cast fit for a slasher as each of them are in their twenties and each of them embodies a different archetype, for the most part, though at least a few of them prove to be a little more layered as the story unfolds. "The Offering" doesn't break continuity at all, but it's not bogged down by it either. It feels perfectly designed to appeal to old fans with a story that is more similar in tone and style to that of *Puppet Master I* and *II,* but at the same time, also brings in new readers by giving them an old story and presenting it in a new way. "The Offering" has several impressive twists and turns, especially when it comes to the way The Bodega Bay Inn is seen by the locals. The offerings of the title are dolls that are brought and left in the hotel to appease the spirits of the puppets that may or may not have committed all those murders so many years ago. For most people, it's nothing more than a local ghost story, which establishes a great atmosphere.

"The Offering" is different from the comic storylines that follow it for several reasons, the most obvious being that it doesn't dig deep into the franchise's mythology or attempt to necessarily answer any of the series' unanswered questions. Instead, "The Offering" is for the most part a back to basics, tried and true *Puppet Master* story. And in its own way, even that proved to be refreshing for fans who hadn't seen a story like that in so long, given the more heroic direction the series had taken after *Puppet Master II.* Like the original *Puppet Master*, "The Offering" reaffirms that the puppets are not evil on their own, unless they are directed to commit evil acts by the person who has asserted themselves as their master. With as many directions as the series had taken by this point, Gabborin made a great effort of clearly establishing the rules of the mythology and presenting them in a way that was easy to digest.

One does not need to read "The Offering" to understand the story of "Rebirth," but the first arc flows into the second quite nicely. The first arc is meant to bring the reader up to speed on exactly what the mythology is while also obviously telling a new and engaging story at the same time. The second immediately gets to work reinventing and expanding that mythology, now that the groundwork has been laid. Nothing is lost on longtime fans of the series. Right from the first few pages, it presents an amazing hook that could have served as its own effective story, as Blade follows a man to a fortune teller who places his soul into the body of an inanimate puppet for a limited time so that he can return home to kill his wife and her lover. This woman is running a business in which she places the souls of people into the bodies of puppets for a limited time so that they can kill anyone they want without leaving a single identifiable trace of evidence. Murder without consequence. Blade spies on her to affirm that the stories they overheard of this fortune teller, Madam Adon, possessing some of Toulon's inanimate puppets to be true. Blade confirms this without telling them of the murders. For the puppets, this is the goal they have always dreamed of: the promise to finally return to the world of flesh and blood and leave their wooden, puppet bodies behind.

From that initial concept, "Rebirth" promised to be the most inventive and imaginative *Puppet Master* story in decades, and it delivers on that promise in spades. At its core, the arc is essentially a "be careful what you wish for" story in the vein of W.W. Jacobs' classic "The Monkey's Paw." The puppets leap at the chance to return to human form and finally start their lives anew, free of bending to the will of a master, free of their small wooden forms. They do not hesitate; they don't think twice to consider passing up the chance to become human beings once again. Since the early entries, the puppets had clearly become the protagonists of this saga. They were the characters everyone showed up to see, but those moments of characterization were brief and were entirely due to the gifted FX artists bringing the puppets to life. Given that the puppets could only make basic noises and could not even speak, there wasn't much that could really be done to explore them as characters.

"Rebirth" has the chance to do that, even if for a limited time, and does not waste the opportunity for a moment. In *Puppet Master III*, we were given the names of most of the characters. Hans Siederman, the Jester; Herman Strauss, Pinhead; and, of course, Elsa became Leech Woman and Hess became Blade over the course of that movie. Tunneler's origin was perhaps the deepest cut here, as his name (Joseph Sebastian) had only ever been given in a *Puppet Master III* trading card. Six-Shooter and Torch, on the other hand, had never had their real names or pre-puppet origins explained. Fans had speculated for years as to who they might have been, how they might have known Toulon or how they became puppets, but "Rebirth" presented the opportunity to finally have some answers in an actual, official *Puppet Master* story. Still, fans were somewhat skeptical after years of their own ideas, so the new comic book storyline would need to prove itself in execution. And that it did.

"I smiled a lot at their interactions," Gabborin says of the chance to give the puppets full-blown dialogue for the first time. "It was nice, growing up as a fan of all these characters, to finally have them talk to each other and finally get to see how they interact."

The characters are all so grateful to return to human life that they do not question how they came about it or whether or not the deal they made with Madam Adon the fortune teller was too good to be true. The first major reveal, though the origin is given out gradually over the course of the four-issue arc, is that Torch is a child. As the story develops, the reader learns that the spirit inside Torch is actually that of Toulon and Elsa's son, Erich. With the couple devoting their lives to the entertainment of children, Erich felt abandoned and unloved, believing that they cared more for other people's kids than for their own. He ran away from home and, though matrilineally Jewish, was adopted into the Hitler Youth because of his blond hair and blue eyes—a trait inherited from his father, if one takes *Retro Puppet Master* into account. As he would almost certainly have been killed for his origins had he not gotten involved with their affairs, Erich was treated as a young Nazi soldier in training. Armed with a flamethrower, he was even sent to kill his own father. Because Toulon had never told the other puppets of Erich, they assumed the boy to be another Nazi soldier and Blade slit his throat. That would make Torch the first puppet to have been killed by another one of the core cast of puppets.

This origin completely brings Torch's entire character into perspective, as fans had always noted how angrier he seemed to be than the other puppets and how he didn't seem to gel with the rest of the group. When Torch is introduced in *Puppet Master II,* he burns Martha just after watching her kill his own mother, Leech Woman. Even Torch killing a child in *Puppet Master II* is completely re-contextualized if he himself is a child. Torch also provides lasting ramifications to Toulon's actions while he was insane and undead in that sequel. Erich is someone how would never have brought into this life had he been in his right mind, as he mentions in "Rebirth." While the other puppets forgave him for that and they have all appeared to move on since then, Torch manages to be the lasting impact of evil, undead Toulon.

Gabborin recalls how and why he settled on the origin of Torch. "For me, it really came down to, 'well, he's making a new puppet and that puppet is rather aggressive.' And who would he, knowing the souls in all these puppets, who would he bring back at that point with his brain so screwed up? And to me, my mind went straight to his kid. There was never a sign that he had a kid or anything, but it just fit to me. When you watch *Part II,* he kills that kid who's yelling at him, calling him a Nazi. He's being told that this woman is the reincarnation of his mother, so he goes after the guy that's sleeping with her. When who he *knows* is his mother in Leech Woman gets thrown in the fire, he flips out and just torches that lady. So to me, it just made sense to tie all that together to give him a reason for being so aggressive toward those particular people. For someone who is the child of someone obsessed with wood to love fire made sense to me too."

Six-Shooter, on the other hand, turns out to be far less of a mystery. Unlike Torch, we don't get too much of his backstory in "Rebirth" nor do we even learn his real name, despite spending time with him as a human character. In this instance, it's a refreshing case of the puppet being a direct reflection of who that human was. Shooter, as he likes to be called, is every inch the smirking cowboy that his puppet counterpart has always appeared to be. The story sees each of them attempt to move on with their lives, splitting up almost immediately. Herman takes to the open road and Hess steps back into being a doctor and it suggests that they are finally returning to normalcy until they start to be picked off one by one by the puppet bodies that they left behind. As the plot unfolds, it becomes clear that Madam Adon is using the Toulon puppets as she used all the others and is allowing people to occupy the puppets in order to hunt down Toulon and his friends, leaving each of their souls to awaken in a Hellish dimension, the home of the demon Sutekh. By the end of "Rebirth" we are introduced to the main antagonist of the comic series, Anapa, son of Sutekh. While they did succeed in killing the elder demon in *Puppet Master 4* and *5*, Anapa claimed that he would take their souls should anything ever happen to him, and now they have returned to the demon's home.

While Anapa is initially drawn to look exactly the same, he does prove to be a very different character from Sutekh as the series progresses. For one thing, Anapa is not remotely interested in protecting the sanctity of the secret of life and killing all those who seek to tamper with it. If anything, he enjoys tampering with it and relishes in people like Madam Adon who corrupt this magic for their own gain. Through much of "Rebirth" fans are led to wonder if Erich is inherently evil, or if he just wants to leave his father and the Toulon legacy behind. That's what makes it such a surprise that, in the end, Erich saves the day by making a deal with Anapa so that they return to their puppet bodies if they essentially do favors for the demon. Even though the status quo is returned by the end of the story, it sets up a larger narrative and proves to have lasting consequences, as all great stories do.

Without a doubt, the best moments of "Rebirth," as big a story as it is, are the small, character moments that play on the franchise's long legacy. It plays to the sentiment of the audience, knowing that that readership is largely built of fans who have been following the series for years if not decades, in the best way possible, allowing for moments that are both heartwarming and heartbreaking in genuinely surprising equal doses. These are best exemplified by a brief scene in which, after they are first returned to human form, Hans asks to keep the Jester puppet much to the surprise of the group. When asked why, he holds the small puppet's hand in his and looks at it warmly as he says, "They weren't all bad times." These are the moments of not just nostalgia, but sincere humanity that Gabborin brought to the story and the characters.

Gabborin reflects on the genesis of the "Rebirth" arc and how it shaped the series as a whole. "One of the things I always try to stick with in writing is the thought that you have to know the rules before you can break them. So I wanted to do 'The Offering,' just a nice traditional *Puppet Master* kind of story, to reintroduce everybody to where in the timeline these stories will take place, and it's for new readers who don't know anything about it. Like, I've had some people that read this that didn't even know there were movies. And that's pretty cool to me, that they were able to get into it and enjoy the stories, not knowing that there was anything more."

The third storyline, "Wooden Boy" attempts to tie up one of the franchise's most prominent loose ends: the cliffhanger ending of *Puppet Master II*. At the end of that film, the puppets are seen with the newly reanimated Camille, who has been transferred into a human-sized puppet body. She's turned them into a traveling sideshow and they are off to entertain the children of the Bouldeston Institute for Mentally Troubled Tots and Teens, but that story is never addressed in any of the sequels and Camille is never heard from again. "Wooden Boy" heads back to the Bouldeston

Institute to explain what happened after *Puppet Master II* as well as highlighting the effect that Camille has had on the institute since that time. Much like the puppets were to the Bodega Bay Inn in "The Offering," Camille has become a ghost story, a sort of local urban legend.

The children at the institute still tell stories about her, some even still claim to see her from time to time. When Toulon and the puppets catch word of this, they return to the institute to see if Camille is actually still alive and still causing havoc. Like, "The Offering" there are still many twists and turns throughout "Wooden Boy" so that the story plays out in truly unexpected ways. Without a doubt, the biggest thing this arc introduces to the ongoing narrative of the series is Anthony, the wooden boy of the title, as he has a wooden leg. By the end of the arc, it's revealed that Anthony is the son of none other than Neil Gallagher, the villain of the original film.

In addition to the main series, Action Lab also released two *Puppet Master* Halloween Specials. The first was set in 1988 a year before the original *Puppet Master*, with Gallagher using the puppets to slaughter a sorority as a way to sort of gauge what they can do. The second, set in 1989 a few weeks after the original, sees a monster sneak into the hotel that the puppets then dispose of, only to realize it was actually a trick-or-treater. Originally, though, that issue was going to have a different ending, touching on one of the few films rarely referenced in the comic series: *Curse of the Puppet Master*. "It was going to end with Megan catching the puppets with this dead body," says Gabborin. "And that would lead to her putting them up for sale, which would have Magrew showing up to buy them. But with that being a one-shot and me not following that up anywhere, I figured I'd just wrap it up. Better for new readers who weren't aware of *Curse*." This is also of note because it would have provided a concrete answer to where in the timeline *Curse* is set, something that fans have speculated about for a long time.

After "Wooden Boy" the comic laid all of the groundwork for its developing plot, which proved to be incredibly high stakes and ambitious, something that could only be done on the comic book page. The puppets found themselves facing off against a host of enemies, from the demon Anapa made flesh to the demon's servants—the same villains previously seen in *Retro Puppet Master*—as well as several new pint-sized enemies. Gallagher and Camille both became recurring antagonists, cementing their place as some of the franchise's Biggest Bads. While the storytelling grew bigger and bigger as the series went on, Gabborin still found the time the give the fans just enough of the small moments and clever references that made this new comic series so great to begin with. It's noted at one point, for example, that Six-Shooter had a checkered past that he kept hidden from the others, including the fact that he sold information to both sides during the war. Because the gift of seeing the puppets in human form was so revolutionary for advancing their characters in "Rebirth," Gabborin devised a way for the characters to still be able to occasionally converse with one another in a psychic communal headspace of Anthony's doing. This allowed them to voice their opinions in clearer ways than having to pantomime them, as well as allowing the puppets to even make their distrust apparent. As the later arc, "Blood Debt" points out, Six-Shooter was absent for several years and they allowed him back into their ranks without question, so he should not be so quick to judge others, according to Blade. This is a direct reference to the fact that Six-Shooter was absent during the events of *Puppet Master I* and *II*. While this is obviously nothing more than a practical error as the puppet was not introduced until the third entry, callbacks like this only highlighted what this comic was able to do at its best. It took these references and plot holes and used them as prompts, not just filling them in but using them as jumping off points for stories that would advance the characters and their respective universes.

The *Puppet Master* comics told stories in a very familiar universe in ways that were completely new, yet still offered so many things for long time fans to be excited about on a monthly basis. The brief appearances of the puppets in human form allowed the readers to see their interplay between one another for the very first time, making friendships that had only been hinted at by two puppets standing close together in the movies into genuine bonds on the page. Andre, of course, always proved to be the key factor, the one person that brought each of them into this. But other friendships, such as those between Six-Shooter and Tunneler or Leech Woman and Blade were delightful to see and offered sincere character moments for people who had never really had the opportunity to have them.

If "The Offering" was not enough to lure in cautious fans, "Rebirth" seemed to do the trick for readers who genuinely wanted to see these characters treated with care and taken in bold new directions. They happily jumped on board as the story evolved from month to month, with the villainous Anapa amassing his own group of nefarious puppets and bringing the young Anthony closer and closer to his mysterious, dark destiny. Fans eagerly bought the new comics as they came out each month. Even as the series entered its twentieth issue, it showed no signs of slowing down, not even for a moment. It even promised to once again go back and address one of the franchise's biggest unanswered question, finally addressing what happened after the events of *Retro Puppet Master* by bringing back those first-generation puppets for an arc titled "Retro Now."

That arc began with issue #19 and continued into issue #20. It once again did what this series did at its best by finding new ways to explore familiar concepts in an old anthology. This arc saw Andre travel with the Retro Puppets to a village called Peterstown, which was founded by a descendant of Peter Hertz, Toulon's young assistant from *Puppet Master III* and the protagonist of *Puppet Master: The Legacy*. Toulon quickly learned upon arrival that the residents of Peterstown were obsessed with the stories of his puppets, which Peter had so fondly told his family over the years. These people came together to form a sort of commune with one common goal: to achieve enlightenment by shedding their shells of flesh and committing a mass suicide to channel their souls into full-sized wooden bodies. Amazingly, after nearly thirty years, this would mark the first cult storyline in the *Puppet Master* mythos and would also simply in its concept be the most genuinely unsettling story ever told within the franchise.

It would also ultimately go unfinished.

After issue #20, the second of the "Retro Now" arc, months and months went by without a new issue of *Puppet Master*. As the series had been licensed for a 30-issue run, fans were growing concerned that the comic book had been cancelled. Months went by without any clear word as to the status of the comic as a whole, let alone the next issue. What was initially believed to be a printing issue—at least on the part of speculative readers—clearly proved to be something greater as the months went on. Eventually, it became clear that issue 20 would be the end and that the series would not be coming back to resume its monthly schedule. For fans who had not only enjoyed reading, but had finally latched onto extremely energetic storytelling from the series they loved, which had been met with lukewarm reactions over the last several on-screen entries. For so many fans, this series had proven to be a dream come true and even if 20 issues were more than anyone had ever expected a *Puppet Master* comic series to run for, it was a blow nonetheless.

Gabborin recalls how "Retro Now" would have played out, had the arc been able to reach its natural conclusion. "The whole town would have gone through the Great Transition," he says, "because Toulon wouldn't have been able to stop them. You would have had most who went willingly and some who would have been forced into it. Basically, you'd have Toulon and the Retros stopping the cult leader and offering everybody, basically, 'You can stay here like this, living in these wooden bodies, and you can keep your noses down, don't bother people, don't attract attention, stay under the radar. Or, we're going to start a bonfire over in that field, if you don't want to stay like this. That's your way out, right now.' And, you know, you'd have some people choosing one way or the other. My intention was to leave the other Retros there as sort of their new guard to help them get used to this, for as long as the Retros would last. Because, to me, they're a different magic set. They drain on Toulon to stay active, so they wouldn't have stuck around forever."

After months of silence it was revealed that the *Puppet Master* comics would be returning in the form of a three-part miniseries titled *Curtain Call,* which would effectively bring an end to the Action Lab era of the franchise's comic book legacy. While far from the originally planned number of issues, this would at least give fans closure in the form of a definitive ending and was thus still something to be excited about.

Appropriately, *Curtain Call* picks up a year after the last issue, as the first issue of the miniseries saw release a year after the last issue of the ongoing title, making the time between comics for fans felt in real time within the series as well. This time, instead of tying up loose ends from the film series, Gabborin was faced with the much more challenging task of tying up all of the loose ends built up over the course of this ongoing comic series in the span of three issues. So many questions had gone unanswered, not the least of them being what had happened to the characters after readers had last seen them in Peterstown. The series had also been building up a new, mysterious villain known only as The Collector, who had fittingly been collecting those puppets that the movies had seemed to discard, from Ninja and Bombshell down to *Curse of the Puppet Master*'s Tank. This villain appeared to have his own motivations and plans for the puppets, which fans had speculated for months.

The opening pages of *Curtain Call* see the puppets under The Collector's employ and forced to kill a great number of people to suit their new master's purposes. During this time, he also reveals in a very quick throwaway line at least part of the explanation for Six-Shooter's absence in the first two films, noting that the puppet had spent several years under his employ without the knowledge of the other characters. This not only explains why Six-Shooter would want to keep the reasons for his absence hidden, but also at least hints at the potential for a larger story that provides layers to the character, simply by the fact that he's the only puppet in the group to serve as a sort of double agent (which was hinted at when it was noted that this was exactly what he had done as a soldier in the war) and provides the others with a legitimate reason not to trust him, even if he wasn't acting against them necessarily. It's something, at least, but it's a story that had clearly been meant to be explored in a larger context rather than a single line. This was the first example to tell fans that *Curtain Call* would do its best to address as many unresolved stories as possible, but that it could not necessarily take the time to deal with all of them.

Curtain Call reveals a surprising answer to Six-Shooter's absence in *Puppet Master I* and *II*, other than the natural answer that he had been created for *Puppet Master III*. That being a prequel, it's noticeable when the puppet is not in the first two but appears in every subsequent sequel. *Curtain Call* reveals that during that time, Six-Shooter had been working under the employ of the mysterious villain The Collector, who had been introduced earlier in the comic as someone collecting those rare living puppets who had maybe only appeared once or twice in the franchise and then had never been seen again. This creates an interesting dynamic between Six-Shooter and the other characters, and adds surprising depth and gray area to the little six-armed cowboy. Gabborin recalls the twist and how it would have played out had the series wrapped up as initially intended. "I mean, I had hinted on it. The biggest was pointed out earlier [in the series] that Six-Shooter had been working both sides during World War II. And it would have been involved with who the Collector is, and that Six-Shooter was working with him even as a puppet, at the time, he was working with him and doing things for him. And that's why Six-Shooter was missing from the first couple movies and showed up after part three, because he finally broke away and got back to the main group."

Despite months of build-up, The Collector is killed right off the bat, his soul placed into an amalgamation of *Axis Rising*'s Nazi puppets known appropriately as The Collection. Anapa and his followers then race back to the Bodega Bay Inn for a final standoff against Toulon, Anthony and the puppets while the demon finally makes his play for world domination. The rest of the miniseries does the tricky, commendable task of addressing unanswered questions and providing satisfying character beats, all during what essentially amounts to an extended action sequence. There are breaks, moments to at least share a few words with one another, but from the moment the action hits the hotel it never lets up, leaving no doubt that this miniseries would at the very least be a finale worthy of the title. *Curtain Call* brings a definitive end to the Action Lab comics and to this small era of the *Puppet Master* saga, bringing finality to the book without necessarily feeling overtly final. There is an impactful and deeply emotional resolution, but there is also an open-endedness to it. The final issue promises in pure *Puppet Master* tradition that this is not necessarily the end, it's simply the end for now.

Curtain Call wrapped up as many loose ends as possible, even if some of them were only mentioned in a single panel and managed to bring a definitive end to the comic series that had already become embraced by so many fans. But there are still some unresolved answers as to *why* it had to be wrapped up this way in the first place. The first and most obvious solution would simply be poor sales. Even though the series was written to bring in anyone with a passing interest in the material, not solely to appease older fans, a *Puppet Master* comic series is in itself inherently niche. It's amazing that it went on for as long as it did in the first place. Piracy also proved to be at least somewhat of an issue, with so-called fans often taking to social media to ask where they could download the latest issue without actually having to buy it—sometimes even stooping to ask this question of the creators themselves. While it might not be the major component that led to the series' cancellation, it certainly didn't help the comic's sales, either.

Even though the series had reached a satisfying conclusion, the ending proved to be bittersweet, as there were still stories left to be told in that universe. Shortly after the end of the *Puppet Master* title, the other Full Moon related books at Action Lab came to a close as well, with the final miniseries appropriately being a comic book follow-up to the studio's second most popular franchise, *Subspecies*. The Action Lab deal had come to a close, and to the shock of most fans, it proved to be something of a blessing in disguise. In early summer 2018, it was announced that even though Full Moon's partnership with Action Lab was no more, two of that publisher's talents—Shawn Gabborin and Brockton McKinney—would be teaming with Charles Band to develop Full Moon's very own comic book imprint, effectively titled Full Moon Comix.

The new imprint launched in August 2018 with the debut miniseries *Dollman Kills the Full Moon Universe*, which saw Gabborin return to write the puppets (along with a slew of other Full Moon characters, including the Demonic Toys) alongside Brockton McKinney, less than a year after the end of the Action Lab series. He also penned a tie-in prequel comic book for *Blade: The Iron Cross*. While the ongoing comic had not ultimately been allowed to run its course, it proved that fans of the franchise were hungry for content like this, that they wanted to see these characters continue on the page. It made it clear that, as they had been doing with so many things in recent years, Full Moon could sustain a comic book imprint of their very own. As Charles Band had so often related the characters to comics and thought of the Full Moon universe as one as interconnected as Marvel or DC, the notion of finally bringing a Full Moon comic book universe to life seemed like something that almost had to happen at some point in time. But the success of the Action Lab comics had taken that hypothetical assumption and made it something tangible. Even if it had been forced to overcome some hiccups and hurdles, the *Puppet Master* comic book series had proven that there was a wealth of new life to be found in comics for these and many of the other Full Moon characters.

Chapter Sixteen

Puppet Master: Axis Termination

While Full Moon struggled to keep up through the early 2010s in a world that had seemed to all but abandon direct-to-video entertainment in favor of VOD, the company announced a completely new and ultimately inevitable direction starting in 2013 with the launch of Full Moon Streaming.[1] In the age of Netflix, Hulu and virtually every company under the sun hungry to produce its own content and create its own streaming service, Full Moon was in some respects ahead of the curve. There are still new streaming services being announced by major companies who are only just now starting to realize the importance of streaming content. But Band, who had already had many of his films available via streaming through Hulu, understood that importance perfectly. Thanks to a number of factors, Netflix among them, the age of the video store was dead and buried. The company couldn't simply keep operating under the same model hoping that a bygone era would come back. Band had always been a producer who had survived by adapting as best he could to the time and by attempting to keep up with—if not ahead of—the curve. In many ways, Full Moon Streaming was a no-brainer. With so many films under his belt through so many different companies, there would be more than enough content to launch with and new favorites would be added all the time. For longtime fans, there was an undeniable appeal to having every Full Moon movie in one place, at their fingertips. But in truth, it was simply the move that the company *needed* to take to survive in this new world.

Other than replicas and other promotional merchandise, *Puppet Master* as a franchise remained mostly on the backburner through 2014 and 2015 as a whole. Through all of this, Band still promised that the third film in the *Axis* trilogy would be coming, but it would take time to get it right, so fans would have to wait. By all accounts, it looked as if they had taken some of the issues fans had had with the previous two features into account and wanted to make sure they took the time to get this one right. The next *Puppet Master* still did not have a title, but Full Moon at least assured those anticipating it that the next movie would be designed to cater to what the fans wanted. The problem with that mentality, of course, is that there has never really been a time in *any* franchise when fans have collectively agreed on anything.

In 2015, Full Moon finally went to work on figuring out what the story for the new entry would be. Finishing off the trilogy, this prequel would be titled *Puppet Master: Axis Termination*, but despite its connection to the previous two in story and title, it was promised to be a very different entry in the franchise than *Axis of Evil* and *Axis Rising*. With a script from Roger Barron, whose only credit to that point had been *Trophy Heads,* Band promised that the new *Puppet Master* would boast the darkest script of any entry in the series to date and that it would also be a much gorier entry than fans had seen in quite a long time. For longtime fans who had been largely dissatisfied with the previous *Axis* movies, this new sequel seemed to hit all the right buttons. At the very least, it looked as if Full Moon was attempting to be ambitious again with their flagship franchise, as difficult as that could be given their financial situation.

Because of that situation, Full Moon eventually took to Indiegogo, launching a campaign on December 4, 2015.[2] As fan-funded as Full Moon had been for so many years, relying on the merchandise and now the streaming subscriptions to keep them going, crowdfunding had honestly been an unavoidable inevitability. It was amazing that it had not happened sooner. Not only was the Indiegogo campaign loaded with perks, from tons of exclusive *Puppet Master* merchandise to the chance to be given an associate producer credit on the film and even the opportunity to appear on screen in the movie and be killed by Blade, but the campaign also dictated what the feature was going to be. If certain goals were met, new things would be added to *Axis Termination* that apparently had not previously been a part of the script. New perks and new goals unlocked new puppet kills as well as the return of several things that harkened back to the glory days of the franchise, so to speak, chief among them being the return of stop-motion-animation. This, above all else, was a stunning announcement. Stop-motion had defined much of the allure of the franchise in its early days, but had not been a part of the series since 1994. Without David Allen, there was simply no way to recreate his particular brand of wizardry, and by this time, stop-motion had essentially long-since disappeared from the industry as a whole.

In 2014, Full Moon also released a ReAnimation Blade replica with a glow in the dark face and a syringe in the vein of *Re-Animator* full of classic green serum replacing the puppet's hook hand. This, if anything, had to be the most direct reference to the similarities between the serum and the reagent formula of *Re-Animator* ever. This new replica also proved noteworthy because, while *Puppet Master: Axis Rising* had had new replicas to tie into it, like the Nazi puppets and Stealth Pinhead and Six-Shooter, this would be the first time that Full Moon announced a new replica to tie-into the upcoming film years ahead of its actual release. The selling point from the moment ReAnimation Blade was released was that it would depict a version of the character that would be seen in the upcoming film.

Devlin remembers the Re-Animation Blade as a similar situation to the previous film's Stealth Six-Shooter and Stealth Pinhead. He explains, "That was a weird thing too, because the Re-Animation Blade replica did come out way before, but I think the script was written before the puppet came out. So we were kind of bound by trying to match it a little bit, but I still wish it looked a little bit better, a little more steam-punk-ish. He just had a big plastic syringe in the figure."

The Indiegogo campaign worked in a very similar way. Many of the various perks, especially the stretch goals, seemed to dictate what the story would be, right down to what puppets would actually be included in the movie. For most fans, the most exciting news and shocking twist from the campaign would be the announcement of the return of Torch.[3] A longtime fan-favorite who had always been included

Chapter Sixteen. Puppet Master: Axis Termination

in the merchandise, Torch had not appeared in a film since 1994's *Puppet Master 5*. People had long wanted to see him return and Band had long said that he wished they could make another movie with Torch in it, but there hadn't been any real financial possibility to include the puppet since the Paramount days. Given both that the puppet was an actual, functional flamethrower and that it required on-set safety in order to pull off, there hadn't been any opportunity to include Torch in any of the later features.

From a story standpoint, one also had to take into account that the *Axis* trilogy had been set during the 1940s and *Axis Termination* certainly planned to do the same, which would be interesting as Torch had not been built until the present day in *Puppet Master II*. Either the movie would provide a definitive origin for the puppet—as the comic series had begun to do at the time—or it would present a glaring continuity error. The scripts for the *Puppet Wars* features had introduced Torch during the World War II era in the second and third installments, so it wasn't as if the idea of creating the puppet during this era would not have precedent. Even the 1990 comic book series showed an early version of Torch being designed while Toulon was still on the run from the Nazis. From the immediate fan response, it became clear that the inclusion of Torch was the number one thing that influenced many fans' decision to donate. Which made the fact that the puppet did not actually appear in the film (as Full Moon reportedly noted the continuity error it would create) that much more unfortunate.

"We were supposed to have Torch in *Termination* and it didn't happen and I don't understand why. I can make Torch. It was very weird. I think it's just residuals of the '90s of knowing how much it cost and how long it takes, but I don't know," says Devlin.

Like *Axis Rising* before it, *Puppet Master: Axis Termination* shot in Los Angeles, which turned out to be a fairly easy way to accommodate people who won walk on roles as some of those who donated turned out to be local, whereas for others a trip to Los Angeles simply proved much easier in the grand scheme of things than places like Romania or China.

Axis Termination would mark Band's second *Puppet Master* entry in a row as director. But even though the film would close out the *Axis* trilogy that had been going for the bulk of the decade, it would also be a vast departure from the previous two movies in many ways. First and foremost among them being bringing back Kip Canyon and Jean Louis O'Sullivan as Danny and Beth, only to kill them in the opening scene. This would send a message to the audience not just to say that all bets were off and that no one was safe, but also to mark that this was a clear departure from a storyline that it seemed fans had yet to fully embrace. This time, the puppets would be joined by an entirely new cast of heroes and villains. For those who had not been overly enthusiastic about the previous two entries, this was no doubt an exciting prospect, but it was also a bizarrely jarring move for what was meant to be the concluding chapter of a three-part story.

Although he did not ultimately return to pen the sequel, *Axis Rising* screenwriter Shane Bitterling notes that he *did* have a concrete plan of where he wanted to take the concluding chapter of the trilogy, had he written it. "I knew exactly where I wanted to take it. When he teased that he was going to be doing the end of the trilogy, everybody kept asking me 'You doing this? Are you doing this? Are you doing this?' but I hadn't heard. Finally, I got tired of everybody asking me, so I called Charlie and said, 'Hey, *am* I doing this? Am I not doing this?'" explains the writer. "Apparently there was an old script for that that he sort of dusted up and polished off and that ended up being the one following me. And while it's fine and it does have some puppet stuff that I wish we had, it didn't address really anything of that trilogy. I think a lot of fans, I personally love the World War II stuff, really love it, but I think a lot of the fans are kind of over it, or at least so they tell me or so I see. I thought it would be the perfect way to end that and then we could start anew with something else, because I was going to have the puppets at the end were going to have to somehow lead into the puppets of the first movie. And they were going to have to turn evil, so they were double crossed and everything and that's how they wind up being the bad puppets of the first *Puppet Master*. I thought that we kind of needed that, but it wasn't even a thing."

Instead, the movie introduces a new protagonist in Brooks, a former army grunt suffering from what would now be known as Post-Traumatic Stress Disorder. Although he is a hard-edged military man, Brooks bears some similarity to Danny Coogan in that both characters are embarrassed by conditions that keep them further from the fight than they want to be. He is joined by Dr. Ivan Ivanov, an occult specialist played by George Appleby, reprising his role form *Ravenwolf Towers*. Ivanov has banded together a unique group of psychics, including his own daughter, to counter the Nazis. The new group of psychics bring the franchise full circle, in some respects. In the original, the puppets were slaughtering humans with extra-sensory gifts and by the time the franchise hit *Axis Termination,* the puppets were teaming up with them.

Replacing the villains of the previous entry were a new batch of Nazi antagonists in Tonya Kay's Gerde Ernst and Kevin Scott Alan's Steiner Krabke, both villains noteworthy because one pushes the mythology in new directions while the other keeps continuity by returning to familiar territory. In many ways, these villains are almost identical to their immediate counterparts Moebius and Uschi, but with one major difference. While Krabke thinks he is in charge and that everyone will simply bend to his will, it's clearly not the case. This time around, the female antagonist is the one with the power. Both of these characters keep the occult Nazi motif going by pledging their loyalties to "The Old Gods." This repeated term could, on one hand, introduce Lovecraftian mythology to the *Puppet Master* mythos for the first time, which would at least be refreshing in terms of opening up the series' horizons in its eleventh official entry. But it also wouldn't be surprising, nor unwarranted, as the interconnected Full Moon universe boasts numerous Lovecraft adaptations. In the context of the franchise, though, The Old Gods may simply refer to the Demon Lord Sutekh. This certainly seems to be the case for Krabke, who possesses the same powers as those last seen in Sutekh's followers of *Retro Puppet Master.*

Ernst is the one who truly opens up the franchise's horizons, as she claims to not only pledge her allegiance to the true Old Gods—beings that, from the sound of it, hail from a time before even Sutekh stumbled into existence—but to (much more impressively) be one herself. Ernst is an endearing concept for a villain and, from a story perspective, the most enticing character in *Axis Termination*. She has lived in several bodies over several lifetimes stretching back thousands of years and is bored with virtually all she sees. She is not even a Nazi, necessarily, she simply wants to see the world burn to ash and the Nazis are the best group to side with in order to make that a reality. If the comics are to be considered canon, one might even wonder if Ernst could be the demon Anapa's mother. Surprisingly, but not in a remotely unwelcome way, Ernst is not even the sole female antagonist of *Axis Termination*.

Joining her would be the sadistic Friede Steitz, a young femme fatale Nazi agent. Steitz made for a striking image in the film's trailer, showcasing her attacking a man with a glove with needles for fingers, those needles full of what appeared Toulon's serum. Although this apparatus *is* used in the actual film, it is only used once and is never explained. In general, it is possible that Full Moon planned to use Steitz for future *Puppet Master* films—or even other projects—as the character actually survives the film. Surprisingly, the actor behind Steitz would be the most famous cast member that any *Puppet Master* film had had in years. Lilou Vos (real name Kirsten Ostrenga) played the character, and had been best known as teenage web celebrity Kiki Kannibal during the heyday of MySpace, where she became known as what was then called a Scene Queen. Because of her dramatic appearance and online antics, Ostrenga had even been the center of a *Rolling Stone* article.[4] Scene culture at that time was defined by colored hair, skinny jeans, bright clothing and celebrating popular music genres of the time including electropop and metalcore. The disconnectedness of MySpace offered something undeniably alluring to insecure teens, a way for those who had difficulty making friends to find thousands of "friends." The still-blossoming Internet provided a place where anyone could be popular, but it clearly became a double-edged sword, as Internet popularity always comes with hateful comments and even death threats. This was certainly the case for Ostrenga. Taking on a feature film role in *Axis Termination* only makes sense, as even over a decade after her time as a Scene Queen, she was very much a public persona, and there are still thousands of online profiles claiming to be the real Kiki Kannibal. It remains to be seen if her new villainess will actually return to the series, given that now that the *Axis* trilogy has come to a close, one would expect the *Puppet Master* series to return to the present.

In 2016, while *Axis Termination* was still in production and in the height of its crowdfunding campaign, a bombshell was dropped—so to speak—on the fans. Texas production company Cinestate announced that it would be developing a *Puppet Master* remake to be written by S. Craig Zahler, who had gained high profile success in the horror community having just written and directed the well received *Bone Tomahawk*.[5] That film had also pulled together incredible talent like Richard Jenkins, Matthew Fox and Kurt Russell. Fans were shocked not only at the out-of-left-field announcement of a *Puppet Master* remake, but also of the talent involved and the production team behind it. It presented a fascinating parallel, as at the same time a Full Moon sequel was struggling to raise the funds to simply finish a microbudget new movie, a high-profile reboot would be coming from the producers of *Transformers* and *The Meg*. Fans could finally hope to see a new entry in the series that would finally have a degree of genuine financing.

For some, this made it harder to look forward to *Axis Termination,* as many viewed the upcoming reboot as a more curious, intriguing and hopeful prospect. Others, meanwhile, found it easier to be more open-minded about the conclusion of the *Axis* trilogy, as even if it didn't turn out well they would have another movie to be excited about following directly on its heels. The announcement of the reboot, though, did nothing to deter *Axis Termination* from its course. Full Moon was still working on the film and there would be at least one stark difference between the promised reboot and the previous non–Full Moon entry *Puppet Master vs. Demonic Toys* in the involvement and approval of Charles Band. While in development and filming *Axis Termination,* Band also took a producer role on the all-new, all-different approach to the concept from Cinestate. Both parties made it clear that this new film would not deter Full Moon's latest sequel and that the original franchise would continue uninterrupted.

And so it did. Dictated by the Indiegogo, *Puppet Master: Axis Termination* shot in the usual short timeframe, but this time promised months and months of post-production work. As these months went by, however, the film began to shift considerably from what many fans felt they were promised when they had pledged their money. First and foremost, one of the biggest draws for fans would be completely scrapped. Realizing (apparently long after announcing his return) that Torch was first built in *Puppet Master II,* decades after *Axis Termination* was set, Full Moon made the formal announcement that there was simply no way around that gap in continuity and that the puppet would not be appearing in the film after all. Those who had paid for a prop Torch from the feature were promised to be reimbursed, but for many fans the disappointment stemmed from the anticipation of awaiting a character they hadn't seen in two decades only to have that swept away from them. There's an irony to the absence of Torch from *Axis Termination,* given that *Puppet Master* had never really seemed to be a continuity conscious franchise, yet caught this glaring continuity error just when the fans clearly didn't want them to.

Other problems with the fulfillment of the Indiegogo perks came about during and after production. Massive death sequences were planned just to fulfill the perks related to them and even though those scenes were shot with every person who had paid for them, there were so many people getting killed as extras in one scene that the scene clearly had to be trimmed down for time, leaving some people in the movie for barely a glimpse. For those completely alien to the film industry, this had to be a doubly crushing blow, being their one shot to appear on screen in their favorite franchise.

The biggest change to *Puppet Master: Axis Termination* still came in the form of the movie's release. While everyone had simply assumed that the feature would be released DTV in the same manner as all the others, Full Moon had been having more and more success with its streaming service, especially when it came to new content. They had tried their hand at in-house streaming series with *Trophy Heads* and *Ravenwolf Towers,* so it only made sense for them to try the same with their flagship franchise. If anything, it had just been a matter of time before they gave *Puppet Master* the serialized treatment. After all, the Sci-Fi Channel had planned to do a series all the way back in 2004. But this decision wouldn't do much to scratch the itch of a *Puppet Master* TV series, which still remains a sensible and viable idea, as it simply consisted of the already completed *Axis Termination* separated into three chapters and released over the course of three weeks. Economically, this made every kind of sense for the streaming service. Being able to see the new *Puppet Master* exclusively on Full Moon Streaming would cause a huge spike in subscribers but having to watch the new film over the course of three weeks would also force them to stick around instead of simply doing a one-week free trial.

The decision to serially release *Axis Termination* felt extremely fitting on at least one level. Like the previous two features, this new one was set in the 1940s and continued on from the style cemented in *Axis of Evil*, in the attempt to recapture the flair of the era. *Axis Termination* pushed that one step further in its segmented streaming release, as the new chaptered version of the feature felt like a full-blown '40s serial. With the exaggerated tone and style of both *Axis of Evil* and especially *Axis Rising*, this turned out to be a fitting move in terms of embracing the tone and style of that kind of wartime storytelling. But it was nonetheless awkward at times to watch, given that it had been shot as a feature film. The incredibly short running time of *Axis Termination*, like most other films in the franchise, also meant that the three segments had to be heavily padded with the movie's complete opening and end credits sequences just to fulfill an even thirty-minute runtime. Eventually, the movie was also released on the streaming service as well as Blu-ray and DVD in its full feature film version.

For fans, whether serialized or as a full feature, *Axis Termination* was as if not more divisive than the last few entries had been. On one level, this was somewhat surprising for a movie that delivered on most of its promises. As promised, this proved to be a much darker and definitely more violent film than *Axis Rising* had been, but it still retained a stylistic quirkiness definitive of late-era Full Moon. There was no mistaking this as anything but a Charles Band movie running simultaneous with the *Gingerdead Man* and *Evil Bong* franchises. At the same time, there is a darkness and harder edge to *Axis Termination* that one normally does not see in a *Puppet Master*. It's much more violent than the immediately preceding movies, with Blade in particular getting soaked in blood multiple times. The Nazi villains are still someone cartoonish but played—with the exception of Steitz—much straighter than the antagonists of *Axis Rising*. The extra angle of cosmic horror in the introduction of the Old Ones also helped to at least attempt to provide an added sense of dread.

Fans were also given the return of Leech Woman and Six-Shooter, as promised. This did not hold as much dramatic weight as the promise of Torch had, however. For most people who had seen the previous movie, it was simply assumed that Leech Woman and Six-Shooter would have a role to play as they had both appeared in that one. Both puppets were stretch goals in the Indiegogo campaign, but when they finally appeared in the finished movie, they only got one scene apiece. Leech Woman only appears during a scene in which Blade and Tunneler infiltrate a Nazi compound, vomiting a leech onto one of the soldiers when the puppets and Ivanov get themselves in a jam. This is the only time in the series that a puppet has made a cameo for a kill sequence without appearing at any other point in the movie. In this one scene her design is much more explicitly creepy than had ever been seen before. That's because her appearance in the movie was based on an Asian Ghost Leech Woman Variant Replica that Full Moon was selling at the time. While fans had expected more Leech

Woman, the stretch goal had specifically called for a brand-new Leech Woman kill, which is exactly what we got in the finished product.

"Actually, the script was filled with Leech Woman," says Devlin. "She was all over the movie. But when it comes down to shooting, we just would move on before we'd get her kill. So then we pulled the plug a couple times. I had even made a full walk-around Leech Woman costume like the Blade and Tunneler ones because she was supposed to be running around on the floor a bunch, and we never got to use it. Leech Woman, she's probably my least favorite puppet to operate or make. They're so hard and so thin and it's so hard to utilize her, so I don't know if I was at all responsible for her not making enough of an appearance in either of those movies but in my mind I could care less because she, to me, is the most unrealistic looking of the bunch. Very hard to puppeteer. She's just a doll and we don't have the money to do it otherwise. That's the problem. She needs to be a foam latex puppet, much like the *Nightmare Before Christmas* stop-motion figures, that's how Leech Woman should be built. We just don't have that time when there's so many other characters to work on that I think are cooler, so maybe that's half the problem, is that I don't put my attention toward her. But also, much like Six-Shooter, Charlie's never happy with any of the Leech Woman puppets and doesn't shoot them."

Devlin also notes that *Termination* marked Jester's shortest amount of screen time to date. "Jester got cut out of that movie, too. Jester's in movie but he's not really *in* the movie, for some reason. You find him broken the one time. But we had a bunch of Jesters. But if I'm proud of one thing in *Axis Rising* it was getting the Jester head spins to work, because doing that on the budget that we had, it was awesome. Just to get it to spin and have that old-style look, I thought that was pretty cool."

For Six-Shooter, it is another story altogether. Six-Shooter never appears to leave the trunk throughout the entire feature and only gets one scene that clearly depicts him as he shoots an invading Nazi officer. He is told early on in the film by Ivanov that they must make repairs on him to restore him to his full strength. This is the only explanation we get for why Six-Shooter never leaves the trunk throughout the entire feature. It wouldn't have been that surprising a move in the past, as Leech Woman did appear all through *Curse of the Puppet Master* without ever being given something to do. But this decision had a very different air about it considering that people had specifically paid for the reward of Six-Shooter's appearance in the film.

The novelty of seeing the Nazi puppets Bombshell, Blitzkreig and Weremacht also does not hold the same excitement factor as it had the first time around, simply because people had already seen it before. In general, these puppets don't have much to do in the film except for a few kill sequences early on. The focus shifts once again back to the puppets fighting Nazis rather than fighting against their evil counterparts. When it comes to the new batch of puppets, all of the most interesting information seems to be what happened between films. Our villains are revealed standing over the body of Dr. Freuhoffer, quickly tying up loose ends from the last movie. Ernst claims that the doctor died of old age, but his body was mangled, which made her story clearly unlikely. Despite coming off as sympathetic by the end of *Axis Rising*, it appeared that he had been using the new puppets to kill several different people across the Los Angeles area indiscriminately.

Overall, Devlin was much happier with the puppet FX on *Axis Termination* compared to the previous movie. "I really enjoyed the animated Blade puppet. And the Pinhead puppet, which you don't get to see enough in the movie. The Pinhead servo animated prop is awesome, he could flex, he could pick things up, he was really cool. And I liked when we used George's hands through the sweater like the old-style Pinhead. And the stuff with Blade at the end of Elisa's bed. When Elisa's carrying Blade and he's alive, it's just something we haven't seen in a long time. He's not just peering around corners, he's sitting at a bed obviously not wired to anything. He's just moving and being alive. That's what I've strived to do with the entire *Blade* movie. There's a part in *Axis Termination* where everyone's just talking in the room and if you look, Pinhead's over there and he's moving and alive and Blade's over there and he's moving and alive. They're not just sitting there like dummies. That I think is the coolest part."

When *Puppet Master: Axis Termination* was released, response was mixed. Many fans who contributed to the Indiegogo felt ripped off after seeing so little of what they had been promised. Some had monumental expectations for the new feature, believing that it would have a much higher budget than the recent movies preceding it, that it would even be a return to the glory days of the first five installments of the franchise. If anything, it proved that those days could never be reclaimed. While it does boast many more puppet FX sequences, *Puppet Master: Axis Termination* does not really look any higher in budget than *Axis of Evil* or *Axis Rising*, when it comes down to it. Some praised its additions to the mythology, noting that the new Lovecraftian elements made the franchise feel fresh again in some respects, while others noted that it felt less safe and much darker than the previous two, a refreshing change of pace back toward the early days of the series. Some diehard Full Moon and *Puppet Master* fans even loved it, noting that it was one of the best the series had offered in a long time. Given how long it labored in post-production, Band has actually said that he is very proud of everything they were able to accomplish with this film.

Still, with the split reaction from fans, it was obvious that people were ready to see this chapter of the *Puppet Master* saga closed permanently. Band had delivered on his promise of the *Axis* trilogy, and now people were ready for something completely new, whatever form that might take.

Chapter Seventeen

Puppet Master: The Littlest Reich

While *Puppet Master: Axis Termination* was still at the height of its Indiegogo campaign, an insane piece of news dropped into the world of horror: hot off the success of his western *Bone Tomahawk*, starring Richard Jenkins and Kurt Russell, among many others, S. Craig Zahler would be writing a reboot of *Puppet Master*. Of course, the idea of a *Puppet Master* remake was not new at the time. In fact, it was something that Charles Band had been discussing as a hypothetical for years. The plan was always to do a new movie with a bigger budget, partnering with a larger studio, that would potentially introduce the characters to an even larger market. At one point, Band even suggested doing a remake in 3D.[1] This was suggested during the height of the remake craze of the late 2000s, which saw successful 3D remakes of everything from *My Bloody Valentine* to *Fright Night*. At the time, 3D was all the rage and with Band always having his finger on the pulse, it made sense for that to be something Full Moon would try and capitalize on, even if it would be on a much smaller scale.

Interestingly enough, this hypothetical remake—which, in this incarnation never came to pass—would not be the first *Puppet Master* 3D treatment. For several years, the original film was available in a post-converted 3D DVD. During the years before Full Moon obtained the rights back from Paramount to redistribute their early movies on DVD and Blu-Ray, there was a brief time when the 3D DVD of *Puppet Master* was the only version that was actually available in the states.

Simply by having a writer like Zahler on board, this new *Puppet Master* reboot would be completely different from every remake avenue Band had explored before. In fact, it became immediately clear that the new film would also be completely different from any *Puppet Master* that had ever been seen before. Zahler had burst on the horror scene with his cross-genre Western *Bone Tomahawk,* but he had always been a fan of cult and exploitation cinema. He brought some of that to the film, an anything-goes kind of Western that seemed like something that couldn't possibly exist today. Despite its high-profile cast and focus on material dramatic enough to warrant actors of that caliber, *Bone Tomahawk* also draws heavily on films like *Cannibal Holocaust* and the movies of Lucio Fulci. It's a melting pot of influences from Sam Peckinpah to the Italian gore-maestros and that's what makes it so unique. For many horror fans, hearing Zahler's name attached to the new film—as writer, no less—was as exciting as it was entirely unexpected. But the reveal of the title promised the biggest departure from the original series of films. Titled *Puppet Master: The Littlest*

Reich, the new movie would see the puppets—long depicted as the victims of Nazis given new life in order to take their revenge—now depicted as Nazis themselves.

The movie was also set to be the first film produced by new Texas-based production company Cinestate, headed by producer Dallas Sonnier. Perhaps even more than Zahler himself, Sonnier had grown up renting the original *Puppet Master* films and loving them, even being influenced enough to want to produce a remake when the pitch came his way. Soon after it was announced that Cinestate would be reviving *Puppet Master* for a new audience, it was also revealed that the company would be reviving another brand, one that was truly dead at the time: *Fangoria.* Resurrecting the magazine while also launching films and books, *Puppet Master: The Littlest Reich* would even be presented under the new *Fangoria* banner. In some ways, this was the most shocking and delightful news of all.

While there was coverage on the original film in *Fangoria* #83, the magazine itself had never had too much love for the series. Even the most celebrated movies of the franchise like *Puppet Master II* and *Puppet Master III: Toulon's Revenge* had earned scathing to lukewarm reviews from the magazine. This seems absurd and unfair to *Puppet Master* fans, naturally, but one has to consider the mindset of the magazine at the time. In the late '80s and early '90s, the horror world was drowning in sequels, especially with the onset of the direct-to-video market. The market as a whole was exhausted by franchise after franchise, where even as a reader it sometimes seemed like all they had to report on were sequels. There was even an issue devoted to covering over 70 upcoming sequels just so that they could play catch-up. Each of the new, burgeoning franchises, especially at the straight-to-video level, must have been highly irritable for the editorial team. Full Moon's love-hate-but-mostly-hate relationship with Full Moon lasted until the 1995 *Fangoria* Chainsaw Awards, where they awarded *Castle Freak* the honor of "Best Limited Release/Direct-to-Video Film" though that did not help further sequels like *Curse of the Puppet Master* or *Retro Puppet Master* to earn remotely positive reviews. With that kind of history, it was astonishing to learn that the new *Puppet Master* movie, when it arrived, would bear the *Fangoria* logo in front of it upon its release.

Obviously, a new *Puppet Master* could not be made without the approval of Charles Band. It would make sense, all things considered, for the shepherd of the franchise to be hesitant to allow it to change hands. He had licensed out the property only once before, for *Puppet Master vs. Demonic Toys,* and had been notoriously unhappy with the results. Over the years, especially during the height of the popularity of remakes, many had approached him about doing a *Puppet Master* reboot. Some of them, according to Band, even made sizable offers, potentially for large theatrical releases. Yet Band had turned all of them down, for one reason above all others: he wanted to remain in the *Puppet Master* business himself.[2] Many of the offers from other studios included acquisition of *Puppet Master,* but that would mean Full Moon giving up its bread and butter. Naturally, they have produced hundreds of movies and have dozens of other franchises, but Full Moon letting go of *Puppet Master* altogether would feel like Marvel getting rid of Spider-Man. It's, in short, unthinkable.

Cinestate seemed to understand that, and so that was never a point of negotiation for them. They clearly wanted to make their movie their way, but not in a way that would force Band to relinquish his hold on the series. With that in mind, they struck a deal. If successful, or if Cinestate so chose, they would be able to make their own sequels to their upcoming remake. But Band and Full Moon would still be able to do whatever they were doing with their own *Puppet Master* franchise, completely unrelated. For Full Moon, it was a win-win. Nothing would change, nothing would affect the movies they were making, but there would also be this *other* film that they would not have to make themselves that could only, if anything, bring them more money. It was a perfect deal. Band gave the excited filmmakers his blessing and went back to work on finalizing funding and preparing to shoot *Puppet Master: Axis Termination*.

The Littlest Reich was off and running. Never appearing to be in the running to direct the film himself, Zahler hand-picked the team of Tommy Wiklund and Sonny Laguna to direct the reboot. The two had previously directed a small-scale independent horror film titled *Wither,* that was essentially a Scandinavian redux of *The Evil Dead.* The film had a manic energy to it and an old-school exploitation feel and Zahler, to his credit, recognized those factors as things that would perfectly match up with the script he had written.

Tonally, Zahler's *Puppet Master* script would be a complete departure from the previous entries in the franchise, especially the original. But elements of the first film are retained. For all its differences, the story for *The Littlest Reich* still sees a group of people inside a hotel being picked off by puppets controlled by an outside, unseen force, just as the original had done. Many of the iconic puppets are still there, as is Andre Toulon, but they are presented in extremely different incarnations than anything fans had ever seen before.

Given Cinestate's location within Dallas, Texas, it only made sense to shoot the film there and so production began gearing up with Wiklund and Laguna at the helm. Even before production began, from the first announcement, fans had their eye on the reboot—horror fans in general, even, whether they loved the franchise or not—simply because the unlikely production team put together behind the scenes piqued the interest of even the more cynical gore hound. But as soon as casting news began to circulate, it became immediately clear that fans truly had not seen anything yet. S. Craig Zahler, a writer and director with a clear love of the genre, was nonetheless not known for horror when he made the decision to pitch and write a totally new incarnation of one of the longest-running franchises. With that in mind, the casting of the film's star seemed completely appropriate.

Even more than Zahler, Thomas Lennon is not known for horror. Prior to this, he had almost exclusively done comedy, with the exception of a few small roles, such as an appearance as Bruce Wayne's doctor in *The Dark Knight Rises*. He is—and will most likely always be—best known as the star of the hit Comedy Central series *Reno 911.* His dry wit and often straight-laced delivery make the transition to horror an easy one, though. Comedians tend to do well in horror, more often than not, as the two genres so often go hand in hand. Like horror, comedy is all about timing and precision and that made Lennon a smart choice as the character who really carries the bulk of the film's weight on his shoulders, a likable but realistic, self-deprecating lead. The character of Edgar is a comic book artist who finds himself returning home to live with his parents after a divorce and the untimely death of his brother. He finds a Blade puppet in his brother's closet, which he then decides to sell at an upcoming auction at a convention celebrating the 30th anniversary of the Toulon Murders.

Edgar's sudden appearance back at his family home is instantly met with ridicule and we first learn of his divorce and his profession through the dialogue of his disapproving and clearly disappointed father. This, if anything, only helps make Edgar instantly more human and relatable. It's one thing to be introduced to a main character and feel like we can grasp something of what he's going through. It's easy to get the audience on your side if you introduce the character in a memorable way, watch them stand up for someone heroically, or introduce them through a joke. But with Edgar, we're in his corner right away and feel something of a connection, because the moment we're introduced to him, we feel *embarrassed* for him.

Jenny Pellicer and Nelson Franklin star as Ashley and Markowitz, the girlfriend and best friend/employer, respectively. Ashley is a quirky girl-next-door, almost at a Manic Pixie Dream Girl level, as she is introduced while walking her cat. But she quickly becomes a much more fully-realized, three-dimensional character who is able to stand up for Edgar in ways that he is not always able to stand up for himself, while also being able to call him on his bullshit, especially when pointing out that the only reason she hasn't read his comic is because she knows that it was based on his ex-wife. When the shit hits the fan—as it does in spades—Ashley actually becomes one of the most capable characters in the film, able to dispose of the Baby Fuhrer puppet when necessary and generally keeping a level head throughout the nightmarish attack on the hotel.

Markowitz, conversely, begins the film as an almost completely unlikable character. He's rude, misogynistic, blunt and generally unkind. He's the kind of friend that you remain friends with because you've known him so long, but often struggle to find reasons as to *why* he's still your friend. Sometimes, in those kinds of friendship, it's all a matter of trying to hold onto the past. And sometimes it's because you know that there's an intensely good person beneath the socially inept, crass exterior. Thankfully, Markowitz proves to be the second option. Like Edgar, we start to relate to Markowitz through humiliation, but it's a humiliation that is more deeply, thematically connected to the core of the film than anything experienced by Edgar. Our first moment to see him as anything more than the self-serving friend standing in between a would-be happy couple is when he is subjected to a much bigger jerk when the hotel manager takes one look at Markowitz's Jewish features and determines his name before actually asking him. It's a moment of profiling that stuns even a character as blunt and awkward as this one. This actually builds throughout the film, with Markowitz eventually serving as the most prominent voice of the oppressed people represented in the narrative. His faith and heritage are things that are revealed to be incredibly important to him, things that he is even willing to fight and sacrifice himself for.

Puppet Master: The Littlest Reich also follows a trend set by many recent reboots by bringing back a member of the original cast. However, the casting of Barbara Crampton stands out as refreshing for several reasons. In most instances, a prominent player in the original comes back to cameo in the reboot. For example, 2013's

Texas Chainsaw 3D brought back original stars like Gunnar Hansen and Marilyn Burns in very small roles. It's a common kind of Easter Egg that always serves as a strong tip of the hat to what has come before. *The Littlest Reich,* on the other hand, subverts this trend in a very clever way. While Crampton was billed in the trailer for the original film, due to the fact that she was well known by the Full Moon audience, but she only actually appears in a single scene that was shot over the course of an afternoon.

In the new film, on the other hand, Crampton actually plays a major role, as a security guard and former police officer who was there on the night Toulon was reportedly killed. It makes sense for the one actor who appeared in the first to return in this capacity, providing the exposition and history. But the role Crampton serves is deeper than that, too. After all, *The Littlest Reich* is wildly different from any *Puppet Master* before it in a number of ways. While it sounds at first like she's bringing the audience up to speed on the backstory, she's actually providing an entirely new history and mythology that we're hearing for the very first time, explaining the different ways this series veered right where the original veered left. She tells us, as the audience, the story of an Andre Toulon who was a Nazi and fled to America when the Nazi occupation ended with the war. It's jarring to hear, but there's a clever respect paid to the original series in that Crampton pronounces Toulon's name completely different from the way it was pronounced in the previous films, and even corrects the other characters every time one of them accidentally uses the original pronunciation. It's a great way to remind the viewer that this is, in fact, a new Toulon in a new world with an entirely new set of rules.

Of course, casting the puppet master himself is never an easy task. The role had not been played by another actor on screen since the passing of Guy Rolfe after the filming of *Retro Puppet Master.* After appearing in four movies, he had become synonymous with Toulon. Even though the role had previously been played by other actors, fans couldn't imagine anyone else in the part. And, in truth, he had probably owned the role since that first extremely empathetic performance in *Puppet Master III*. Rolfe gave Toulon a kind and gentle, if broken, spirit. There was a complexity to his character that people gravitated toward every time he was on screen. In a sequel or prequel in the original franchise, it would have been difficult to see someone else in the part. A reboot, however, offers a clean slate in more ways than one. *The Littlest Reich* brought out its biggest gun, its most known and unpredictable genre star, casting veteran actor Udo Kier as the new Toulon.

While previous portrayals were layered and empathetic, Kier's Toulon is cartoonishly evil. He is, after all, a Nazi and the film goes out of its way to show that bigotry is his *only* character trait. Every line feels as stylistically blunt and mean as Zahler is known for, and yet at the same time, every single thing that comes out of Kier's mouth feels as though it could have been entirely improvised. In his first and only scene in the film, Kier's Toulon offers his own lemon for his water and runs out of the room to throw up when he realizes that he is talking to a lesbian couple. It's a perfect reminder right out of the gate that this is not the Toulon fans have ever known. There's no sympathy for this man, it would be hard to even imagine *how* one could possibly feel any kind of empathy toward him, but Kier plays it somewhere between Fritz Lang in *M* and Christopher Lloyd's Judge Doom of *Who Framed Roger Rabbit?* While peppering in his own unique idiosyncrasies, of course.

Fabio Frizzi, another legend of the genre, was brought on to compose the score for the film, another smart move for multiple reasons. Frizzi is best known for composing the scores for most of Lucio Fulci's films, including *Zombie, City of the Living Dead, House by the Cemetery, The Beyond* and so many more. In some ways, Frizzi—and to an extent, Kier, are actually the elements of the new film that bring it back to the style of the original. After all, Frizzi isn't the first longtime Fulci collaborator to work on the franchise, as Sergio Salvati—who shot all of the movies listed above—was the cinematographer on the original *Puppet Master.* While it's possible that this was an intentional call back to the origins of the franchise, it seems more likely that Zahler and Co. simply wanted someone who felt like a callback to the video store era that *Puppet Master* represented. That, if anything, feels like what *Littlest Reich* is meant to recreate more than anything that ever actually appeared within the *Puppet Master* franchise. It's about the feeling that so many fans felt as children, simply seeing the box art in the video store and feeling like they were seeing something that they were not supposed to be looking at. *The Littlest Reich,* simply in terms of approach, is meant to provide that same feeling of something that is unpredictable and unsafe. Frizzi's score echoes that, both moody and intense and often almost whimsical, sounding very much like a classic Frizzi score. Perhaps the most exciting thing for longtime fans, musically, is that the end titles track is actually composed by Richard Band. With an actual orchestra this time, it reimagines the classic *Puppet Master* theme as a war march, an appropriate distinction for the reboot's new approach.

Of course, like any *Puppet Master* movie, the stars are always the puppets themselves. While it boasts a strong cast, *The Littlest Reich* is no exception to the rule in at least this one regard. With a higher budget than any previous entry in the franchise, it stands to reason that the reboot boasts more puppets than had ever been seen on screen before. Even though there was money enough for all eight "classic" puppets and then some, however, only four puppets from the original film series appear. While fans were left wondering for months exactly which of their favorite puppets would appear in the new film, it was revealed at Texas Frightmare 2017 that Blade, Pinhead, Tunneler and Torch would be the chosen ones to appear in the reboot, even showing off the brand-new Blade and Tunneler puppets from the film. Of all the puppets to appear, the most exciting for longtime fans was clearly Torch, as that particular puppet had not appeared on screen since 1994's *Puppet Master 5,* despite being a fan favorite. It was smart of the creative team to choose to include this puppet, as they had more money to work with than the previous features, and budgetary limitations had been the only thing keeping Torch from appearing in the original franchise sequels.

Tate Steinsiek, best known for his appearances on SyFy's *Face Off,* was hired to design the new puppets and took a very practical approach to the work. He noted that, to him, the puppets of this franchise had never really felt authentic, even in the original.[3] To Steinsiek, they never actually looked or moved like marionettes, and never looked to be believably made of wood. That was something he wanted to change even as he was watching the movies as a kid and got his chance when it came to designing the new puppets for the reboot. Each of the four main puppets are clearly recognizable as the original ones that they are based on, but each of them bears many differences as well. Blade's sly grin is replaced with an almost alien frown. There's something much more German Expressionistic about the design of the new Blade, which only makes sense when considering the new Toulon and what his influences may have been. Pinhead, on the other hand, has an appearance that mixes his classic look with something similar to Quasimodo of *The Hunchback of Notre Dame*. Tunneler bears the most similarities to the original, save the uniform now being blue and displaying a swastika and an iron cross. Torch does not have the stocky build of the original puppet and has a green jacket instead of the classic tan, though his biggest change is that he has two hands, with one of them popping off to reveal the flamethrower.

None of these are set in stone, however, and all of them have subtle differences because—in possibly the biggest departure from the original series—there are multiple versions of each puppet. There are at least three Blades, two of which are drastically different in appearance. There are two Pinheads and possibly three Tunnelers, it's honestly hard to keep count of just how many puppets appear in the movie. In some ways, this completely changes the experience of watching the puppets. From the original film, we had begun to watch the series for the puppets' personalities. Much of that was due to the success of David Allen and his team, making these little FX creations feel like individual characters. But it became further cemented when *Puppet Master III* provided a concrete explanation for these individual identities by noting that they had each been humans cut down by the Nazis, whose souls were transported into wooden bodies.

In *The Littlest Reich,* there are no individual personality traits to any of the puppets, which makes sense with the insane number of puppets that appear in the film. There would be almost no way to characterize them. But the reboot actually goes further, somewhat. This mythology is totally new, after all. It's not forced to obey any of the same rules as the earlier movies and it doesn't, to the point that the puppets in the new film don't appear to technically be alive, at least not in any similar way to how the earlier puppets were alive. Instead, they appear to be controlled telepathically by Toulon via the mysterious iron rods and occult circuitry he has set up inside of his crypt. It's an approach that's actually much more similar to David Schmoeller's pre–*Puppet Master* collaboration with Charles Band, *Tourist Trap*. It also provides totally new context and viewing experience for the puppets themselves. Originally, *they* were the icons. But here, they're not characters within the film at all, and are actually the murder weapons that Toulon is using to carry out his hate crimes from beyond the grave. In this instance, Blade isn't Michael Myers, he's Freddy Krueger's glove, still iconic, but as a deadly tool and *not* a character.

This changes things, without a doubt, but it—along with the multiple versions of each puppet—opens up a new thematic wheelhouse that might be the smartest commentary *The Littlest Reich* provides on the *Puppet Master* franchise as a whole. After all, the movie is set at an auction. Most of the side characters we meet once we get to the hotel are collectors. The different versions of the classic puppets aren't just different versions, they're actually referred to in the film itself as "variants." That is a perfect way to comment on the collector mentality that has defined the series for so many years. It obviously began with the action figure variants, of which there were numerous ones for each puppet, but even since then there have been variant replicas, variant comic book covers, statues and more. The *Puppet Master* fandom is defined by a constant search for the most rare, impressive variants one can find. *The Littlest Reich* comments on this directly, as it is in some ways about collectors being overwhelmed and assaulted by their own habits grown out of control. Some of the different variants seen in the movie even look as though they're inspired by some of the classic action figure variants.

"Skull Blade," for example, is a puppet that featured heavily in the movie's marketing and promotion. While it doesn't look like any other version of Blade, it bears a striking resemblance to The Mortician, a figure that was a Full Moon Direct exclusive in the early 2000s. Actually a variant of *Retro Puppet Master*'s Dr. Death, The Mortician features a totally black and gray aesthetic, which Skull Blade echoes with its much more realistic skull face and gray/black design. One of the Pinheads has a blue sweater as opposed to the traditional brown, which the Japanese variant figure also features. While there's only one Torch in the film, his green sweater is the same color as the Preview's Exclusive variant action figure, which totally makes sense in this context. The multiples of the new puppets feature different tweaks between them as well. There's even a teddy bear with a top hat that hides a drill similar to Tunneler's.

The new puppets seen in the film come in all different shapes and sizes and each of them seems to fit a wildly different purpose. Autogiro, for instance, is a flying puppet that uses its propeller to slice people down. Happy Amphibian is a frog puppet that looks harmless but appears to shoot something like acid, and a Mantis puppet also serves a similar function. On the most extreme side of things, there's Baby Fuhrer, a puppet that looks like an actual baby version of Hitler that crawls up inside a human host, to control them like a puppet, which is an interesting and surprising spin on the overall concept. And there are certainly more than that, as well.

It stands to reason that more puppets would allow for more carnage, but that's more true than anyone ever probably expected going in. *Puppet Master: The Littlest Reich* is an incredibly gory film to the point that it was actually released unrated. The gore goes for broke, trying to achieve Herschell Gordon Lewis levels of splatter. This is where the movie most echoes the "unsafe" horror titles in the video store, of which it was meant to be a throwback to. It's like seeing *The Toxic Avenger* for the first time all over again. There's a scene that depicts a man urinating on his own severed head, a child who gets his hands cut off, and in the most graphic sequence by far, a puppet tears a woman's unborn child from her uterus by crawling up inside of her and forcing its way out. *Everything* about *Puppet Master: The Littlest Reich* is about being as extreme as possible and pushing boundaries until there are absolutely none left to push. It's an experience in shock value that, to its credit, never tries to be anything else.

This is first established by the fact that the puppets are picking off minorities. The people being targeted in this film are gay, lesbian, black, Hispanic, Jewish people and everything in between. For some, this was seen as shockingly offensive and for others, it's at least a stark departure from where the series had originated. But it's done from the mindset of putting the focus on the characters rather than the puppets themselves. It would be one thing if the puppets were still the stars of the show this time around, but they're definitely not. They're not the main characters, and we are at least given characters who we want to root for, that we want to survive even when most of them don't. Whether or not there is an inherently racist streak to *The Littlest Reich,* there is *absolutely* a nihilistic one, without a doubt. As a reader says to Edgar at the end, after reading the comic that Edgar wrote about his experience at the hotel, "a lot of horrible things happened to people who don't deserve it." And if there's any real point to the movie, it's that and only that. That horrifying things happen and usually to people who really don't deserve them. There are definitely cathartic moments in the film, satirical enough to be funny instead of mean-spirited, like Marokwitz tossing the Hitler puppet into an oven and saying "See how you like it." But even still, many people were split on that element of the feature's focus, and there are probably better ways to express it than—in a cast this diverse, in a movie about diverse groups of people being killed—it doesn't feel like the best way to handle it than for virtually the movie's only straight, white and non–Jewish male to also be its only survivor, excluding Cuddly Bear's "surprise" survival in a post-credit scene.

The reaction, despite that, proved to be largely positive upon its initial festival release, from people that one would not normally expect to even *see* a *Puppet Master* movie let alone favorably review one. *Puppet Master: The Littlest Reich* premiered in October 2017 at the New Orleans Horror Film Festival and from there, it hit the festival circuit and began growing a reputation as one of the most bonkers, shocking and enjoyable horror efforts of 2018, but mostly from people who were totally unfamiliar with the franchise. Within months, more people were talking about *Puppet Master* than ever before. People were saying that it needed to be seen for the kills alone. Many of the major horror sites reviewed it as the best of the franchise. As this reputation grew and grew, Cinestate announced that it would do the unthinkable: a *Puppet Master* movie, a film in a franchise that had been built as a platform solely to launch home video distribution, was going to get a theatrical release.

That release in August of 2018 proved to be limited to only a handful of cities, for one night only, but it was still more than any *Puppet Master* had seen before. It represented something powerful, a shift in the marketplace that there might actually be a hunger for something like this again, that people were ready for bizarre, tasteless and generally weird horror that the early years of the decade really didn't provide. Even though few got to see it in its brief theatrical release, *The Littlest Reich* still played at almost every major horror festival—or even film festival in general—throughout the first half of the year. Genre sites and magazines began reporting on every new detail surrounding the release. *The Littlest Reich* saw reviews in publications like *Newsweek* and a 60 percent on Rotten Tomatoes when some entries of the franchise still don't even have a score. Charles Band, credited as an executive producer on the feature, was interviewed in Entertainment Weekly to promote the new film.[4] It was a level of popularity that no *Puppet Master* had ever come close to seeing before.

For many diehard fans of the original franchise, it's hard to even see it as a *Puppet Master* movie just on the grounds that it is so different and that it's not interested

Chapter Seventeen. **Puppet Master: The Littlest Reich**

in retreading the same ground. It's not even necessarily meant for people who love the franchise. It's designed to cater to people who don't, to win over a new audience by showing them things they've never seen before, and even to give people something that they never got out of the earlier movies. After all, there is an interesting subset of *Puppet Master* fans who don't actually like any of the movies at all. Like everyone else, they got into it because of the designs of the puppets, which are so striking and iconic on their own. These are fans who collect all of the merchandise, the toys, the replicas, but don't happen to enjoy the movies. It's surprising, it's something that no other horror franchise really has, but it does make sense on some level. The tagline of the original movie states "Evil comes in all sizes" and none of the features really deliver on the promise of that poster. *Puppet Master II* is the closest as it's the one the feels the most complete as a horror film of its era. It's the goriest of the original series and definitely the most mean-spirited. *The Littlest Reich* is definitely for people who love the puppets and what to see what kind of carnage they could truly unleash if they were just absolutely let loose but doesn't feel as if it's so much for people who love the *Puppet Master* movies in general. It's kind of nice, even still, that a group of fans so long overlooked would actually be able to have something cater to them for the very first time in this franchise.

This is also, I think, what won over so many genre critics, most of whom were not *Puppet Master* fans.[5] Many voices within the genre were always put off by the quirkiness of the series, and especially the safeness that stemmed from the puppets most often being depicted as antiheroes. In *The Littlest Reich,* the whole appeal is that anything can happen, that it's not so much about watching a *Puppet Master* movie, but watching unbelievable kill scenes that hadn't been accomplished on the big screen in decades. It's about seeing something shocking and revolting and, ideally, seeing that with a crowd. As some great critics have pointed out, it's the kind of film that you need to see with an audience just to assure you that you're all actually *seeing* what you're seeing. That appeal transcended the franchise and broke through.

Puppet Master has always been a series that people were conscious of, even if they didn't entirely know what it was. Since the late 2000s, the films have only become more and more widely available, going from being out of print for years to being sold at gas stations. But with *The Littlest Reich, Puppet Master* broke through into the mainstream in a way it truly never had before. Even if it's not the same timeline or the same franchise, it's the same brand, and Band was ultimately smart to wait until filmmakers came along who cared enough to allow him to continue on with the property. It was an impressive deal, because the success of *The Littlest Reich* can only help Band moving forward. More people are aware of *Puppet Master* than ever before, and even in his low budget world, it allows the films to reach a bigger and bigger marketplace. In some ways, it feels as if the excitement over the franchise, which had been waning for years as the budgets dwindled and the releases became more sporadic, has been entirely renewed. There's a hunger for new *Puppet Master* and even if Band doesn't jump on it right away, it's impossible to imagine he would not capitalize on that.

Chapter Eighteen

Blade: The Iron Cross

Even with the crowd-funding for additional FX, the budgetary realities of the *Puppet Master* series had begun to show themselves in the more recent sequels. *Axis Rising* and *Axis Termination* were small-scale in scope, but nonetheless ambitious. Both involved not only six of the main Toulon puppets, but an entire crew of Nazi puppets as well. In recent years, Full Moon production schedules had begun to move more quickly than ever. Tom Devlin had proven up to the task, but these were smaller and smaller victories resulting in the puppet creations that were simply the best that could have been built under the circumstances, and it's no small miracle that they were even made at all. After all, these were puppets made in only a little over a week's time. For *Axis Termination,* the script called for six Toulon puppets and three Nazi puppets, and with at least three to four of *each* to execute everything the characters needed to do on screen. As the budgets had gotten smaller and smaller and the schedules shorter and shorter, this kind of work—even when pulled off perfectly—began to look more and more impossible.

After the release of *Puppet Master: Axis Termination,* fans were left to wonder as to what direction the franchise would take from there. After all, *Axis of Evil* had been the start of a promised trilogy. Each entry after that had therefore contained a vague promise of what direction it would take, each sequel felt like it had somewhere to go. But after *Axis Termination,* that trilogy was effectively completed, and there was no telling where or how Full Moon's series would continue, only the simple promise that it *would* continue. It seems a ridiculous thing to even have to say, but *The Littlest Reich* had begun filming before *Axis Termination* even saw release. Fans had only naturally begun to wonder if the start of one franchise meant the abandonment of another. Cinestate had, after all, made an equally clear promise that their rebooted *Puppet Master* would become a franchise, with *The Littlest Reich* even ending on the words "To be continued."[1]

Both parties turned out to be correct in their promise that they would be separate franchises with separate goals and ideals. While *Aryans Ahoy,* the prequel to *The Littlest Reich,* was announced, Full Moon wasted no time keeping good on its promise to keep the original franchise alive. In 2018, they organized the clip show *Puppet Master: Blitzkrieg Massacre,* another greatest hits compilation, this time bookended by a motion comic. They continued to sell more replicas, including an incredibly expensive 30th anniversary Blade replica, much higher in quality than anything they had produced before and with the price tag to prove it. It was the next announcement, though, that proved to be far more ambitious.

Chapter Eighteen. Blade: The Iron Cross

In April 2019, Full Moon announced the biggest endeavor of its entire history, an experiment called The Deadly Ten.[2] This was, on one hand, simply a development slate. But even that proved incredibly ambitious, as Full Moon hadn't made ten movies in a single year's time in decades. Then came the reveal that each of the Deadly Ten movies would be live-streamed throughout the entire production. This would be a great way, especially for fans quick to criticize the newer movies, to see exactly what filmmaking at this level looks like. The highs and the lows, the nuts and bolts, everything would be live-streamed throughout the entire filming. Even that, though, was not the most exciting news, at least for Full Moon fans. No, that honor fell to the slate of films in particular.

The announced Deadly Ten slate included not just one or two, but nearly *every* movie that Full Moon had promised to make over the years, but had never delivered on. Chief among them were the sequels *Bride of the Head of the Family* and *Subspecies V: Blood Rise,* which had both been promised for over twenty years, but had never seen the light of day. Sequels to *Sorority Babes in the Slimeball Bowl-A-Rama* and *Necropolis* were also announced, alongside original productions like *Weedjies: Halloweed Night.*

Tom Devlin notes just what a massive announcement the Deadly Ten was, to the point of sounding completely impossible. "I said 'no' to *Weedjies*. I said, 'There's absolutely no way I'll do that movie.' Danny called me, the director, and I said, 'I can't do it, Danny. This is going to be stupid, I can no longer make crappy *Evil Bong* movies where people are going to think that's all I can do.' And then I read Shane's script and I said, 'This is not a crappy *Evil Bong* movie, this is awesome.' Then we all got on the same page. I also said 'no,' because I didn't imagine John Lechago would direct *Blade.* They came at me with *Weedjies* before they even announced they were doing a *Blade* movie, but as soon as John told me he was going to direct *Blade* that changed my tune about the Deadly Ten, because I knew I *had* to do *Blade.* And then I heard Charlie was doing *Head of the Family 2* and that's really enticing. Then of course Dave DeCoteau with *Sorority Babes 2,* that's a huge film from my youth. So they hooked me in as a fan. Of course, I tell everybody, as much as I complain about the budgets and the time, if I say 'no' to one of these movies, twelve-year-old me would jump through a time portal and kick me in the nuts."

Also in the mix as part of the announced Deadly Ten slate was *Blade: The Iron Cross.* Just as the title suggests, a spinoff solo venture for the franchise's most popular puppet—and very likely the most popular Full Moon character in general. That, if anything, made the decision to give Blade his own movie a no-brainer. Blade's had been the face plastered on video boxes to move rentals in the earliest days of the studio's history. Blade had become a top-selling action figure, a sought-after replica and—by this point—everything from a plushie to a bobble head to a Halloween mask and a lighter. Blade's popularity almost seemed to transcend the franchise itself. It's almost akin to the early popularity of Wolverine in the *X-Men* titles. After the response to that character had grown and grown over time, a solo adventure began to seem like more of an inevitability than anything else.

It made even more sense from a practical standpoint, though. With the pressures to create so many puppets on a short schedule for a single *Puppet Master* film, the idea of spinoffs for individual puppets becomes an incredibly smart prospect. One movie focused on one character means that the FX department only has one puppet to focus on and has every opportunity to get that singular puppet perfect. Even if the glory days of Paramount and David Allen were long behind Full Moon, this kind of scaled-back approach certainly marked the greatest chance to recapture some of the magic of that era. And Tom Devlin no doubt proved up to the task, beginning work on a Blade animatronic to be the star of the small puppet's self-titled outing, long before the Deadly Ten slate was announced.

The decision to give Blade his own movie also spoke to the larger film climate at the time as well. Since the teasing

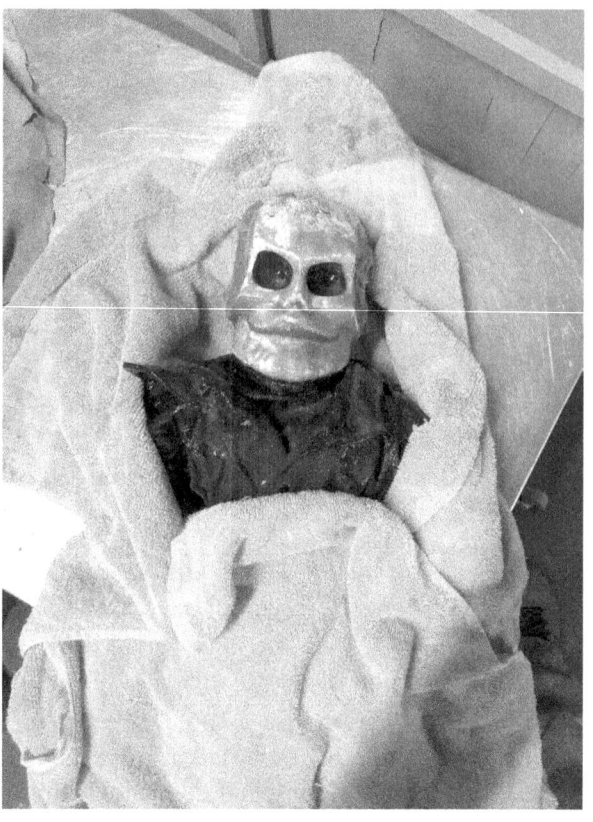

Bloody Blade in a blanket (courtesy Tom Devlin).

begun in 2008's *Iron Man* had successfully led to *The Avengers,* every major studio had begun to attempt some variation of a cinematic universe, from larger team-ups to solo ventures for individual characters. But this was only yet another major studio model that Full Moon had originated. From the early years of the company, characters would cross over from film to film, to allow these movies to feel like one weird, singular shared world. Band was even very much influenced by Marvel, and by the original comics themselves. Since the early 1960s, characters who starred in one team book would be known to carry their own title as well, and heroes from different titles would cross paths on a nearly monthly basis. *Dollman vs. Demonic Toys* was a sequel to three entirely different Full Moon features, with the third being *Bad Channels,* and that was only the tip of the comic book iceberg that Band had announced as being part of the overall plan as early as the Video Zone for *Puppet Master II.* If anything, it's surprising that a *Puppet Master* spinoff, especially for this character, hadn't happened sooner.

Puppet Master also yields itself to spinoffs because, as well as the characters work as a group and each bring a different kind of flavor to the table, they each have a very distinctive gimmick. Each puppet has a unique look and talent that could easily make them the star of their own movies. They're all incredibly different characters with incredibly different talents. The recent comic book series only helps that

Chapter Eighteen. Blade: The Iron Cross

case, having been able to delve into the backstories of each individual puppet and explore their personal lives more than the movies had ever had the chance to do before. Because of that, it was no surprise when Full Moon announced *Blade: The Iron Cross* would have a tie-in comic book prelude penned by the *Puppet Master* comic series' scribe, Shawn Gabborin.

Unsurprisingly, the one-shot *Blade: The Iron Cross* prequel comic book is terrific. Releasing in September 2019, several months before the release of the film its promoting, the story clearly sets up the events of the feature while also easily standing on its own, especially to long time fans. The comic technically takes place during the end of *Puppet Master III,* just before Toulon and Peter board their train to Switzerland. It's Blade's first night as a puppet, as he prepares to leave his old life behind by destroying any remaining evidence of the dangerous work he had done as Dr. Hess, not realizing that one of the Nazi soldiers has made off with the notebook containing Hess' research, thus setting up the plot of the new movie. It easily fits in just with the comic book canon as well, as the desire to make amends for both his past life and some of his actions as a puppet are traits that define Blade as a character in the Action Lab series.

Blade suit actor gets into character on set (courtesy Tom Devlin).

As for the film itself, it was revealed that despite being a standalone spinoff, *Blade: The Iron Cross* would nonetheless serve as a direct sequel to *Puppet Master: Axis Termination*. In fact, Tania Fox even returns to star as Elisa Ivanov, the clairvoyant daughter of Ivan Ivanov, who has somehow shifted gears to become a war journalist in the passage of time between films. While the prospect of a returning heroine held promise, this did nothing to sway those who had hoped that, with the *Axis* trilogy having finally been concluded after nearly a decade, the franchise would abandon the 1940s and finally return to the present. The plot synopsis quickly revealed that to not be the case, but there were plenty of factors to make up for it, first and foremost that the synopsis promised a plot that would dig deeper into Blade as a character. The plot revolves around a mysterious Nazi doctor and a darkness from Blade's own human past as Doctor Hess that is now coming back to haunt him in the present, thanks to his work within reanimating the dead when he was forced to work under the Nazis.

Even still, the most surprising announcement may have been its director. After *Axis Rising* and *Axis Termination* it seemed reasonable to assume that Charles Band had finally slipped into the role of director on his flagship franchise and never planned to leave. But that clearly turned out not to be the case as John Lechago was announced to helm the spinoff. Lechago's best known work at Full Moon would have to be the *Killjoy* franchise, which is certainly among the most celebrated of the company's recent output, as well as possibly being its best kept secret. After all, the first two *Killjoy* entries were seen as being among Full Moon's schlockiest, but the franchise took a turn toward embracing the weirdness of its concept and feeling as big as a recent movie for the company possibly could. Even genre sites that would often come down hard on the *Evil Bong, Gingerdead Man* and especially late-era *Puppet Master* movies had given Lechago's *Killjoy* sequels a pass with some regularity. In that respect, he was already somewhat known as a director for taking a series that had garnered a kind of lukewarm response and reinvigorating it, injecting new life and flavor—and above all, a totally different energy, that it turned out it had desperately needed.

The only concern, if only judging a director on their previous work, would certainly be that the *Killjoy* movies were completely different in tone from the much more serious *Puppet Master* franchise. Thankfully, that was dispelled almost immediately thanks to the Deadly Ten's opportunity to allow each director to introduce their movie and the livestreamed events—such as the casting—leading up to the actual shoot. In those appearances talking about the film, Lechago not only showed a clear love of the franchise, but also a deep—almost profound—understanding of Blade as a character, noting that he was instilled with the soul of the good Dr. Hess but molded in the image of the evil Major Kraus and that that represented an interesting kind of dichotomy for the character, which they planned to explore in the movie itself.

"That's what I love about John," says Tom Devlin. "It's not even a joke that he can make a pencil interesting. He will take this character, this doll, and give him so much meaning and purpose and turmoil. That's why I say I'm excited to work with him, because it's not just 'OK, put the puppet in the back and have him look around.' It's not that. It's a character in his movie that basically I was cast to be, or create. I'm honored."

Devlin goes on to explain the things that excite him most about working on this particular film and what sets *Blade* apart from the other entries in the franchise. "Focusing on one puppet. And working with John as a director. I've only ever worked with Charles Band directing a *Puppet Master* movie. Although he was there from the beginning, he was a producer. You had Schmoeller, who's an incredible director, you had Dave Allen—and I think *Puppet Master II* is my favorite *Puppet Master* of all time—Jeff Burr, these are great fucking directors! John Lechago is to me that caliber of a director and if ever given the budget and time, he could make *Aliens*. John is a great director. Charles Band is a phenomenal producer. I think the opportunity to get to work with a different director with the puppets is probably my favorite part about it. Because John has something to prove, too. This is a franchise and a known character, like I've said, that people have action figures and comic books of. John wants to leave his mark. He turned the *Killjoy* series around. Nobody cared about *Killjoy*. But he wanted so badly to give some legitimacy to the demon and some lore, and now he *is Killjoy*. And that's what he's going to do to Blade. He's got so many ideas. He wants to give Blade some lore and to really start understanding, 'Why was Blade a bad guy then a good guy?' Hopefully, we can define all that in this movie."

Joining Tania Fox in the movie would be Vincent Cusimano as Detective Lieutenant Jonas Gray. Known largely for short films, *60 Seconds to Die* and *Mega Shark vs. Mecha Shark*, viewers got to watch Gray's audition via the live-streamed casting session on the Deadly 10 website. Returning alongside Fox would also be most of the crew from *Axis Termination*, including cinematographer Howard Wexler. Ultimately, this is unsurprising as Band is well known for liking to do most of his work in-house and *Blade: The Iron Cross* has clearly proven to be no different on that particular front.

Blade raises his knife (courtesy Tom Devlin).

Roy Abramsohn was also announced as the movie's lead villain, the Nazi doctor Erich Hauser, who has picked up where Doctor Hess left off and has—as expected and feared by Hess in *Toulon's Revenge*—furthered those experiments for the worst kind of evil. With a wealth of television guest roles under his belt, Abramsohn is nonetheless no doubt known for his starring role in the risky independent horror film *Escape from Tomorrow*. For those unfamiliar, *Escape from Tomorrow* was an imaginative, no-budget psychological horror movie shot inside Disney World without the studio's awareness, poking fun at the studio's mega-corporate nature while also telling an imaginative and scary mystery, no small miracle considering the budget and (especially) time. The movie was shot quickly with not only the cast, but the entire crew disguised as tourists, who would have to stop any shot at any time whenever it looked as if people might be noticing what they were doing.

For fans nervous that watching the entire production of a movie would give away the entire thing, it turned out that they needn't have worried because everything is so quick, so DIY and so blunt to the realities of guerrilla independent filmmaking that it really wasn't a concern. The ultimate goal, it seemed like, was for the Deadly Ten features to showcase the realities of making a film on a low budget and as such it certainly succeeded. More than anything, there's also the fact that production hours are long, especially on movies of this type, and it's easy to assume that almost no one tuning into the production stream of *Blade: The Iron Cross* watched the entire production from beginning to end, uninterrupted.

Where the franchise goes from *Blade: The Iron Cross* is anyone's guess. It's a safe bet that Full Moon will return with a full-blown *Puppet Master* sequel in the near future, whether it returns to the present or sets the stage for a new *Axis* trilogy or something like it. If response to *Blade* is strong, it could lead to sequels, similar to the Marvel Cinematic Universe structure of, say, *Avengers* and *Captain America* franchises running concurrently. Given why the timing felt so right to do a solo film now, so that the budget could be focused on getting a single puppet to look great, it would only make sense to try and look into *other* spinoffs for the franchise as well. That remains an enticing prospect. A Leech Woman movie and a Tunneler movie would be totally different from one another. Cost, more than anything, has prevented Torch from being a part of the franchise for a very long time, but if he was given his own feature, the cost of creating all of the other puppets would be stripped away. That would make bringing him back—in a Full Moon production, at least—much more feasible.

Tom Devlin also notes why spinoffs make so much sense for the franchise at this point in time. "You've got those two different fans: the ones who just want to see something they've already seen and then you get the ones that *want* a little bit more of the story and a little more with the puppet. To us, this is a solo film for a reason: to focus on Blade. It's more than just saying 'Blade is based on Richard Lynch.' We're going further. We're giving him more emotion, mental breakdowns, whatever. I don't know how much I'm allowed to say about the movie, but I can say that we're giving the puppet personality in physical, practical ways."

While *Blade: The Iron Cross* is still brand new at the time of this writing and Full Moon has surely made no statement as to when or how it plans to carry on the franchise after this latest entry, there are a wealth of reasons as to why this *one* spinoff was at the very least a good idea. If it is successful and provides a new model that seems to work, then it would be worth it to speculate that the future of *Puppet Master* may, for the time being, lie in spinoffs. At the very least, the character-focused approach shows the influence that the comic series of the past few years has begun to have on the films themselves, and that can only be a good thing. With two franchises running concurrently, between Full Moon and Cinestate, making a *Puppet Master* movie now almost feels like the wild west. Truly, anything goes. Anything could happen from here and none of it would be surprising, but then, that's not the first time one could say that about this series and it probably won't be the last. Whatever Full Moon has in store for the puppets after *Blade: The Iron Cross*, though, the fans will no doubt turn out to see it. No matter the release. Streaming service, VOD, Blu-ray, etc. The days of simply seeing a bizarre title and even weirder cover art in the video store and picking up a Full Moon title by chance are gone. If the Deadly Ten has proven anything, it's that the company has survived by catering directly to its own fan base, and it's a model that definitely seems to work, at least for now.

Blade hangs from the window (courtesy Tom Devlin).

Blade: The Iron Cross proves beyond a shadow of a doubt why spinoffs were a smart approach. It *does* look better, feel more accomplished than other recent entries when there are not a dozen other puppets to focus on. And to have seen the whole production live-streamed, to know the circumstances and to know how cheaply it was made and that it principal photography lasted only four days, to know all that and for the movie to still look at good as it does is honestly a phenomenal achievement.

Tom Devlin animates Blade (courtesy Tom Devlin).

The film is much tighter than the *Axis* movies, both in terms of the story and narrative focus as well as the actual technical craft. This is the first modern *Puppet Master* that feels bigger than it actually is and looks at least as expensive as *The Littlest Reich* when it in fact has an astronomically smaller budget. More importantly, especially for fans, is the fact that there is a reason why this is Blade's movie. Rather than simply devising a flimsy excuse for only using this puppet—although there is a bit of that, as protagonist Elisa notes that they are running low on the serum that gives them life—returning writer Neal Marshall Stevens (who wrote both *Curse of the Puppet Master* and *Retro Puppet Master* under the pseudonym Benjamin Carr) provides a personal stake for the character. The Nazi who serves as the central villain was a colleague of his when he was alive, as Dr. Hess. The notes that they are using to further their experiments with reanimating the dead are his own, it's his notebook from *Puppet Master III*. Even though the puppet is silent, as always, this makes him feel like a genuine character again. Like *Puppet Master III* before it, it genuinely feels like it has a point to make, particularly with the fact that the story shifts slightly from German Nazis to American Nazis, who have infiltrated many offices, including the police department and the district attorney. And with *Blade* perhaps being the best *Puppet Master* movie since the end of the Paramount era in *Puppet Master 5*, the future of the franchise feels genuinely promising for the first time in years.

Chapter Nineteen

The Fans

Puppet Master belongs as much to the fans as to the filmmakers themselves—perhaps even more so, considering the fact that it's the fans who ultimately determine the direction of the series, and ultimately whether or not it is allowed to keep going and thriving. The fans feed directly into Full Moon, more than other franchises and studios, because it's the sales of replicas, t-shirts and any and all other kinds of merchandise that keep the company alive and able to continue producing features. As Full Moon has gone through so many changes as a company over time, even licensing out the property to other studios at times, *Puppet Master* has become, for all intents and purposes, an entirely fan-funded franchise. The merchandise and the movies have become completely intertwined. Not only do the selling of replicas and other tie-ins fund further sequels, but those new characters and designs also make it into the sequels to sell further replicas and toys. The experience of being a *Puppet Master* fan is entirely cyclical. The merchandise and the movies are one and the same and they have been for a long time, and that's what it takes for an independent horror franchise on such a small-scale as this one to survive for as long as it has.

Fans have dictated the direction of the course of *Puppet Master* throughout the run of the series. First and foremost, it was the enormous popularity of the original's home video release that even made a sequel possible. The fondness for the Leech Woman character led to her being reintroduced into the series even after having been decisively killed off. The popularity of the puppets in general led to a new direction shifting them away from villains and into antiheroes, a direction that seemed to stick, with the obvious exception of the 2018 reboot *The Littlest Reich*. After it became clear that *Puppet Master III* had become the apparent fan-favorite entry, the series shifted gears to make World War II era prequels almost exclusively in order to attempt to recapture some of that success.

But for the diehard fans, that love of the series extends well beyond the movies themselves. Some fans have collections including not just all of the toys and comic books, but even props from the films themselves. Many, many more fans extend that love toward making their own creations. There is an entire, devoted subset of the *Puppet Master* fan community creating truly exceptional handmade replicas that look as good—or even better—than the puppets used in some of the actual feature films. Fans write their own stories, create their own artwork, there are horror fans who adore *Puppet Master* as deeply as some people adore pop culture institutions like *Star Wars*. Obviously, the fan base is smaller, but while one is tempted to just call it small in general, we're seeing more and more that that's clearly not true. From new posters and replicas and T-shirts to, especially, new movies, the *Puppet Master* audience is bigger now than it has ever been.

Sometimes, fans of this franchise pop up in the most unexpected places. Acclaimed filmmaker Kevin Smith, for example, said that *Puppet Master* and a steady video store diet of the early Empire and Full Moon pictures served as the chief inspirations behind his tongue-in-cheek genre throwback, *Yoga Hosers*.[1] While mostly known for comedy and lately directing episodes of shows like *The Flash, Supergirl* and *The Goldbergs,* Smith made a turn to horror in more recent years and made his love of the genre more outspoken, directing genre fare like *Red State* and *Tusk*. The inspiration of *Puppet Master* on *Yoga Hosers* is abundantly clear when watching the film itself, as the feature includes several miniaturized Nazi-themed villains—played by Smith himself, no less—that run around incoherently mumbling. Everything about the little creatures, dubbed Bratzis, screams of a Charles Band movie.

Podcasts have also shown a fondness for the franchise that many of the older magazines never did. F This Movie and Revenge of the Pod People are just two noteworthy podcasts that have deep dived the *Puppet Master* series with entertaining results, especially for the uninitiated who weren't as familiar with the series beforehand.[2][3]

But the most exciting and inspiring will always be the fan creations, some of which are the result of thousands of dollars and painstaking hours of hard work to create the most screen-accurate replicas imaginable, down to the smallest details. These obsessive fans produce stunning, quality work with a time and budget that the Full Moon films don't always have the luxury of having. There are even fans who have taken it upon themselves to create replicas of every puppet to have ever featured in the series, down to the characters that might only have ever been glimpsed for a scene or two, like the original's Shredder Khan or *Curse of the Puppet Master*'s Tank. With the nearly 40 new puppets offered up by *The Littlest Reich,* that's become an even bigger undertaking of late. Fans often create their own, wholly original puppets as well, which only makes sense. There's an element of watching the puppets and seeing what they can do on the screen that lends itself to the age-old question "If you were a superhero, what would your power be?" The only difference is that these "powers" inevitably take a much more macabre direction when contextualizing them alongside characters who vomit leeches or have drills on top of their heads.

Fan art has taken it a step further, imagining not only original puppets, but original versions and new spins on the classic puppets. It's amazing to see characters like Blade and Pinhead drawn in anime style, or drawn as humans, as superheroes, in the style of *The Simpsons, South Park,* Steampunk, the list goes on and on. These are the moments, looking at how the fans have taken something and run with it, that truly show how popular the franchise has become, the kind of reach that it has and the lasting impact that it continues to show.

Perhaps the most stunning fan creation in recent years would have to be a fully functional, playable video game for the PC from October Games. A very legitimate, real gaming team, the developers at October Games created an immersive multiplayer game that looks as good as any official game on the market. The characters and locations are true to the movies, allowing players to take on the role of a puppet or a human, with all but Six-Shooter (of the main eight, at least) being playable within the game. Players can team up or go head to head as either humans vs. puppets or puppets vs. puppets in the game's two multiplayer modes, while a single player "interactive demo" was used to unofficially launch the game and show people what this unofficial but impressive game was capable of.

Things like this, things that look and feel as authentic as any officially licensed product on the market, truly show how much the line between fan and creator has been blurred over time. That transition from fan to creator shows most clearly with Shawn Gabborin and the *Puppet Master* comic series, as Gabborin had been a long-time fan of the series who had developed the same questions as many other fans had and sought to address them in a story that would also be engaging for readers. The comic book he created is much more than simple fan fiction or fan theory, he not only found ways to make his own speculation canon but to turn it into genuine storytelling that compelled new readers while furthering the narrative and mythology of the franchise as a whole. More and more fans, it seems, have grown up to be passionate storytellers, and have put that passion back into the franchise that inspired them.

We see that not only through the recent film and the comics, or through the practical effects wizardry, but through the unofficial creations as well. Things like the video game and the homemade replicas showcase a profound level of fan devotion to this thing that they love so much that they are driven to create their own. In an official capacity or not, fans feel as though they are a part of the franchise. That's especially true of *Puppet Master*, probably for a couple of different reasons. For one thing, Charles Band has always had a direct line to speak to the fans, even before the days of the Internet, through the Video Zones attached to every Full Moon release. Those continue even now in the form of the monthly vidcasts. Band has always engaged with the fans as directly as possible, whether it be in this way or through the roadshows or numerous convention appearances. And he has never been shy about admitting that it is the fans, and only the fans, that ultimately keep Full Moon going.

This is a two-way street of course, as it has always allowed fans a platform to speak as candidly as possible about the films and the studio. *Puppet Master* is an interestingly split fan base. There are fans who fundamentally feel that the glory days of the series are well behind it now. That the films were only good with the Paramount backing, or that there was a magic in the series that was never recaptured after the loss of David Allen. And there are others who limit it even further. While *Puppet Master III* is widely considered to be the most beloved entry, there are fans who consider that to be the downward turning point for the series, believing that even if the puppets were never inherently evil, the concept only ever worked when they were villains. There's merit in this, naturally, simply the baseline fact that it's easier for *Puppet Master* to function as a horror franchise if the puppets are the ones committing the horrors. Obviously, *Puppet Master: The Littlest Reich* marked a distinctive return to this mentality and direction for the franchise, to an even more extreme degree than had ever been seen before.

There are also *Puppet Master* fans—many of them, it seems—who believe that the new era of Full Moon and the new films are not up to par with what the series used to be, that the studio simply lacks the time and resources to pull off their more ambitious ideas. Yet, on the opposite side of that same coin, there are fans passionate about even the new Full Moon entries—the *Axis* trilogy—who believe that the newer entries are as good as anything that's ever been seen in this franchise before, if not better. These are the people who continue to drive and strengthen the Full Moon brand through thick and thin. In some cases, these fans seem to be a minority, but that's not entirely true. The truth is, most fans are casual. The die-hards are the minority and every fandom, and there's always much to be said for the people who simply see that a new entry in the franchise has come out and say "Oh, hey, a new *Puppet Master*." These are never voices to be discounted as they are almost all the majority.

At this point in time, however, something has happened in the *Puppet Master* fandom that has really never happened before: it's blown up. Since 2018, more people have been talking about *Puppet Master* than ever before, thanks almost entirely to both the larger platform and the critical success of *The Littlest Reich*. Thanks to the reboot, *Puppet Master* is now a celebrated title on almost every major horror site. *Puppet Master* has graced the cover of *Fangoria* for the very first time. While the title appeared in issue #83, there was no image on the cover. But the first issue of the newly relaunched Fango proudly displayed an image of Torch (or Kaiser, as he's referred to in the film itself) on the cover of the magazine. This is thanks mostly to the fact that the reboot was produced by *Fangoria*, with the logo even being featured before the movie itself.

While its release was limited to one night in select cities, *Puppet Master: The Littlest Reich* was nonetheless the very first theatrically released *Puppet Master* film ever. It also played many of the major film festivals, which was where it first started to draw so much attention. Even if it was mostly limited to the horror community, *The Littlest Reich* gave *Puppet Master* more exposure than it had ever really seen before. That exposure has brought so many new people to at least an awareness of the franchise, considering how many people love the reboot entry. At the very least, this will bring people to the franchise that might never have really given it a chance before.

Availability is also a major factor when considering the growing *Puppet Master* fan community. When I was just discovering the series as a child, the Paramount deal had ended, so all of the films were currently out of print. The video store was the only place to really discover *Puppet Master,* and that makes sense, looking back, as that was where the success of Full Moon had always truly lied. Now, things could not be more different. Thanks to deals with companies like Echo Bridge, *Puppet Master* movies are available in DVD multipacks everywhere from Walmart to Family Dollar to 7-Eleven and local supermarkets. These movies went from being available nowhere to being completely unavoidable. Blu-Ray releases from both Full Moon and 88 Films also helped the early films to look better than they ever had and be rediscovered with a new fondness from old and new fans alike. Having been so used to VHS and low-quality full screen DVD transfers for so long, the Blu-ray releases felt like fans were truly being given the opportunity to see their favorite entries for the first time all over again.

Streaming has also come to define so much of how movies are watched in the present day, and the *Puppet Master* movies have been available to stream at Hulu, Netflix and Amazon Prime with varying frequency. Once again, Charles Band recognized a lasting trend and had his finger on the pulse of that trend when he created Full Moon Streaming. That service continues to provide new content and both the Blue Underground and Surrender Erotica libraries pull in viewers outside just the standard Full Moon fans. This leaves us in a time where people aren't just rediscovering *Puppet Master* for the first time since their youth, but where even more people are discovering the movie and the series as a whole for the very first time. With fourteen films and counting, it's no shock that people love *Puppet Master* as much as they do.

However we came to it, however we love it, we *love it*. As big as it's become, *Puppet Master* is still a small ripple in the waters of the horror community. That's ultimately, what brings us together and keeps us together. When you ask someone if they've heard of *Puppet Master,* more people are saying "yes," than ever before, but not enough that you ever actually *expect* them to say "yes," and are therefore obviously delighted every time that they do. It's a loyal fan base and a rabid one, to the point where someone would write a book about a series that did not actually have a single theatrical entry until it was thirty years old. There's something about the nicheness of *Puppet Master* that allows its fans to wear its obscurity as a particular badge of pride, and to cherish the fact that other people simply love this thing even half as much as they do. Because of that, it doesn't matter if someone only loves the movies where the puppets are villains or only loves the movies where the puppets are heroes. It doesn't matter if some people think *Retro* is a better prequel than *Puppet Master III*, if some people feel that *Puppet Master vs. Demonic Toys* was far from the crossover they wanted or the comedic shot in the arm that the series needed at the time. The arguments aren't what matter, what matters is the passion behind them. What matters is the love for the one common ground that every fan shares: the love of the puppets themselves, whether they're good, bad, morally ambivalent or totally inanimate. We love them, the marionettes that put Full Moon on the map and the faces that launched a thousand sequels. And at the end of the day, they're the reasons we always come back for more, and they always will be.

Chapter Twenty

The Future

Where *Puppet Master* could go from here is truly anyone's guess. In the past, there have been ebbs and flows for the franchise, periods where it has sat for years and periods where it has seen rapid-fire success, even releasing more than one entry in the span of a single year. This happened more than once during what most fans consider to be the golden age of the series. *Puppet Master II* and *III* were both released in 1991, one at the very beginning of the year and one at the end. Then, of course, *Puppet Master 4* and *Puppet Master 5* were shot at the same time and thus released a little under a year apart. We've seen the same thing happening right now, but it feels bigger than ever. *Puppet Master: Axis Termination* came out in November of 2017 and just a few months later, *The Littlest Reich* began playing festivals. From its premiere at the New Orleans Horror Film Festival, the reboot became an immediately notorious "you have to see it to believe it" kind of film. There was a hunger for it that had never been seen for a *Puppet Master* movie before, at least not on this scale. For Full Moon, wrapping up the *Axis* trilogy already felt like something of a milestone, at least for the current era of the studio. It had spent years in development, from finding the right script to putting together the indiegogo and raising the funds that went into the feature's visual effects shots, most of which still didn't win over skeptical fans who had not been wowed by the previous two entries in the saga.

Puppet Master: The Littlest Reich completely overshadowed the previous film's release simply by bringing so many people into the franchise who had been completely unfamiliar with it beforehand. Thanks to the availability of the entire series, the promotion of the *Fangoria*-helmed reboot and the widely available comic book series, more eyes have been drawn toward *Puppet Master* in the past year or so than any other time I've seen as a fan. The series shows no signs of stopping. If anything, it's been revived, not unlike the puppets—or their master, for that matter—themselves. It's been given new life. There are now two totally divergent timelines, two mirror universes not unlike (even *exactly* like) those depicted in *Star Trek*. In one timeline, the puppets were the victims of Nazis, crafted to take their revenge on their oppressors. In the other, the puppets are the creations of a Nazi and are the weapons he uses in the spread of his hateful agenda. These are two wildly different approaches to the same concept and allowing both to continue does something that most fans have long considered impossible: it bridges the gap. The *Puppet Master* fan community, for all of its smaller factions and microchosims, has always essentially been split into those who love the puppets as antiheroes and those who very much do not.

Chapter Twenty. The Future 229

Now both sides are happy in a way that probably no one ever could have predicted, with two separate franchises being firmly established to appeal to these two wildly different bases. With that in mind, however, the question remains as to where the series—singular or plural—goes from here? By the time of this writing, Full Moon has already technically released a new *Puppet Master* feature. Running just over an hour, *Puppet Master: Blitzkrieg Massacre* is the first in Full Moon's *Bunker of Blood* series. Like *Puppet Master: The Legacy* and *When Puppets and Dolls Attack* before it, it is a clipshow of standout moments from the series, now including clips from the *Axis* trilogy which had yet to be made when those earlier compilations were edited together. The unique thing about the *Bunker of Blood* approach is that it uses a combination of comic book art and voiceover narration to weave a wraparound story that is stitched throughout each of the *Bunker of Blood* clipshow films. *Puppet Master: Blitzkrieg Massacre* distances itself from *The Legacy* by not tackling the series in a linear fashion, instead providing a much more random mixtape, essentially putting all of the series' greatest hits on shuffle. It also has the added bonus of being released after the entire series had been remastered, so that all of the clips look their best. Films like the original *Puppet Master* and *Puppet Master 5* that were almost entirely absent from *The Legacy* are given a fair shake this time around, at the very least, while *Retro* goes entirely unrepresented and *Curse* is given only one scene. It's obviously hard to seriously consider *Blitzkrieg Massacre* to be a true "new" *Puppet Master* movie, given that it's much more of a "greatest hits" collection, but some of the clips are very cleverly edited together, regardless.

Full Moon will, for sure, approach an actual new *Puppet Master* at some point down the line. When that could be, exactly, is anyone's guess. They seem to be unlikely to let it rest, at least for a little while, but Charles Band made it very clear while promoting the reboot that his own franchise at Full Moon is entirely unaffected by the deal with Cinestate and that fans can rest assured that the original series will continue. Many fans have been asking for years for *Puppet Master* to return to the modern day after several prequels. With *Axis Termination*, Band has fulfilled his promise of a trilogy set in World War II, so it's possible. There still seems to be an interest on Full Moon's part in exploring that era more, even outside of the franchise, in recent efforts like *Ravenwolf Towers*. But with the reboot timeline having such a Nazi-specific focus, perhaps that will shift gears for Full Moon to differentiate with their own films to bring the puppets back into the modern day with a new focus. It's hard to say exactly what that direction could be, but for the first time in a long time, Full Moon's potential with the *Puppet Master* franchise feels fresh and open-ended. At this point, limited budget permitting, anything could happen.

One hopes the recent success of the comics will continue, and there will be toys and replicas as there have been for almost twenty years running. This is as much the world of *Puppet Master* as any film, and maybe even more so. The merchandise is inseparable from the franchise, it feeds into the series and the success of the series feeds back into it, in turn. Recently, there have been vinyl figures in addition to the 3¾-inch Blade action figure. There's a Blade Halloween mask by the very popular Trick or Treat Studios, as well as a mask of Pinhead. *Puppet Master* has never been obscure. It's always been within eyesight of people who had no idea what it was, but their attention is being directed toward it more than ever before. There are soundtrack releases and T-shirt collections from the likes of such successful companies as Terror Threads and Cavity Colors. In an age based around nostalgia, more people are going back to their own roots and rediscovering their childhood love of this franchise. Full Moon smartly tapped into that with their VHS Blu-ray re-packaging of the original *Puppet Master* in a Blu-ray box set designed to emulate the look of a classic "big box" VHS, a popular style tape that was created by Band himself in the early days of Wizard Video.

Puppet Master benefits from the cult horror Blu-ray renaissance, now that more fans are talking about thirty-year-old films than ever before and discussing them with fresh eyes. *Brain Damage* and *Frankenhooker* are now part of the everyday horror conversation, as are the Full Moon films that so many people grew up with. But of course, *Puppet Master* never disappeared. Even during times when it felt like the franchise would never continue, the longest time between films has only ever been the six years between *Puppet Master vs. Demonic Toys* and *Puppet Master: Axis of Evil*.

The series might not have toys in every major specialty retailer in the U.S., as it did in 2000, but nonetheless *Puppet Master* feels in some ways bigger than ever. Even still, there are the ebbs and flows. Full Moon's history has always been cyclical. Things sometimes do very well, and sometimes they go away for awhile. At this moment in time, with two freshly released entries in the franchise, it's hard to imagine *Puppet Master* disappearing anytime soon. But it has before. When Full Moon Toys closed its doors, that company felt like it was on top of the world, at least in the horror specialty market. Full Moon's success has always been bigger in the long term than the short term. In the thirty years since the original film's release, Full Moon has had to go through several different incarnations just to keep itself and its properties alive, even losing its name at one point. There have been sacrifices, the loss of the Romanian studio, the end of the distribution deal with Paramount, the creation of Shadow Entertainment, the deal with the Sci-Fi Channel and so on and so forth, and each one of them has only ever been made for one purpose: to keep this franchise, and this brand, alive. To make sure that Full Moon would continue however it could, and that the people who loved and supported these films would only get the chance to continue to do so.

Yes, anyone who worked on a Full Moon film even during their heyday would attest to the small budgets and schedules and the general realities of low-budget filmmaking. Compromises were certainly made. But the company continues to this day while so nearly every other home video production label of its era vanished years ago. Full Moon has found a new model that, over the past few years, has proven to be stable. Full Moon Streaming has provided them the opportunity to share a wealth of different material, all niche and exploitation stuff well within their banner, that they can deliver directly to the consumer. Their original content premieres on their own platform first before an eventual DVD/Blu-Ray release. While there might be experimentation every now and then—from original streaming series to serialized versions of their latest feature films—it's a model they've clearly decided to stick with and it is one that certainly seems to be working. If the tides of content distribution should change, as they always do, there's no doubt that Full Moon will find a way to adapt if and when the time comes to do so.

But where does that leave *Puppet Master*? Over the last thirty years, it has undergone several incredibly different incarnations. It began as a moody, quirky, meaner version of *Dolls,* a straightforward tale of puppets that could be used for incredible evil before becoming the story of a sympathetic old man's revenge on his Nazi pursuers. The puppets, initially used for evil by their masters in the first two films, became antiheroes by the time the third movie rolled around and took the leap into full-blown superhero territory with the third and fourth. *Curse of the Puppet Master* provided something of an anthology entry, a standalone mad scientist tale meant to deliver the puppets back to their villainous roots, while *Retro* flipped right back to tell a tale of heroic beginnings, even bearing the PG-13 rating the features had been leaning toward for some time. Like any long-running sitcom stuck in a rut, *The Legacy* served its purpose by bringing fans up to date on what had come before, while *Puppet Master vs. Demonic Toys* melded two of Full Moon's most iconic brands into a made-for-TV kids movie—a move that, given the amount of young fans, was truly not without merit—and the *Axis Trilogy* sought to recapture the magic of the beloved *Puppet Master III,* this time mixing in elements of irreverence and exploitation that have come to define the modern era of Full Moon Features. Now, with the gonzo, bizarre gore-fest that is *Puppet Master: The Littlest Reich,* the franchise has split. Whether Cinestate will continue to make its planned prequel, *Aryans Ahoy,* is unknown. Full Moon will undoubtedly continue to make its movies in the original timeline, and with the success of *Blade: The Iron Cross,* the future looks more promising than ever.

By all accounts, Full Moon was happy with the work that was done on *Puppet Master: Axis Termination* and *Blade: The Iron Cross.* With *Termination,* Band has fulfilled the promise he made over a decade ago to do a *Puppet Master* trilogy set in World War II, something that fans certainly did not believe at the time. The next *Puppet Master,* at least from Full Moon, seems completely open-ended. Would it continue to explore World War II, even after the events of the *Axis* trilogy? It's possible. Full Moon has established a recent hunger for that kind of material, not just in the recent *Puppet Master* films, but things like *Ravenwolf Towers* as well. The title *Puppet Master: Blizkrieg Massacre* does not seem to suggest any plan to abandon the Nazi elements of the franchise any time soon. *Blade: The Iron Cross* also showed a clear decision to stay within that era. But it's still entirely possible that this could all be abandoned in the next entry in favor of a fresh direction. The success of that entry would also lead one to wonder if more spinoffs may be in the cards, considering how well this one turned out.

There are also dozens of abandoned projects that never saw the light of day, though none of them appear closer to ever happening. Even though it's astonishing to see Full Moon dust off and complete *Primevals* after decades since its production was shut down at the end of the Paramount era, the same treatment could never be given to something like *Puppet Wars.* For so many fans, that trilogy is the holy grail of unmade *Puppet Master* projects, it's still the number one thing that so many dream of seeing. But everything that had already been shot for that project made it into *Retro*

Puppet Master. And over the years, so many other films (especially the *Axis* movies) have borrowed so heavily from the unfilmed *Puppet Wars* scripts that it would almost seem moot to actually attempt to make them. We've already seen so much of them at this point that parts of those scripts, if filmed now, would feel as if they were ripping off things that they actually inspired, especially to new or unfamiliar viewers.

Fans have also spent years clamoring for a sequel to *Retro Puppet Master.* That film definitely suggested that the journey did not end there. The movie only told the very general origin of the magic and Toulon's introduction to it but set the stage for another story explaining what became of the Retro Puppets themselves. Twenty years later, we haven't seen any kind of follow up nor even a mention of those events in the later sequels, save for *Puppet Master: The Legacy.* There is so much ground to cover there, even now. Looking at the timeline chronologically, several decades pass between when we meet the young Toulon in *Retro Puppet Master* and when we see him again as an old man in *Puppet Master III*. With the massive success of *The Disaster Artist,* it would make sense to try and bring back Greg Sestero as a slightly older Toulon to help fill in that large chunk of time that still remains uncovered. This, too, seems unlikely, especially considering the fact that *Retro Puppet Master* was not a hugely successful entry in the franchise as well as how much it would cost to produce a pre–World War II period piece.

The most celebrated movie in the franchise, *Puppet Master III,* also pulled its basic concept from a comic book. In recent years, there have been a wealth of incredible comic book stories that could make for exciting and impactful movies on their own. It would be incredible, if unlikely, to see any version of "Rebirth," one of the best *Puppet Master* stories since *Toulon's Revenge,* to be told on the screen. Even a loose adaptation of *The Offering* would be an interesting return to something like the *Curse of the Puppet Master* formula. There are so many different stories, characters, bits of backstory, origin, explanations for abandoned plot threads, that could be pulled from the comics and brought to the screen if Full Moon so chose. That, again, seems unlikely, but one can always hope.

No matter what form the next iteration of *Puppet Master* takes, one thing is certain: it *will* continue. That is perhaps clearer now than it has ever been. *Puppet Master* is not going anywhere. It has survived so much over so many years, from bankruptcies to the death of the video store market it was created to capitalize on. The franchise has survived so much, and for the moment, it's actually successful again. *Puppet Master* is back on top in a way that it hasn't been in decades. These tides always turn. The history of the franchise has shown that over and over again. But this is a moment that appears to be lasting, and it is a moment that is certainly worth celebrating.

It could be two years before Full Moon's next *Puppet Master* sequel. It could also very well be a decade. It changes nothing. *Puppet Master* will always continue. Sometimes it thrives, sometimes it simply survives, but it is a franchise that has shown— as I think we've proven here—a remarkable adaptability. It perseveres. There's room even still for it to go down as the longest-running horror franchise, but even if it doesn't stake that claim, *Puppet Master* has already proven itself as the most resilient franchise in horror history. It is a series that can survive anything because, essentially, it already has.

Chapter Twenty. The Future

There are fourteen movies and surely more on the way and each one offers something different. So many appeal to wildly different tastes. The high camp antics of *Puppet Master 4* and *5* might not appeal to someone who loves the sheer mayhem and bloodshed of *The Littlest Reich,* and vice versa. No matter how different the movies might be, they share the common denominator of a low-budget B-movie flair, they gleam with independent spirit. And for those who recognize and enjoy that kind of cinema, the series truly does offer something for everyone. There is no other horror franchise like it and it seems reasonable to think that there probably never will be. *Puppet Master* is entirely its own beast, even within the Full Moon niche of killer dolls and toys. Because it's never just a killer puppet series—and sometimes it abandons the killing altogether—and it is a series that continues even now to constantly redefine itself.

Why *Puppet Master*?

Because it is the epitome of the low-budget spirit, the horror franchise equivalent of *Rocky,* a series that gets back up every single time it gets knocked down and finds a way to keep pushing forward.

Why *Puppet Master*?

Because it is most resilient franchise in the genre's history and because, at the end of the day, the puppets themselves are among the most visually striking horror icons of the last thirty years.

Why *Puppet Master*?

Because a film franchise that had never had a theatrical entry up to that point created characters so striking that their action figures, Halloween masks and more were sold in malls, comic book shops, Suncoast, Spencer's, FYE and specialty shops around the world.

Why *Puppet Master*?

Because a pioneer of stop-motion animation was hired to create these puppets years after stop-motion FX work had lost its mainstream popularity and designed stunning visuals that *still* wow new viewers and that people continue to feel nostalgic for over three decades later.

Why *Puppet Master*?

Because it's *great*.

Chapter Notes

Chapter One

1. "About Charles Band." charlesband.com.
2. Campochiaro, Michael. "The Legend of Demi Moore's Backside, Or: I Stripteased On Your Grave." aftermoviediner.com February 24, 2020.
3. "EMPIRE PICTURES Presents *PARASITE II*." *Variety*. May 4, 1983.
4. Brody, Meredith. "We Killed 'em in Chicago." *Film Comment*. February, 1987.
5. Gallagher, John A. "Stuart Gordon, Past, Present & Future." *Bloody Best of Fangoria #6*. 1987.
6. Simpson, MJ. "Interview: Charles Band" *Cult Films and the People Who Made Them*. January 21, 2007. mjsimpson-films.blogspot.com
7. Jay, Dave; Wilson, William S.; Dewi, Torsten. *It Came From the Video Aisle: Inside Charles Band's Full Moon Entertainment Studio*. Schiffer, 2017.

Chapter Two

1. Sellers, Christian. "Interview With David Schmoeller (*Puppet Master*)." *Love it Loud*. love-it-loud.co.uk. February 28, 2010.
2. Jay, Dave; Wilson, William S.; Dewi, Torsten. *It Came from the Video Aisle: Inside Charles Band's Full Moon Entertainment Studio*. Schiffer, 2017.
3. "The Man Behind *Tourist Trap*: An Interview With David Schmoeller." Terror Trap. terrortrap.com. November, 1999.
4. Schweiger, Daniel. "David Allen: The Real Puppetmaster." *Slaughterhouse Magazine #3*. 1989.
5. McGee, Mark Thomas. "Puppet Master II." *Cinefantastique vol. 21 #5*. April 1991.
6. Progcroc. "All Scream for Irene... The Irene Miracle Interview." House of Freudstein. houseoffreudstein.wordpress.com. December 8, 2015.
7. "No Strings Attached: A Behind the Scenes Look At the Making of *Puppet Master*." Paramount/Full Moon Entertainment, 1989.
8. Warren, Bill. "The Puppet Master and His Pals." *Fangoria #83*. June 1989.
9. "The Video Eye of Dr. Cyclops." *Fangoria #90*. February 1990.
10. Bloom, John. "Puppet Master." *Joe Bob Goes to the Drive-In*. https://www.angelfire.com/mn/nn/Puppetmaster.html September 8th, 1989.

Chapter Three

1. "*Puppet Master II*." Video Zone. Paramount Pictures/Full Moon Entertainment. 1991.
2. "Malibu Hotline." *Puppet Master #1*. Eternity/Malibu Publishing, 1990.

Chapter Four

1. "Charles Band Commentary." *Puppet Master II*. Blu-Ray. Full Moon Features, 2012.
2. Simpson, MJ. "Interview: David Pabian." *Cult Films and the People Who Made Them*. mjsimpson-films-blogspot.com August 1, 2015.
3. McGee, Mark Thomas. "Puppet Master II." *Cinefantastique vol. 21 #5*. April 1991.
4. Barton, David P. "Puppet Master And His Victims." *Gorezone #21*. Spring 1992.
5. Shapiro, Marc. "She Works Horror for the Money." *Fangoria Horror Spectacular #8*. 1993.
6. "*Puppet Master II*." Video Zone. Paramount Pictures/Full Moon Entertainment. 1991.
7. McGee, Mark Thomas. "Puppet Master II." *Cinefantastique vol. 21 #5*. April 1991.
8. "The Video Eye of Dr. Cyclops." *Fangoria #105*. August 1991.

Chapter Five

1. "David DeCoteau & C. Courtney Joyner Commentary." *Puppet Master III: Toulon's Revenge*. Blu-Ray. Full Moon Features, 2012.
2. "Hard Times Give New Life to Prague's Golem." Bilefsky, Dan. *Prague Journal*. nytimes.com May 10, 2009
3. "Albert Band, 78; Producer, Director Worked With Huston." Times Staff Reporters. *Los Angeles Times*. June 29, 2002.
4. "David DeCoteau & C. Courtney Joyner Commentary." *Puppet Master III: Toulon's Revenge*. Blu-Ray. Full Moon Features, 2012.
5. *Puppet Master #1*. DeVries, David; Lumsden, Glenn. Eternity/Malibu. 1990.
6. "*Puppet Master III: Toulon's Revenge*." Video Zone. Paramount Pictures/ Full Moon Entertainment, 1991.

7. "The Video Eye of Dr. Cyclops." *Fangoria #105.* August 1991.

Chapter Six

1. Unknown. *Full Moon Catalogue.* 2012.
2. Dave, Jay; Wilson, Willam S., Dewey, Torsten. *It Came From the Video Aisle: Inside Charles Band's Full Moon Entertainment Studio.* Schiffer. 2017.
3. "Seedpeople." *Video Zone.* Paramount Pictures/Full Moon Entertainment. 1992.
4. Dave, Jay; Wilson, Willam S., Dewey, Torsten. *It Came From the Video Aisle: Inside Charles Band's Full Moon Entertainment Studio.* Schiffer. 2017.
5. "Puppet Master III: Toulon's Revenge." *Video Zone.* Paramount Pictures/ Full Moon Entertainment, 1991.
6. "Jeff Burr Commentary." *Puppet Master 4.* Blu-Ray. Full Moon Features, 2015.
7. "Puppet Master 4." *Video Zone.* Paramount Pictures/Full Moon Entertainment. 1993.
8. "Puppet Master 5." *Video Zone.* Paramount Pictures/Full Moon Entertainment. 1994.

Chapter Seven

1. "Puppet Master 5." *Video Zone.* Paramount Pictures/Full Moon Entertainment. 1994.
2. Woelfel, Jay. "*Puppet Wars: Curse of the Puppet Master* Production Notes."jaywoelfel.com.
3. "Backlash: Oblivion 2." *Video Zone.* Full Moon Pictures, 1998.

Chapter Eight

1. "Lions and Tigers and Puppets… Oh My!" *Lee's Action Figure News and Toy Review #57.* July 1997.
2. "The News." *Lee's Action Figure News and Toy Review #79.* May 1999.
3. "Poor Jim's Toy Almanac." *Lee's Action Figure News and Toy Review #79.* May 1999.

Chapter Nine

1. Jay, Dave; Wilson, William S.; Dewey, Torsten. *It Came From the Video Aisle: Inside Charles Band's Full Moon Entertainment Studio.* Schiffer. 2017.
2. Green, Adam, Lynch, Joe. "Stuart Gordon." *The Movie Crypt.* 2015.
3. "Puppet Master." *Lee's Action Figure News and Toy Review* #63. January 1998.
4. "David DeCoteau Commentary." *Curse of the Puppet Master.* Blu-Ray. Full Moon Features, 2017.

Chapter Ten

1. "*Puppet Wars: Curse of the Puppet Master* Production Notes." Woelfel, Jay. jaywoelfel.com.
2. Sestero, Greg; Bissell, Tom. *The Disaster Artist: My Life Inside The Room, The Greatest Bad Movie Ever Made.* Simon & Schuster. 2013.
3. "Greg Sestero Interview." *HorrorHound.*
4. Sestero, Greg; Bissell, Tom. *The Disaster Artist: My Life Inside The Room, The Greatest Bad Movie Ever Made.* Simon & Schuster. 2013.
5. Nelson, Mike; Murphy, Kevin; Corbett, Bill. "Retro Puppet Master." *RiffTrax.* 2017.
6. "*The Disaster Artist* Trailer: James Franco is Making the Worst Movie Ever." *Filmsane.* filmsane.com. July 19, 2017.

Chapter Eleven

1. Jay, Dave; Wilson, William S.; Dewey, Torsten. *It Came From the Video Aisle: Inside Charles Band's Full Moon Entertainment Studio.* Schiffer. 2017.

Chapter Twelve

1. "Seedpeople." *Video Zone.* Paramount Pictures/Full Moon Entertainment. 1992.
2. "*Puppet Master III.*" *Video Zone.* Paramount Pictures/Full Moon Entertainment. 1991.
3. "*Puppet Master II.*" *Video Zone.* Paramount Pictures/Full Moon Entertainment. 1991.
4. "Win a Trip to Hollywood and Be a Film Extra in Puppet Master vs. Demonic Toys: The Movie." *Tomart's Action Figure Digest #74.* April 2000.
5. Brehmer, Nat. "Exclusive Interview: C. Courtney Joyner Talks Lurking Fear, Puppet Master And More!" Wicked Horror. www.wickedhorror.com. June 20, 2016.

Chapter Thirteen

1. Hill. "Hill's Charles Band Interview—Part 2." ween.net/puppetmaster.
2. Jay, Dave; Wilson, William S.; Dewey, Torsten. *It Came From the Video Aisle: Inside Charles Band's Full Moon Entertainment Studio.* Schiffer. 2017.

Chapter Fourteen

1. Jay, Dave; Wilson, William S.; Dewey, Torsten. *It Came From the Video Aisle: Inside Charles Band's Full Moon Entertainment Studio.* Schiffer. 2017.
2. "Puppet Master Forever." fullmoonhorror.com. 2011.

Chapter Fifteen

1. D'Andria, Nicole."SDCC: Action Lab Entertainment to Create New Puppet Master Comic Series." comicmaven.com. July 26th, 2014.

Chapter Sixteen

1. Wells, Mitchell. "Full Moon Features Announces Full Moon Streaming!" www.horrorsociety.com. August 20, 2013.

2. "Full Moon's Puppet Master Film Sequel Axis Trilogy." indiegogo.com.

3. Gelmini, David. "Puppet Master: Axis Termination Indiegogo a Huge Success." www.dreadcentral.com. January 29, 2016

4. Erdely, Sabrina Rubin. "Kiki Kannibal: The Girl Who Played With Fire." rollingstone.com. April 15, 2011.

5. Marshall, Andrew. "Puppet Master Remake Announced." starburstmagazine.com. May 5, 2016.

Chapter Seventeen

1. Miska, Brad. "Charles Band to Remake Puppetmaster in 3D." bloody-disgusting.com. March 9, 2009.

2. Murphee, Zach. "Full Moon Madness: An Interview With Charles Band." www.horrorgeeklife.com. August 13th, 2018.

3. Brehmer, Nat. "Breaking Down the New Designs of the *Puppet Master* Reboot." www.wickedhorror.com. May 11, 2017.

4. Feldberg, Isaac. "Charles Band on *Puppet Master* Reboot *The Littlest Reich* and 28 Years of Tiny Terrors." ew.com. August 19, 2018.

5. Foutch, Haleigh. "*Puppet Master: The Littlest Reich* Review—Nazi Puppet Grand Guignol." collider.com. August 17, 2018.

Chapter Eighteen

1. Hamman, Cody. "S. Craig Zahler Plots *Puppet Master: The Littlest Reich* Prequel *Aryans Ahoy.*" www.joblo.com. May 8, 2018.

2. Fouch, Haleigh. "Full Moon Features to Live-Stream the Making of 10 Horror Movies With *Deadly Ten.*" collider.com. April 19, 2019.

Chapter Nineteen

1. Smith, Kevin. Tweet. twitter.com. June 2, 2016.

2. Bromley, Patrick. "Full Moon Fever: Puppet Master II." F This movie.fthismovie.net. May 30, 2017.

3. Vanderbilt, Mike; Rife, Katie. "The Puppet Master Saga—Part I." Revenge of the Pod People. revengeofhtepodpeople.libsyn.com. October 28, 2015.

Bibliography

"About Charles Band." charlesband.com.
"Albert Band, 78; Producer, Director Worked with Huston." *Los Angeles Times*. June 29, 2002.
"Backlash: Oblivion 2." *Video Zone*. Full Moon Pictures. 1998.
Band, Charles. "Charles Band Commentary." *Puppet Master II*. Blu-Ray. Full Moon Features. 2012.
Barton, David P. "Puppet Master And His Victims." *Gorezone* #21. Spring 1992.
Bilefsky, Dan. "Hard Times Give New Life to Prague's Golem." *Prague Journal*. nytimes.com. May 10, 2009.
Bloom, John. "Puppet Master." *Joe Bob Goes to the Drive-In*. https://www.angelfire.com/mn/nn/Puppetmaster.html. September 8, 1989.
Brehmer, Nat. "Breaking Down the New Designs of the *Puppet Master* Reboot." www.wickedhorror.com. May 11, 2017.
Brehmer, Nat. "Exclusive Interview: C. Courtney Joyner Talks Lurking Fear, Puppet Master and More!" Wicked Horror. www.wickedhorror.com. June 20, 2016.
Brody, Meredith. "We Killed 'em in Chicago." *Film Comment*. February 1987.
Bromley, Patrick. "Full Moon Fever: Puppet Master II." F This Movie. fthismovie.net. May 30, 2017.
Burr, Jeff. "Jeff Burr Commentary." *Puppet Master 4*. Blu-Ray. Full Moon Features. 2015.
Campochiaro, Michael. "The Legend of Demi Moore's Backside, Or: I Stripteased on Your Grave." aftermoviediner.com. February 24, 2020.
D'Andria, Nicole. "SDCC: Action Lab Entertainment to Create New Puppet Master Comic Series." comicmaven.com. July 26, 2014.
"*The Disaster Artist* Trailer: James Franco Is Making the Worst Movie Ever." *Filmsane*. filmsane.com. July 19, 2017.
DeCoteau, David. "David DeCoteau Commentary." *Curse of the Puppet Master*. Blu-Ray. Full Moon Features. 2017.
DeCoteau, David; Joyner, C. Courtney. "David DeCoteau & C. Courtney Joyner Commentary." *Puppet Master III: Toulon's Revenge*. Blu-Ray. Full Moon Features. 2012.
DeVries, David; Lumsden, Glenn. *Puppet Master #1*. Eternity/Malibu Publishing. 1990.
"EMPIRE PICTURES Presents *PARASITE II*." *Variety*. May 4, 1983.
Erdely, Sabrina Rubin. "Kiki Kannibal: The Girl Who Played with Fire." rollingstone.com. April 15, 2011.
Feldberg, Isaac. "Charles Band on *Puppet Master* Reboot *The Littlest Reich* and 28 Years of Tiny Terrors." ew.com. August 19, 2018.
Fouch, Haleigh. "Full Moon Features to Live-Stream the Making of 10 Horror Movies with *Deadly Ten*." collider.com. April 19, 2019.
Fouch, Haleigh. "*Puppet Master: The Littlest Reich* Review—Nazi Puppet Grand Guignol." collider.com. August 17, 2018.
Full Moon Catalogue. 2012.
"Full Moon's Puppet Master Film Sequel Axis Trilogy." indiegogo.com.
Gallagher, John A. "Stuart Gordon, Past, Present & Future." *Bloody Best of Fangoria* #6. 1987.
Gelmini, David. "Puppet Master: Axis Termination Indiegogo a Huge Success." www.dreadcentral.com. January 29, 2016
Green, Adam; Lynch, Joe. "Stuart Gordon." *The Movie Crypt*. 2015.
"Greg Sestero Interview." *HorrorHound*.
Hamman, Cody. "S. Craig Zahler Plots *Puppet Master: The Littlest Reich* Prequel *Aryans Ahoy*." www.joblo.com. May 8, 2018.
Hill. "Hill's Charles Band Interview—Part 2." ween.net/puppetmaster.
Jay, Dave; Wilson, William S.; Dewi, Torsten. *It Came From the Video Aisle: Inside Charles Band's Full Moon Entertainment Studio*. Schiffer. 2017.
"Lions and Tigers and Puppets … Oh My!" *Lee's Action Figure News and Toy Review* #57. July 1997.
"Malibu Hotline." *Puppet Master* #1. Eternity/Malibu Publishing. 1990.
"The Man Behind *Tourist Trap*: An Interview with David Schmoeller." terrortrap.com. November 1999.

Marshall, Andrew. "Puppet Master Remake Announced." starburstmagazine.com. May 5, 2016.
McGee, Mark Thomas. "Puppet Master II." *Cinefantastique* vol. 21, #5. April 1991.
Miska, Brad. "Charles Band to Remake Puppetmaster in 3D." bloody-disgusting.com. March 9, 2009.
Murphee, Zach. "Full Moon Madness: An Interview with Charles Band." www.horrorgeeklife.com. August 13, 2018.
Nelson, Mike; Murphy, Kevin; Corbett, Bill. "Retro Puppet Master." *RiffTrax*. 2017.
"The News." *Lee's Action Figure News and Toy Review* #79. May 1999.
"No Strings Attached: A Behind the Scenes Look at the Making of *Puppet Master*." Paramount/Full Moon Entertainment. 1989.
"Poor Jim's Toy Almanac." *Lee's Action Figure News and Toy Review* #79. May 1999.
Progroc. "All Screams for Irene … the Irene Miracle Interview." *House of Freudstein*. houseoffreudstein.wordpress.com. December 8, 2015.
"Puppet Master." *Lee's Action Figure News and Toy Review* #63. January 1998.
"Puppet Master 5." *Video Zone*. Paramount Pictures/Full Moon Entertainment. 1994.
"Puppet Master Forever." fullmoonhorror.com. 2011.
"*Puppet Master 4*." *Video Zone*. Paramount Pictures/Full Moon Entertainment. 1993.
"*Puppet Master III: Toulon's Revenge*." *Video Zone*. Paramount Pictures/Full Moon Entertainment. 1991.
"*Puppet Master II*." Video Zone. Paramount Pictures/Full Moon Entertainment. 1991.
Schweiger, Daniel. "David Allen: The Real Puppetmaster." *Slaughterhouse Magazine* #3. 1989.
"Seedpeople." *Video Zone*. Paramount Pictures/Full Moon Entertainment. 1992.
Sellers, Christian. "Interview with David Schmoeller (*Puppet Master*)." *Love it Loud*. love-it-loud.co.uk. February 28, 2010.
Sestero, Greg; Bissell, Tom. *The Disaster Artist: My Life Inside the Room, the Greatest Bad Movie Ever Made*. Simon & Schuster. 2013.
Shapiro, Marc. "She Works Horror for the Money." *Fangoria Horror Spectacular* #8. 1993.
Simpson, MJ. "Interview: Charles Band" *Cult Films and the People Who Made Them*. mjsimpson-films.blogspot.com. January 21, 2007.
Simpson, MJ. "Interview: David Pabian." *Cult Films and the People Who Made Them*. mjsimpson-films-blogspot.com. August 1, 2015.
Smith, Kevin. Tweet. twitter.com. June 2, 2016.
Vanderbilt, Mike; Rife, Katie. "The Puppet Master Saga—Part I." Revenge of the Pod People. revengeofhtepodpeople.libsyn.com. October 28, 2015.
The Video Eye of Dr. Cyclops." *Fangoria* #105. August 1991.
"The Video Eye of Dr. Cyclops." *Fangoria* #90. February 1990.
Warren, Bill. "The Puppet Master and His Pals." *Fangoria* #83. June 1989.
Wells, Mitchell. "Full Moon Features Announces Full Moon Streaming!" www.horrorsociety.com. August 20, 2013.
"Win a Trip to Hollywood and Be a Film Extra in Puppet Master vs. Demonic Toys: The Movie." *Tomart's Action Figure Digest* #74. April 2000.
Woelfel, Jay. "*Puppet Wars: Curse of the Puppet Master* Production Notes." jaywoelfel.com.

Index

Aarniokowski, Doug 74
Abercrombie, Ian 65–68
Abramsohn, Roy 220
Action Lab Comics 185, 187, 189, 190–94, 217
Afzel *(Retro Puppet Master)* 130, 135, 136, 145
Allen, David 2, 8, 13, 17, 19–20, 24, 29, 38, 42, 46–49, 51, 54, 59, 63, 67, 74–75, 82, 87, 95, 98, 117, 124–26, 128–30, 173, 196, 210, 216, 219, 225
Allen, Sage 47
American Graffiti 21
Anapa 189–93, 199
Argento, Dario 21, 89
Aronowitz, Greg 70, 100
Autogiro 211

Baal 92, 155, 157, 163
Band, Albert 7, 55, 57, 60, 115
Band, Charles 2, 7–15, 17, 28–31, 33, 35–38, 40–41, 43–44, 46–47, 50, 53–55, 58, 60–62, 64, 68–70, 72–75, 77–78, 85, 87–91, 95–96, 99–101, 113–17, 119, 122–23, 126, 129, 135, 137, 139–44, 152–53, 155–56, 163, 165–69, 171, 173–76, 179, 182–85, 194–98, 200–1, 203–6, 209–10, 212–14, 216, 218–19, 224–25, 227, 229–32
Band, Richard 15, 29, 44, 122, 173, 209
Bandcompany 14, 55, 75
Barton, David P. 42–43, 129
Bates, Ralph 65–66
Bergschneider, Christopher 127–29, 163, 180, 182
Bernsen, Collin 45
Bernsen, Corbin 45
Bey, Ahmed 91, 178
The Beyond 7, 15, 209
Bielefeld, Robin 86
Billy *(Puppet Master II)* 49
Bilson, Danny 77
Bitterling, Shane 176–77, 181–82, 197
Blackehart, Stephen 134–35
Blade 1, 3, 17–19, 24–27, 36, 41, 45–48, 52, 60, 61, 62, 66–68, 70, 75, 79, 85, 91, 92, 94, 100–102, 104, 105, 107, 108, 110, 112, 113, 117, 121, 127, 134, 140, 149, 152, 155, 159, 162–64, 173, 180, 182, 187, 188, 191, 194, 196, 201, 202, 203, 207, 209, 210, 211, 214–224, 229, 231
Blade: The Iron Cross 19, 155, 194, 210, 214–15, 217, 219, 220–21, 231
Blitzkrieg 180, 214, 229
Blockbuster 99, 141–42, 167
Blood Dolls 126, 129, 139, 176, 179
Bloomsfield, Joanne 65
Bodega Bay Inn 17, 21, 23, 33, 35, 38, 84, 93, 123, 144, 170, 186, 190, 193
Bombshell 95, 180–82, 192, 199, 202
Bookwalter, J.R. 123, 140–41, 145, 155
Bouldeston Institute 53, 189

Bramwell, Carolyn 43–45, 51, 53
Bramwell, Patrick 44
Buechler, John Carl 8, 13, 162–63
Burr, Jeff 55, 75, 78–79, 82, 85–86, 88, 119, 219
Butler, William 169

Calzada, Yancy 38
Cameron *(Puppet Master 4)* 80–84, 121
Cannon Films 55, 66
Carpenter, John 11, 47
Castel Studios 116
Castle Freak 89, 105, 107, 112, 114, 127, 139, 168, 205
Castle Green 23, 86
Cavity Colors 230
Celentano, Jeff 45, 152
Cellar Dweller 15, 129
Children of the Puppet Master 35–36
Child's Play 1, 180
Child's Play 2 21
Cinefantastique 20, 42, 51
Cinestate 5, 199, 200, 205, 206, 212, 214, 229, 231
City of the Living Dead 15, 209
Claire *(Puppet Wars)* 90, 92, 177
The Collector 192–93
Comb Queen 111
Coogan, Danny 170–72, 179, 197–98
Cook, Randy 47, 79, 81
Corman, Roger 8–9, 13, 156
Crampton, Barbara 207–8
Crash & Burn 37–38, 40, 43–44, 152
Craven, Wes 81, 89, 169
Crawlspace 15, 18
Creepozoids 38, 40, 54
Critters 153, 170, 177
Currie, Gordon 80, 148
Curse of the Puppet Master 90–91, 96–97, 105, 110, 114–26, 130–32, 136–37, 139, 142, 145, 148, 157, 172–73, 178, 183, 185, 190, 192, 202, 205, 224, 232
Cyber Puppets 110–12, 153, 154–63

Da Sacco, Michela 186
Dau, Brigitta 133–34
David Allen Productions 38, 47, 49, 59, 87, 126
The Dead Hate the Living 89, 126
The Dead Next Door 123, 140
Deadly Ten 215–16, 218, 220–21
Decapitron 41, 77–78, 80, 84, 85, 87, 105, 110, 145, 173, 185
DeCoteau, David 14, 38, 54, 57, 60, 62, 64–66, 75, 96, 117, 119, 121, 124, 129, 130–31, 138, 170, 173
De Meo, Paul 77
Demonic Toys 31, 45, 73, 77, 92, 110–12, 139, 149–65, 167–69, 171, 173–74, 176, 181–82, 185, 194, 200, 205, 216, 227, 230, 231

241

Devlin, Tom 113, 180–81, 183, 196–97, 202–3, 214–22
DeVries, David 31–33
Dion, Debra 13, 57
The Disaster Artist 132, 138, 236
Disney 9, 17, 115, 133, 220
Dr. Alien 14
Doctor Mordrid 57, 72, 76, 176
Dollman Kills the Full Moon Universe 1, 194
Dolls 10–11, 14, 17, 33, 62–63, 71, 153, 231
Donaggio, Pino 15, 28
Donner, Jack 135
Douglas, Sarah 64–66, 133
Dracula 42, 50, 66, 90–94, 178
Dreamaniac 38, 54
The Dungeonmaster 8, 9, 12–13

Eisenberg, Aron 69
Eliminators 58
Empire Pictures 7–11, 13–15, 23, 28, 29, 33, 37–38, 55, 57–58, 62, 73, 75, 77–78, 129, 157, 159, 169, 175, 224
The Empire Strikes Back 4, 93
Endicott, Chris 18, 20, 23, 26, 28, 38, 40–41, 46–49, 51–52, 59, 61, 63–65, 70, 74, 76, 78–79, 81, 83–87, 124, 143, 147
Eternity Comics 31, 33, 35–36, 60, 67, 170, 185

Fangoria magazine 10, 18–19, 24, 29, 46, 53, 71, 110, 114, 205, 226, 228
Farley, Jeff 127–29, 131–33, 135–38, 149–50, 155, 157, 159, 160, 162–66
Feldman, Corey 160–61
Fenn, Sherilynn 37, 40
Fletcher, Joel 87
Flower, Buck 47
Forrester, Frank 21–22, 25–27, 45
Frankenstein 63–64, 66, 73, 78–79, 90, 93, 95, 119, 158
Franklin, Nelson 207
Frates, Robin 21
Friday the 13th 38, 44, 80, 89, 137, 146, 155, 160
Frizzi, Fabio 209
From a Whisper to a Scream 55, 75
From Beyond 10–11, 210
Fulci, Lucio 7, 15, 17, 89, 120, 204, 209
Full Moon Comix 194
Full Moon Entertainment 12, 114, 169
Full Moon Fan Club 46, 73, 100
Full Moon Features 69, 169, 175–76, 231
Full Moon Streaming 195, 201, 227, 230
Full Moon Toys 3, 99, 105, 107, 108, 110–13, 115, 126, 139, 153, 230

Gabborin, Shawn 185–90, 192–94, 217
Gallagher, Anthony 190–93
Gallagher, Megan 21, 24, 27, 35–36, 43, 190
Gallagher, Neil 21–22, 24, 26–27, 35, 51, 85, 190
Gentry, Paul 47
Ghoulies 11, 13–14, 112, 157, 170
Ghoulies II 15, 17
Gingerdead Man 112, 144, 169, 170, 183, 185, 201, 218
The Golem 60
Goosebumps 3, 119
Gordon, Dennis 17, 78
Gordon, Stuart 10, 17, 33, 37, 78, 89, 105, 115, 141, 153
Gotell, Walter 65, 67
Goyer, David 152
Grand Guignol 19

Hadley, Dana 21–22, 25–27, 45
Hall, Kenneth J. 13–15, 17–19, 58, 98
Halloween 4, 7, 62, 146
Halloween III 137, 157–58, 161
Happy Amphibian 211
Head of the Family 115, 139, 168, 176, 179, 215
Hellraiser 19
Hertz, Peter 69, 144–45, 191
Hess, Dr. 61–62, 67–69, 120, 178, 187–88, 217–18, 220, 222
Hickey, William 23, 62, 68, 120
Hitchcock, Alfred 23, 27, 68
Hitler, Adolf 58, 60, 188, 211, 212
Howling VI: The Freaks 38

*I Spit o
In Your Grave* 7
Indiegogo 196, 200–4, 228
Inferno 21
Intruder 11, 142
The Invisible Man 37, 43, 50
Ivanov, Elisa 203, 217, 222

Jack-O 123, 128
Jennings, Laurence, Dr. 83–84, 121
Jester 17, 23–25, 27, 41, 44, 63, 85, 101, 104–6, 108, 112–13, 117, 122, 147, 162–64, 173, 183, 187, 189, 202
Jones, Gary 165
Joyner, C. Courtney 55, 57–58, 60, 63, 65–66, 69, 75, 95, 143–44, 146, 156, 159–61, 177

Kier, Udo 208–9
Killjoy 112, 169, 180, 218–19
Kinney, Camille 44–45, 51, 71, 189–90
Kinney, Michael 45, 51
Kinski, Klaus 18
Kraus, Major 61–62, 65–68, 81, 90, 134, 171–72, 178, 218
Kron, Colonel 90, 92–94, 177
Krueger, Freddy 3, 29, 146, 158, 210
Kushner-Locke Company 99, 137, 139–40

Lance *(Puppet Master II)* 43, 45–46, 152
Laserblast 8, 17
Lauren *(Puppet Master 4)* 80–82
Leatherface: The Texas Chainsaw Massacre III 42, 75
Lechago, John 180, 215, 218, 219
Leech Woman 19, 24–27, 32, 40–41, 47, 55, 60–51, 64–65, 67, 70, 85, 93, 101–2, 108, 110, 123, 134, 173, 180, 182, 187–88, 191, 201–2, 220, 223
Lee's Action Figure News & Toy Review 101, 107, 110, 116
Leguna, Sonny 206
Le Mat, Paul 21, 35, 63
Lennon, Thomas 206
Leroy 25, 35
Lom, Herbert 66
Lords, Traci 155
Lumsden, Glenn 31–33, 35
Lynch, Richard 65–66, 220

Maclain *(Puppet Master: The Legacy)* 144, 148–50
Maclellan, Elizabeth 43–44
MacLeod, Lee 13, 29, 107, 112
Magrew, Dr. 120, 121–23, 146, 190
Magrew, Jane 120–23, 25
Malibu comics 31–32
Manoogian, Peter 8, 77
Martha *(Puppet Master II)* 41, 47, 188
Marvel 31, 33, 72, 73, 194, 205, 216, 220

Mathew *(Puppet Master II)* 41, 47
McBain, Diane 82–83
Media Home Entertainment 7, 11
Melvin & Howard 21, 35
Mephisto 4, 65, 105
Meridian 37–38, 40
Miracle, Irene 21, 63
Mr. Sardonicus 63, 79
Moebius, Commandant 177–78, 182, 198
MPAA 27, 136
Mueller, General 32, 67–68
Muir, Brian 170, 176–77
The Mummy (film) 38, 42, 91
The Mummy 50, 90–91
Myers, Michael 29, 210
Myers, Rick 77, 80–82, 148
Myhre, John 17
MySpace 199

Naha, Ed 10
Nazis 35, 49, 57–58, 60, 64, 66–68, 81, 90–92–94, 134, 171, 177–82, 188, 193, 196, 198–99, 201–2, 208, 214, 217–18, 220, 222, 224, 228–29, 231
Neame, Christopher 66
Netflix 175, 195, 227
Nicolau, Ted 8, 158–59, 161
The Nightmare Before Christmas 3, 23, 202
A Nightmare on Elm Street 53, 81, 89, 146
Nightmare Sisters 13
Ninja 172–73, 192

October Games 224
Ogilvy, Ian 83
O'Neal, Ron 82–83
O'Reilly, Kathryn 21–22
Origins of the Puppet Master 98
Ozu 171–73, 177

Pabian, David 37–38, 40, 42
Paramount Pictures 12, 15, 87, 95–96, 98–99, 113–15, 137–41, 151, 153, 159, 169, 173–74, 197, 204, 216, 222, 226, 230–31
Parker, Dave 88–89, 91, 95–97
Perello, Hope 38
The Phantom of the Opera 43, 105
Phares, Rick 99–102, 104–5, 107–8, 110, 112, 116, 126
Pinhead 15, 17–20, 24, 26, 41, 44–45, 60, 61, 70, 79, 86, 91–92, 102, 104, 107–8, 111–12, 117, 121, 134, 143, 149, 152, 162–64, 173, 181, 187, 196, 203, 209–10, 224, 229
Plush Buddies 113
Power Rangers 89, 121
Prison 11, 55, 121, 129
Project Metalbeast 77
Pugh, Willard 83–84
Puppet Master (film) 1–8, 10, 13–30, 32–33, 35–38, 40, 42, 43–45, 47, 50–51, 53–54, 58, 60, 62, 68–75, 77, 80, 82, 85–88, 92–94, 108, 120, 124, 143, 146–47, 149, 152–53, 170, 173–74, 186, 190, 198, 204, 205–10, 229–30
Puppet Master (TV series) 159–61, 165, 200
Puppet Master II 31, 35, 37–47, 49–51, 53–54, 58, 61, 64–65, 71, 75, 78, 85, 88–91, 93, 102, 105, 122–24, 127, 145–49, 152, 185–86, 188–90, 197, 200, 205, 213, 219, 228
Puppet Master III: Toulon's Revenge 10, 32–33, 53–73, 75, 77–78, 81–82, 87–90, 95–96, 98, 101, 117, 120, 125, 127, 130, 134, 137, 143–46, 149, 156, 168, 170–71, 174, 178, 187, 191, 2015, 208, 210, 22–23, 225, 227, 231–32

Puppet Master 3D remake 204
Puppet Master 4 70–88, 93–94, 102, 105, 108, 117, 121, 123, 135, 142, 156, 173, 182, 189, 233
Puppet Master 5 74, 79, 82–89, 101, 114, 116, 121, 124, 136, 142, 148, 176, 197, 209, 222, 228–29
Puppet Master: Axis of Evil 168–76, 178–80, 182–84, 195, 201, 203, 214, 220
Puppet Master: Axis Rising 90, 113, 175–84, 193, 195–97, 201–3, 214, 218
Puppet Master: Axis Termination 47, 101, 113, 195, 197–201, 203–4, 206, 214, 217–19, 228–29, 231
Puppet Master: Blitzkrieg Massacre 214, 229
Puppet Master: The Action Figure Series 99–101, 103–7, 109, 111, 113, 114, 123, 126, 126, 153, 183
Puppet Master: The Legacy 140–51, 156, 162, 173, 176, 185, 229, 231–32
Puppet Master: The Littlest Reich 204–14, 222–26, 228, 231, 233
Puppet Master: The Movie 73–75, 116
Puppet Master vs. Demonic Toys 73, 110, 111, 112, 139, 149–65, 168, 173–74, 176, 182, 200, 205, 227, 230, 231
Puppet Wars 88–89, 91–99, 101, 114–16, 120, 131, 138, 143, 168–70, 177–78, 182, 197, 231–32

Ragdoll 88, 114
Rappaport, Mark 17, 38, 42, 117, 125, 130, 149, 173
Ravenwolf Towers 198, 229, 231
Rawhead Rex 11
Re-Animator 9–11, 14, 28, 41, 55, 68, 196
Replica 1, 49, 68, 77, 112–13, 175, 181–83, 195–96, 201, 211, 213–15, 223–25, 229
Retro Puppet Master 4, 63, 97, 107, 112, 126–31, 133–40, 142, 145, 149, 153–54, 156, 158, 173, 183, 188, 190–91, 198, 208, 211, 222, 232
Rey, Fred Olen 13, 123
Robot Jox 37, 78
Roe, Matt 21
Rolfe, Guy 10, 62–68, 78–80, 96–97, 120, 131, 133, 135–36, 208
Romania 62, 90–91, 94–95, 116, 125, 130, 133, 135, 140–41, 159–60, 171, 197

Salvati, Sergio 15, 17, 209
Schmoeller, David 14–15, 17–18, 24–25, 29, 75, 210, 218
Seedpeople 88–89
Sestero, Greg 132–33, 138, 145, 232, 236, 239–40
Shadow Entertainment 141–42, 151, 168, 175, 230
Shredder Khan 224
Shrieker 105, 119, 123, 126
Simmons, Patrick 42, 129
Six-Shooter 3, 18, 41, 42, 58–60, 67, 68, 70, 77, 85, 94, 98, 101, 104, 107, 108, 110, 130, 134, 152, 162–64, 166, 172, 181, 185, 187, 188, 190–93, 196, 201, 202, 225
Skaggs, Jimmie F. 22, 27
Smith, Kevin 224
Sorensen, Cindy 17
Sorority Babes in the Slimeball Bowl-a-rama 40, 54, 215
Spradling, Charlie 37, 45–46
Sssssss 119, 157
Stamford, Clarissa 21–22, 25–26, 45
Steinsiek, Tate 209
Steitz, Friede 199, 201
Stevens, Neal Marshall 96, 119, 127, 142, 222
Strange, Dr. 31, 72, 76
Subspecies 62, 74, 91, 93, 105, 126, 137, 139–40, 152, 159, 168, 194, 215
Sutekh 75–77, 82–83, 86, 130–31, 134–35, 189, 198

Index

Talbot, Nita 45
Tales from the Crypt 23, 68, 128
Tank 120–23, 192, 224
Tempe Entertainment 123, 139–42, 155–56
Terror Threads 230
TerrorVision 11, 159
Teska, John 17, 38, 51, 65
The Texas Chain Saw Massacre 4, 7, 146
Theresa 22, 24–25
Tooker, Melanie 165
Torch 35, 41–42, 45, 47, 49, 54, 61, 70, 76, 80, 84–85, 93–94, 104–6, 108, 110–11, 113, 152, 172, 187–88, 197, 200–1, 210–11, 220, 226
The Totem 74, 80, 82–83, 85–86, 101–3, 108, 129, 136
Toulon, Alex 161
Toulon, Andre 10, 17, 19, 22–24, 31–33, 35–38, 43, 50–51, 53–55, 57–65, 67–71, 75–76, 78, 80, 88, 89, 90–94, 96, 98, 104, 111, 120, 123–24, 127, 129–34, 136, 144–50, 153, 170–71, 178–79, 181, 187–93, 197, 199, 205–8, 210, 215, 217
Toulon, Elsa 32, 38, 43, 51, 58, 60, 64, 67, 130, 133–34, 145, 172, 187–88
Toulon, Erich 188–89
Toulon, Robert 157, 160–61, 163
Tourist Trap 8, 14–15, 29, 53, 55, 210
Toys "R" Us 1, 108, 112
Trancers 77, 82, 100, 176
Trancers II 57, 66
Trancers III 57
Trancers 4 74
Trancers 5 74
Trancers 6 89, 141
Trick or Treat Studios 229

Troma 134, 184
Tunneler 18, 25–28, 41, 43–44, 51, 61–62, 70, 91–92, 101–3, 107–8, 110, 112, 121, 127, 173, 180, 187, 191, 201–2, 209, 210–11, 220
Turkel, Ann 66

Video Zone 50, 72, 78, 80, 87–88, 152–53, 216
Von Sholly, Pete 86
Voorhees, Jason 3, 29, 80, 146, 155, 158
Vos, Lilou 199

Walton, Jeff 123
Wanda *(Puppet Master II)* 45–47
Webb, Greg 44
Wells, Steve 50, 62
Weremacht 180, 202
Wexler, Howard 214, 231
Whitaker, Duane 83–84
White, Brett 17
Whittaker, Alex 21, 24, 27, 35–36, 38, 44, 82
Wiklund, Tommy 206
Willard, Fred 160
Wiseau, Tommy 132, 138
Wizard Entertainment 168, 169, 175
Wizard Video 7, 8, 11
Woelfel, Jay 88–92, 94–98, 141

X-Men 3, 17, 215

Yuzna, Brian 10, 115, 121

Zahler, S. Craig 199, 204–9
Zombie Flesh Eaters 7, 209

www.ingramcontent.com/pod-product-compliance
Lightning Source LLC
Chambersburg PA
CBHW060339010526
44117CB00017B/2895